ENCOUNTERS
with JESUS

ENCOUNTERS
with JESUS

The Man in His Place and Time

ADRIANA DESTRO
and
MAURO PESCE

Translated by
Brian McNeil

Fortress Press
Minneapolis

ENCOUNTERS WITH JESUS
The Man in His Place and Time

L'uomo Gesù. Giorni, luoghi, incontri di una vita

English translation copyright © 2012 Fortress Press. All rights reserved. Except for brief quotations in critical articles or reviews, no part of this book may be reproduced in any manner without prior written permission from the publisher. Visit http://www.augsburgfortress.org/copyrights/contact.asp or write to Permissions, Augsburg Fortress, Box 1209, Minneapolis, MN 55440.

First publication: *L'uomo Gesù. Giorni, luoghi, incontri di una vita*
Original copyright © Arnoldo Mondadori Editore S.p.A., Milano.

Some scripture quotations are based on the New Revised Standard Version Bible, copyright © 1989 by the Division of Christian Education of the National Council of the Churches of Christ in the USA. Used by permission. All rights reserved.

Cover image: Funeral portrait (2nd century c.e.), Fayum, Egypt. Erich Lessing / Art Resource, NY
Cover design: Laurie Ingram
Book design: The HK Scriptorium, Inc.

Library of Congress Cataloging-in-Publication Data

Destro, Adriana.
 [Uomo Gesù. English]
 Encounters with Jesus : the man in his place and time / Adriana Destro and Mauro Pesce ; translated by Brian McNeil.
    p. cm.
 "First publication: L'uomo Gesù: giorni, luoghi, incontri di una vita. Milan: Arnoldo Mondadori Editore S.p.A., 2008"—T.p. verso.
 Includes bibliographical references and index.
 ISBN 978-0-8006-9845-4 (alk. paper)
 1. Jesus Christ. I. Pesce, Mauro. II. Title.
 BT203.D4713 2011
 232.9'01—dc22

2011009203

The paper used in this publication meets the minimum requirements of American National Standard for Information Sciences—Permanence of Paper for Printed Library Materials, ANSI Z329.48-1984.

Manufactured in the U.S.A.

15 14 13 12   1 2 3 4 5 6 7 8 9 10

CONTENTS

Introduction: On Jesus' Lifestyle ... ix
Lifestyle as the First Message ... x
The Historical Reliability of the Gospels ... xii
The Necessity of Research into the Historical Jesus ... xiv

1. Jesus on His Landscape: Mental Maps and Real Territories ... 3
   Jesus and His Land ... 3
   Far from the Cities ... 5
   Jesus in Galilee, in Judaea, and outside the Borders ... 11
   Jesus' Attitude toward Jerusalem ... 16

2. Jesus on Foot: A Life in Continuous Movement ... 25
   An Identity without Networks ... 26
   Not a Nomad, Not a Traveler, nor Yet a Pilgrim ... 29
   The Code of the Itinerant: Do Not Sow or Reap,
   *   Do Not Toil or Spin* ... 33
   Walking and the Time of the Itinerant ... 35
   Solitude and Flight ... 37

3. Jesus Face to Face: Encounters ... 41
   On an Equal Footing ... 41
   The Encounter with the Baptizer ... 42
   The Followers ... 48
   The Twelve ... 53
   Meetings with Relatives: Closeness and Conflict ... 57
   Friends and Supporters ... 62
   The Women ... 65
   Sinners, Those Possessed by Demons, and the Sick ... 69
   An Array of Adversaries ... 69
   "Rich" and "Poor" among the Addressees of Jesus ... 71
   The Lost Sheep of the House of Israel ... 72
   Jesus' Preference for Direct Encounters ... 74

Contents

4. **Jesus at Table: Eating Together** — 78
   - *Coming Together to Eat: Building Up Society* — 78
   - *In the Houses of the Rich* — 84
   - *Eating along the Way* — 85
   - *At Table with His Followers* — 87
   - *At Table with Friends* — 89
   - *Miracles to Feed the Hungry: The Sign of Abundance* — 90
   - *Eating Together in the Parables* — 91
   - *The Symbolic Complexity of Conviviality* — 94
   - *The Future Banquet* — 99

5. **Jesus Leaves Home and Is Made at Home with Others** — 102
   - *Without a House of His Own—in the Houses of Others* — 102
   - *The Variety of Houses: Styles and Relationships* — 104
   - *A Group without a Place of Its Own* — 107
   - *The Individual Call* — 109
   - *The Adult Generation Abandons Home* — 110
   - *Conflicts among the Members of a Household* — 116
   - *An Interstitial Strategy* — 125

6. **Jesus and His Body** — 128
   - *The Place of Corporality* — 128
   - *Bodies Procreate: Jesus' Genealogical Position* — 130
   - *When His Contemporaries Looked at Jesus, What Did They See?* — 134
   - *Other Looks, Other Appearances* — 139
   - *The Body Is Taken Prisoner* — 141
   - *An Inclusive Subject: The Crowd* — 143
   - *The Body in Danger* — 148
   - *The Body of Jesus and the Healings* — 150

7. **Jesus and Emotion: Feelings and Desires** — 155
   - *How Do We Get to Know the Inner Life of Jesus?* — 155
   - *The Cultural Meanings of Emotions* — 155
   - *Jesus' Compassion* — 157
   - *Anxiety and Sadness* — 159
   - *Indignation and Anger* — 161
   - *The Power of Silence* — 162
   - *The Problems Involved in Leave Taking* — 163

Contents vii

Will, Desire, Decision	166
"I have come in order to . . .": Jesus Expresses His Desire and His Interior Passion	168
Conclusion: The Concrete Reality of a Radical Life	170
Notes	177
Bibliography	221
Index of Authors and Names	237
Index of Ancient Texts	242
Index of Subjects	249

TRANSLATOR'S NOTE

Biblical texts are usually taken from the New Revised Standard Version, but occasionally a more literal translation is given in order to bring out the authors' meaning.

Introduction

ON JESUS' LIFESTYLE

The life of Jesus closed with a violent death. But this death did not extinguish his voice, which has continued to kindle the hearts and minds of many people at the same time as it has moved others to reject him. What was there in his person, in his behavior, and in his words that prompted both the enthusiasm of so many followers and the extreme hostility of those who killed him? To what extent was his activity born of a profound crisis that affected not only his own environment but also vast sectors of society in classical antiquity? The historical and cultural figure of Jesus is enormous, and there is no risk of exhausting the significance of what it represents. New questions continually arise—and as soon as they appear, discussions and debates rage.

This book is the fruit of a long collaboration between an anthropologist (Adriana Destro) and a historian (Mauro Pesce). It takes its position within the principal currents of research that have renewed scholarly work on Jesus and on the origins of Christianity in recent decades. Our epoch is characterized by big questions and new goals for knowledge. Our hope is to contribute to the emancipation from presuppositions or paradigms that correspond only poorly to the drive for knowledge that animates our age. Jesus belongs to the heritage of humanity, and his story involves us all. What is needed, however, is a reflection that employs ever more appropriate tools of analysis and methodologies in order to give him a place in the sphere of today's intellectual debate. This can help establish a contact between his story and our own culture, which is still being shaped by Christianity.

The starting point for our investigation is the fact that his death, which is the incontestable proof of his life and of the way in which he led it, did not succeed in halting his message. We do not analyze this fact; we simply recall it. This is where we start the task of recovering and analyzing his life, wherever this is possible.

Lifestyle as the First Message

Jesus kindled hopes, mobilized consensus, and brought people together. Were the hopes and expectations that he had aroused diminished by his death? Were his followers faithful to his message? It is difficult to give a clear and decisive answer to these questions. Gerd Theissen thinks that "popular expectations of Jesus of Nazareth included everything the people expected of charismatic leader figures at that time: he was to be an interpreter of Scripture who expounded Torah more convincingly than other interpreters; a prophet who not only announced a better future but actually brought this about; a messianic king of the people, who restored freedom to the Jews. And yet, Jesus shattered all these expectations and roles."[1] Doubtless one sector of the population, that which was closest to the learned men and the theologians, was capable of sharing these Judaic religious concepts, but the expectations of the majority were much simpler, more urgent.

The clearest impression that the reader of the Gospel of Mark receives—an impression that the other Gospels do not negate—is that at one particular moment in his life, in the fullness of his adult existence, Jesus made a radical choice and that he staked his whole existence on this fundamental choice, right to the very end of his life. One other fact is essential, however. He pursued his objective in just one way: by going to meet the people to whom he belonged, the Judean[2] people, and taking his place among them.

At the center of our reflection, therefore, is the fact that Jesus addressed real persons with his words and his actions. He had taken on the task of solidarity with ordinary people in order to help them, to heal them, and to give them a concrete hope. Every day, he encountered crucial existential situations: domestic life, the narrow and absolute horizon constituted by family interests, the sickness of the poor, the insolent arrogance of the rich, the invasive power of the Romans. And it was the concreteness of these situations that he constantly addressed, making use of his own word and the power of his own body. His lifestyle is marked by two basic needs: the overturning of the coercive conditions that afflicted the existence of the people, and the expectation— in a "tomorrow" that was imminent—of a radical rebirth determined by God's dominion over the world.

It is precisely by penetrating into the depths of Jesus' lifestyle and habitual actions that we discern the secret of his person. On the one hand, he did not refuse to be physically present to people; but, on the other hand, his firm intention was not to have roots in any place, not to settle down in any environment. Jesus knew how to safeguard his own freedom of action and his complete independence. And because of this independence, which often took the form of a search for solitude, it is possible to reconstruct his life only in part. Many of his most intimate experiences remained unknown even to his disciples, and important segments of his existence were not captured in the writings that have come down to us.

Many books about Jesus center on his message, his words, or his most important public actions. Ed Parish Sanders, in *Jesus and Judaism*, attempts to base the historical portrait of Jesus not so much on his words, which are difficult to reconstruct in their original form, as on elements that are historically more certain, "facts about Jesus' career and its aftermath."[3] The novelty in our own research consists in the identification of an even more solid and certain foundation, what we call the "practice[4] of life" or the "lifestyle" of Jesus, that which shaped and determined his way of living. We have been guided by an anthropological intention in our investigations into the texts of earliest Christianity. When we speak of the lifestyle and practice of life of Jesus, we mean the cultural forms on which he based his life, the mechanisms by means of which he organized his existence and his means of support, the logic of his actions, and the modalities of his contacts with people and with institutions. We have used the word "practice" to indicate that the center of his personality consists not only in ideas but in a constant way of acting—a style of life. We want to find out how his concrete actions produced new realities and turned things upside down in the lives of the persons who encountered him. We want to identify the precise social environments in which his words, which were born in the interior of his existence, circulated, thanks to direct contacts.

His true message, therefore, is the message transmitted by his way of living, by the way in which he positioned himself in the world. His teaching passed through the various events of his career within a complex cultural context which is anything but transparent. His religious vision is incomprehensible outside his practical experience and his share in the life that people led. An utterance such as "Foxes have holes, and birds of the air have nests; but the Son of Man has nowhere to lay his head" (Luke 9:58) has very little significance if it remains outside the real meaning of the practice of Jesus' life, if it is not understood in the light of the fact that he was a man who had abandoned home, goods, and work. He entered people's houses and taught within domestic reality. This provoked conflicts, for example, between the two sisters Martha and Mary (Luke 10:38-42). When he tells them that only one thing is necessary for a woman—listening to the message—he is not formulating an abstract principle. A different way of evaluating individual behavior has made its way into the working relationships of a domestic unit.

Cultural anthropology teaches us that a cultural configuration coincides with an ensemble of behaviors and of relationships that are based on patterns that condition the existence of individuals precisely in their singularity.[5] Accordingly, our first task has been to show how Jesus positioned himself with regard to the social forms of his time, and to identify the substance of the innovations he proposed. Without examining his concrete actions and the way in which he was in contact with real human life stories, it is impossible to clarify whether his project corresponded to people's expectations. Did this project affect only a few persons or only the people of Israel, or did Jesus envisage a social transformation embracing the whole of humanity? Did he call into question the cultural and religious basis of the Judaic society of his time, or did he appeal to this basis against those who did not respect it? Without examining the details of his way of living, it is pointless to ask what meaning he attributed to his own proclamation and what essential reason led him to put his own life utterly at risk. Accordingly, we have sought to discern how Jesus met people, how he was physically involved in the crowds that came together and thronged around him, what the forms of association were that he preferred or with which he came into conflict. We have not resisted the temptation of shedding some light on his interior life, his emotions and feelings; the task is difficult, but not impossible. Ultimately, we have found ourselves facing an astonishing figure and a lifestyle that is personal, radical, and alternative.

The Historical Reliability of the Gospels

In the task of reconstructing the historical figure of Jesus,[6] the Gospels of Mark, Luke, and Matthew and the Gospel of John are indispensable. But the so-called Jewish-Christian Gospels are also important: the Gospels of the Nazarenes, of the Hebrews, and of the Ebionites. The *Gospel of Thomas*, which is certainly extremely ancient in its first redaction, offers significant help, although its contents primarily concern the words of Jesus, which are not the principal object of this book. We have drawn on the seven authentic letters of Paul, especially on 1 Corinthians, Galatians, and 1 Thessalonians. Useful information and a stimulus to further analysis are offered us by the Letter of James and the *Didache*, which transmit a sizable repertoire of words of Jesus and, in the case of the *Didache*, indications about the form of the Lord's Prayer, about the

Eucharist, and about the eschatological expectations that were linked to Jesus. A work from the close of the first century, the *Ascension of Isaiah*, is important because it helps us understand the eschatological scenarios and the experiences of contact with the supernatural that were widespread among the first disciples. The Acts of the Apostles provides essential information about the refraction of Jesus' action by the various currents of followers who came into existence after his death.

In the absence of Jesus and his world, which have now disappeared, anthropological analysis too must turn to these ancient written texts, products of the mentalities of an age that has passed away, texts that share the perspectives of that age. These are very distinctive works that appear to most of today's readers (or are presented to them) as closed and untouchable. Anthropology looks in them for the traces of a world that was real but is now vanished; for the references that concern the author and the addressees; and for the concrete aspects of the life of Jesus and the cultural context of these aspects. Anthropology endeavors to uncover the strategies and the elements of challenge that (often in a way that is scarcely visible) characterize the world of human relationships. In this way, anthropology gives a voice and a visibility to elements and situations that allow the reconstruction of an entire human and social order. We must supplement a tendency among scholars who are, in general, reluctant to shed light on ordinary cultural contents that they regard as possessing scanty cognitive value. In this way, we can delineate what was required in an environment that was governed by matters of custom.

The questions that anthropology puts to a text are not purely literary or theological. On the contrary, these questions follow an interpretive process that gives priority to the factors and events that shape a person's life. We have chosen a methodology that interweaves different models and structures of anthropological analysis,[7] looking at the places and the dislocation of persons, the domestic units, the phenomena of associations, and the distribution of the primary means of sustenance (from food to housing). The more open the dialogue among these interpretive models, the more the various cultural factors will converge in a plausible image of the human life of Jesus that is truly integrated into a precise human context. We are interested above all in spatial and temporal dimensions (where and when Jesus worked); in his personal relationships, circumstances, and contacts (how he related within and outside kinship groups and how he dealt with the transactions of giving and receiving on which these groups were based); in his private and public roles and gestures (how he used his body, the itinerant life, the periods of isolation); and in his interior states (how he expressed his feelings). Along these lines, an attentive investigation of the materials offered by the Gospels—materials that are sometimes highly stratified, and not explicit[8]—leads to the discovery of an extraordinary quantity of information and supplements the results of historical or literary and exegetical approaches.

The Necessity of Research into the Historical Jesus

Why is it necessary to reconstruct the historical figure of Jesus? The answer lies in two sets of facts: the nature of the documents and the divergences that exist among them. The documentation that permits us to know about Jesus consists essentially of texts. Like any written work, the texts of earliest Christianity must be examined critically.

All texts are cultural products, and written texts are among the most refined instruments that human culture has ever produced. But they do not simply reproduce the facts: they *propose* facts by making use of points of view and interpretive patterns. They offer, first of all, visions or give glimpses of their authors and of their projects. There is, therefore, an ineradicable difference between the historical reality and the texts that document it.[9] This makes it necessary to undertake a critical analysis of the nature of the documents, the paths they take, and their intellectual structures.

The sources that we have used are not documents from an archive. They are not texts that were laid down in a written form to become in some way or other a fetish. They are not novelistic productions nor works of fantasy, and they are certainly not philosophical. They are expressions of persons and of human groups that mirrored themselves in these texts and constructed their own memory and their own convictions. They are not neutral texts, because they take a stance; but they are truthful texts, in that they reproduce the authentic beliefs or the religious points of view of those who wrote them.

The Gospel narratives are the result of a lengthy process of accumulation and selection of information that was passed from person to person. Interpretive, anthropological, and historical methods cannot avoid taking account of the choices that shaped the processes of memory. Anthropology offers paths to analyze the transition from event to text, including the technique of recording and the need to forget.[10] No transmission, whether oral or written, is truly literal. The value of many diverse aspects in a transmission—from formal discourses to occasional

Introduction   xv

speeches, to reported speeches, to gossip and rumors—can be extremely variable. There is no material that is uncontaminated or totally truthful and authentic. This necessary interdependence between memory and forgetfulness, between speaking and keeping silent, should be neither suppressed nor overestimated, for it is, in fact, obvious that a narrative concentrates its attention only on some elements that its author judges relevant to the goals he or she has sought to realize—and such goals are always partial. Let us give only one example. In some cases, the author was limited by the scarcity of certain and verifiable information, of memories that can safely be accepted. If all we had was the Gospel of John, we would not know the Lord's Prayer. On the basis of the oldest form of chapter 16 of Mark, we would not know about the appearances of the risen Jesus. And in Mark, many of the words that Luke and Matthew attribute to Jesus are absent. Some parables, such as the celebrated story of the Good Samaritan, are transmitted only by Luke. The anthropologist's awareness of the process of memorization demands the critical reconstruction of the history, of the persons involved, of the environments, and of the goals (often implicit) pursued by the authors of a text.

Let us now look at the second aspect that makes it necessary to carry out research into the historical figure of Jesus. Earliest Christianity in its first two centuries was characterized by a multiplicity of currents that give us diverse images of him. None of these can claim to be more authentic or unequivocally exclusive vis-à-vis the other images. At least for the first one hundred and fifty years after the death of Jesus, different tendencies coexisted within emerging Christianity; there was no normative Christianity recognized by all. It is in the second half of the second century that for the first time we find the idea that the deviation from a certain norm that emerged in one precise historical form is to be considered open to censure as a "heresy." It seems that it was Justin, shortly after 150, who gave the Greek word *hairesis* the meaning of an opinion that was to be condemned—a heresy.[11] Before Justin, this term signified one distinct free opinion that was admitted on equal terms with all other opinions. However, the need for an orthodoxy—a fact that is culturally relevant and reveals a change of perceptions and expectations—does not mean that there was universal agreement about the doctrines that were to be considered "orthodox." And another century again had to pass before the New Testament was formed, the collection of twenty-seven normative works that were regarded as inspired by God.[12] The writings of the New Testament are necessary for the reconstruction of the historical image of Jesus, but they are not sufficient for this task. It is a partial collection full of gaps. It gathers together only some of the Christian works written in roughly the first one hundred and twenty years, and this means that it excludes various images of Jesus that are scattered in other writings, some of which are lost today, although they were widespread in the first century.

Furthermore, the twenty-seven writings included in the New Testament can be used only on certain conditions. First and foremost, one must free oneself of the idea that the four canonical Gospels were known by everyone in the first or second century. It cannot be taken for granted that, at that period, the readers of the *Gospel of Thomas* or the *Gospel of the Hebrews* or any other of the many existing Gospels would have known Matthew or Luke or Mark. Justin, in the mid-second century, speaks of "the memoirs of the apostles" (*1 Apol.* 67; *Dial.* 103.106), but continues to make use of words of Jesus transmitted by noncanonical gospels and texts.[13] The *Didache*, probably redacted toward the end of the first century and contemporary with the Gospels of Luke and Matthew, is close only to the Gospel of Matthew, but without being dependent on it. The community of Rhossus (in the southeast of today's Turkey) knew the *Gospel of Peter*, but not the others.[14] Despite this, some of the Synoptic Gospels had become points of reference that were widely consulted toward the middle of the second century, as seems to be demonstrated by the *Gospel of Judas*.[15] But this does not mean that the canonical Gospels were considered normative all at once. In the first century, Mark was not more important than *Thomas*. The fact that Luke had recourse to sources of his own when he wrote his Gospel (Luke 1:1-4) shows that he did not consider the others normative—not even the Gospel of Mark.

It is the differences among the Gospels that oblige us to ask about the words pronounced by Jesus or the actions performed by him. Here, we limit ourselves to a few remarks by way of example. (a) According to the Gospel of Mark, followed by Luke and by Matthew, Jesus went to Jerusalem only once, after having preached only in the north of the Land of Israel; but according to the Gospel of John, he went there several times and worked extensively in Judea. In John, Jesus expels the merchants from the Temple near the beginning of his activity, but in Mark, Luke, and Matthew, he does so at the end. (b) The order of the facts concerning the life of Jesus varies among the three Gospels of Mark, Luke, and Matthew. (c) It suffices to examine accurately the three versions of the parable of the banquet that have come down to us[16] to see that the Gospel of Matthew has profoundly modified the original parable of Jesus, and that the versions of Luke and the *Gospel of Thomas* are more reliable. The comparison with the *Gospel of Thomas* allows us to affirm that sometimes the parables were adapted in order to express the supernatural role that the earliest Christian communities attributed to Jesus. This is the case with the parable of the murderous tenants in the vineyard.[17] (d) The Gospels of Matthew and John have a tendency to place lengthy discourses on the lips of Jesus, but the exegesis of every detail of the text shows that the discourses of Matthew are made up of individual sayings of Jesus that the earlier tradition had handed on separately, while those of John seem profoundly influenced by the theology that was typical of the Johannine community.

We could easily multiply such examples of divergences. But to say that the Gospels sometimes present discordances does not imply that these words are historically untrustworthy. As a matter of fact, the Gospels very frequently converge, and their documentary value is extremely high, as is also that of those other texts that the communities would later regard as apocryphal. Critical analysis must be made on a case-by-case basis, just as in the historical investigation of any document. Our starting point is the presupposition that the Gospel documents are reliable, but only to some extent, and we seek to understand the motives that led their authors to omit or to modify what they had received from others.

Faced with the divergent testimonies in earliest Christianity, there is no alternative but to trust in the traditional methodologies of historical criticism and in anthropology's competence in the analysis of the complex of relationships and experiences. There is, however, a specific debate about the criteria that should be applied to research into the historical figure of Jesus. Here we limit ourselves to a presentation of the criteria that we have followed in the present book.

There is an immense gap between today's culture and the culture of Jesus. The first criterion that we have adopted systematically here consists in reading the way of life, the actions, and the words of Jesus within his own culture and environment. Our theory about the three levels of depth of the text[18] allows us to identify in the Gospels deep cultural strata that are the most solid base for showing us how Jesus related to the world around him. We could call this the criterion of continuity, or conformity with regard to the culture of his environment; and of discontinuity, or lack of conformity, with regard to today's culture. We have taken on the anthropological view of one who observes from afar,[19] aware of our own distance from the ancient world and, at the same time, of the contemporary values that we bear and of the analytical experiences that have been elaborated in our own historical-cultural context.[20]

Some contemporary tendencies in theology reject the necessity of recognizing the distance and the cultural gap, insisting on the fact that the texts of earliest Christianity were produced by persons and communities who believed in Jesus, just as today's faithful believe in him. They infer from this that only faith—a faith that traditionally is presumed to be uniform and unvaried—makes it possible to understand these texts. In reality, this affirmation is not very helpful. It is true that the writings of earliest Christianity were produced by persons who believed in Jesus and intended to propagate their faith, but from the very beginning, the *faiths* in Jesus were many—just as the faiths of today diverge greatly from one another, and some churches accuse others of not being faithful to the will and the message of Jesus. This shows why we need an anthropological and historical approach that attempts to grasp what was in fact the faith of Jesus, and what was the faith of his disciples.[21] Anthropologists and historians are aware that their own reconstructions are partial and depend on their own points of view. But it is precisely this ineradicable subjectivity that gives value to their research and provides the energy for further investigations.[22]

The second criterion we have followed consists in taking account of the difference between the ideas and actions of Jesus and the ideas and actions of the first communities of his followers. We regard as authentic the attribution to Jesus of words and actions when these contrast or are not in harmony with the words and actions of the first Christian groups, for it is improbable that the original communities would have arbitrarily ascribed to him actions that contradicted their own practice and customs.[23] The distance of Jesus from his own environment is also important. In some individual instances, we encounter actions and words in which he criticized certain aspects of his own Judaic context. Nevertheless, we must always seek to grasp to what extent the attribution to Jesus of a critical attitude is determined by the polemic that the communities subsequently elaborated against the Judeans.

We regard as certainly historical those sayings attributed to Jesus in which there is no affirmation about his salvific function or his special supernatural dignity. For example, the petition in the Lord's Prayer, "Forgive us our debts, as we also have forgiven our debtors" (Matt 6:12), must be considered authentic because it attributes the forgiveness of sins exclusively to God and to the behavior of human beings—not to Jesus' death on the cross. For the same reason, it is highly probable that the following words that Luke ascribes to Jesus are authentic: "Unless you repent, you will all perish as they did" (Luke 13:3).

It is often the case that an action, a saying, or a parable of Jesus is attested by only one source, but this is not a sufficient reason to dismiss it as unhistorical. For if the contents of these actions and words converge with other actions and words in which it is difficult to doubt the historicity, they are to be considered reliable.

The attempt to reconstruct a plausible image of Jesus always encounters one obstacle: namely, the fact that no source puts us in direct contact with him. None of the Gospels is the work of eyewitnesses, but only of followers from the second or subsequent generations. However, eyewitness testimony, which is the basis of ethnographical reconstruction, has a relative value, and it is accompanied in anthropological analysis by other strategies of verification. The interweaving of appearance and reality, of the invisibility and the visibility of the phenomena, is at the center of wide-ranging discussions of the reliability of the observer's eye. It is well known, on the one hand, that "the testimony of the next day"—which reports after a brief lapse of time something that happened in the past—opens up a whole series of historical and interpretive problems. On the other hand, a faithful transcription contemporary with the event itself is an extremely rare thing, and it entails the risk of incompleteness and of the momentary impression made on a person.

The authors of the Gospels were persons who belonged to the Hellenistic-Roman culture, but their works portray the career of a Galilean Judean who spoke Aramaic. Since they spoke and wrote in Greek, they do not record for us the words that Jesus may perhaps have spoken in his own language. The authors of the Gospels made use of narratives that originated in persons who had a direct relationship with him or who had been informed indirectly about him. It is certain that the comparative examination of the Gospels permits us to go back to the common sources of their authors and to what these sources contained; but it does not permit us to go back to Jesus himself, to what he in fact said and did. We can reconstruct with a certain amount of reliability the form that his parables, his sayings, or the stories about him had before they were reworked and entered into the various formulations of the Gospels. But it is obvious that we cannot go back to a phase more ancient than that of those who supplied the information to the authors of our Gospels. There is an empty space, a distance, between the testimonies on which the Gospels are based and Jesus—and this gap is not filled by any intermediary testimony accessible to the historian. Nevertheless, we reject a skeptical attitude, since that would be unjustified. The data that emerge from the earliest Christian sources are numerous, and their convergence allows us to reconstruct a sufficiently convincing image of the historical figure of Jesus. Although it often remains hypothetical, it possesses a significant degree of reliability.

The primary need that moves us to begin this investigation of the historical figure of Jesus is the conviction that is possible even today to appeal to Jesus as an indispensable basis of our culture and our morality.

Research into the historical Jesus bears within itself the possibility of a regeneration of the religious world for which he is the point of reference. It is not true to say that shedding light on the contrast between the historical Jesus and the later churches and their dissonant interpretations amounts to an attack and a denial of Christianity. To argue in this way would mean yielding to a fundamentalist mentality that holds that the churches of today have always been faithful in every way to the lifestyle and teaching of Jesus, and that they put into practice a great inheritance that is monolithic and untouchable—and improbably uncoupled from the evolution of history. Anthropological and historical research brings out the complexity of many cultural aspects and the reasons for the historical change that is always going on. These data can have a constructive influence on doctrinal reflection (as happened, for example, in Christian theology in the decades after the Second World War) and even on the conceptions of religion and religiosity.

In this book, we maintain that Jesus practiced his traditional religion and was not the founder of a religious system different from that in which he was born. His lifestyle and his message, the movement that he created during his existence, were not a religion (a concept absent from the Judaism of his time).[24] Rather, he invited people to change their behavior in order to bring about a profound renewal within the Judaic world in which he lived.

The figure of Jesus became detached totally from Judaic culture only at a time when the great majority of his followers were non-Judean. People lost sight of his human dimension when they began to regard him primarily as a divine being. His figure was transformed at that time from the authentic believer that he was into the figure of an innovator and reformer who was critical of his own culture. In this way, people began to lose their appreciation of his fidelity to God and of his expectation that God would intervene. It is from this time on that a wedge was inserted between the historical Jesus and the Jesus of the later churches.

Encounters
with Jesus

1

JESUS ON HIS LANDSCAPE

Mental Maps and Real Territories

Jesus and His Land

Jesus is always imagined in a place: by the Jordan, at Capernaum, in the Garden of Gethsemane. These are either places mentioned in the Gospels or places revealed to us by historians and archaeologists. These localizations correspond to a need for mental order, which always links a person to a place, an existence to a residence, a body to a locality.

Besides this, the anthropological interpretation of written texts[1] emphasizes that our social imagination situates every individual in one particular space and time and within one specific social action. In his discussion of the ecology of culture, the anthropologist Tim Ingold sees human subjects as organisms that live and act within one particular existential situation of which they, together with other living beings, form an integral part.[2] In this perspective, a house is necessarily a container of human activities; a street is a route followed by travelers; and a field is the place where agricultural activity is carried out. It is the function that the individuals perform in a given context that allows us to understand its social physiognomy. It is an incontestable fact that no person exists without space. The individual characteristics necessarily manifest themselves and become concrete in the act of appropriating and modifying the spaces that are available to each person.[3]

Everyone possesses mental maps[4] that are closely linked to the place where he or she lives, and everyone has in mind a geography of the internal structure and the external boundaries of the world in which one exists and in which others exist. This mental construction cannot be transmitted or reproduced by any geographic map. By means of places, the individual ultimately appeals to an existential meaning and an order,[5] because as Marc Augé argues in *Non-Lieux*, the place is at one and the same time "a principle of meaning for the people who live in it and also a principle of intelligibility for the persons who observe it."[6]

Not only must Jesus be located in precise places. He must also be regarded as a person who has points of view about his own material and geographical environment. In order to reconstruct the territory in which he lived and moved, which is distant from our own idea of territory, we are dependent on archaeological, historical, and anthropological research and, in particular, on documents of early Christianity, namely, the Gospels, which were written decades after the events of his life. This means that we are obliged to move among various maps: those of today's archaeologists, historians, and anthropologists. In all of these instances, the map depends on the conceptual universe and the experience of the one who drew it. The archaeologist and the historian give preference to certain elements (borders, communication routes, centers of habitation, monuments) and neglect others. The archaeologist who draws a map of first-century Galilee has certainly conceived an image of the region. This image guides his work, without taking an explicitly material form in the maps he draws. The historian cannot avoid the necessity of picturing (at least implicitly) the scenery within which the events that he wants to reconstruct take place. Likewise, the authors of the individual Gospels possessed a mental map of the places they mentioned in the narrative. How is it possible to get behind their social imagination, so that we can find access to Jesus' mental map? The difficulty in answering this question is caused by the fact that we are obliged to make use precisely of these Gospels and of the data that the historians, archaeologists, and anthropologists offer us.

The mental maps of a territory are constructed on the basis of a social practice and a vision of reality. The evangelists' maps are generated by the practice of the preaching of Jesus' first followers and by the memory these followers had of the events of his life. What conception and what practice generated the mental map of Jesus? When we answer this question, we must bear in mind the methodological perspectives mentioned above, and especially the ecology of culture, because place obliges every individual—and hence Jesus too—to mobilize forms of integration, of appropriation, and of use. Everyone internalizes images and symbols of the natural environment that surrounds him or her (mountains or plains, rivers or lakes, cities or villages), and everyone experiences these individually.

Far from the Cities

In the archaeological maps of the Land of Israel (to borrow the name used by the Gospel of Matthew 2:20-21), great importance is attributed first of all to the cities with their impressive structures, their forms of habitation, and the great roads that facilitated communication. Recent historical study has shown that the construction of cities and roads[7] was one of the principal objectives of the political and administrative authorities and of the highest social strata. The world of the first century, in which we must locate Jesus, saw new urban centers arise several times alongside the centers that already existed. If we begin with Galilee,[8] or at any rate with the northern zone of the Land of Israel, we find the cities of Bethsaida, Tiberias, and Hippos-Sussita situated along the Sea of Tiberias, on its northern, western, and eastern shores respectively. Ptolemais, Dor, and Caesarea Maritima were situated on the Mediterranean coast.[9] Continuing toward the central and southern zone of the land of Israel, we find the following coastal towns: Apollonia, Ashkelon, Antedon, Gaza, and Raphia. The urban centers on the coast were city-states. In the central hinterland of Galilee were Sepphoris and Scythopolis (Beth Shean). The latter town, like Hippos, belonged to a territory known as the Decapolis, made up of ten cities situated mostly to the east of the Sea of Galilee (including Gadara, Gerasa, Pella, Philadelphia, Raphana). A network of great roads united the cities and linked them to Jerusalem and to the principal urban centers outside the Land of Israel. For example, Josephus speaks of two important roads leading to Jerusalem, the "principal road" from the north and the "public road" from the coast.[10] The large-scale system of Roman roads is thought to be later than the time of Jesus.[11]

The literary documentation and the socio-anthropological approach combine to show us how the higher social classes in the first century, both Judean and Roman, moved around, especially among the major centers and along the principal communication routes. In the eyes of these elites, the Land of Israel, and Galilee in particular, looked like a collection of cities linked by great roads that avoided the minor centers. The villages were linked by a multitude of secondary routes and paths that basically followed the configuration of the territory and served the ordinary needs of the populace.[12] Networks of roads around the lake and navigational trajectories across it have been identified.[13] The archaeologist James F. Strange has demonstrated that there was "an extensive specialized agricultural and industrial production" in first-century Galilee, as well as a "trade network . . . that connected the villages, towns, and cities of Lower Galilee, Upper Galilee, the rift and the Golan."[14] Vessels of terracotta, of ceramic, and of glass were produced and sold, as well as agricultural products and wine. This presupposed the existence of a network of unpaved roads and footpaths that linked the various production sites to the urban centers.

The map reconstructed by archaeologists is limited to the cities and to the principal roads, and this certainly means that it provides an important backdrop to the life of Jesus. It gives us little information, however, about the places where he actually moved, since the immediate objective of his existence and his place of action seem to have been almost exclusively located in rural areas and in centers of habitation that were not very important in urban and political terms. Jesus must have regarded the villages as the real vital ganglia of the territory where he preached; their complex and swarming life influenced his perceptions and his mental pictures. Although the places he frequented lay outside the major communication routes, they were crowded with people and were exposed to a great variety of influences. The fact that the greater part of production took place in the villages established a close link between them and the cities that it was their task to supply. This made them satellites of the urban centers or the important provincial capitals. John Dominic Crossan underlines this fact by pointing to Nazareth, which was united to Sepphoris by two roads that presumably saw a great deal of traffic.[15] All this explains why the villages were anything but isolated environments closed in on themselves. Lower Galilee was at the center of complex commercial trajectories. The archaeologist Eric M. Meyers maintains that "the isolation often associated with the Galilean personality is therefore quite inappropriate when we speak of Jesus of Nazareth, who grew up along one of the branches of one of the busiest trade routes of ancient Palestine."[16]

There can be no doubt that we must turn to the Gospels in order to discover how Jesus imagined his own places and related to them. At once, however, we encounter a methodological problem that is well known to exegetes and affects every attempt at research into the historical figure of Jesus. Very frequently, his actions or his words are reported by more than one Gospel, but each of them locates these in different places and at different times. This is because the spatial and temporal locations offered by the Gospels are late and are not at all certain.[17] The same applies to the overall geographical scenarios of the activity of Jesus, which vary from one Gospel to another. This means that it is far from certain whether any particular action actually occurred in the place where a Gospel narrative locates it. What the Gospels present, however, is not some abstract truth, but a truth linked to the concrete life of a man, and this makes it essential for them to attempt to transmit the memory of the times and the places at which the events occurred. Maurice Halbwachs correctly affirms that "remembering" requires more than merely general ideas: it is necessary to have recourse to facts that actually happened, since "a purely abstract truth is not a remembrance." A remembrance takes us back to concrete events of the past, whereas "an abstract truth has no point of contact with the succession of events."[18] The historical reliability of a memory is made problematic by the fact that it arises when the event is already distant in time, and verification is difficult.

The Gospels agree on one point, namely, in not locating Jesus' activity in the big cities. This has one fundamental consequence for the historical reconstruction—that his life acquires its meaning outside the urban centers and without their help. This makes the investigation harder, since there is little information about the non-urban centers in the historical documentation; at the same time, Jesus' deliberate wish to keep away from the large centers ought to make us cautious about applying to him the urban scenario on which the historical and archaeological reconstruction of the first century has usually concentrated.

Mark's Jesus is indubitably a man of the village[19] who looks at the big cities and at the rest of the Land of Israel from a peripheral viewpoint.[20] He seems to choose marginality not as an expedient or a renunciation but as a point of strength. The villages of Galilee were not places where Romanization was suffered in a simply passive manner; and besides this, we are more aware today than ever before of the creative and active roles played by local and marginal conditions in the processes of inclusion or globalization.[21] Here, we have in mind above all the political and juridical aspect of the concept of city rather than its spatial or urban dimension: we are referring to the *civitas*, not to the *urbs*. It is the political and juridical element that characterizes the Romanized cities of Galilee and the Land of Israel at the time of Jesus. The city is defined not so much by its buildings and its walls as by the body of citizens, who have the right to participate in the assembly and the senate, to which only the landed proprietors belong. Lellia Cracco Ruggini has shown how "the political bond of urban society had a primarily juridical nature, while at the same time the cities constituted only one modular element within a more complex structure." In the Roman Empire, of which the Land of Israel formed a part, "society was broken down into a series of concentric circles. One of these was the city, as an intermediary link between the family and the state." Accordingly, the Roman imperial city was not a "structure of participation in the conduct of communal affairs" but "increasingly a structure of integration" of the provincial districts "in keeping with a broad range of duties, rights, and privileges." The empire ruled and exercised control primarily by means of the cities; for this reason, the Romans carried out "an intensive work of urbanization":

> The new provincial cities—i.e., those recognized as such by Rome—were ranked according to juridical hierarchies that were subtly graded. On the formal level, these sanctioned corresponding hierarchies of relationships of dependence and privilege vis-à-vis the Roman power, which employed this instrument consciously to nourish local patriotisms by distributing favors and juridical promotions.[22]

Jesus was profoundly alienated from the city *qua* nucleus of juridical structures constituted by the urban elites who aimed at integration into the empire. From this point of view, he was an unintegrated man. The Gospel of Mark clearly shows the pre-eminence of the village environment, and this is confirmed by Matthew and Luke. It is, however, true that these two Gospels attach a greater importance to the cities, as, for example, when Luke ascribes to Jesus the following words: "I must proclaim the good news of the kingdom of God to the other cities also" (4:43); but the noun *polis* in these two Gospels can also designate what in fact were only large villages.[23] But we are never told that Jesus lived in, or even entered, Sepphoris and Tiberias, or Caesarea and Scythopolis. Of all the big cities, Jerusalem is the only exception here. It is true that Mark and Matthew state that Jesus went to the "region" of the city of Tyre, that is, its surrounding territories (Mark 7:24; Matt 15:21), but they do not write that he actually went *into* the city. One saying reported by both Luke and Matthew (and thus probably originating in Q, the sayings source)[24] appears to assume that Jesus was active in the cities of Chorazin and Bethsaida: "Woe to you, Chorazin! Woe to you, Bethsaida! For if the deeds of power done in you had been done in Tyre and Sidon, they would have repented long ago, sitting in sackcloth and ashes" (Luke 10:13/Matt 11:21). This saying probably shows us the mental map of Jesus, rather than of the evangelists. By contrasting two cities in Galilean territory with two cities in Phoenician territory, he may have expressed a symbolic contrast between Galilee (personified in Chorazin[25] and Bethsaida[26]) and the non-Judean regions.[27] In the case of Bethsaida, Mark tells us that Jesus entered this city (8:22), but the narrative underlines that the miracle Jesus worked on that occasion took place outside the city. Indeed, Jesus tells the blind man whom he has healed to return home without going back to Bethsaida, where he had probably been begging (Mark 8:22-26). According to the Gospel of John, no less than three of Jesus' followers—Andrew, Simon, and Philip (1:44; 12:21)—came from Bethsaida, which means that this town formed a part of the identity of those who accompanied him. According to Luke 9:10-17, the place where Jesus withdrew in private and then worked the miracle of the multiplication of the loaves for five thousand persons was near Bethsaida, but not inside the city.[28] To sum up, it seems unlikely that Jesus would never have entered Bethsaida; but the city as such does not constitute the real-life scenario, still less the mental scenario, of his activity. On the other hand, Mark relates that Jesus entered the city of Sidon, to the north of Tyre on the Phoenician coast (7:31), and the city of Jericho (10:46).

Capernaum (*Kephar Nahum* in Aramaic) is a case on its own. Scholars have debated whether this inhabited site was very large or rather small:[29] Was it a small village or a city?[30] Luke and Matthew call Capernaum a "city" because they are dependent on Mark; they do not seem to have had any direct information about the place. But Mark did not have a precise concept of "city." He uses this noun to designate inhabited territory as opposed to deserted or wild places (Mark 1:35, 45; 5:14; 6:32-33). Jonathan Reed concludes that "a Markan inference that Capernaum was a polis, and the later explicit label by Matthew and Luke, should in no way count as evidence that Capernaum was a polis in any technical sense.... Its population of 600–1,500 was, related to the surrounding Galilean cities, modest. As a political entity on the Galilean scene, it was unimportant and peripheral."[31]

John confirms the image of a Jesus who, with the exception of Jerusalem, frequented small settlements (for example, Bethany and Ephraim). The cities are bearers of historical and institutional signs that are inappropriate to the project of Jesus.[32] It is in the villages that he establishes his relationships and that the paradigms that give him identity are developed. We should not, however, overemphasize the hypothesis that Jesus categorically refused to enter the cities.

Village life is anything but simple. To frequent the villages means becoming immersed in a daily life that is both composite and problematic. In village societies and rural areas,[33] the local situations are always determined by relationships of a familiar, personal, economic, and work character. These relationships are often characterized by tensions and make an incisive impact on individual lives. There can be no doubt that a great variety of stimuli and conditioning occurs in small, restricted areas such as villages. Despite the variety in people's emotions and relationships, however, there are many similarities in terms of material goods and of individual lifestyles. We may, therefore, suppose that there was a high density in the network of relationships in the places Jesus visited, and that this network was constrictive, since it was often generated by situations of daily life from which the individual could not escape. In order to grasp the situation that confronted Jesus, we must bear in mind that political and administrative activities, such as the collection of taxes,[34] judicial business, and military controls, were located in many villages. Jesus, however, seldom worked in the places where these institutional activities were located.

The fact that Jesus was a man of the village who avoided the cities has raised a number of questions. E. P. Sanders notes that Jesus "offered the kingdom to outcasts and sinners, including tax collectors and prostitutes" and that one "would think that such a mission would have taken him to Tiberias, the capital city. He might have gone to Sepphoris to protest against the wealth of the aristocracy. A desire to summon Israel might have sent him to the major population centres." Yet Jesus "worked among his own: the residents of villages."[35] What are we to make of this behavior?

Research into the socio-economic situation of Galilee emphasizes the existence of a contrast between city and countryside, which was exploited by the landed proprietors who lived in the urban centers. This must not be reduced to the contrast between Gentiles and Judeans, since many Judeans lived in the big cities, and some of them were wealthy proprietors.[36] As we shall see more clearly below, this contrast emerges in Jesus' own sayings and parables. We can grasp his strategy more precisely if we look at some general aspects of the relationship between city and countryside. The urban centers are certainly social poles[37] that govern, celebrate, legislate, and legitimate; they treat the periphery in terms of their own interests. They also lay claim to long histories, which they employ to define the persons and groups who reside in these centers. In the eyes of the dominant urban classes, the rural villages are not bearers of identities and recognizable historical ancestries: they are only suppliers or subordinate producers. Jesus demurs from this way of looking at things, and indeed opposes it. For him, the village is the primary locus of Judean identity. He saw the rural units as the basis on which the entire socio-cultural structure rested.

Jesus in Galilee, in Judaea, and outside the Borders

The Gospel of Matthew gives us a piece of information that allows us to enter into the image Jesus had of his own land. This can be gleaned from the prohibition that he addressed to his disciples when he sent them out on a mission: "Do not go onto the road of the Gentiles, and do not enter into the town of the Samaritans" (10:5).[38] These words are extremely important, since they disclose precious information about the choices made by Jesus and his disciples. Most exegetes do not take seriously this prohibition against going along one precise type of road, and restrict themselves to a discussion of whether Jesus did indeed forbid preaching to non-Judeans.[39] But the "road of the Gentiles" is a real road, just as the "city of the Samaritans" is real. The forbidden road of which Matthew writes cannot be one of the Roman roads, which were not built before the beginning of the second century.[40] It is possible that the "road of the Gentiles" corresponds to what Josephus, writing at a period not far distant from Matthew, calls the "principal road" (*leōphoros*) from the north to Jerusalem, which we have mentioned above. When Jesus goes to Jerusalem, according to Mark and Matthew, he avoids this road and passes through Peraea on the far side of the Jordan. He seems to prefer the minor roads that were taken by the Judeans when they moved from one village to another. This suggests that his presence in the territory was selective, limited to certain places; he was a stranger to the great currents of political-administrative communication. Jesus avoided the roads frequented by non-Judeans because he reserved his attention for the social milieus to which he himself belonged. In short, although his aims include the entire population of Israel, Jesus becomes a leader of the social strata that populate the villages—and the only way to meet these persons is to go to where they live.[41]

We must now ask how Jesus envisaged the extent of the territory of the Judeans. In order to answer this question, we must concentrate our imagination on the geographical map of all the places—internal and external, central or peripheral—that he visited; and here too we encounter a significant methodological problem. Jesus goes to places that seem to lie outside what modern scholars think of as the borders of his land. In the case of Galilee, some scholars refer to the political borders laid down by the Romans, while others look exclusively to the geographical borders. But how did Jesus conceive of the boundaries of his own territory? Did he think basically of Galilee, or did he regard the entire

"Land of Israel" as his own? And did he understand the boundaries as territorial, or were they defined for him by the de facto spread of the population? When modern scholars assert that he went "beyond the borders," are they arguing on the basis of a territorial criterion of their own, or was it Jesus himself who thought he was crossing a boundary?

It is possible that any attempt at an answer will fail to provide a definitive solution, but it may at least help clarify the essential problems. The first of these is the concept of the "Land of Israel," which seems to be related to an ideal land with boundaries that are not clearly defined and change from time to time. The kingdom of David is not exactly the same as the Hasmonaean kingdom or the kingdom of Herod, and the religious leaders in the various periods imagined it in diverse ways.[42] The Gospel of Matthew speaks of the Judean territory as the "Land of Israel" with a vague extent that includes both Judea and Galilee (2:20-22). The northernmost boundaries that Josephus ascribes to the Land of Israel are farther to the north than the Roman delimitation of Upper Galilee; and a rabbinic document that may have been written in the Roman period, the so-called baraita of the borders, envisages different borders than those on the map on p. 2. For Josephus, the northernmost place is Niqbata of 'Ayun (the Pass of 'Ayun), roughly forty kilometers to the east of the Mediterranean coast, thirty kilometers north of the Sea of Galilee, and ten kilometers north of Tyre.[43] This means that the eastern border of Upper Galilee is contiguous with the territory of the city of Tyre. Although it is difficult to say how Jesus envisaged the borders of the Land of Israel, it is improbable that he felt bound to accept the territorial demarcations of the Romans.

Jesus rarely speaks of his land. He does say who will possess it: "Blessed are the meek, for they will inherit the land" (Matt 5:5), but only the Gospel of Matthew records these words. The Acts of the Apostles attribute to him the desire to "restore the kingdom of Israel" (Acts 1:6), but this passage says nothing about its extent.

Jesus and his group go beyond the Roman borders of Galilee both to the northwest and to the east. Mark writes that Jesus "set out and went away to the region of Tyre" (7:24), and we see that he covers long distances outside Galilee: "Then he returned from the region of Tyre, and went by way of Sidon towards the Sea of Galilee, in the region of the Decapolis" (7:31). The description of this route is somewhat obscure,[44] but it does tell us that Jesus also crossed non-Judean territories.[45] There were, in fact, many Judeans there. Judeans certainly lived in the Decapolis, since the Hasmonaean kings, and especially Alexander Jannaeus, had taken possession of many cities there.[46] Josephus writes that there were substantial Judean communities in Ptolemais, Tyre, and Sidon.[47] Many Judeans lived in Tyre, and to the south of this city lay the thirteen "forbidden" villages of which the Judean tradition speaks, where numerous Judeans lived.[48] It is therefore possible that Jesus' journey to these regions may have been motivated by the desire to address the Judean groups who resided there. We find it plausible that Jesus looked for the lost sheep of the house of Israel also in the territories to the north, the east, and the west of Galilee, and that he believed that the restoration of the kingdom of Israel[49] must include these regions too.[50]

Recent studies have insisted strongly on locating Jesus in Galilee, defining him as a "Galilean Jew."[51] Galilee, which was divided into Upper and Lower Galilee, was not a large region.[52] Lower Galilee, where Jesus' activity may have been more intense, was more densely populated and was traversed by heavy traffic of goods and persons between the Mediterranean coast and the cities of the Decapolis. An important role was played by the districts around the cities founded by the Herods. The harbors and the numerous docks along the shores of the lake are evidence of the flourishing activity in this region.

Although he reports that Jesus crosses the border in the direction of Tyre, Sidon, and the Decapolis, Mark believes that Jesus was active primarily within Galilee. It is only on the occasion of his one journey to Jerusalem (Mark 10:32) that Jesus "went to the region of Judea and beyond the Jordan" (10:1). Matthew confirms this, but Luke corrects it[53] in 4:44 when he tells us that Jesus preaches in the synagogues of Judea at the beginning of his public activity. Luke, however, knows nothing of Jesus' journeys in the regions of Tyre, Sidon, and the Decapolis.[54] Luke's Jesus reaches Jerusalem by way of Samaria and Judea instead of avoiding these regions by going through Peraea on the far side of the river Jordan, as he does in Matthew and Mark.[55] We must add that all the Gospels, including John, agree that Jesus never went south of Jerusalem and Jericho. He does not enter south Judea, does not go to Bethlehem and Hebron, nor does he go to the southern Mediterranean coast.

We find a profoundly different pattern, incompatible with that of Mark, Luke, and Matthew, in the Gospel of John, where Jesus' activity extends to Judea—which indeed becomes the major setting for his activity. The chronological sequence of events likewise changes. After choosing five of his disciples, Jesus leaves the south of the Land of Israel and goes to Galilee, not to Nazareth (as Matthew relates), but to Cana. He then goes to Capernaum not only with his disciples but also with his mother and his brothers and stays there "only a few days" (2:12). Immediately after this, he goes to Jerusalem for the Judaic feast of Passover

(2:13), where he expels the merchants from the Temple—an episode placed by the Synoptic Gospels at the end of his life. He then leaves Jerusalem and goes through the whole of Judea (3:22). He and his disciples[56] baptize, in concomitance with John the Baptizer ("He must increase, but I must decrease," 3:30). John gives us further details about the presence of Jesus in Judea. For example, he tells us that Jesus was in this region on the occasion of a feast that is not precisely identified (5:1).[57] It is true that this Gospel says that Jesus preaches throughout the whole of Galilee, but this seems to be for a brief period when he wanted to avoid Judea (7:1). He returns there for the feast of Tabernacles in the fall (7:10) and preaches in the Temple (8:59). John gives a lengthy account of his activity during this visit to the city, relating the miracle of the healing of the man born blind and the parable of the shepherd (9:1—10:21). He is at Jerusalem for the feast of Hanukkah (the dedication of the Temple, 10:22). After this, "he went away again across the Jordan to the place where John had been baptizing earlier, and he remained there" (10:39).[58] Not even after the raising of Lazarus does he return to Galilee: "he went from there to a town called Ephraim in the region near the wilderness" (11:54). From this point on, we see him in Bethany (12:1), which also lies in Judea, and then in Jerusalem, where his life ends. The Synoptic Gospels do not mention all these moves, with the exception of the statement in Luke that Jesus initially preached also in Judea. Finally, John does not tell us about any journey to the north of the Land of Israel in the direction of Tyre or Sidon or the regions to the east of the Sea of Galilee.

What are we to make of such significant differences? If the author of the Gospel of John knew the other Gospels, or at least Mark,[59] we are forced to hypothesize that he wanted to write a different story that would integrate and correct the other accounts. If, however, he did not know them, we are forced to admit that disparate groups of Jesus' disciples may have had no communication with one another for many decades, and that they preserved highly divergent historical memories.

It is at any rate clear that the Synoptic Gospels and John allow us to see two areas exposed to the influence of Jesus. These appear to be dependent on different groups of his disciples, who apparently possess divergent maps of his activity. One of these is set in the north, in Galilee, and events tend to take place around the Sea of Tiberias. The other, in the south, is centered on Jerusalem, the incomparable religious place, but also on the places where the Baptizer worked. The two maps may have been drawn up with two different perspectives. The Synoptic Gospels collect impressions of a world often (although not exclusively) constituted by fishers, craftsmen, and workers on the land; John, on the other hand, reflects a milieu that often relates itself to the Temple and to Jerusalem, that is, to places of great symbolic importance; and this Gospel has few references to concrete scenes of daily life. The fact that the "beloved" disciple, the nameless follower of Jesus to whom this Gospel traces its own tradition (John 21:24), is thought of as a person who has good relations to the high priest (18:15) and thus appears to be close, at least to some degree, to priestly circles,[60] leads to the hypothesis that the perspective of the Fourth Gospel was born in a medium-high cultural milieu[61] that was involved in the life of the city. On the other hand, John locates the internal life of Jesus' group in only *one* place in the city, namely, in an unknown dwelling with rooms of Hellenistic-Roman type in which the Last Supper is held, followed by Jesus' discourses and his final prayer. In his presentation of the gathering at the supper, John takes the symposium as his model and gives it a prominent position in his narrative;[62] but there is nothing here that betrays any specific knowledge of Jerusalem on the part of the Fourth Evangelist. On the contrary, the official milieus of the Romans and the priesthood that John mentions are also present in the synoptic passion narratives.

We could perhaps conclude that there was a double enclave in the movement. The enclave of the north seems to have had deeper social roots in the population of the region. The Synoptic Gospels frequently speak of settlements without giving their names, but they describe scenes that could take place only in one specific type of village. The situations to which they refer are plausible. In John, we often have precise indications of places, but no events are linked to them. The Fourth Gospel contains many markers of time and space, but without any realistic connotations. To sum up, the enclave of the south seems to construct its pictures in a somewhat intellectual and abstract manner, offering us symbols that omit the territorial and concrete character of real life.

The references to the synagogues may shed light on the place occupied by Galilee in Jesus' mental map. According to Mark (1:21-29, 39; 3:1; 6:2), Jesus teaches in a number of Galilean synagogues, and important episodes take place there (Mark 12:39/Luke 11:43; 20:46). A first-century inscription from a synagogue in Jerusalem, the inscription of Theodotos, shows that synagogues (understood as buildings) already existed in the Land of Israel during the lifetime of Jesus, as John S. Kloppenborg has convincingly affirmed in a recent study. This inscription can be dated to the Herodian period or the first Roman period. It is thus earlier than 70 c.e.,[63] and the fact that the builder of the synagogue was not only "head of the synagogue" but also a son and grandson of "heads of the synagogue" proves that synagogue buildings existed at an earlier date. The synagogue of Theodotos had several functions: the reading of Torah, instruction in the commandments, and hospitality for strangers in rooms specially destined for this purpose. Luke pays more attention to the scenes set in the synagogue.[64] In 7:5, he mentions that the synagogue of Capernaum was built under the patronage of a centurion. In 8:41, he calls Jairus an *archōn* ("ruler") of the synagogue. As in Mark, the synagogues in Luke are places where important episodes in Jesus' life take place. Luke's attentiveness to the synagogues may perhaps be due to the diaspora situation in which he was writing. At any rate, he shows us Jesus preaching in synagogues in Judea too. The different perspectives may be due to the situation in which their authors were working, or perhaps to the materials they were using, rather than to the viewpoint of Jesus himself. It remains difficult to reconstruct his mental map in any detail.

We can still accept the idea that his primary horizon was that of Galilee, but we must ask whether he subsequently left this behind. Large amounts of data compel us to conclude that Jesus' environment, on the basis of which he constructed his image of his own land, was that of the Galilean villages through which he passed. It also included some places in Judea, especially the holy city, which were important to him.

Jesus' mental map was based not primarily on the territory per se, but—as we shall see below—on the people who inhabited it. His project was to seek out "the lost sheep" of all the house of Israel, wherever they were, even outside the borders laid down by the Romans. And he saw Jerusalem as the symbolic center of the Land of Israel.

We have written above that much of the identity of a person is revealed by the way in which one passes through places, making spaces one's own and "dwelling" in them. Our conclusion is that Jesus had an extremely personal and innovative ability to pass through places and dwell in spaces. His independence and opposition to the customary social patterns made him an extraordinary reorganizer of space.

Jesus' Attitude toward Jerusalem

Why, then, did Jesus adopt the strategy of avoiding the big cities? Why did he adopt an anti-urban attitude? Recent studies of global processes have alerted us to the fact that no export of cultural models from the center to the periphery is ever received passively or accepted automatically.[65] On the contrary, there is almost always a variety of responses in the local situation.

Jesus on His Landscape

In the first century of the Common Era, the Land of Israel experienced political events and cultural transformations linked to the process of Romanization and to the client relationship of the local authorities vis-à-vis Rome. Recent research has shown that the effects of Romanization were not purely negative.[66] As in the case of Hellenization two centuries earlier, reactions to Roman rule were mixed. It led to conflicts in the local Judean culture, and it is impossible to dismiss the idea that Jesus' movement was one of the attempts within Judaism to respond more or less directly to this situation.

Socio-historical studies of the various regions in the Land of Israel at the time of Jesus offer us a complex picture of the transformations that were taking place.[67] Here, we recall only the transformation by Herod the Great (37 B.C.E.–4 C.E.) of Jerusalem and various places in Samaria and the Judaic territory into a "Great Judea" with the construction of theaters, amphitheaters, hippodromes, and villas. The Temple itself underwent restoration, and Jerusalem became one of the most celebrated urban centers in the ancient world. His son Antipas (tetrarch of Galilee and Peraea, 4–39 C.E.) intensified this process. In Galilee, he reconstructed the city of Sepphoris, renaming it Autocratoris.[68] In 20 C.E., he founded Tiberias.[69] Both names were chosen in honor of the emperors Augustus and Tiberius. This "apparently introduced Greco-Roman urban culture to Galilee for the first time,"[70] and inevitably entailed a disruption of the life of the adjacent Galilean villages. Their rhythms and internal processes were changed through these interventions by the governing authorities. "It appears that in order to provide the appropriate population for a completely new royal city [that is, Tiberias], Antipas moved the populations of the nearby villages."[71] Bethsaida too, which was transformed into a city by Herod Philip, underwent a process of Romanization in the 20s.[72]

The presence of new or reconstructed cities, where some of the elite probably also spoke Greek[73] and the Roman architectural patterns became established, also altered the existential horizons of the rural population and their relationship to the political powers. The villages entered a period of uncertainty and weakness. As Richard A. Horsley has remarked, "It is precisely in such circumstances, in face of the disintegration of the communities," that social and prophetic movements of revolt are born. One example is that of the prophet Theudas, who led a crowd out into the desert, like a new Moses, in 44 C.E.[74] This episode, however, took place after the death of Jesus. We know nothing of anti-Roman revolts in the two decades before the arrival of Pontius Pilate, who was certainly present in the Land of Israel from 26 to 36;

but popular dissatisfaction and discontent seem to have increased under his rule.[75] A distinction must be drawn between Romanization and the Roman military or political presence in Galilee. Many scholars today tend to the view that "the Roman presence in pre-70 C.E. Palestine was minimal."[76]

The society to which Jesus belonged is thus characterized by processes of growth and transformation, but also by strong tensions and waves of discontent. The uncertainties and disequilibrium, however, cannot be explained simply by referring to a situation of poverty, since we find both deprived persons and flourishing family units.[77] A considerable part of the population lived in impressive urban centers. This means that the various currents and movements that were active in the world of Jesus involved milieus of varying economic strength and social importance. As in any other place, the modalities and the gradations of this situation were linked to specific or local factors. Jesus was in contact with a composite society that was in ferment and exposed to processes that ranged from uprooting to social renewal. Although he did not live in the urban centers, he was involved with people who were "sensitive to the processes of social ascent and descent."[78]

The fact that Jesus belonged to rural Judean milieus does not mean that he was ignorant of the life and problems of the cities. Indeed, his anti-urban attitude makes sense only as a critical response to situations that he knew and rejected. Scholars have pointed out that it is highly improbable that he was unacquainted with Sepphoris or Bethsaida, towns that are so close to Capernaum, or that he lacked any information about their most important institutions (the theater, the political buildings, the places of recreation, or the gymnasium).[79]

The rural population had strong links to Jerusalem thanks to the pilgrimages and the solemn festivals—and Jesus was no exception. It is inconceivable that he never went to Jerusalem at any point in the period before his public preaching, at least on the occasion of one of the more important feasts. The city was the seat of religious and political power and the site of unique and irreplaceable religious rites. Economic activities were linked to the Temple, although it appears that certain forms of commerce were absent, or subject to restrictions.[80] The Temple was the symbol and the economic motor of an entire society. This made it necessary to accept living together and to cultivate a relationship both to the supreme political authorities in the land and abroad, and to the middle and lower social strata. Gerd Theissen has argued that the political attitude of the inhabitants of Jerusalem was moderate: their aim was to maintain "the status quo of the city and the Temple," and they were "linked to the Temple by material interests."[81] In Jerusalem, the choice was between integration and alienation, and Jesus could not evade this inescapable alternative. His attitude—a radical criticism of certain ways of understanding the Temple and the religious traditions—inevitably led him to adopt a stance that was out of sympathy with the population of the city.

Jesus certainly went to Jerusalem during his public activity, but John and the synoptics portray his visits differently. The Johannine Jesus went to Jerusalem as often as five times, following the Judaic festal calendar; the other Gospels report only one visit. What can we say about the historical reliability of these two divergent accounts? As we have seen, Luke relates that Jesus had preached in Judea too, even before he chose his first disciples (Luke 4:44), and this may mean that the evangelist knew traditions about events in Jesus' life that took place in Jerusalem. It is difficult to see why we should prefer one account rather than the other.

We should not forget, however, that the two versions agree at least on one point, namely, that Jesus went to Jerusalem to take part in the feast of Passover. This means that he appeared to some extent integrated into this feast alongside the pilgrim masses that made their way to the city. He looked like an observant Judean who fulfilled a ritual duty dictated by tradition: he accepted the representative character of the places and of the religious system.

Let us leave aside here the question why he went to Jerusalem. We shall look only at his relationship to the city. He was a man of the village—how much information did he have about the city in its institutions and mechanisms, and how did he in fact experience it? It is possible that he concentrated on particular places in Jerusalem, either because of his own spiritual attitude or because of his social position, but the Gospels say nothing in detail about how Jesus lived in the city. We gain information about his behavior in Jerusalem from the discussions with the groups that met him and engaged in polemic against him (Pharisees, scribes, priests), rather than from precise events that occurred in the city. Prior to his dramatic arrest, our information concerns the human subjects rather than the *places* or the public events in Jerusalem—and as we have seen, the mention of places in the Gospel narratives is historically less reliable than the narrative of the events that are located there. As Maurice Halbwachs writes, to speak of particular places helps to reinforce the memory of actions and events that are now finished and far away.[82] This means that the localization may often be the effect of a mechanism of memorization mobilized long after the events took place; this may be the case with the miracle at the pool of Siloam or the presence of Jesus in the portico of Solomon (John 9:7 and 10:23), as well as with the location in the Temple of the discussion about purity that survives in an otherwise lost Gospel.[83] The primary purpose of these localizations is to recall a miracle or an important discussion.

We do not know enough of Jesus' relationship to particular locations, but the same is not true of his attitude toward this city: he behaved like a person who did *not* belong to it. He never on any occasion led the life of an established citizen of Jerusalem who was at home there. We see this from the fact that during his visit, he entered the city in the morning, but left it at the close of day (Mark 11:11-12; 13:3; 14:3; 14:26; Luke 21:37; 22:39; Matt 21:17; 26:6; 26:30), and was welcomed in milieus or by persons he knew. He did not even have friends in the city with whom he could stay overnight, but he had such friends in the nearby village of Bethany (according to Mark), or in the village where a man made ready an ass[84] for his so-called triumphal entry into Jerusalem.

Several episodes shed light on Jesus' attitude toward Jerusalem. All the canonical Gospels describe his activity in the holy city in the days before he is arrested and put to death (Mark 11:1—14:11; Luke 19:28—22:6; Matt 21-25; John 12:12-50), but there is an enormous difference between John's narrative and that of the other three Gospels. The great discussions that Jesus had in Jerusalem according to Mark, Luke, and Matthew are entirely absent in John. In the Fourth Gospel, Jesus went to the city five days before the Passover feast (12:12). In addition to the Last Supper with the disciples (chs. 13–17), John relates only three episodes: the triumphal entry (12:12-19), the scene in which Jesus hears a voice from heaven (12:20-36), and a discourse delivered in a place and at a time that are unspecified (12:44-50). If we add the scene in Bethany where Mary anointed him with perfumed oil, we have a total of four episodes. In the synoptics, on the other hand, we find a total of fourteen episodes before the arrest,[85] and some of these give us detailed information about Jesus' attitude to the city.

Jesus was perhaps in the village of Bethany in the house of Simon the leper (Mark 14:3-11). He wanted to be in the city for the Passover, so he sent his disciples (Mark 14:12-17/Luke 22:7-14/Matt 26:17-20) to Jerusalem to look for a suitable place, giving them only one direction: "A man carrying a jar of water will meet you" (Mark 14:13). Once this man had been identified, Jesus led the guests to a room already prepared on the upper floor of the house. It is symptomatic that people offered Jesus what was necessary for the customary rites, now that the Passover was at hand. In Mark and Luke, Jesus seemed to have some acquaintance with the city: he knew the habits of the city and he was aware that he could count on someone to offer him a room for supper with his disciples. It is possible that his host was one who accepted Jesus' message, but this is not mentioned in the narratives. The fact that he sends two disciples into the city agrees with his custom of sending people ahead of him to the places where he wanted to receive hospitality (cf. Luke 9:52). According to the Synoptic Gospels, Jesus *wanted* to celebrate the Passover supper in Jerusalem: he seemed to regard the location of the celebration as essential.[86]

In another incident, while he was walking around in the Temple the day after he had expelled the merchants, the chief priests, the scribes, and the elders came up to Jesus and asked him "what authority" he had for interfering with what went on in the Temple precincts. Here the Gospels (Mark 11:27-33; Luke 20:1-8; Matt 21:23-27) present a confrontation between Jesus and those who governed the sanctuary and were not willing to permit anyone else to exercise authority over the cultic spaces. This is why they protested against Jesus, who appeared to possess authority but was completely foreign to the system constituted by the Temple.

In yet another instance, the Synoptic Gospels stage the confrontation between Jesus and his adversaries by means of a parabolic narrative that relates how the tenants forfeit their right to cultivate the vineyard (Mark 12:1-9; Luke 29:9-19; Matt 21:33-41). It is highly likely that the Markan version is a theologization of the original parable. Kloppenborg has suggested that Jesus told a story about a wealthy landowner who lived in a city far away from his vineyard and attempted in vain to get the fruits of the harvest from the vine dressers.[87] The context of the parable would thus be the antagonism between the city and the countryside. Mark localizes it in the Temple in order to use it with reference to the antagonism between Jesus and the religious authorities, and Matthew accentuates this perspective even more strongly. It is improbable that Jesus did in fact tell this parable in the Temple, although it is likely that clashes and debates with the religious authorities occurred during his preaching activity.

Another episode relates to the occasion when Jesus "watched the crowd putting money into the treasury." We find this in Mark 12:41-44, followed by Luke 21:1-4. The donations by pilgrims were a normal action in the city, something that happened every day as part of a series of religious acts supervised by those who were responsible for the Temple. It was normal for those who could give large sums to draw attention to what they were doing. Jesus commented on this scene by praising the merits of the poor woman who donated only a few small coins (Mark 12:41-44).[88] We are told that Jesus addressed these reflections only to his own disciples, but his comment expressed a harsh criticism of what goes on in the sanctuary. He revealed an attitude that was utterly alien to the administrative apparatus of the Temple—an attitude that is closely parallel to the gesture of violent wrath directed against the merchants. This confirms that although Jesus felt that he did not belong to the city, he was not indifferent to its cultic and identity functions. It was the symbolic importance of Jerusalem as an irreplaceable religious center that impelled him to oppose the system of urban living, while at the same time demonstrating his attachment to the fundamental value of the Temple.

Two actions that certainly took place in Jerusalem reveal the extreme importance of the city and the Temple in the eyes of Jesus: the royal entrance into the city and the expulsion of the merchants from the Temple. The Synoptic Gospels agree in situating the latter event at the end of Jesus' life, while John puts it almost at the beginning of his narrative as a kind of overture to the drama that will subsequently unfold; but all four Gospels place the triumphal entry of Jesus to Jerusalem, sitting on an ass, at the end of his life. Both these actions betray a tense and openly polemical relationship to the urban world.

In reality, Jesus needed Jerusalem because it was the locus of the most important religious symbols of the people of Israel, and it was there that the projects he was pursuing had to be publicly manifested. But he could not avoid clashing with the conservative milieu of the city and the current religious practice there. His anti-urban attitude was reinforced by his critique of the way in which the traditional religion was practiced, and this ineluctably led to a situation of conflict that found expression in words reported by Luke and Matthew (who found them in Q): "Jerusalem, Jerusalem, the city that kills the prophets and stones those who are sent to it! How often have I desired to gather your children together as a hen gathers her brood under her wings, and you were not willing!" (Luke 13:34; Matt 23:37). This exclamation was polemically directed against the political and religious authorities of the city, because Jesus drew a distinction between the Jerusalem "that kills the prophets" and prevented him from acting, and its "children" whom he wanted to "gather."

In Jesus' eyes, urban society was a world apart. One example of his hostility to this foreign world of cities in general is the parable of the son of a wealthy rural landowner who foolishly squandered his goods in the city and was ruined (Luke 15:11-31).[89] He found salvation by returning to his father's house, from which he had wanted to emancipate himself—and where he found natural and definitive protection. In this parable, Luke locates the message of Jesus in the scenario of antagonism between the city and the countryside, where the city expresses the negative pole of values in which one can get lost. The city has the power to ruin or destroy the individual. It also appears as a place where the traditional laws, such as the prohibition of eating pork, are not respected: the son became the slave of a man who kept pigs. Once the son of the wealthy man lost all his possessions, he was compelled to serve a pig breeder in the city.

Jesus' distance from the urban world was similar to his distance from the Romans.[90] His contacts with their world seem to have been exceedingly rare, and perhaps not taken on his own initiative; the case of the centurion (Luke 7:1-10) is an exception, and is presented as such. Some scholars have doubted whether this man was a Roman, since neither Luke nor Matthew (Matt 8:5-13) specifies this, and the imperial military presence in Galilee was small at that time; the term *hekatonarchēs* could also apply to a non-Judean official of Herod's army.[91] According to the Gospel of Luke, the encounter with this official is surrounded by considerable reserve and a complex ceremonial. Jesus offered his services only in order to heal the centurion's servant; no political motives were involved. This attitude of distance is confirmed by his criticism of the Herodian milieu, if we are to believe Luke when he tells us that Jesus called Herod a "fox" (Luke 13:32). And this shows how profoundly suspicious Jesus was of the Romanization that relied on Herod's clientele. Some scholars see an affinity between the Cynic philosophy and Jesus' preaching, or the convivial Greco-Roman style that he sometimes seemed to practice (on this, see below); but this remains an indirect influence. It is not evidence of a positive view of the imperial authority and politics. It is true that the Roman governors had a direct relationship with the Judean population only in those territories that they administered directly, but the Roman influence (though indirect) was decisive also in the regions governed by Herod Antipas or Herod Philip: Romanization permeated every aspect of life, generating transformations that became irreversible.

Although no one can avoid the cultural influences of a globalizing society, it remains possible to react against this society and even to oppose it within certain limits. The style and the behavior of Jesus seem distant from the Roman milieu, and this is not surprising, since the urge to refuse integration is generally stronger where an innovative response can be seen. Jesus' reaction to the central system and to the urban world tended to be located in the villages and the rural areas where he judged it still possible to combat integration or to resist Romanization.

Jesus took his place in a somewhat limited territory in the world of his days, that is, in the Land of Israel; and he invited the village people to remain rooted in this territory—without migration, without territorial expansion, and without making any conquest.

2

JESUS ON FOOT

A Life in Continuous Movement

Jesus was not a man of the city, but neither was he a sedentary inhabitant of a village. He frequented the small centers, but none of these became his stable residence.[1] He chose to live only briefly and provisionally in any one location and moved about from place to place. Walking was the way in which he entered into contact with people.

Although the Gospels do not agree on the geographical parameters of his movements, his continual movement remains a constant element in all the narratives. This lifestyle constitutes an extremely significant historical fact. This is the fundamental scenario and the starting point for understanding everything that he does. The fact that the details given of the places or settlements visited by Jesus are often not particularly reliable concentrates our attention on his style of moving about, rather than on the specific facts of his itineraries and their exact chronological sequence. Accordingly, our aim here is to bring out the social and religious logic of this way of life within the historical context of the Land of Israel at that time.

We may wonder why Jesus began this way of life. He kept on going to new places—what did this mean to him? An anthropological analysis of places and mobility allows us to get a better grasp of his experience. Marc Augé has attempted to comprehend displacement by means of a stimulating reflection on the use of the spatial dimension. Understanding what displacement means allows us to identify the continuous process whereby experience is transformed.[2] From this perspective, Jesus' refusal of a stable residence can be defined as a continuous calling into question of the relationships and the bases of human existence.

An Identity without Networks

The uncertainty and precariousness that characterized the existence of Jesus are elements that go to the very roots of his story. In order to visit the villages, he went out from his original stable situation and underwent a deracination. The incessant movement from one place to another exempted him from the institutional rules that governed life in society, for example, the daily duties regarding one's family and work. Jesus abandoned everything. He freed himself from the obligations of obedience vis-à-vis the head of the domestic group or any political or religious authority, since such obligations had local roots. Since he was no longer involved in the networks of work and family, as an uprooted individual he had a much weaker basis for his identity, a basis no longer dictated by his household and his work; at the same time, however, he found himself immersed in new interpersonal bonds in the places through which he passed. He was thus compelled to construct new perspectives and carry out new activities. The repeated act of moving away thus entailed a profound disturbance to the ordinary structure of life both of the one who moved around and of those who received him. Jesus created new spaces in the places he visited and passed through.[3] Wherever he arrived, a space had to be created in order to welcome a delocalized identity that lacked the normal criteria of reference.

We can see some outlines, contours, and specific areas in the nonstability of Jesus. He avoided certain circumstances or situations (for example, we never find him in a marketplace) and accorded primary importance to others (for example, the situations created in the houses of those who gave him hospitality). The fluidity of his movements, the change of place and horizon, brought about a selection of factors that shaped his identity (for example, he resolved to address only "the lost sheep of the house of Israel") and determined what needed to remain as it was (for example, a son needed to stay with his widowed mother), what had to be constituted (that is, the group of the Twelve), and what had to be preserved in memory (for example, the action of the woman who poured out precious perfume on his body).

When Jesus arrived in a village that he had never visited before, he was presumably regarded as a foreigner, as one extraneous to that place. It was not possible for the local people to perceive him through the normal network of personal local connections, because Jesus did not belong to this. Unlike those persons who were settled inhabitants of the village or city, Jesus was not bound by the customs, the calendars, or the local activities and cyclical rhythms. At the start of the encounter, there was no pre-existing understanding of the person of Jesus, because people related to him only through the patterns of their own antecedently defined relationships.

This means that Jesus not only underwent a deracination, he was also constantly obliged to reposition himself. In every place, he was obliged to enter into a new horizon and to take up a different position within the new system of relationships; it was one thing to find himself in a house in the region of Tyre, and something else to find himself in Peter's house in Capernaum. As a transient person who merely passed by, his identity and his perspectives were not determined by his origin in terms of kinship, work, and religion: anyone who met him on the road and wanted to follow him saw in him only the preacher and the worker of miracles. His links to his origin were shaken off, and other constructive processes came into view, gradually growing in intensity and producing different results with regard to Jesus' identity and activities. He found himself in a variety of situations, for example, in the houses of the Pharisees who invited him or in the houses of followers such as Levi, Martha, or Simon the leper. The interaction could change greatly.

It is, in fact, this absence of a network of pre-existing relationships that gave those whom he met greater freedom to welcome or to reject his message and his lifestyle. He brought new things from outside their own daily lives, and these may have appeared highly attractive; but he was also a foreigner, and he could be expelled without fear of consequences. This was what happened in the case of the Gerasenes, who asked him to leave their territory (Mark 5:17). The polarization between a very favorable reaction and a violent rejection was made possible not only by the power and the originality of the message and of the actions that Jesus performed but also precisely by the absence of a network of relationships that might perhaps have presented an obstacle to accepting him, or have toned down the rejection. One who lives in continuous mobility like Jesus creates a situation that we can define as a constant and persistent "flexibility."[4]

If one relies on a purely religious explanation, one will tend to understand the welcoming or rejection of Jesus' message as the manifestation of antithetical positive and negative moral attitudes, or of antithetical doctrines and principles, or even as the embryonic expression of the difference between Judaism and Christianity (when the interpreter projects onto Jesus the religious differences of subsequent centuries). In our view, there is a *cultural* explanation that illustrates the dynamics with regard to society and identity. No one can escape these dynamics, and they enlarge our cognitive horizon here. Jesus' continuous moving around created spaces of unusual experience both for him and for other persons in the places through which he passed and in the domestic environments he frequented. Thanks to his presence, these places became subject to a transformation, even if only for a limited period of time. The transient visit of a cultural subject like Jesus permits and motivates new alignments that modify local existence.

One essential point is that Jesus removed himself from his own family and his own village, exposing himself thereby to instability, uncertainties, and criticisms. He was against stability, against certainty. He chose a life with no inclination to take root in a secure and comfortable context. On the contrary, he did not organize his own life in physical terms on the basis of a residence or a home of his own. His custom was to chose specific places for his own dwelling, but only for brief periods. These were temporary bases, and he left them to move around or to go to another place in the region. At Capernaum, for example, according to the Gospel of Mark, he seemed to use a dwelling that was not his own, the house of Simon and Andrew. He stayed there on two occasions, the first time for one single night, and then again, briefly, a long time afterward (cf. Mark 1:29; 9:33).[5]

The fact that there was no fixed dwelling for Jesus and those who accompanied him signals that their identity was not subject to borders between organized territories. This state of affairs is emphasized by the saying in which Jesus affirmed that "The Son of Man has nowhere to lay his head" (Matt 8:20) and by the fact that his disciples needed to look in every village for a house that would receive them.[6] Typically, they had to search for temporary lodging in other people's homes.

Jesus' desire not to remain in the places where he has already worked is well expressed by the Gospel of Mark. "And Simon and his companions hunted for him. When they found him, they said to him, 'Everyone is searching for you.' He answered, 'Let us go on to the neighboring towns, so that I may proclaim the message there also; for that is what I came out do to.' And he went throughout Galilee, proclaiming the message in their synagogues and casting out demons" (Mark 1:36-39; Luke 4:42-43). The list of his movements reveals that Jesus felt an immensely urgent need to spread his message everywhere. Mark incessantly relates the laborious comings and goings not only through the villages and countryside, but also along the shores of the Sea of Galilee: "After some days, he returned to Capernaum" (2:1); "Jesus went out again beside the sea; the whole crowd gathered around him, and he taught them. As he was walking along, he saw Levi" (2:13-14); "Jesus departed with his disciples to the sea" (3:7); "He went up the mountain" (3:13); "Then he went

Jesus on Foot

into a house; and the crowd came together again" (3:19-20); "Again he began to teach beside the sea" (4:1); "On that day, when evening had come, he said to them, 'Let us go across to the other side'" (4:35; this leads into the scene of the tempest that Jesus calms and the miraculous cure of the man possessed by demons); "Jesus crossed again in the boat to the other side" (5:21); "He left that place and came to his hometown" (6:1); . . . and the list could be extended. There can be no doubt that the quick succession of movements from place to place indicates his intention to cover all the parts of a territory. This urgent desire was the precondition for the success of Jesus' undertakings.

It has been calculated that in one day, walking on foot on unpaved roads and paths, it would be possible to cover ca. ten Roman miles (ca. fifteen kilometers). The radius of activity depended, however, on the location of the villages. James Strange calculates that in Lower Galilee one could find a village or some other locality every six square Roman miles.[7] This means that in the course of one day, it was possible to reach between one and three villages; but if we think rather of movements radiating out from one single location in order to reach all the inhabited centers around it, the number of villages that could be visited in the course of one day increases.

Not a Nomad, Not a Traveler, nor Yet a Pilgrim

An itinerant life that is totally uncertain excludes fixed relationships. It can be envisaged as a strategic choice of new situations that are always unknown beforehand, of brief encounters followed by partings. This multiplies the possibilities of creating networks and contacts; and although these are hardly ever fixed, this does not mean that they are not influential. Mobility always generates relationships and potentialities. It creates a lived and intensified "habitat" that changes the way people belong and defines their identity. The itinerant life of a preacher like Jesus, however, must be distinguished from nomadism, which is linked to the need to move around in order to find new pastures, to cultivate and harvest food. Nomadism involves a form of the provision of resources between more or less restricted (but not unknown) territories. Transhumance too is different from a simple wandering around, because it consists in an oscillation between fixed places. Above all, however, the nomad and the transhumant are different from the wanderer because they are legitimately rooted in social systems that welcome them. On the other hand, a sage, a philosopher, or a preacher who intends to bring a message of wisdom or of truth is a transient in ever new places in which he possesses no legitimation. This creates a major problem: people can accept him or reject him, leave him alone or gather around him. He may appear to be inspired, or, on the contrary, he may appear guilty of falsehood and imposture.[8] Ultimately, the preacher's moving around implies evaluations of acceptability, compatibility, and authority that are not entailed by nomadism or any other kind of moving around. Georges Hubert de Radkowski has recalled that, even for nomads, the experience of a dwelling, as a center of their habitat, remains fundamental. For sedentary persons, the dwelling is fixed, while for the nomad it is mobile; but the relationship between a dwelling, established as the center, and the habitat remains structurally identical in both cases.[9] In his dislocation, Jesus breaks the bond between dwelling and habitat. He and the disciples who follow him have no dwelling, not even a mobile dwelling, that would constitute the center of their relationships with the surrounding world.

In the ancient world, there existed a number of types of itinerant activity that have often been compared to that of Jesus. There were various figures of sages and philosophers with no fixed abode—not only the Cynics, who have most commonly been compared to Jesus. Religious personalities such as Apollonius of Tyana led a life that was at least partly itinerant. Halvor Moxnes has drawn attention to the Galli, the itinerant worshipers of Cybele.[10] But few scholars have attributed the correct importance to the itinerant craftsmen, who included carpenters. Jesus could have belonged to this category before becoming a preacher. In a peasant society, these mobile figures, who are not subject to control by the higher strata of society, constitute channels of innovation and instability. They make the picture of social stratification more complex, since this cannot be reduced to the antithesis between rich and powerful persons on the one hand and poor and subordinate persons on the other, with the latter group bound to the routine and immobility of a life in one and the same locality. To this picture we must add beggars, vagabonds, and uprooted persons of various kinds. These moved around without any rule and possessed no money.

When the Gospels relate the circumstances and the trajectories of Jesus' movements—what Moxnes has called "the challenge of dislocation"[11]—they never tell us about any reintegration of Jesus, even if only partial and momentary, into particular milieus, places, or groups. This is important, if we are to clarify the concept of the itinerant life and avoid confusing it with the concept of a voyage. In the modern sense of the word, a voyage entails a visit to see cities, natural and artistic sites, exotic objects, and foreign populations. There is, however, also the voyage of the merchant and the business trip, the voyage of the researcher and of the ethnographer, of the politician and of the soldier. Cultural analysis tends to emphasize that the voyage includes not only the idea of departure from a place of residence but also the idea of returning to one's own habitual situation after an experience one has had elsewhere. The voyage also implies the need to construct, on one's return, a memory or a narrative of what one has experienced elsewhere.[12] In the kind of mobility practiced by Jesus, one does not depart from a place temporarily, or from time to time, because of some dissatisfaction or restlessness, nor does one set out on simple visits of exploration or to pay courtesy calls. One does not travel in order then to return home.

Some of the characteristics of the concept of voyage are found in a parable of Jesus in the Gospel of Mark, in connection with the theme of return.[13] A householder has set out on a voyage after leaving his residence and assigning a task to each of his servants. Accordingly, his return home appears as the final moment of the voyage, which takes the form of a temporary absence of the householder from his own dwelling and his duties. Similarly, in a parable of Jesus transmitted by Luke (19:12), a man of high social rank goes off on a voyage to a great country to obtain the kingly dignity, and then returns home. Before leaving, he gives orders to his servants to make use of a certain quantity of money. Implicit in these stories is the expectation of local society that the return will be the crowning and the conclusion of an absence. The voyage has the appearance of a suspension of the domestic life of the householder, who is replaced by the slaves. Their duty is to look after his affairs and to prepare for his return.[14] We may sum up as follows: the scenario of the voyage implies the possession of a house, the entrusting of temporary tasks to others, and the resumption of ordinary life. None of these elements characterized the life of Jesus.

Jesus did not travel. He moved from place to place, he pressed forward. He went quickly—not to see places but to meet persons. It is highly probable that the inhabitants of the small villages had rather limited mobility, and that this was in fact the only way to meet them. It is true that agricultural production and the small industries that tended to be located in the villages entailed moving from place to place in order to sell goods,[15] but most of the population led a very settled (though not isolated) life that was tied to the soil or the lake. Their life was turned inward upon their own domestic environment and the spaces that were necessary for their work. Accordingly, anyone who wanted to meet the country people had to go where they were. Jesus was a religious leader who did not expect people to come to him: it was *he* who set off on foot to meet them.

Jesus' moving around is thus not a voyage; but neither is it a pilgrimage.[16] A pilgrimage is a movement toward one precise place in which alone it is possible to have contact with the divine that will give appropriate satisfaction to the religious longing of the believer,[17] for example, a place where there is a miraculous spring or where an event occurred in which the divine benevolence was manifested, or a place where people believe that a particular supernatural force resides. Pilgrims seek elements that will reinforce their own religious experience, in symbols and spaces consecrated to the divinity. These symbols and spaces are reactivated in a cyclical rhythm, and individuals can make them their own, obtaining thereby confirmation of a necessary and satisfactory relationship to the supernatural powers. The pilgrim does not bring his own world with him. He detaches himself from this world in order to have an encounter with the divine, and usually then returns to his own country and his own customs, although he bears with him a new status and some kind of transformation of his identity. The pilgrimage is one of the phenomena that Marcel Mauss has defined as the "total social facts" to which many forms of cultural and religious socialization are linked—forms that can pass from one epoch to another and permeate entire continents.[18]

Jesus did not move around in order to encounter some place that had been made sacred by a divinity or by events connected to a supernatural power. His aim was not his own religious renewal or the acquisition of a new status thanks to his pilgrimage to the sanctuary. The main difference between his experience and that of the pilgrim is that he believed that he himself was the bearer of words and the author of actions that provided a "salvation" that included escape from evil, from despair, and from destitution. This salvation was linked to his word—it was not something that resided in places where one would have to go. Jesus was convinced that it was urgently necessary to spread the words that transmitted this salvation, bringing them from place to place.[19] In his moving around, he expressed the firm conviction that his primary task was the personal aid of his neighbor, wherever this neighbor might be.[20] His itinerancy is the exact opposite of the pilgrimage. The pilgrim goes toward the sanctuary in order to encounter the sacred. Jesus was convinced that he knew the will of God, and he went toward people in order to proclaim this.

Jesus did probably go on pilgrimage to Jerusalem, but what is described in the Synoptic Gospels as well as in John are not the typical acts of contact with the divinity, but the acts of one who wanted to bring messages and words about change—in addition to carrying out commandments.[21] He went to Jerusalem because he wanted to carry out his own mission in the religious center of the Land of Israel, the Temple. It is there that he needed to ensure that this message was publicly acknowledged.

The Code of the Itinerant: Do Not Sow or Reap, Do Not Toil or Spin

For Jesus, the itinerant life necessarily entails stripping oneself. This project has high costs in terms of detachment, of distance, and of insecurity. It is carried out in a climate of weakness and of constant uncertainty. There is no palpable objective that one reaches and on which one can rely thereafter. This condition can be seen in an urgent recommendation that Jesus addressed to his disciples:

> Do not worry about your life, what you will eat, or about your body, what you will wear. For life is more than food, and the body more than clothing. Consider the ravens: they neither sow nor reap, they have neither storehouse nor barn, and yet God feeds them. Of how much more value are you than the birds! And can any of you by worrying add a single hour to your span of life? If then you are not able to do so small a thing as that, why do you worry about the rest? Consider the lilies, how they grow: they neither toil nor spin; yet I tell you, even Solomon in all his glory was not clothed like one of these. But if God so clothes the grass of the field, which is alive today and tomorrow is thrown into the oven, how much more will he clothe you—you of little faith! (Luke 12:22-28)

Every day, Jesus starts walking again. He realizes his plan afresh, sustained by his hope in God. The consequence of this lifestyle is the desacralization of places, activities, materials, and environments. Work, property, and family are no longer the highest values to which a person must submit: they are relativized, and one plays with these values in a succession of challenges. The things that are the most important in ordinary life no longer form the center of interest in his project or his lifestyle. He abandons them, because they are no longer needed.

What is the reason for this detachment on a person's part, and for this kind of decrease in value? It is because family and work imply tying oneself to a modality of production that is localized and constricting. Family and work lead one to direct one's activity to serve the interests of a group that will tend to come into conflict with other groups about its own identity, or that will face constant challenges from other groups. We should also note that detachment is not the same thing as a denial or an indiscriminate rejection of the places and persons, or of the activities linked to family and work. Giving up work means that the primary goal of one's life is not gain, material solidity, or a certain future for oneself and for one's own domestic group. But this choice does not entail the denial of shared feelings of solidarity.

For the Jesus portrayed in the Gospels, the act of abandonment can be seen as a liberating act that allowed him to draw near to individuals in their concrete existence, wherever they were. It allowed him to concentrate on their needs and on their aspirations for justice, where these were not respected. The only person who does not represent the *partial* interests of groups and social layers is the one who is detached from his own domestic group. He withdraws from the responsibility and the risk of representing any kind of powers and interests. If the proclamation of the kingdom of God came from one family, from one social layer, or from one place, it would no longer be the expression of the will of God—and it is this that Jesus wanted to make concrete.

In conclusion: Jesus seemed to live under an imperative. He had to legitimate his own existence, but without a basis in the presuppositions or the boundaries of a family. His primary definition and means of support were not to be found in the resources of a family. He seemed impelled by the need to furnish a basis of his own for the diversity of his experiences. Sometimes he was playing for high stakes; on every occasion, it was his individual resources—those that were available to him as person—that made what he did meaningful.

Two considerations can show us more specifically the effect that Jesus' mobility had on his milieu. First of all, welcoming Jesus and his disciples into a house and giving them food was not in the least an obligation or an easy task, although it was not anomalous in the context of the practice of hospitality at that time. Jesus and his followers did not belong to any recognized institution that involved obligations incumbent on everyone (as would be the case with a religious order in a Christian society or with itinerant monks in a Buddhist milieu). Jesus' moving around was not linked to any official religious structure—neither to the Temple nor to the synagogues. This meant that extending hospitality to Jesus, and *a fortiori* to the itinerant preachers he sent out to announce the kingdom of God, was a personal decision that implied some form of adherence to a message of renewal and salvation with no guarantee of institutional credibility. It signified that one entered into a logic of transformation. The fact that an itinerant preacher, not recognized by any institution and without the support of a network of relationships in the village, presented an unusual message must inevitably evoke doubts about the truth or falsehood of what he was saying. Inevitably, discussions and clashes arose with regard to the validity and reliability of his words. The lack of institutional criteria to which people could refer was a structural difficulty that generated the question of authenticity and legitimacy, opening the door to conflicts.

Another difficulty encountered by Jesus was the size of his group. His itinerant life involved the movements of more than one person. Mark's narrative shows us that from a certain point onward, Jesus was accompanied by many followers. This means that his itinerancy, with all its consequences, was the story of a group, sometimes numerous, that acted and moved around in small inhabited centers.[22] The arrival of a conspicuous number of persons in a village caused a considerable change in the conduct of daily life. It created repercussions and reactions. Nor was this all. Jesus moved around with a retinue that also included women (Luke 8:1-3; cf. Mark 15:41), and this mixed group may have appeared risky to those who might offer hospitality. Besides this, Jesus' arrival in a place meant that people from the surrounding places would come in the hope of meeting him. This intensified the problems and may have created extra inconveniences for the village that welcomed him.

Walking and the Time of the Itinerant

Walking obliged Jesus to follow the temporal rhythm of each day. This meant that there was no stability in the sequence of events. The walker's itinerary is always subject to adjustments owing to unforeseen events (rain, heat, meeting others on the road, or various obstacles). The Gospels, however, scarcely ever speak of this; we have only hints. As he moved across the countryside, Jesus had ordinary experiences in a peasant milieu. The panoramas that he constantly observed are mentioned in some of his sayings and parables. It seems that he walked along fields of grain close to rural farms (Mark 2:23-27; Matt 13:24-28; Luke 12:16-21; 16:1-8; cf. John 12:24), beneath trees (Matt 21:19; cf. Matt

7:16-20; 13:31-32; 21:8), and along hedges (Luke 14:23) and beside vineyards (Matt 21:33), and that he was often on the shores of the lake.

How regular was Jesus' daily walking? How far was it subject to adjustments? Here, we cannot get beyond hypotheses. Jesus had one single aim, and we can say with a measure of certainty that if his march was not to become pointlessly arduous, it must have been fairly regular. He must have had a program: it is obvious that he did not just wander at random, going ahead and then retracing his steps. Instead, he always had a starting place and a point of arrival. Jesus' intention was to reach the very borders of his own land, in expectation of the coming of the "Son of Man" (Matt 10:23).

The activity of walking imposes an order on time and on the sequence of days. When we walk, we enter into a time that is regulated by necessary rhythms. The length of the day is measured by the walking: a day's walking is followed by a night, and a night is followed by a day's walking. This alternation of times may supply another element that helps us to understand how Jesus' walking conditioned his perception and his organization of time.

In a celebrated study of social history, Jacques Le Goff has illustrated the changes in the conception of time that are due to diversity in social and economic practice.[23] Like the activity of the merchant, Jesus' continual moving around was a social practice that had a considerable influence on his conception of time. This practice led him to a confrontation, sometimes taking the form of a violent conflict, with the various ideas of the households, the synagogues, and the Temple about the individual day or the temporal cycles. What we have in mind is not a contrast between the cyclical time of the activities linked to the earth and the seasons of the year on the one hand, and on the other hand that the Judaic conception of time was dominated by the expectation of the arrival of a final outcome of history. We refer here to something much more concrete, namely, to how the organization of daily time changes in the life of a preacher once he is detached from family and work and moves around in order to reach villages.

The life of the itinerant Jesus involved concrete practices. Presumably, he awaited daylight before setting off. He began his walking very early in order to move to new places each day, to preach either in the villages or, by way of exception, in open spots where people gathered to meet him. His presence and his activity did not form part of the expected daily rhythm of the household, and his preaching clashed with the timetables of work. Along the road, Jesus called people from their work to follow him: there was a collision between two trajectories, two practices, two conceptions of time. While he was in people's houses, he did not interrupt his preaching and his action: he continued to teach, turning upside down the rhythm and customs of the household. Besides this, Jesus' time was not cyclical. His itinerancy had unforeseen elements— his withdrawal, his lengthy prayer in inaccessible places, periods of isolation in territories beyond the borders of Israel. His conception of time was totally dominated by something urgent: the kingdom of God is close at hand, and he will not have gone through all the cities of Israel "before the Son of Man comes" (Matt 10:23). He needed to leave one place early in the morning in order to reach another place quickly. It was the sense of the urgency of time that made him walk, made him push on farther. Jesus had little time, and he could not waste the time that still remained to him.

Solitude and Flight

Being on the roads, in the synagogues, and in people's houses was not the only relevant aspect of Jesus' moving around. The Gospel narratives also relate his recurrent need to find an escape route into solitary and hidden places. His life alternated between being "together" and "in" the villages and departing from them (cf. Mark 1:36, 40), between remaining close to the people and being distant from them, "hidden" (Mark 7:24) or "away" (Mark 6:30-32). This double rhythm was indisputably a feature of the itinerant life of Jesus, marking the various phases of a biography that lacked a uniform rhythm and was in fact unpredictable.

We have two historical sources, largely independent of one another, that bring out this emblematic aspect of the story of Jesus: the Gospels of Mark and of John. Jesus often withdrew. He was off the beaten track in secret and isolated places in order to escape the pressure of the crowds or the dangerous attacks of his enemies. He had a variety of strategies to avoid being in the open. Sometimes he withdrew on his own, sometimes with his followers[24] or with a small group of those who were closest to him (Mark 3:17-18; 9:2). The Gospel of John tells us several times that he escaped in order to protect himself from enemies who wanted to seize him: "After this Jesus went about in Galilee. He did not wish to go about in Judea because the Judeans were looking for an opportunity to kill him" (John 7:1; cf. also John 8:59; 11:54, 57; 12:36). Mark too seems to say that Jesus withdrew in order to escape from those who wanted "to destroy him" (Mark 3:6-7). Certain periods of isolation seem to be chosen precisely in the context of conflicts or situations of risk in order to gain temporary security.

Flight is a strategic expedient with the aim of saving one's life. It is completely different from the recourse to solitude in order to safeguard one's own identity and to be able to concentrate within one's own self. Jesus sought to strengthen his certainties and to take refuge in his own inner life. He had recourse to solitude in order to be able to pray and communicate with God before he preached. Mark tells us, "In the morning, while it was still very dark, he got up and went out to a deserted place, and there he prayed" (Mark 1:35). Before moving on, Jesus interrupted the contact with his followers in order to pray. If they wanted to find him, they had to find out where he was in his solitude, in his own intimate dimension. How are we interpret this action by Jesus? Mark underlines it as a characteristic element of his behavior. We must not underestimate the significance of this search for solitude, because it shows us that Jesus was very much aware of being different from others. It is the symptom of his need to situate himself in a space and a time of his own. At the same time, it is also a communicative gesture that establishes a link between himself and the others. When he interposed space and silence between himself and his own milieu, he communicated his intention of undertaking an intense personal search that could not be shared with anyone else, but was for the good of all.

Jesus' prayer was an extraordinarily relevant and strategic action. It was not the same as the withdrawal into meditation by the sage or the hermit, nor did he give himself over to the contemplation of nature. It was impossible for his prayer not to be directed to the God of the Judaic tradition.[25] It inevitably entailed a relationship between the divinity and the construction of his own existence.

Was this a question only of moments of prayer, or also of visions, revelations, ecstasies? It is difficult to know exactly what these experiences were, but this difficulty should not lead us to ignore them or to eliminate them from the historical picture of Jesus. On the contrary, they should be considered an essential element that can lead us to the very heart of the story of Jesus. The visions are a part of his solitary experience.

His fame did not always benefit him—it compelled him to move off suddenly, perhaps on occasion against his own intentions. After he had spoken or worked prodigious deeds, his fame forced him to take other roads than those he had envisaged. In these instances, it was not only a question of retiring from the scene but also of a prudence that obliged him to modify his relationships with particular places and persons.

It seems that in some cases, Jesus ordered people to keep silent about what he was doing,[26] but his fame spread nevertheless. This made him less able to control popular reactions to his actions; and this became an additional factor that he had to take into account. Mark tells us that a leper whom Jesus healed "began to proclaim it freely, and to spread the word, so that Jesus could no longer go into a town openly, but stayed out in the country; and people came to him from every quarter" (Mark 1:45). The places where Jesus worked his wonders were full of people—and this meant that he could not lodge there, any more than he could lodge in the places where his enemies attacked him. He expected and proclaimed the decisive action by God that would change everything; but he seemed to be constrained to act in accordance with the assent and the attacks of other people. Jesus himself had no control over the reactions and responses evoked by his action. He was exposed to the ineluctable course of events. He could, however, choose spaces of his own, where he could act or withdraw. Solitude was essential, because only so was it possible to clarify to himself his ultimate goal. In certain circumstances, Jesus was a solitary. In other circumstances, he was a master who addressed the people. His entire religious experience moved between the two poles of attention to the people and concentration on his own inner life.

We can see these two poles, which characterize Jesus' itinerant activity as a whole, in the alternation between his moving around to meet ever new groups of people and his care to reserve moments of solitude for himself. An individual like Jesus, who has broken the links with the roots that usually serve to construct the basis of the person (residence, household, work, possessions), needs to find a basis in his own individuality. And the only place he can seek this is in an "other" space, in solitude, not in a group of persons (even of his own disciples). If he did not find his roots in a solitary or "empty" place in which he could locate his own otherness, he would have to abandon the alternative that this solitude represents. But if he were to renounce solitude as the foundation of his own personality, he would lose his way. It is the solitude—not only the intinerancy—that made Jesus an "alternative" person, locating him in a state of marginality without defined places. Scholars who have studied his itinerancy almost always overlook Jesus' search for solitude, although this was an integral aspect of his life. Jesus was a man who insisted on his own autonomy. He insisted that the center of his life was in his own self,[27] not only in the encounters with other persons.

This is because Jesus' itinerancy did not aim at founding a separate institution. It occupied only interstices, entering into a dialectic with the fundamental structures of society, namely, the family and the domestic group, the synagogue and the Temple, the political institutions. The religious forms created by Jesus himself—his way of praying and of relating to God, where he found the very foundation of his person—were born of the logic that was inherent in his itinerancy.[28] The same is true of the way he presented himself: as one uprooted and marginal, never "embedded" and "situated," but present where people live and come together.

Jesus did not establish a center of power to spread his message. But he did create a practice of life that would make it possible for God to intervene.

3

JESUS FACE TO FACE

Encounters

On an Equal Footing

As he passed through the Land of Israel, Jesus met an extraordinary variety of persons. Those with whom he entered into dialogue were not some occasional part of the scenery, but were his objective. A cultural analysis of his interlocutors shows that these are not mere extras put on the stage by the evangelists in order to present the teaching and the supernatural character of their protagonist.[1] We see that meeting people is the programmatic goal of Jesus' incessant moving around from place to place.

Whenever a large number of persons meet and interact, the social dynamics that are created in these encounters always go beyond the intentions of the one who seeks them. And this is what happens in the case of Jesus. The reactions of the persons who swarmed around him, the formation of groups that was a result of his physical presence in a place—these were situations over which Jesus himself had only a limited control and that could have far-reaching and largely autonomous developments. Although it is difficult today to reconstruct these repercussions, we should not forget that they played a central role in the life story of Jesus, both in the spread of what he preached and in the events that led to his death. Nor should we forget that his intentions could be very different from those of his interlocutors.

A history of earliest Christianity cannot overlook this perspective. A theological reading of these early years often tends to take autonomous developments that were neither sought nor controlled by Jesus himself, and to transform these into events that are alleged to have happened under the direct guidance of divine providence. Jesus exercised influence on his world by means of relationships that unfolded in a lively environment that was exposed to a great variety of stimuli. He virtually never employed strategies or mechanisms that would set the seal on the "correct" version of his words and perpetuate them, or that would direct popular reactions in one way rather than another. All he did was to launch a message that shook people. As the Gospels present it, his message takes on a different form depending on each specific situation that Jesus encountered. This is why it is impossible for us to really know the effects his preaching had. Undoubtedly, one of these effects was his arrest and his violent death. But this was not the only possible outcome, and we do not know how the various repercussions of his activity intermeshed to produce *this* outcome, the dramatic end.

Jesus made contact with persons on whom his destiny depended. Similarly, their personal destinies often depended on him. These included followers, members of his family, people he met in occasional encounters, the authorities, and many others from a great variety of social milieus. Dependence on others—material, but also mental and emotional—is one of the fundamental aspects of human existence. Dependence on other individuals involves both learning and teaching; a person is trained for combat and learns how to reach objectives or to give up the idea of reaching them. Relationships are established, open or hidden, and sometimes long-lasting; and constructive processes are mobilized.

It is impossible to paint a complete picture of the relationships that Jesus had with others because the Gospels do not give us sufficient information, and we have no other documents that would supply greater detail and permit us to perceive the real impact that Jesus had on people. Nevertheless, we can offer a description of the variety of persons with whom he had contact. Jesus related on an equal footing to ordinary persons who spoke to him and gathered around him, rather than to established groups. In order to grasp the meaning of Jesus' "face-to-face" meetings with people, it is essential to bear in mind both his welcoming attitude and the types of people whom he sought to meet, as well as those who would determine his fate. Jesus took his message everywhere, addressing persons individually.[2] His approach varied in keeping with the variety of his interlocutors. There were mutual influences and repercussions between Jesus and the persons with whom he came into contact.

The Encounter with the Baptizer

Jesus' encounters must be seen in the context of a tormented situation of social uprooting, where many prophetic figures and resistance movements were at work. No socio-cultural approach can give an exhaustive account of how this uprooting was experienced by individuals, but it is easy to imagine the powerful attraction some movements could exercise vis-à-vis certain social strata. According to Theissen, "In all the renewal movements within Judaism that recruited their members from among the socially uprooted, there was the intention to criticize society. Wealth and possessions were criticized in various ways."[3] In this situation, where did Jesus stand? One item of information transmitted not only by the better known Gospels, but also by those of the Nazarenes, the Ebionites, and the Hebrews, was that Jesus began his preaching after the encounter with John,[4] a man who invited people to conversion and to an inner renewal, and who practiced a purifying immersion in water. From that point on, the whole of Jesus' life was determined by this one initial encounter.

The John whom Josephus and the Gospel narratives present to us is defined exclusively by his activity and by the way in which he carried this out.[5] He is *baptistēs*, "the baptizer" (Mark 6:25; 8:28; Luke 9:19; 7:20, 33; Matt 3:1; 11:11-12; 16:14; 17:13; Josephus, *Antiquities* 18.116). He has no patronymic, nor does the way he is named mention any family relationships, although this was the most common way of presenting a person in the first century of the Common Era. According to Josephus, John was simply a "good" man. It is only Luke who tells us that he was the son of a priest named Zechariah (Luke 3:2), but we are entitled to doubt the historicity of the information on which this is based. John's religious physiognomy seems to resemble that of Bannus, the hermit who lived in the desert of Judea and in whose company Josephus himself spent part of his youth.[6]

John's eccentric clothing is a deliberate signal of his identity (Mark 1:6; Matt 3:4). Another element in the picture we have of him is his choice of a location in other dimensions than those of religious institutions and family, far away from ordinary life, in various marginal areas around the Lower Jordan, where he led a solitary existence. The baptizer linked his identity to the activity of an outsider. He acted like a person "out of place."[7] We know nothing, however, of the events that preceded and could explain the picture of John that is transmitted to us: we know nothing at all of his history. A number of scholars have maintained that he had an experience like that of the Essenes of Qumran, which he then abandoned; in that case, his distance from other movements would underline his own independence and originality. The Baptizer is not the representative of any traditional authority. He is defined by his eccentricity and marginality. "John was, then, an apocalyptic prophet like, but also somewhat unlike, many others to follow in the decades leading up to the First Roman-Judean War in 66 C.E."[8] His preaching was critical of existing society (Matt 3:9), but it was addressed to the entire Judean population (Matt 3:7-10). His ritual practice was intended to summon the people to a vigorous renewal, to wipe out sins, and to create bodily purity by means of a ritual immersion in water.[9] John was convinced of the imminent end of this world: he expected the last days. This implies some kind of connection with the attempts to discover the dating of the "last events," which were widespread in some Judaic milieus in John's day.[10]

No early Christian document explains why Jesus went to meet John: was this because a revelation prompted him to do so, or was he linked to John in some way? The only exception is the *Gospel of the Nazarenes*, which attributes to Jesus' mother and brothers the initiative that led to the initial contact: "Behold, the mother of the Lord and his brothers said to him: 'John the Baptizer is baptizing for the remission of sins. Let us go and be baptized by him.' But he said to them: 'In what have I sinned, that I should go and be baptized by him?—Unless what I have said just now is ignorance.'"[11] The only clear point is that it was not John who went in search of Jesus, but vice versa. Accordingly, this is an encounter that Jesus wanted, not something suffered passively or merely accepted with resignation. Jesus seemed to be in search of a religious experience; he was looking for a project that involved what John was doing, and we can imagine the kind of religious life to which Jesus aspired here only if we attempt to understand what the baptism of John was. Jesus submits to the rite of immersion, like the others who flock to the Baptizer. After this, it seems that he lived with him for a certain period, but we do not know for how long (Mark 1:14; John 3:22-24; 4:1-3).

Are we meant to think that he submitted to this rite in order that he too might obtain pardon for his faults (Josephus, *Antiquities* 18.117; Mark 1:4; Luke 3:3)? This question opens up a whole series of questions. The authors of the Gospels seem to have found a positive answer to this question disturbing, since they seek to demonstrate that Jesus accepted the immersion in response to the divine will and that the Baptizer explicitly confessed his own subordination to Jesus (Luke 3:16; Mark 1:7; Matt 3:14-15; John 1:15; 1:26; 1:29-34; 1:35; 3:26-30). But the most plausible explanation seems to be that Jesus wanted to experience an act of conversion, and that on this occasion he received a revelation and a supernatural consecration that determined the course of the rest of his life. At the beginning of the public story of Jesus, then, there is the consciousness of the value of conversion—not the idea of an unredeemable sin.

If the beginning of the public events in his life is linked to a great religious figure, this must mean that his experience did not consist in a doctrinal reflection or in the reading of sacred texts. He was attracted by the concrete proximity, face to face, of a person who denounced his own world and invited people to change and renewal.

It is important to recall what Mark tells us: "Now after John was arrested, Jesus came to Galilee, proclaiming the good news of God" (Mark 1:14). This means that Jesus spent a lengthy period of time with the Baptizer, and that he returned to Galilee and began his own independent religious activity only after John was arrested. This information appears to agree with what the Gospel of John tells us, namely, that before the Baptizer was arrested, Jesus baptized in a similar manner, and even in competition with John:

> After this Jesus and his disciples went into the Land of Judea, and he spent some time there with them and baptized. John also was baptizing at Aenon near Salim because water was abundant there.... John had not yet been thrown into prison. Now a discussion about purification arose between John's disciples and a Judean. They came to John and said to him, "Rabbi, the one who was with you across the Jordan, to whom you testified, here he is baptizing, and all are going to him." John answered, "No one can receive anything except what has been given from heaven. You yourselves are my witnesses that I said, 'I am not the Messiah, but I have been sent ahead of him.'" ... Now when Jesus learned that the Pharisees had heard, "Jesus is making and baptizing more disciples than John"—although it was not Jesus himself but his disciples who baptized—he left Judea and started back to Galilee. (John 3:22-28; 4:1-3)

This shows that it is not the history of ideas and of thought (whether Judaic or not) that can take us to the *center* of Jesus' experience but rather the analysis of the relationships and the dynamics that link individuals. It is these that make the ideas and the lifestyles meaningful and indeed shape them.

The link established to the Baptizer highlights the fact that Jesus was located outside the ordinary life of family and work. And since John's immersion in water took place out in the open, in places that were not officially designated for any religious function, this link also underlines Jesus' location outside the normal religious institutions. This means that Jesus too will face questions and criticisms from the representatives of the religious institutions that both he and John ignored. Like John, Jesus lacked any institutional legitimation. The two men are linked by a second trait, namely, the conviction that God was about to intervene directly in the world, with the consequence that people must at once orient their lives to this imminent and decisive fact. A third element they appear to have in common is the radicality and the critical power of their preaching, and the fact that their direct contact with the people created a critical distance vis-à-vis the established authorities. It is above all the transgressions of the rich and the powerful that the Baptizer denounced (Matt 3:7-10; Luke 3:7-14; Mark 6:18). And Jesus not only proclaimed the mercy of God, in view of the final judgment that is now close at hand; he also declared that he came to bring fire, or the sword, or division (Matt 10:34; Luke 12:49-51; *Gospel of Thomas* 16 and 82). Nor was he sparing in his use of severe warnings: "But woe to you who are rich, for you have received your consolation. Woe to you who are full now, for you will be hungry. Woe to you who are laughing now, for you will mourn and weep" (Luke 6:24-25).

An attentive reading of the Gospels thus shows us the close link between these two innovative figures, as well as the difference between them and the subsequent independence of Jesus, who is depicted as initially preaching with John, but then as parting company with him on a number of fundamental points. The Baptizer saw bodily purity as important,[12] but Jesus appears to regard this aspect as wholly secondary. Jesus differed from John above all in his lifestyle and in his itinerant preaching. The Gospels put on the lips of Jesus a revealing saying that defined the specific character of his life: "John the Baptizer has come eating no bread and drinking no wine[13] . . . the Son of Man has come eating and drinking" (Luke 7:33-34; Matt 11:18-19). The point may be not that John simply abstained from food. He did not move from house to house or from village to village in order to preach.[14] It is precisely his mobility that made Jesus' lifestyle different. People flocked to meet the Baptizer in the place where he was, but Jesus moved around to meet the people where they were. Jesus did not let himself be integrated, nor did he settle down—not even among the persons whom he had sought out.

The Gospels and early Christian literature (see Acts 19:1-7) also show us that the Baptizer's movement and the group of his disciples did not dissolve when Herod Antipas had him arrested and executed; it continued to exist for a long time. The Gospels depict not only a controversy between the group of Jesus' followers and those of the Baptizer, as we have seen in the Gospel of John (3:22-24; 4:1-2), but also an uncertainty on the part of the Baptizer himself about the role and the destiny of Jesus:

> The disciples of John reported all these things to him. So John summoned two of his disciples and sent them to the Lord to ask, "Are you the one who is to come, or are we to wait for another?" When the men had come to him, they said, "John the Baptizer has sent us to you to ask, 'Are you the one who is to come, or are we to wait for another?'" . . . And he answered them, "Go and tell John what you have seen and heard: the blind receive their sight, the lame walk, the lepers are cleansed, the deaf hear, the dead are raised, the poor have good news preached to them. And blessed is anyone who takes no offense at me."[15]

The Baptizer's uncertainty in this episode is in open contrast to the affirmations ascribed to him in some of the Gospels, where he declared that he was inferior to Jesus (Matt 3:14; Mark 1:7; Luke 3:16). Accordingly, the theory of the subordination of the Baptizer seems to be a late explanation that ill accords with the totality of the testimony. The fact that Jesus gave a positive response to the question whether he was "the one who is to come" is important: he accepted the ideas of John's movement, and it was within this movement that he attained a consciousness of who he was.

We agree with Theissen that the Baptizer's movement was one of the "renewal movements within Judaism which in view of the great pressure for change that emanated from the over-powerful Hellenistic culture attempted to preserve Jewish identity or to redefine it."[16] Luke transmits a significant saying of Jesus: "At that very time there were some present who told him about the Galileans whose blood Pilate had mingled with their sacrifices. He asked them, 'Do you think that because these Galileans suffered in this way they were worse sinners than all other Galileans? No, I tell you; but unless you repent, you will all perish as they did'" (Luke 13:1-3). One who does not repent will be subject to divine punishment. This saying, in which Jesus said nothing about his own work of salvation or of intercession for sinners, can certainly be attributed to him. It shows that he shared the ideas of the Baptizer for rather a long time.

To sum up: the decisive encounter with the Baptizer's movement (to which Jesus' first disciples also belonged) locates Jesus in the midst of religious movements and groups that proliferated in the Land of Israel and in the Judean diaspora. Some of these had an itinerant social form.

For example, the Pharisees too seem to have had a high level of mobility and continual dislocation.[17]

THE FOLLOWERS

Jesus was surrounded by many persons. The places where he preached and the habitual scenes of his life were crowded with people, and his followers played a special role here. The way in which Jesus met his first disciples is related differently in Mark (followed by Matthew) and in John. In the earliest Gospel, he entered into contact with four persons whom he seems not to have known beforehand. He met Simon, Andrew, James, and John in their place of work and invited them to follow him. With an authoritative command, he took them away from their work: "Follow me, and I will make you fish for people" (Mark 1:17). Typically, Jesus was not speaking here to persons whom he met in cultic sites or persons who followed some religious leader. In any case, the population of the villages consisted of peasants, fishers, and craftsmen, not of people who were eagerly awaiting the arrival of preachers and masters. John, on the other hand, relates that Jesus met the five persons who would be his first followers (the unnamed disciple, Andrew, Simon, Philip, and Nathanael) in a religious context, not at work. It was not Jesus who called the disciples. Rather, two disciples of the Baptizer went to him, and he then invited them to follow him (John 1:35-39).

Although these two accounts are highly divergent, they agree on the fact that after his baptism, Jesus organized a group of his own followers. The main difference is that in the first case four persons are "called" by Jesus, and we have the impression that the encounter with him took them by surprise, while in the second case it was the future followers who looked for Jesus in order to become his pupils. These were persons in search of a guide, of an innovative project of living; and they were persons who had already experienced the lifestyle of another master. Perhaps they were already familiar with what it meant to lead a precarious itinerant life outside the accredited structures. Most likely, they were persons inclined to take a radical attitude.

In the Synoptic Gospels, all the disciples (not only the first group) were introduced into a situation that was extraordinary for them. They were not idlers, still less beggars, sick persons who had been cured, or (with the possible exception of Mary of Magdala) persons from whom evil spirits had been exorcized. They appear to belong to the active, mobile, and resourceful sector of society.[18] For example, the sons of Zebedee were members of an association of fishers,[19] and the fact that they had salaried dependents demonstrates their ability as businessmen. The insistence by Jesus in Mark, Luke, and Matthew that the one who follows him must abandon family and work and sell his possessions means that his closest disciples belonged to a relatively prosperous class, which in some instances was on the rise. Their involvement in professional groups or commercial milieus exposed them to cultural influences and to various forms of communication. They were part of a network of commerce centered on the fish market, which was probably organized by merchants who were dependent on the Romans.[20]

A closer look at the differences between the texts helps us to perceive the kind of contacts Jesus had with the persons who followed him. In Mark, the details that accompany the names of the disciples point to individuals who have a stable place in society. Simon and Andrew, James and John (Mark 1:16-20; Matt 4:18-22) are two pairs of brothers. In this context, they represent networks of family relationships that Jesus did not break. Initially, he met the first two; then, going on a little farther, he saw James the son of Zebedee and John his brother in their boat "mending the nets." Here too, it is emphasized that Jesus was dealing with two brothers. He called them both, "and they left their father Zebedee in the boat with the hired men, and followed him." The persons who stand out in this scene are thus linked both by strong bonds of family relationship (brothers, father, and sons) and by a shared commercial enterprise: there are hired workers, who may perhaps have been employed on a day-to-day basis. Jesus wanted the fishermen whom he called to be transformed into another kind of worker, who would take care of the people and their needs in a new way. The family relationship between the brothers is used as the basis of a new solidarity, whereas it appears that the father was left behind with his helpers to continue the work he had been doing up to now.

Despite its differences, the narrative of Luke (5:4-11) agrees with Mark that Jesus called the first disciples while they were fishing. Indeed, the context of work plays a more central role here than in Mark, since Luke presents Simon as a "partner" of James and John, thus revealing a whole network of economic relationships. In his account, however, Luke places the call of the disciples after a rather lengthy period in which Jesus appeared *on his own*, preaching and working miracles both in Judea and in Galilee (Luke 4:16; 5:2). Subsequently, he is not alone, and we see that when Jesus was at Capernaum, Simon was close to him on two occasions (Luke 4:38; 5:2), although he has not yet been called to follow him as a disciple. It is only when they show that they basically believe in him, despite their bewilderment—"Go away from me, Lord, for I am a sinful man!" (Luke 5:8)—that Jesus calls Peter, James, and John to accompany him on his way (Andrew is not mentioned in Luke's account). They responded by bringing their boats to shore and leaving them there. They moved from regular work to the state of uncertainty that is typical of the itinerant life.

The network of relationships is even more complex in the Gospel of John. His list of the first disciples agrees only in part with Mark's list, since only Andrew and Simon appear in both Gospels (John 1:40; Mark 1:16). As we have seen, John appears to know a story of how the disciples left the Baptizer for Jesus: "The next day John again was standing with two of his disciples, and as he watched Jesus walk by, he exclaimed, 'Look, here is the Lamb of God!' The two disciples heard him say this, and they followed Jesus" (John 1:36-37). Here, Jesus is an unknown man who is "walking by." He turned and asked what they were looking for (John 1:37-39). This scene does not contain a genuine call or a direct invitation. The two disciples were moved to initiate a relationship with Jesus by the words of John the Baptizer, and only later by Jesus himself. The context has nothing to do with work, and Jesus does not require any separation from their family or work.

It is clear that the idea of the itinerant life underlies both the synoptic accounts and that of John, and that this concerns not only Jesus but his disciples too (who in John already seem to be far away from their own home). An important element in both versions is that certain persons see Jesus on the road and decide to follow him: we see this both in the Gospel of John (1:35-39) and in the three stories related by Luke (9:57-62).[21] This suggests that the image of Jesus surrounded by disciples is a certain historical fact, although (unsurprisingly) it has generated different memories. What then can we reconstruct of Jesus' first encounters with the disciples on the historical level? Can we choose to attribute historicity only to those elements that are common to these two traditions? Must we opt for Mark's picture, with the corrections made by Luke?

In the Gospel narratives, the persons who follow Jesus are called in Greek *mathētai*, which is normally translated "disciples."[22] In reality, this term would be more appropriate to a philosophical school with a master resident in one place. It is not impossible that Mark and John have retouched the historical reality of Jesus to some extent, under the influence of the language used by the philosophical schools that they knew, and it is probable that some resemblances affected the terminology the evangelists employed. The scene in John's Gospel where the Baptizer points out Jesus to two of his disciples as he passes along the road, and they then follow him, has points of similarity to the later story of Zeno, who became a disciple of the philosopher Crates.

Zeno, who by now was thirty years old, was sitting in a bookseller's shop. He was reading the second book of Xenophon's *Memorabilia*, and he was seized with such a strong emotion that he asked where it was possible to meet men of that high moral stature. By a happy coincidence, Crates was passing by at that very moment, and the bookseller, pointing to him with his finger, said to him: "Follow that man." From then on, he was the disciple of Crates and dedicated all his energies to philosophy.[23]

Unlike some philosophical schools, Jesus lacked a stable location for his teaching. In this, it resembled certain aspects of the preaching of the itinerant Cynics. His teaching was addressed to everyone and was always and exclusively presented in a contingent manner: Jesus did not require people to take courses over a fixed period, nor did his teaching generate abstract elaboration or systematic presentations.[24] Jesus' primary aim was direct action; he announced coming events and waited for them to take place. Those who accompanied him are called first and foremost to follow him, and this means that "follower" is a more appropriate term than "disciple."

It is possible that the number of followers could vary over the course of time. For example, the Gospel of John tells us that on one occasion Jesus lost many of those who followed him (John 6:66). With the obvious exception of the Twelve, we know little about the social composition of the group of disciples. We are indebted to Theissen for the classical presentation of the division of Jesus' followers into two categories, namely, the itinerants who constantly followed Jesus (after abandoning their houses, their families, and their work, and selling their possessions) and the so-called sedentary followers.[25] This second group was made up of the innumerable persons who accepted his message but remained in their own homes and continued their own work, such as Levi (a contract tax collector), Joseph of Arimathea, or Martha and Mary and their brother, Lazarus (about whom John gives us no concrete information).

The Fourth Gospel also mentions a third category of secret sympathizers, who include Nicodemus, a Pharisee who is "a leader of the Judeans." The evangelist states that many of the leaders believed in Jesus, but did not declare this openly (John 3:1; 12:42). To these we must add the followers whom Jesus rejected, and those who were afraid. For example, the Synoptic Gospels tell us about some who wanted to follow Jesus but were sent away by him, such as the man whom he freed from possession by evil spirits (Mark 5:18-19), the man who wanted to follow him, but wished first to go and bury his father (Matt 8:22),[26] or the rich man who lacked the courage to sell all his possessions (Mark 10:22). Another, larger group was the people as a whole, since the message was meant for all the Judeans, and it was from them that Jesus recruited his adherents.[27] He formed the restricted group of itinerant disciples in order to bring back and to save the whole population of Israel (see Mark 1:17; Matt 10:6).

The non-itinerant followers constituted in reality the basis of Jesus' movement. They were the primary fruit of his preaching and his activity. Since they were not linked by any fixed network of connections, they constituted a rather loose group. They were important because they helped Jesus to carry out his activity and to recruit followers. They did not form one specific social group or class; they were individual persons or family units who accepted the message of Jesus individually and spontaneously.[28] The existence of this group of followers shows that Jesus did not intend to organize a separate community and give it a code of behavior and beliefs, still less to initiate a new religious movement. Theissen describes very well the reciprocal relationship between the followers who moved around and those who stayed in one place. Without the help of the latter, the itinerant preachers could not survive; and without the preaching, the sedentary followers could not exist.[29]

It was well known that Jesus' retinue was a mixed group that also contained women, who are described not in terms of professions or associations connected to work but of the places they came from or family membership. Luke gives us a list: Mary of Magdala, Joanna the wife of Herod's steward Chuza, Susanna, "and many others" (8:1-3), and there is confirmation of the existence of this feminine component in Mark (15:40). Studies of the role of these women have emphasized that they must be recognized as female disciples, not simply as helpers.[30] The evangelists often fail to mention their presence and their role, perhaps because this diverged from the conservative habits in their own milieus. Nevertheless, some memories have remained, like erratic blocks not transformed by the conservative attitude of the early churches, bearing witness to this characteristic aspect of Jesus' retinue. We shall see this in greater detail below.

Although a number of scholars have underlined the religious role played by women in various sectors of the Greco-Roman world,[31] the participation of women in the activities of an itinerant religious leader is a phenomenon that still awaits explanation.[32] We have suggested elsewhere that the absence of older heads of families in Jesus' movement may have given greater space for the participation of women.[33] Ross Shepard Kraemer has proposed another hypothesis: the conviction that this earthly world would soon be over may have led Jesus to regard many of the conventions of his age (for example, marriage, the transmission of goods to the next generation, and procreation) as less important. It is precisely when all these "are invalidated that women stand to achieve significant parity with men" also in the movement of Jesus.[34]

The Twelve

Traditionally, Jesus is pictured in close contact with the Twelve, an entourage that has a special place and is distinct from the larger group that accompanied him. Luke tells us that the Twelve were chosen as the result of an explicit decision and by means of a ritual process of nomination in two stages.[35] First, Jesus ascended an unnamed mountain to pray, probably alone. When day came, he called his followers and chose twelve of them (Luke 6:13). This suggests that the decision to establish the Twelve is the result of a reflection that has matured in prayer rather than a decision that Jesus had taken before he went up the mountain. Luke does not tell us what criteria determined the choice of these disciples. Mark writes: "He called to him those whom he wanted, and they came to him" (3:13), and then tells us that Jesus established the Twelve. It is not easy to grasp what criteria Jesus followed, but the all-decisive factor is how he evaluated each of those whom he selected.

According to Mark, Jesus intended to establish a group of persons "to be with him, and to be sent out to proclaim the message, and to have authority to cast out demons" (3:14-15). Matthew adds another task: "and to cure every disease and every sickness" (10:1). Luke confirms that they were given power over the demons and illnesses (9:1-2). How does Mark understand "being with him"? Is it simply a question of being physically close to him, of living together as his counselors and moving around with him from place to place? Or does it involve being his immediate representatives and the privileged addressees of his discourses? "To be with him" entails accompanying Jesus constantly in an intimate relationship with the master. Luke too, in a completely different context, appears to share this picture when Jesus says that the Twelve "are those who have stood by me in my trials" (22:28). There is an indirect confirmation in John when he writes that after the disciples abandon Jesus, only the Twelve remain with him (6:66ff.). And this confirmation is interesting, because John does not record the setting up of the group of the Twelve, nor does he have a list of their names.

We do not know to what extent Jesus' choice changed the life of the Twelve, nor to what extent they took on and shared a precise function. In fact, scarcely more than half of them take on a distinct personality in the Gospel narratives: Peter, James, John, Andrew, Philip, Thomas, Judas. After the death of Judas, the Twelve as a formal group disappears completely, although the Acts of the Apostles relates that Judas Iscariot was replaced by Matthias (1:21-26). We do not know how it was possible for the Twelve to work miracles. Were they charismatic figures with powers of their own? Mark does not explain how Jesus transmitted his own power to them, but he does not suggest that they were charismatic figures before Jesus charged them with a special task.

According to the synoptic narrative, Jesus' choice of the Twelve as addressees and direct interlocutors was situated not at the very beginning of his public activity, but in an early and constitutive phase of the relationship between Jesus and his followers. It is, of course, permissible to doubt the historicity of this account; but if we accept it, we may hypothesize that he wanted to reward the disciples who had already received his teaching. He trusted them and had great hopes for them.

Since the members of the group of the Twelve[36] belong to the circle of those closest to Jesus, we are interested in knowing their names. We have basically two lists, which differ slightly (Matthew depends on Mark's list, and the Acts of the Apostles on that of Luke).[37] The names and brief descriptions of the Twelve allow us to see something of the relationships that bound them to Jesus.

Our primary interest here is in the persons who belonged to Jesus' most intimate circle. The Twelve and the itinerant followers were part of a network with many points of intersection. This network was centered on a leader and personal dependence on him.[38] Among the descriptions of the identities of the Twelve we find that of being someone's "brother." As we have seen, this is the case of John in relation to James (Mark 3:17; Matt 10:2) and of Andrew in relation to Simon Peter.[39] Another description is "son of" someone, as with James the son of Zebedee and James the son of Alphaeus (according to Mark 3:17 and Matt 10:2, but not according to Luke). In Luke and in Acts, we find a "Judas the son of James" who does not appear in Mark and Matthew (who instead have the name Thaddaeus/Lebbaeus). In Mark and Matthew, James and John are called "sons of thunder," perhaps because of their character, perhaps because they were at the center of some particular heavenly revelation, or perhaps because they had a special tone of voice. Matthew is called "the tax gatherer" in the Gospel of Matthew. In the Synoptic Gospels, Judas Iscariot is always specified as the one who "betrayed" or "handed over" Jesus.[40] It is highly likely that some of these descriptions were necessary in order to distinguish members of the Twelve who had the same name. There may have been four persons called in Greek *Ioudas,* "Judas," in the larger circle around Jesus. Finally, Simon Peter is distinct from the Simon whom Mark calls "the Cananaean" and whom Luke calls a "Zealot"; it is, however, uncertain whether Mark and Luke are, in fact, referring to the same man.

The brief descriptions of the Twelve emphasize a characteristic of the person, his professional work, or his political tendency, and allude to voluntary choices. The variety of the descriptions reveals a lack of social homogeneity that must inevitably have influenced their relationships.[41] Far from weakening the group established by Jesus, however, this lack of homogeneity may, in fact, have been a source of strength. The unity of the group depended on the personal relationship between each individual and the leader, not on a uniform identity on the part of the members. When one disciple is described as brother of another, this may imply a certain solidarity and unity of intention; on the other hand, it also indicates a certain hierarchy. And this brings us back to the fundamental factor: it is the direct relationship between each individual and Jesus that is at the center of every relational construction or network. This is why the exit of Judas does not break up the group. All that is lost thereby is *one* of these relationships between Jesus and an individual.

When Jesus changed the names of some of them, he specified, amplified, or transformed the image of that person. This is further evidence that the group was held together basically by the position of each individual disciple vis-à-vis the leader. The surnames Cephas for Peter and Boanerges for James and John attribute to these three a wholly personal identity that is not shared by others. And it is precisely these three, according to Mark, Luke, and Matthew, who have a more intense and close relationship to Jesus.

In addition to the problems connected with the identity of the Twelve, we must ask why Jesus set up this group. They were an essential instrument for preaching, both at present and in the future.[42] The fact that this choice had a future dimension may mean that Jesus wanted to act in public surrounded by a group that could give him support. His intentions may be clarified by a saying that is transmitted by Luke and Matthew and shows signs of being very early.[43] Jesus said that the Twelve would have the function of judging the twelve tribes of Israel before the imminent coming of the kingdom of God.[44] The institution of the Twelve is a further clear confirmation that Jesus' perspective looked solely to the people of Israel. In the kingdom of God, Israel consisted of the twelve tribes of Judah, as in the period before the Israelite monarchy. This brings out the anti-monarchist ideal of Jesus, who ascribed to God alone sovereignty over Israel. In the vision attributed to Jesus, it appears that the final transformation would take place very soon: the Twelve would still be alive at the day of judgment.[45]

As far as the internal logic of social relationships is concerned, the choice of the Twelve brings about a change in the relationships between Jesus and his most assiduous followers—a change in positions and in links. Jesus decided to share some of his powers with a small and select group, giving them his own abilities to heal and to perform exorcisms, and this could not leave his own milieu unaffected. The Twelve as a group were the expression of a level of organization that was more elaborate than a simple, spontaneous coming together of individuals. Their size made them an influential body, within which there were specific relationships to the head or guide. As an elite within a larger circle of followers, the Twelve had to some extent a representative function vis-à-vis outsiders. They could have considerable influence in every concrete local situation, because as itinerants they were independent of the groups based on kinship and of territorial and residential communities. The fact that the constitution of this elite depended on a decision by the leader and that they were chosen to "be with him" explains why the group disappeared shortly after Jesus' death: the Twelve did not possess any features that guaranteed a lasting existence.

If Mary Douglas is correct in stating that the character of a "group" can be measured by the extent to which the life of the individuals is absorbed by their membership in the group and is sustained by it, we can certainly speak of the Twelve as a group. These analytic categories help us to grasp how the Twelve differs from other social formations. Jesus has asked them to leave their own homes, but he has not established any place of residence for the group. In this way, he embedded the totality of their existence in a common activity (preaching and their share in his healing power), so that they lived exclusively from the resources of the group (and as we shall see, these resources consisted basically of the hospitality they received). Detaching his disciples from domestic systems meant withdrawing them from the influence of their families and their future as husbands and fathers, and making them highly dependent on the group headed by Jesus. While this gave them an internal logic and cohesion, the detachment prevented Jesus' followers from exercising any control over family, kinship, and political matters. Douglas writes that a group is stronger, the more it involves the individuals in a common residence, in work, and in shared resources.[46] On this count, we must say that the Twelve were a very weak group.

It is only the Gospel of Luke that tells us of Jesus' decision to give seventy (or seventy-two) disciples the task of going "in pairs to every town and place where he himself intended to go" (10:1). This is similar to the task that had been assigned to the Twelve shortly before (cf. Luke 9:1-6). Here, it is likely that Luke has imagined this institution on the basis of his own picture of Jesus' preaching. It is clear that he had no other information about this event, since he applies to the seventy the same norms that Jesus had given to the Twelve. In agreement with the majority of exegetes, François Bovon holds that the number seventy or seventy-two symbolizes the seventy non-Israelite peoples.[47] If this event recorded by Luke is historical, it would mean that Jesus further differentiated the functions within the group of his closest followers and that he envisaged varied roles for them in the kingdom of God that was soon to be inaugurated. However, the fact that neither the sources earlier than Luke nor those after him ever speak of the seventy, while they speak very often of the Twelve, argues against the historicity of Luke 10:1ff.

Meetings with Relatives: Closeness and Conflict

Jesus' relatives are not obvious members of his entourage, and their presence there is not something taken for granted. It is possible that his break with his own family roots created a situation of distance. Nevertheless, his relatives did play a significant role in his life, even if they were not the most important persons in the group. Here, we must look at two questions: the influence of his relatives on Jesus himself, and the relationships between these persons and the disciples.

It is no easy task to draw up a list of the members of Jesus' family milieu.[48] The domestic environment from which Jesus came remains obscure, because it is seldom mentioned or presented overtly. But information is not completely lacking, and, in fact, the Gospels mention indirectly the closest relatives of Jesus who were active during his life.

In the earliest Christian writings, Jesus' family members sometimes seem not to be part of his retinue, and in disagreement with it. At other times, they seem to belong to the circle of persons who were very close to him during his itinerant life, and this is an important point. After his death, his brother James had a central function in the group of followers in Jerusalem, where he was the head of the community and had an influential function in the entire movement.[49] The followers of Jesus who may have been present in Jerusalem after his death included the sister of his mother, who may have been the wife of Clopas (John 19:27); according to a late tradition,[50] he was the brother of Joseph. Simon the son of Clopas appears to have played a rather important role in Jerusalem after the death of James. This chain of Jesus' relatives challenges the image of a total distance between Jesus and the members of his family. Indeed, it raises the possibility that he was integrated almost by necessity into the family network.

The Gospel of Mark focuses its attention on the memory of Jesus' family when it recounts the preaching of Jesus in the synagogue in his hometown, Nazareth: "Is not this the carpenter, the son of Mary and brother of James and Joses and Judas and Simon, and are not his sisters here with us?"[51] The domestic milieu described here includes the mother, four brothers, and more than one sister, but no father. The narrative does not tell us whether these relatives were present in the synagogue and why. At any rate, it is certain that Jesus was recognized and judged by his closeness to one particular family group and by precise bonds of relatedness. We can only speculate about the reciprocal influences between Jesus and these persons, but we can be sure that such influences are present in Mark's social imagination.[52]

We learn what Jesus thought of family relationships in a scene where his relatives were looking for him but could not reach him because he was surrounded by a large crowd. His words, "Whoever does the will of God is my brother and sister and mother,"[53] denote a critical distance between Jesus and his domestic group—not only because he refused to interrupt what he was doing when he was told that his mother and his brothers had arrived but also because this little group of relatives seemed to arrive "from the outside," from some other place. They were not in his company when he was preaching. In this scene, the family group was not small in numbers, nor was it uninterested and inactive with regard to Jesus. His relatives attempted to communicate with him. Doubtless, they had their reasons. Perhaps they came to him in order to get information, or to ask him directly, about what he was doing; perhaps they wanted to invite him to return home. It is probable, even if not certain, that they were uneasy, or indeed that they disapproved of his behavior. The fact that they arrived all together and "send to him and call him" (Mark 3:31) may mean that they intended to exercise their authority as a group closely related to Jesus. We do not get the impression that they wanted to listen to him. Here too, the Gospels diverge. Luke states that his relatives only wanted to see him (8:20), while Matthew says that they wanted "to talk to him" (Matt 12:46). Jesus put a considerable distance between himself and them by replying that "doing the will of God" makes those who listen to him his sister, his brother, and his mother. It seems that he was reacting decisively to a family that was visible and present. These blood relatives were not actually putting pressure on him, but they claimed the right to take charge of him, and he wanted to remove himself from them.

This scene in Mark is preceded by the story that "those around him" (Mark 3:20-21) had learned that so many people were thronging around Jesus and his disciples that they had no time even to eat. They wanted to go to him because they thought that "he has gone out of his mind." It is not completely clear whether this thought is attributed to the disciples, to the relatives of Jesus, or to unidentified persons. If Mark has the relatives in mind, that would mean that they made a grave judgment about Jesus; at the same time, they wanted to protect him.[54] This Gospel typically specifies that they wanted to "take hold of him," to "seize him" forcibly. To restrain Jesus in this way would imply serious opposition.[55]

At any rate, we cannot eliminate from Mark's narrative the idea of incomprehension between the family and Jesus (3:31-35). This is an important structural fact. In Jesus' unequivocal reply, the fundamental task is to do the will of God, and a mother has no prerogatives of her own that would take priority over this. Jesus did not allude to the possibility that a new metaphorical family could take the place of the real family: the familial terms are employed polemically. Whoever does the will of God is Jesus' brother or mother. Obedience to God takes the place of obedience to one's parents. It is this that makes all human beings, including Jesus, brothers and sisters.

The group of Jesus' relatives is present in John and interacts with Jesus on several occasions. His mother, who is not given a personal name in John, appears at the wedding in Cana (2:1-11). After this, she, the brothers, Jesus, and the disciples go to Capernaum (2:12). We find the mother again at the foot of the cross, when she is entrusted to the unnamed disciple (19:25-27). Her influence is decisive in the wedding scene.[56] It appears that she is the one who was invited to the wedding; Jesus was invited afterward, and it may be that John thinks that Jesus' mother took the initiative to get him invited: "There was a wedding at Cana in Galilee, and the mother of Jesus was there. Jesus and his disciples had also been invited to the wedding" (2:1-2). On the level of formal relationships, therefore, we see the mother here as the instrument of the socialization of her son on a solemn occasion. Her influence is clear: it is she who invited him to take note of the lack of wine and to supply it. But we also see clearly the distance that Jesus established vis-à-vis his mother: "Woman, what to me and to you?" (2:4). Nevertheless, this distance is overcome when he then decided to follow her counsel.

Other passages shed a more penetrating light on the network of relationships with the brothers. In chap. 7, John presents a scene where they intervene in Jesus' decisions and regard themselves as entitled to give him advice. The Gospel underlines that "not even his brothers believed in him" (7:5); they may have been influenced by the fact that "many of his disciples turned back and no longer went about with him" (6:66). Their place is in the larger circle of those who had doubts about the miracles, or who felt the need to see Jesus acknowledged by the rest of the world. The idea that Jesus went on pilgrimage to Jerusalem with his brothers implies habitual close relationships and a reciprocal trust; it may also imply that they belonged to his movement.[57] This episode reveals a greater distance between Jesus and his brothers than that between Jesus and his mother in Cana. First, he told them he did not wish to go to Jerusalem, and allowed them to leave on their own. Later, he went there alone (7:10).

John's narrative thus depicts a more central presence of the relatives in Jesus' movement. In the first stages, it seems that his mother and his brothers were an integral part of his group, since they moved to Capernaum with him. And the fact that at the end of his life, his mother was entrusted to the unnamed disciple at the foot of the cross is extraordinarily interesting, since this episode agrees with the rest of the narrative in illustrating how important she has been for Jesus ever since the wedding feast at Cana. Jesus said to his mother, "'Woman, here is your son.' Then he said to the disciple, 'Here is your mother.' And from that hour the disciple took her into his own home" (John 19:26-27).

These data are compatible with the presence at Jerusalem of the mother and the brothers of Jesus after his death, as related in the Acts of the Apostles,[58] and with the guiding function that James assumes in Jerusalem at some date (Acts 12:17; 15:13; 21:17; 1 Cor 15:7; Gal 1:19; 2:9; 2:12). It is more difficult to explain these facts on the basis of the synoptic texts, which seem rather to posit some distance between Jesus and his relatives. We must, however, recall that John never mentions one central piece of information: he never speaks of the detachment from family that Jesus demands of his disciples. It looks as if John's more positive image of the role of Jesus' relatives depends on a lack of knowledge of the breach of which the Synoptic Gospels more faithfully preserve the memory. We should, however, note that John does not speak of the family of Jesus in an undifferentiated manner: in his Gospel, the mother has a much more pervasive and binding role than the brothers.

Taken as a whole, the four Gospels relate interventions by the family that aim to restrict the public activity of Jesus (Mark 3:21, 31-35; John 7:2-11) rather than to give it their support or unconditional approval. The data that emerge from the various testimonies paint a picture in which he is compelled again and again to face up to his family, who keep on reappearing in problematic situations. Some traditions are more critical than others with regard to the family. This situation does not permit us to recover the historical facts with certainty, but we believe that what we might call their "dialectical" presence and their strong link to the movement of Jesus are well attested. And we believe that on this basis we can accept a historical picture of the life of Jesus where his relatives played a certain role—though not necessarily a homogeneous role.

It is important to note that the role his relatives play is not the role that Jesus wanted for them. This discrepancy between their positions has a socio-cultural character rather than a theological or institutional character. Jesus did not want the members of his family, merely because they are his relatives, to have an excessive impact on his actions and on his movement. They on their part intervened, guided by the controlling role they attributed to themselves and by the social prerogatives that relatives normally exercise and defend. Sometimes, they intervened in his path to put the brakes on him, and attempted to give him counsel. Jesus' reaction was not directed to them as persons, but to their claim to be able to act as his brothers, sisters, and mother. He rejected the narrowness associated with kin relationship.

It is possible to restrict the role of the family members as long as the leader of the group is alive. But, after the leader's death, following the relationship between religious movements and the fundamental structures of society, kinship inevitably gains the upper hand, acquiring a number of significant functions. But also when a movement of this kind is transformed into a socially recognized body, the position of the family and the institutions never goes completely unchallenged: there will always be a competition between family structures and institutional structures to determine who will guide or control this body.

Bearing this in mind, we must look at the role attributed by various testimonies to James after the death of Jesus.[59] The *Gospel of the Hebrews*[60] relates the appearance of the risen Jesus to James:

But the Lord, after he had given the linen cloth to the servant of the priest, went to James and appeared to him. For James had sworn that he would not eat bread from the hour in which he drank the cup of the Lord until he had seen him rising again from those who sleep. And again, a little later it says: "Bring a table and bread," said the Lord. And immediately it is added: He brought bread and blessed and broke it and gave it to James the Just and said to him, "My brother, eat your bread, for the Son of Man is risen from those who sleep."[61]

In this Gospel, James is the first one to whom Jesus appears, and this event is related as a testimony to his importance in the earliest period of Jesus' movement after his death. The synoptics do not relate this appearance, but Paul records it in his First Letter to the Corinthians (15:5). In Saying 12 of the *Gospel of Thomas,* Jesus assigns an extraordinarily important role to James: "The disciples said to Jesus, 'We know that you will depart from us. Who is to be our leader?' Jesus said to them, 'Wherever you are, you are to go to James the righteous, for whose sake heaven and earth came into being.'"

It is significant that independent sources such as Paul, the *Gospel of the Hebrews,* and the *Gospel of Thomas* attribute such a prominent position to James. Josephus relates that James, "the brother of Jesus," was stoned to death under the high priest Ananus in 62 C.E. (*Ant.* 20.200). John D. Crossan has suggested that this action may have been one of the reasons that led to the high priest's deposition after the intervention of persons who were strict observers of the law.[62] But this is only a hypothesis; the reality is that the available information does not allow us to give convincing answers to the questions that the historical data oblige us to ask. It is hard to believe that the indubitable historical role played by James was not rooted in the life story of Jesus and in their mutual relationship; but although he was a leading personality, we know very little about James. Our conclusion is that it seems legitimate to suppose that James and the mother of Jesus were religious figures who enjoyed some measure of autonomy vis-à-vis Jesus, not simply persons who owed everything to his initiative and to his life story.[63]

Friends and Supporters

If we were to follow Theissen in reducing all the relationships between Jesus and his interlocutors to the distinction between disciples (whether itinerant or sedentary) on the one hand and adversaries on the other, this would entail an excessive simplification of the relationships Jesus evoked and sought. There is, in fact, a vast spectrum of interpersonal relationships: sympathy, devotion, friendship, clientship, foreignness, antipathy, opposition, hostility, and so on. We must ask, for example, whether Jesus had friends and supporters other than those who were his more or less faithful followers and were conscious adherents of the way he lived.

In the Synoptic Gospels, friendship never appears as an object of reflection or a proposed model for the relationship between two persons.[64] It is only the Gospel of John that speaks of a relationship of friendship between Jesus and another person, namely, Lazarus of Bethany (John 11:11). According to the image constructed by John, Lazarus belongs to the circle of sedentary disciples, as do his sisters, Mary and Martha. Jesus weeps over his death and then raises him to life. It is difficult to attribute historicity to this feeling in regard to Lazarus, among other reasons because the Gospel of Luke knows Mary and Martha but does not locate them in Bethany; nor does Luke mention a brother. Nevertheless, the fact remains that the Fourth Gospel finds it normal that Jesus should have had friendships. Indeed, in chap. 15 he suddenly resolved to call his disciples "friends," canceling out the relationship between teacher and disciple, which was similar in many respects to the relationship between master and slave.[65] John is also the only evangelist to tell us that Jesus "loved"[66] the unnamed disciple who plays an extraordinarily prominent role in the entire narrative; but the love felt by a teacher does not seem to be an aspect of friendship, which is something different from the bond between teacher and disciple.

Friendship creates a reciprocal fidelity that is independent of family membership and political ties. In this relationship, this fidelity lies on a higher level than fidelity to the ethical code that governs the behavior of a family or a group. This means that Jesus, who has broken his links to work and family and the "political" alliance with his domestic group, could have been particularly open to the tie of friendship, which passes over all these other bonds. On the other hand, we must remember that obedience to the will of God is the only criterion Jesus follows when he establishes relationships with others. And this means that friendship must remain something foreign to his own life, since friendship seems to create a social relationship that can also disregard the need to obey God's will. According to the synoptics, therefore, there is no place for the bond of friendship in the relationship between the master and the disciple. The Gospel of John, on the contrary, does not see a contradiction here and does not posit the same absolute priority.

The Gospels do not lack instances where Jesus encounters sympathy, or where favor is shown him, but these are presented implicitly or in a veiled manner. For example, we see an attitude of sympathy when persons from various social strata open their own homes to him, displaying generosity or a sense of duty to Jesus. Some people express a desire for his company; others want to see what he is able to do. This is true of Pharisees, who invite him to their houses on two separate occasions in the Gospel of Luke (7:36-50 and 14:1-24). In the second episode, "a leader of the Pharisees" invites Jesus without any intention of becoming his follower. He seems torn between the attraction that Jesus evoked in him and his distrust of Jesus' behavior, for Luke underlines that the Pharisees were observing Jesus closely to see whether his actions would confirm their distrust. More is involved than the satisfaction of their curiosity. Luke closes the account of this invitation with the parable of the banquet, which indirectly reveals a very negative verdict, though not a condemnation. According to Luke, these Pharisees belonged to a group of persons who were uncertain and struggled to arrive at an evaluation of Jesus. He tells us that some Pharisees went to Jesus to warn him against Herod Antipas: "Get away from here, for Herod wants to kill you" (13:31). Here too, we have individuals who were not adherents of Jesus, but nevertheless were not hostile to him and indeed sought to give him good advice. And after Jesus' death, we find Pharisees in the earliest community that came together in Jerusalem (Acts 15:5).

Similarly, Mark relates an episode in which a scribe who put a question to Jesus displays an attitude of sympathy. He was not a follower of Jesus, nor did he wish to become a follower, but he agreed with him and said, "You have spoken truly." And Jesus replied: "You are not far from the kingdom of God" (Mark 12:28-34). This dialogue is an authentic face-to-face encounter with a person outside the movement who took a favorable view of it.

The intermediate category between followers and adversaries was surely both extensive and composite, if we are to give credence to the story in Mark of the man who was not one of Jesus' followers but performed exorcisms through the power of his name. The words with which Jesus defended this exorcist—"Whoever is not against us is for us" (Mark 9:38-40)—indicate the existence of persons who remained outside but were positively attracted by the movement and imitated its style and its intentions. This group may have included Joseph of Arimathea, "a member of the council." Mark tells us that "he was also himself waiting for the kingdom of God" (15:43). He is not mentioned before this, and he appears not to have exercised any function in the Sanhedrin during the trial of Jesus. It is only after his death that Joseph went to Pilate to ask for permission to bury the body. It is difficult to decide whether Joseph was an outsider with a positive view of the movement of Jesus or a non-itinerant follower, but the statement that "he was also himself waiting for the kingdom of God" aligns Joseph with the fundamental belief of Jesus' followers. After the death of Jesus, despite the fact that he was dead and defeated, they did not stop expecting God to establish his kingdom. For Mark, it is clear that the kingdom has not yet arrived (cf. 1:14). If we ask whether Joseph of Arimathea was a follower of Jesus, it is probable that the correct state of affairs is formulated by the Gospel of John when it states that "many, even of the authorities, believed in him" but did not confess this publicly (John 12:42). This could be, therefore, a clandestine adherence on the part of a member of the upper strata.

All these individual cases are sociologically plausible. They give us glimpses of the attitudes and the very varied responses that the presence of Jesus evoked in different groups of people. The plausibility is connected with the complex relationships that Jesus established with his interlocutors. If we look closely at these interactions, we can grasp how the various groups reacted. An abstract examination of their theological doctrines does not take us very far: in one and the same religious group, for example, among the Pharisees, the scribes, or the members of the Sanhedrin, we find both opponents and sympathizers. This means that abstract theological divergences or contradictions were superseded in the concrete interactions with Jesus.

In addition to itinerant and sedentary followers, therefore, we also find sympathizers, clandestine adherents, imitators, and outsiders who showed a positive and generous attitude that is often independent of the norms and customs of the groups to which they belonged. We also find persons and groups who were torn between attraction and rejection. Finally, we find genuine opponents. We shall attempt in a later section to outline their characteristics and their orientations.

The Women

We have already said that the group of Jesus' followers included several women. Women and children were certainly present in the great crowds that gathered, for example, among the five thousand and the four thousand who were fed miraculously (see Matt 14:2 and 15:38). Here, we shall look at the direct encounters with women who cannot be regarded as followers of Jesus. We have a series of face-to-face encounters that acquire prominence because of their exceptional character. One particularly moving episode is related three times in various ways. For Luke, this is the story of an unknown woman, a "sinner" in an unidentified city, who unexpectedly entered the house of a Pharisee (Luke 7:37). For John, she is Mary, one of the sisters of Lazarus at Bethany;[67] for Mark and Matthew, she is an unnamed woman who is present in the house of Simon the leper at Bethany (Mark 14:3; Matt 26:7). She anointed Jesus with a precious ointment while he was taking part in a banquet. Luke's version emphasizes that Jesus attributed no importance to the fact that the woman was regarded as a "sinner" (perhaps a prostitute). Here, he disregarded something that was very important to the prevalent masculine ethos.[68]

In other situations, the women were present as the mothers of disciples, and possibly were themselves followers of Jesus. We find Mary the mother of James "the less" and of Joses, and Salome (Mark 15:40), whom Matthew (27:56) may take to be the mother of the sons of Zebedee. Mary and Salome stood with Mary of Magdala both at the foot of the cross and beside the empty tomb on the morning after the burial of Jesus (Mark 16:1; cf. Matt 28:1 and Luke 24:10). "Many other" women followed Jesus as he went up to Jerusalem, but we know nothing about their names or their social status (Mark 15:41; cf. Luke 23:49; 23:55—24:10).

In another episode related only by Luke,[69] Jesus accepted the hospitality of a woman named Martha. While she bustled around making all the necessary preparations for receiving him, her sister Mary listened to his teaching.[70] When Martha asked him to rebuke Mary and to get her to help in serving, Jesus objected. The words "Mary has chosen the better part, which will not be taken away from her" (Luke 10:42) seem meant to defend women and to refuse to let them be reduced to a purely servile function in subordinate domestic roles. If the episode is not historical, we would have to conclude that whoever created it wanted at the very least to criticize the masculine mentality that was prevalent in some groups of Jesus' followers. It would be evidence of a positive attitude to the exercise by women of non-subordinate public functions. Many hypotheses are possible here, but we find it more likely that the origin of this positive attitude is to be found in Jesus himself rather than in the evangelist.

With respect to life within the houses, Carolyn Osiek recalls that women were traditionally responsible for hospitality and that testimonies in the Greco-Roman world of antiquity speak of the hospitality offered to members or friends of the family who ask for a place appropriate to their social position (or even simply for a safe place to stay).[71] Women would have had the primary roles in the practical work of welcoming visitors, itinerant preachers, or prophets. In the First Letter to Timothy (5:10), the function (or "ministry") of hospitality is entrusted to widows, who had the onerous duty to receive travelers and pilgrims. The widow's house as a place of hospitality thus bore witness to a more general custom in the society of that time. It is likely that the women in the villages Jesus visited had the same task of taking care of guests. We should therefore envisage a female milieu much larger and more important than the Gospel texts suggest.

The women whom Jesus met had various horizons, needs, and requests. One woman suffered from hemmorhages and mingled with the crowd in order to draw near to him (Mark 5:21-34/Luke 8:40-48/Matt 9:18-22). She wanted to get close enough to touch him surreptitiously, and she stood behind his back so that she could take hold of his cloak. She was healed instantly but was then compelled to give a public explanation of this gesture, which may perhaps have been considered disrespectful. This encounter with Jesus seemed so inappropriate that she was forced to justify it.

In another case, handed down only by Luke (7:11-17), we see Jesus' concern for the status of socially disadvantaged women without support. That is what moves him to raise the only son of a widow who has just died: "The Lord had compassion and said, 'Do not weep.' And he came and touched the coffin" (7:13-14). Even in Jerusalem, he points out to his disciples that a widow, living in poverty, put two pennies in the treasury of the Temple—that is, all that she had to live on (Mark 12:41-44; Luke 21:1-4). One may wonder if the attention to widows shown by the groups of followers of Jesus after his death (Acts 6:1; James 1:27) is rooted in the social need of a category of women who were very vulnerable to abandonment and exploitation.

Luke also records the words of a woman who listened to Jesus and exclaimed: "Blessed is the womb that bore you and the breasts that nursed you!" (11:27). Here, Jesus was confronted with the exemplary model of the mother. Motherhood, the supreme (or only) glory of a woman, as well as something that ties her down considerably, can be the source of her prestige or of her shame. Jesus paid no attention to these ambiguous qualities that were attributed to the world of women. He compelled his interlocutor to widen her horizon, shifting the attention to the will of God, which is greater than either motherhood or the values connected to it: "Blessed rather are those who hear the word of God and obey it!" (11:28).

A more complex attitude to the world of women is revealed in the words he addressed to the women who surrounded him and wept over him while he was going to his execution. Jesus rejected their lament: "Daughters of Jerusalem, do not weep for me, but weep for yourselves and for your children. For the days are surely coming when they will say, 'Blessed are the barren, and the wombs that never bore, and the breasts that never nursed'" (Luke 23:29). These words were addressed to a group of women who were carrying out their normal social functions: it may well be that these specific persons had the function of ritual weeping, of public lamentation on the occasion of bereavements and tragedies. Jesus did not disavow this function, any more than he disowned the link that bound mothers to their children. But he offered a polemical reevaluation of sterility—the female drama par excellence. In this way, he opens a wider perspective to women's lives. The maternal bond must not absorb women to such an extent that it is the ultimate horizon of their existence. Jesus invited them to reflect on their own future in the light of the imminence of the kingdom of God.

We find, however, an attitude of great concern for motherhood when Jesus encountered a foreign woman. The suffering of a non-Judean, a Syro-Phoenician woman, because of her sick daughter is so great that it moved Jesus to interrupt the solitude into which he had withdrawn. He healed the daughter[72] and restored her to the mother, freeing both of them from their pain.

The episode in which he prevented the stoning of a woman caught in adultery (John 8:2-11), hindering a public execution, tells us about a concrete intervention on Jesus' part rather than an instruction. Many social codes linked to the sexual behavior of women are woven into this scene. This dramatic episode that is emblematic of female weakness reaches a remarkable conclusion when the woman is liberated and sent away.[73]

One indirect piece of evidence helps us to grasp better the relationship between Jesus and women. Some women felt moved to break the established customs of a society dominated by the family networks in which masculine power was exercised in order to have direct contact with Jesus. In her own home, in the context of her relationship to her own sister, Mary had to overcome the barrier that kept women separate, busy with serving the guests. And this was possible only because Jesus decided to accept the hospitality of a woman and be listened to by a woman. Similarly, the woman who suffered from hemorrhages made use of the crowd in her successful attempt to reach Jesus. She breached every customary boundary between men and women and touched him. The "sinner" resolved to expose herself to the danger of finding her path blocked in public and being sent away. She broke the rules. She entered uninvited; she took the risk of being in the house of a Pharisee, because what matters was to have a direct encounter with Jesus. The Syro-Phoenician woman overturned both the ethnic-religious barrier and Jesus' desire for solitude, because what mattered was to obtain a miraculous cure. On the other hand, the woman taken in adultery was resigned to her fate. Faced with the prospect of being stoned, she did not undertake any strategic move. Perhaps we could say that breaking the rules that give a woman a subordinate status is easier for a woman whom the masculine ethos is sometimes compelled to treat well. But it is more likely that these breaches of the rules took place because these women seemed to know that Jesus would have compassionate and that he would cast his mantle (so to speak) over their insubordination.

Sinners, Those Possessed by Demons, and the Sick

Scholarly research into Jesus emphasizes the fact that he is said to have healed, freed people from demons, and worked miracles.[74] The attempt has sometimes been made to construct a contrast between the social distress of the poor and the sick and the purely religious intention of Jesus, who is alleged to have had a very different concern. In reality, however, one cannot posit this antithesis between his religious intention and the crowds' plea for healing, because he himself, according to Mark, charged the Twelve not only to preach, but also to drive out the demons (3:14-15).

Whenever the crowds assembled and went in search of Jesus, two things happened. He announced a message and he healed (Mark 2:1-12). The people indeed admired his teaching (see, for example, Mark 11:8; Matt 7:28), but what they were looking for was the healing of sickness or the liberation from evil powers. This double attitude added a measure of complexity to the relationship between Jesus and the crowds. As we shall see, Jesus' healing activity during his lifetime had an enormous impact; but the desires of the crowds went still further and did not coincide with those of Jesus. The two trajectories did not go in the same direction. His healing activity called forth reactions that he neither envisaged nor wanted: it generated a trust and an attachment to the person of Jesus, rather than an acceptance of the religious message he proclaimed.

An Array of Adversaries

Our aim here is not to present a complete reconstruction of the adversaries of Jesus and of their motivations, but only to show how he met them. We are interested in the opposition that is revealed through (or in the course of) direct contact with him. Among those who proved hostile we find, above all, members of religious movements and groups such as the Pharisees and Sadducees, members of a particular category such as the scribes, and political personalities such as the Herodians. Before Jesus' arrest, there were no clashes with individual Romans or with the Roman political and military authorities, and it would be wrong to say that the genesis of the opposition to Jesus lies here.

The clashes with Jesus' enemies were not located exclusively in Jerusalem, where the synoptics present a series of encounters that became increasingly bitter. Even before this, while he was on the road, Jesus often met signs of opposition (see, for example, Mark 2:6; 2:18; 2:24; 3:6; 3:22; 7:1; 8:11; 8:31). He worked among the people, and neither the positions he took or the program he proposed threw down the gauntlet *directly* to the political and religious hierarchies. Nevertheless, their presence in the places he frequented is a very significant factor. It is they who asked questions about what Jesus was doing in the marginal areas, in the interstices, where he clearly was addressing anyone at all who was willing to listen to him. Jesus confronted the seats of power and the legal and religious structures only when he was compelled to do so. It seems, however, that he gradually accepted the inevitability of situations in which he was challenged and threatened.

According to Mark, Luke, and Matthew, Jesus had contact with the institutions of the Sanhedrin and the Temple only at the end of his life. This late confrontation confirms that he was not primarily interested in the authorities, since he did not regard them as his most important interlocutors, as persons he must face up to. The Gospels attribute to him sayings against the movement of the Pharisees, but not against the priests.[75] The clashes with the institutions prior to his arrest took place above all when he was in Jerusalem, in the Temple, and it is the others who took the initiative to challenge him.

Apart from the unease caused by his preaching in his hometown of Nazareth, the Synoptic Gospels do not present instances where individual persons are hostile to Jesus. One exception can be found in Luke (13:10-16), when the leader of the synagogue was indignant that Jesus healed a sick woman on the Sabbath day: here, Luke speaks of the "opponents" of Jesus. John, on the other hand, ascribes to the Judeans a recurrent hostility that made them want to kill him (John 5:18; 7:1; 7:19, 20, 25; 8:37, 40; 11:53). In all likelihood, here as elsewhere in John, this is an interpretation rather than a historical fact. In one of the phases of the redaction of this Gospel or of the tradition on which its editors depended, the antithesis between *hoi Ioudaioi* ("the Judeans") and "us" (the group to which the redactor belongs), which erupted decades after the crucifixion, was backdated to Jesus' own lifetime.[76]

After his arrest, Jesus was confronted by a number of adversaries: the Roman soldiers who arrested and tortured him, the Judean religious authorities (for example, Annas and Caiaphas), the political authorities (such as Herod and Pilate), the crowds in Jerusalem who mocked him, and those who preferred Barabbas and demanded that Jesus be put to death. It is necessary to apply a rigorous critical sense to the evaluation of the historicity of the individual episodes, given that the Gospel narratives are not based on eyewitness testimonies and seem to have an apologetic motive, as we can see (to take only one example) in the terrible words that Matthew attributed to all the people: "Then all the people answered, 'His blood be on us and on our children!'" (27:25). Despite questions of detail, however, the picture as a whole is historically plausible. The major elements are all probable: namely, that some of the inhabitants of Jerusalem shouted insults against a man condemned to death; that the soldiers treated a defenseless man cruelly; that influential religious authorities accused him unjustly; that they held a discussion with him about their irreconcilable views; and that the Roman authorities got rid of a man whom they regarded as dangerous, or whom their political allies portrayed as a threat to the power of the state.[77]

"Rich" and "Poor" among the Addressees of Jesus

Many studies have attempt to reconstruct an economic history of the Land of Israel in the first century of the Common Era, and of Galilee in particular, in order to identify the social strata to which the followers of Jesus and those whom he influenced belonged. The socio-economic categories employed by these researchers are highly analytic,[78] but the Gospel texts employ generic categories. They speak of the "rich" or of persons who possessed "many goods." The terminology varies in the Gospels. Luke speaks eleven times of the "rich" (*plousios*, plural *plousioi*), and six of these occurrences are in parables. John never uses the term; Mark uses it twice, and Matthew three times. Without a detailed examination, it is difficult to determine what these words meant in the categories of that time.

We should note that it does not seem to have been easy for "the rich" to join the movement of Jesus. In Mark, a man "who had many possessions" declined to follow him (Mark 10:22; cf. Matt 19:22), since he was dismayed by Jesus' demand that he sell everything and give it to the poor (*ptōchoi*). Luke says that this man was "very rich" (Luke 18:23). With reference to this man, Jesus affirmed that it is easier for a hawser to pass through the eye of a needle than for one who is rich to enter the kingdom of God (Mark 10:25).[79] There were exceptions, however, such as Zacchaeus, whom Luke described as "rich" (19:2). He was converted, made reparation for his earlier fraudulent behavior, and offered half of his goods to the poor. Besides this, Jesus' retinue included women who were certainly rich (Luke 8:1-3).

The contrast between "rich" and "poor" defines the entire human world. For Luke, these categories are necessarily antithetical, as we see in the following words in the Sermon on the Plain: "But woe to you who are rich."[80] The same antithesis is present in the scene of the people who made donations of money in the Temple treasury (Luke 21:1-2; Mark 12:41-44).

In the Gospel of John, there is no condemnation of the rich. The unnamed "beloved" disciple in this Gospel seems to be a rich man, who possessed a house in Jerusalem, and possibly belonging to priestly circles.[81] And the same Gospel informs us that Jesus recruited some members of the upper strata, not indeed as itinerant disciples, but at any rate as sympathizers, namely, Nicodemus and "many of the authorities" (3:1; 12:42). There is, therefore, no reason to dismiss as historically improbable the affirmation that rich persons became disciples of Jesus. But the lack of sensitivity to poverty is John's shortcoming, not Jesus'.

The Lost Sheep of the House of Israel

Let us make one final observation. Jesus wanted to meet only members of the people of Israel, not other persons. It is true, as we have seen, that the Synoptic Gospels relate that he cured non-Judeans; but these cures were exceptional, and they are presented as such. And it is highly probable that his visits to the territories that the Romans regarded as lying outside the borders of the Land of Israel were motivated by the desire to encounter Judeans there too.

We must therefore recognize that most of those whom Jesus met were Judeans. He privileged the relationship with the people of Israel. We have already indicated the importance of his words in Matthew: "I was sent only to the lost sheep of the house of Israel" (15:24). Similarly, he commanded the Twelve not to take "the road of the Gentiles" nor to enter into the "town of the Samaritans." Rather, they were to go to "the lost sheep of the house of Israel" (Matt 10:5-6).[82] It is difficult to deny the historical veracity of these data, because it is precisely this Gospel that clearly wishes to affirm that the message of Jesus must be addressed to non-Judeans too after his death (Matt 2:1-2; 28:19). Furthermore, the Gospel of John, which is so different from Matthew, confirms this general picture, despite its opening to the Samaritans. The legitimacy of preaching to non-Judeans was a highly disputed issue for the first generation of Jesus' disciples, as we see from the debates in Paul's Letters (Gal 2:3-16) and the Acts of the Apostles (10:1-48; 15:1-29). This was a problematic departure from the life practice of Jesus, and it needed to be justified.

As we have seen, Jesus did not intend to found an association of his own detached from the places and the social forms (in particular, the domestic units) in which people led their lives. He wanted to address all the people of Israel, to prepare them to enter into the future kingdom of God by means of a radical renewal of daily life in their houses.

An obvious question, therefore, is why the Gospel of Matthew puts on the lips of Jesus the celebrated words addressed to Simon Peter: "You are Peter, and on this rock I will build my church [*ekklēsia*]" (16:18). These words have been used over and over again in support of the thesis that Jesus wanted to found the church, a religious entity that is very distinct and autonomous. We must, however, bear in mind that most exegetes recognize that these words do not go back to Jesus. The evangelist has attributed them to him roughly fifty years after his death. The Catholic exegete Joachim Gnilka does not hesitate to ascribe these words and the brief passage into which they are inserted (Matt 16:16-19) to the initiative of Matthew, who is the only evangelist to report them.[83]

We agree that it is hard to imagine that Jesus himself could have uttered this saying. The Gospels of Mark, Luke, and John quote more than a hundred sayings, parables, and discourses of Jesus, but the word "church" (*ekklēsia*) never occurs in any of them. The Gospel of Matthew likewise quotes a large number of sayings of Jesus, but it places this word on his lips only twice. We have just quoted the first instance; the second is more elaborate and eloquent:

> If your brother sins against you, go and point out the fault when the two of you are alone. If he listens to you, you have regained the brother. But if you are not listened to, take one or two others along with you, so that every word may be confirmed by the evidence of two or three witnesses. If he refuses to listen to them, tell it to the church [*ekklēsia*]; and if the offender refuses to listen even to the church, let such a one be to you as a Gentile and a tax collector. (Matt 18:15-17)

In this second passage, Matthew refers to a community organization that did not exist during the lifetime of Jesus. He envisaged a situation typical of his own period, the last quarter of the first century, when communities have already taken shape and regulations for internal conduct exist. In Matthew's days, the word "church" had already become established. We find it very frequently in the canonical writings of the New Testament that speak of the life of the communities of Jesus' followers several decades after his death. It is found, for example, more than sixty times in the letters attributed to Paul. It is in this historical climate that the various communities began to pose the question of their own legitimacy and their link to the authority of Jesus. Matthew 16:18 is one of several texts that attribute a particular function to Peter, but we also have texts that give James or Thomas particular functions. But Jesus himself saw things very differently. He did not aim at the organization of an autonomous body but at the renewal of the whole people of Israel in the expectation of the new reality that God would soon inaugurate.

Jesus' Preference for Direct Encounters

It is obvious that the persons whom Jesus met had their own way of looking at the world and pursued their own specific personal objectives. This obliged him to take account of individual, social, and political situations that varied greatly. It forced him to look at each individual in his or her own particularity. There is no passage anywhere in the Gospels—and this is an important fact in our analysis—that shows Jesus choosing any other strategy than the direct face-to-face encounter.

One problem arises when we look at his method of communicating: Jesus spoke, but why did he not write anything? We can now attempt an answer. He was certainly capable of writing, or of asking others to write for him.[84] His reason for not doing so was that writing is a means employed by one who does not enter into a personal dialogue, by one who is not exposed to the immediate reaction of his or her interlocutor. In Jesus' days, poets, novelists, philosophers, and politicians chose to communicate by means of writing, without entering directly into contact with those for whom they wrote, and without knowing their particular feelings and emotions. The written work interposes itself between the author and the intended reader. One who reads enters into contact with the author only by means of an instrument that is highly elaborate and complex, and that is rarely unequivocal. The text can be used by many persons. Jesus, on the other hand, wanted to enter into a concrete and unique exchange. Writing has a quality of permanence: it endures over the course of time. The personal encounter is brief and need not imply any continuity. It can be improvised and can end abruptly. Jesus aimed at evoking a response and a decision that involved the totality of a person's existence, and that must be immediate. Only the spoken word can communicate how urgent it is to make this response, and can elicit adherence or dissent.

Was this attitude on Jesus' part dependent on the imminent coming of the kingdom, or by the fact that only his person was able to communicate the power inherent in this kingdom? One who writes fears that time is slipping away, and wants to preserve the message for the future. But it seems that Jesus was unafraid that time might destroy what he was doing. The sands of time are running, but the passing of time does not make meaningless the decision that Jesus wants to provoke. What is happening *now* is decisive. The present moment is what exists and what counts.

Social analysis shows that in all religious experiences, the most important and effective factor is the personal encounter that takes hold of a person's life and reshapes it, making it completely different from what it had been up to that moment. Without appealing here to fixed paradigms, we can say that, often, religious experience is channeled through a direct relationship between individual agents: a master and a disciple, an inspired person and an aspirant.[85] The analysis of religious phenomena teaches that one who senses a profound need will turn personally to the one who can satisfy it (a healer, a guide), or will go to a sacred place in which one can be bodily taken hold of by supernatural powers.

Jesus was interested in contact with every type of person in the immediate situation. He looked intently at people and understood them. He shared in their lives, observing their faces and listening to their voices. He experienced feelings of identification with them. He perceived their problems and made them his own. A face-to-face encounter means that each is mirrored in the other. Jesus produced an instantaneous magnetic effect and possessed a special power to convince others precisely by means of his face, by the way he looked at people (Mark 10:21) and the way he spoke. It is highly likely that his voice and his gestures, and the charismatic power of his person, were able to elicit exceptionally strong reactions—including aversion and rejection.

The encounter with people, in its various forms, was essential for Jesus, because it was there that his role and his abilities could be revealed. We must regard him as an unofficial preacher, that is, as one who lacked any recognized authority. He was not legitimated by the institutional authorities, and thus had no credentials. The only way for him to find recognition was through the direct reaction of the people. In some, Jesus evoked attraction and the hope of being able to realize their own aspirations through him. In others, as we have seen, he evoked interest, doubt, or suspicion. Finally, in still others he evoked an opposition that was lethal.

If we analyze the dynamics of these encounters, we invariably find an intense and deep relationship. For some, Jesus felt love, or a sense of sharing their lot; for others he felt compassion and the desire to restore them to a state of normality in their own families. He rejected and condemned others, subjecting them to sharp criticism.

People's reaction was the only instrument that allowed Jesus to see where he stood. The reactions oscillated between the opposing poles of attraction and rejection. He must have seen the attraction and love that some persons showed as a confirmation of his function. He held that the dedication of the persons who followed him ought to take the form of a radical detachment from the households to which they belonged and from their foundational relationships. Systemically speaking, his relationship to his itinerant followers was based on a reciprocal recognition. The follower recognized in Jesus the guide; and Jesus recognized in the follower an affinity to his own self. Where he was rejected, Jesus took an unambiguous stance of opposition. This rejection entailed a radical conflict, since Jesus' vision of the situation in which he lived was highly conflictual. The alternatives were affinity or a radical distance, love or hate.

Jesus sought out the greatest possible number of persons who belonged to the people of Israel. He wanted them to give their lives an orientation that would allow them to participate in the new reality that was beginning. He announced the "kingdom of God" in which he believed and which he expected.

It is possible that the questions the crowd themselves asked about the future kingdom went unanswered, or that such questions nourished uncertain and unending expectations. People sought out Jesus in order to have a personal encounter with him, to receive an orientation for their lives, to follow him, or to be healed or protected by him. Women drew near to him in order to break the barriers that kept them on a subordinate level or in separate locations. His relatives sought him out in order to control him. His adversaries wanted to see in person whether their doubts were justified, or to challenge him, or to seize him by force. After his miraculous actions, people were enthusiastic and wanted to spread the news of the extraordinary deeds. All this confirms, on the level of the network of relationships, that his own person was at the center of people's interest. They sought in him the satisfaction of their needs and the fulfillment of their hopes. The primary aim of all those who drew near to him was most likely to get access to his power. Once health and security were attained, once they had eaten their fill, the rest followed.

Jesus' trajectory and the trajectory of the people went in contradictory directions. Jesus directed individual persons to God, but people sought Jesus.

Jesus can be envisaged only in the midst of the group that surrounded him and listened to his words—sometimes words of consolation, sometimes words of provocation. Jesus and his followers constituted, therefore, a Judean movement among many other Judean movements. Their aim was the definitive and radical liberation from the daily restrictions that dominated every sector of the population.

Without the reactions of the people in all their variety, the figure of Jesus remains obscure, misty. Those who reacted are the "historical," real people whom Jesus made the center of his own existence. These were the people who were to take part in the construction of the kingdom, and these were the ones whom Jesus invited to take hold of the eschatological moment that would soon begin. Jesus promised not only an end to distress, nor did he promise only egalitarianism. He promised a new era.

Most probably, the people were largely unaware of what Jesus wanted and hoped, and of the events that he envisaged as a consequence of his public activity—not least because he had communicated his most intimate convictions only to a very small number of his disciples when he was alone with them. He often kept silent about his deepest experience, and sometimes forbade his followers to speak about what they had seen. Jesus' encounters with people are an essential element in all the possible reconstructions of his figure. In many respects, however, they remain hidden under a veil of silence.

Jesus was not the leader of a destitute mob, as in the movements of revolt. The central issue is the fissure that existed in Jesus, the contradiction between his being a real and effective leader of the people he encountered and his attempt not to be a leader and to withdraw from every leadership role, as he waited for God himself to intervene and to assume power directly.

4

JESUS AT TABLE

Eating Together

Coming Together to Eat: Building Up Society

Both in public and in private contexts, eating together allows the participants to have special encounters and exchanges, or to reach agreements.[1] By preparing food, by giving it to others, and by accepting it as a gift—here we recall the structure of exchange elaborated by Marcel Mauss[2]—people offer, receive, and give back. Often, a meal is the way of solemnizing special events and moments. Sharing food, however, permits people to pay due honor to the supernatural world and to make friends with the human world. Those who are admitted to a banquet measure their own interests against those of the other participants and find a balance between them, since they must also reflect on how they can continue to be invited and to invite. Reciprocal or repeated invitations rekindle the mechanisms of social life and are a proof of one's social standing. Without invitations of this kind, the agreements reached would risk a gradual weakening that could lead to their cancellation. Every kind of banquet confirms and reinforces one's alliances with those partners who can offer the best protection or promotion. The act of eating and exchanging food always has repercussions on people's future projects.[3]

One who receives guests and offers food is in a certain sense a producer and distributor of symbolic goods. The guest, who has neither produced nor procured the food, is given the opportunity to accept and to share in consuming another person's goods. The relationship between offering and accepting is not a relationship of equality in producing, giving, receiving, and sharing, since there is no equilibrium in the situations and functions of the persons involved. The act of eating together has the merit of establishing a relationship between individuals who are in unequal situations. The "debt side" of food is seldom equal to the "credit side" in importance or quantity, and this is why the contacts and exchanges are continually renewed. This disequilibrium guarantees the continuation of the reciprocal relationship in the exchange of invitations.

While it is true that food brings people closer, it is also clear that it *draws distinctions* and isolates wherever it cannot be freely accepted and distributed. When an individual or a group wishes to remain distinct from the surrounding environment on which it depends, and with which it has relationships, it has recourse to a different style of eating together. It manipulates, innovates, and changes the canon of its dietary practices, insisting on precise prohibitions. If it does not possess the means to keep itself distinct, it must accept dietary usages and customs of some other type, and this poses a risk to its identity. Accordingly, we may say that the various groups in a society express their reciprocal difference by means of the specific character of the occasions on which they come together to eat.

In conclusion, the food that is offered is a gift carefully measured out and presented as a means to achieve pacification and agreement. It is also possible, however, for the offering of food to be a deliberate and institutionalized challenge between individuals and groups. Food eaten together, and organized with a greater or lesser degree of solemnity, is not only the place of sharing and of a reciprocal gift. It is also the place where dissent or conflict becomes evident and explodes. The place where the greatest closeness is realized is also the place where the greatest division is possible. As we shall see in the case of Jesus, the food that is exchanged constructs domestic life and the primary duties in the life of households. This is why our analysis must center on the domestic sharing of food, which is less visible but no less influential than the public sharing.

We shall see below that eating together is one of those activities that, according to Maurice Godelier,[4] are of their nature enigmatic, since it is in them that the functioning and the prosperity of society are rooted. A primary principle is that the things offered at table must belong to the category of that which one is allowed to exchange, and they must be appropriate to the one who receives them. They must also possess an explanatory meaning, in the sense that the fabric and the stratification of society are either confirmed or overturned by what is eaten. The one with a higher social position eats first and keeps the better parts of the food and the most comfortable and sought-after place for himself. To eat together while respecting the structure of society and not challenging it means that one accepts this structure out of conviction, by means of a pact of fidelity that is confirmed again and again. But sharing food can become a time of extreme tension, leading ultimately to rupture, when the inequalities and the social duties that are imposed become intolerable.

In classical antiquity, there were many different types of banquets, promoted and supported by individuals and by groups, with a mixture of styles and social functions. Dennis E. Smith lists the following elements in the tradition of the Roman banquets that are relevant to the milieu in which Christianity had its origin: the Roman symposium, the philosophical banquets, the sacrificial meals, the funeral meals, the meals of groups of adherents of mystery religions, and the communal and festive Judaic meals.[5] Other scholars, such as David Balch and Carolyn Osiek,[6] present a list of the situations in which early Christians met to eat together. We should add the meals taken in common by various voluntary associations, such as those of professional or religious groups.[7]

We may take as our starting point the hypothesis that in the various cultural milieus in which the movement of Jesus and early Christianity emerged eating in common was an expression of distinct goals that depended on the type of group or the social occasion. In the religious sphere that interests us here, the practice of shared meals could express the relationship between the human and the superhuman, or between the living and the dead, or the functions of the ritual actors, or the relationship between master and disciple. Moreover, shared meals of voluntary associations or on particular occasions allowed people to cut through and overcome distinctions of religion or wealth. Eating together confirmed moral customs and states of purity or impurity. Max Weber underlined that "totemic brotherhood" found expression in table fellowship with borders laid down by dietary taboos that distinguished one group from another.[8]

This means that whenever people meet to take their normal daily food or to use food to celebrate an event (births, marriages, funerals, festivities, sacred meals), the codified models of a society are transmitted, and light is shed on the elements on which the society is based. The sharing of food expresses symbolically—and influences—the organization of any kind of society. The persons who take part, the order in which they take their places, and the food that is chosen for the meal—all these factors function as a symbolic synthesis of a social group, of its hierarchies, and of its values.

Jesus was uprooted from work and the domestic unit and continually moved from place to place. This meant that he had a concrete need to be welcomed as a guest by landed proprietors and householders, by simple workers, or by women, and to receive help toward his sustenance. This, however, did not deprive him of the possibility of assuming a dominant role vis-à-vis his host. When the group made contact with those who could offer them food, they demonstrated their dependence; but at the same time, they offered something in exchange. First and foremost, the disciples whom Jesus sent out were to proclaim peace and well-being: "Whatever house you enter, first say, 'Peace to this house!' And if anyone is there who shares in peace, your peace will rest on that person; but if not, it will return to you" (Luke 10:5-6). Jesus appears to think that the welcome received by the itinerants should be considered a legitimate recompense for their labors: "Remain in the same house, eating and drinking whatever they provide, for the laborer is worthy of his hire" (Luke 10:7).[9] The dependence here is that of a salaried worker, not of a beggar.

Despite their cultural, geographical, and chronological distance from Jesus' lifetime, the Gospel texts agree in giving considerable space to the scenes in which he is "at table"[10] with various kinds of persons. Sharing food is a characteristic of Jesus' way of life, and we will take a closer look at those with whom he has contact. The Gospels present him as one who shares food in a great variety of forms: banquets in people's homes, scenes in which thousands of people eat together, but also intimate moments in which he eats with the group that is closest to him, as, for example, in the final chapter of John, in which he invites the disciples to eat the fish he has cooked on a charcoal fire on the lake shore (John 21:12). And there can be no doubt that the Last Supper, so rich in action, bears elaborate symbolic meanings.[11]

Another proof that the practice of eating together is a characteristic aspect of the itinerant lifestyle of Jesus is the fact that meals in common become the object of reflection in the parables. This narrative material makes use of elements that are central to the social imagination of Jesus. Examples (of which we will speak below) are the scenarios in the parables of the banquet (Luke 14:16-24; *Gospel of Thomas* 64; Matt 22:2-10), of the rich man and the beggar "at his gate" (Luke 16:19-31), or of the slave who comes back from working in the fields and must serve his master at table before he himself can eat.[12]

Jesus also attributes an important symbolic meaning to eating in common in relation to the central element of his message about the kingdom of God.[13] It seems impossible to deny the historicity of sayings in which the banquet becomes the paradigm of the kingdom of God. Even the Gentiles will come from every region of the world to sit at table with Abraham, Isaac, and Jacob. Jesus himself declares at the Last Supper that it is only in the kingdom of God that he will drink anew of the fruit of the vine (Mark 14:25; cf. Matt 26:29; Luke 22:18).

After the death of Jesus, the gatherings at table became the place where the essential values of the movement were conserved and idealized. Some scholars regard a number of the convivial scenes, whether in the Gospel narratives or in the form of parables, as lacking historical reality. They argue that such scenes were composed in order to reinforce the memory of the sayings of Jesus, and that they shed light on the ideal of the earliest communities, which were influenced by models of conviviality in Greco-Roman culture. For example, Smith argues:

> My argument is that what is being identified as the historical Jesus at table is more likely the idealized characterization of Jesus at table produced in the early Christian community. The social realities of such meals are still being correctly assessed, but the one who presents parabolic messages by means of meal practices is more likely the idealized Jesus than the historical Jesus. . . . The social realities defined by these meals, in which table fellowship is equated with a new community self-consciousness, are more likely those of an already developing early Christian community than those of the motley crowds who came to hear Jesus teach.[14]

We believe that it is possible to argue for the opposite view. Indeed, there is nothing erroneous in the hypothesis that many of Jesus' sayings may have been spoken by him in a context of shared meals, even if they were subsequently detached from the original context and transmitted without any genuine reference to the meals. And even authors such as Smith do not deny that the original convivial context of many sayings of Jesus finds confirmation in the cultural centrality of meals and the symbolism of eating in contemporary Judaic culture. The context of Judaic commensality is present in a number of sayings in which Jesus seems to be stating his own position with regard to questions and internal debates in Judaism about dietary customs.[15] Furthermore, while it is correct and necessary to differentiate between the commensality of the early communities and the practice of Jesus himself, it is also true that some measure of continuity between his customs and the traditions of the early churches is undeniable. These arguments, however, are on a secondary level that does not go beyond a comparison of the concepts in the early church, the Judaic environment, and Jesus. The principal argument is that the practice of commensality was absolutely necessary for Jesus, for the simple reason that he was dependent on the resources of those who welcomed him into their houses. He was surrounded by followers who were likewise uprooted from their own homes and had no possessions of their own. They depended exclusively on what they might receive on the road.

In any case, it cannot be doubted that Jesus practiced commensality. The fact that he ate what people put before him was a choice that differentiated him from his master, John the Baptizer. We have seen that John is presented by the Gospels as a man who practiced abstinence from food. The customs of the early communities after the death of Jesus are certainly inspired by the historical reality of a person who did not refuse food and drink (Luke 7:33-34). Despite this, a certain discontinuity in the specific forms of eating may well have become necessary. On this point, the difference between Jesus and the customs of the early communities was due to the fact that they soon abandoned the itinerant lifestyle and the specific form of sharing food that was linked to this. When customs change, there is simultaneously a change in understanding and in the symbolic meanings of eating.

Since the Gospels paint divergent pictures of how Jesus ate, we must ask which of these could correspond to the style of life he actually led. We must also ask about the types of persons with whom he ate. Accordingly, we shall look separately at different kinds of gatherings: (a) meals in houses of a certain social level, or on the occasion of important banquets; (b) meals with his disciples on the road; (c) meals that involve only Jesus' own group in people's houses, including the Last Supper; (d) meals with friends and people close to Jesus' movement; (e) scenes in which Jesus feeds the crowds miraculously; (f) depictions in the parables of eating together or of a banquet.

Scholars do not regard all these situations as equally historical. There is a general consensus that Jesus' custom of eating with his disciples and with "tax collectors and sinners" is historical. While Smith agrees with this view, he holds that the stories of miraculous feedings of the crowd are the outcome of idealizations, and are thus historically dubious. Similarly, the meals with Pharisees are to be attributed to Lukan redaction.[16] We, however, believe that it is impossible to deny the reliability of the numerous occasions on which Jesus asks for hospitality for himself and his followers. This historical reliability attaches not to the precise chronological or geographical situations of the narratives but to

Jesus' *habit* of asking for food from persons who belonged to a variety of social strata, of sharing in the domestic customs of their milieu, and of sharing food with a large variety of unknown persons.

In the Houses of the Rich

After Jesus' lifetime, many of his habits were subject to a re-elaboration and charged with symbolic meanings. In Luke 14:1-24, Jesus is invited to eat in the house of "a leader of the Pharisees." This means that the house must have been rather large and that the banquet was on a grand scale. Jesus accepted the invitation, and the story shows that he went there not only in order to eat, but also because the meal offered him a good opportunity to reveal his message and his lifestyle. Luke paints a broad picture that shows Jesus as a man who thoroughly understood the symbolic system of the meal and who openly expressed criticism of the current practice.

Luke emphasizes that the Pharisees were "observing" Jesus on this occasion[17] to see what he would do and teach. Luke's Jesus accepted the challenge, and his reaction takes place in three successive moments. First of all, there is his anomalous behavior in performing a healing on the Sabbath day. When he was criticized, he replied that this deed was not only permitted but was in fact obligatory, just like saving one's son or an animal that has fallen into a well, even when this happens on a Sabbath day.[18] During the meal, Jesus presented his teaching polemically in a parable about "the places" at table about priorities and about the honor that is gained or lost, depending on whether one is at one's own place or at the place that belongs to others. Luke's Jesus appears aware of what eating together expresses about the order of society, about the difference between rich and poor and between masters and servants, and about the gradations of honor in the upper strata. The meal taken in common is understood precisely as sanctioning the stratification and the social exclusion, and this is why Jesus proposed to the Pharisee that he should not invite friends, brothers, relatives, or neighbors. He asked him to welcome the poor, who would not be able to offer him anything in return, nor to reciprocate his invitation. Finally, Jesus told the parable of those invited to the banquet.

There can be no doubt that this scene as a whole is a literary elaboration by Luke, who brings together different elements of the tradition of Jesus' words and actions in order to form one single treatment of the topic of eating together.[19] It is hence highly unlikely that the text is a literal reproduction of Jesus' healing and his teachings, or that they took place in this sequence during a meal in the house of a leading Pharisee. The backdrop of this whole scene in Luke is a meal in the style of a Greco-Roman symposium, where it was normal for a discussion to take place—a discussion that might well be heated and controversial.[20] There is nothing improbable in Jesus' historical context about the idea that he could have accepted an invitation from a leader of the Pharisees to a grand banquet, or that he could have taught and started a discussion during this meal. And it is likely that Jesus uttered the two parables and the polemic about the places at table precisely in the course of meals taken in common. In the last quarter of the first century, when Luke was writing, it was no longer possible to reconstruct the historical circumstances.

Another scene in Luke's Gospel (19:2-9) illustrates well the relationship between different social actors and between their intentions and expectations. The situation is defined by the fact that Zacchaeus, a rich man, was the chief tax collector. He climbed a sycamore tree because he wanted to see Jesus. When they met, Jesus said to him: "I must stay at your house today." It seems, therefore, that this involved more than just a meal: Jesus would stay overnight in a house that is presumably large. His decision was criticized: "All who saw it began to grumble and said, 'He has gone to be the guest of one who is a sinner.'" But Jesus told the householder, Zacchaeus: "Today salvation has come to this house." The generosity Zacchaeus showed to an itinerant preacher led to his "salvation." As a consequence, Zacchaeus changed his life.

The scenes in houses belonging to the rich show us Jesus pursuing the goal of a precise and profound renewal of the life of the households. On the one hand, he shows that he trusts the rich; at the same time, however, he criticizes them and suggests that they must change their lives in a radical manner.

Eating along the Way

Jesus' custom of eating along the road is particularly important.[21] This is implicit in Mark's narrative (8:14-21) when the disciples have "only one loaf" with them and are afraid that this will not be enough—thereby revealing how precarious their situation was. Mark seems to think that, just as Jesus has given the crowd food in a miracle, he can now give the disciples food even if there is no bread available. In the ensuing discussion, he invites the disciples to distrust the yeast[22] of the Pharisees and of Herod. The word "yeast" shows how the teaching of Jesus in a context of commensality refers to the essential elements of food. The entire narrative presupposes that it was normal for the group to have a small reserve of bread with them, and to stop at some point along the road in order to eat together.

This detail is very significant, because it brings us closer to the practice of Jesus. He reveals himself above all through what he does. His message is contained in his words, but it cannot be reduced to what he says.[23] Often, one who writes a text or sends a message is silent about precisely those aspects of daily living that are the most obvious. For a reader today, accustomed to a radical decontextualization and spiritualization of the figure of Jesus, such aspects—which were obvious in their early Christian environment and were typical of the ancient world—are not obvious. Indeed, they are often obscure.

The Synoptic Gospels relate that one Sabbath day, along the road, the disciples began to pluck ears of grain in the fields and ate them (Luke 6:1-5/Matt 12:1-8/Mark 2:23-28). Once again, this is a simple form of eating together that offers a realistic glimpse of the life of a man who was continually moving from place to place. This very rustic act of eating is accompanied by a teaching: Jesus justified the behavior of the disciples, maintaining both respect for the Sabbath and a certain liberty of conduct on the weekly day of rest.

The style of eating is the object of reflection on another occasion, related by Mark and Matthew,[24] when the Pharisees accused Jesus' followers of eating without washing their hands in accordance with the dietary customs followed by some groups. In these two instances, the criticism was directed not at Jesus but only at his followers: it is they who plucked the ears of grain, and it is they who did not wash their hands. In another situation presented by Luke, it is Jesus himself who did not wash his hands before he ate in the house of a Pharisee (Luke 11:37-41). We are entitled to doubt whether Jesus himself practiced a certain liberty on this issue, since the fact that only his followers were accused may mean that the earliest Christian groups had these customs (and were therefore challenged by other Judean groups). They would then have justified themselves by creating stories in which Jesus authorized them to do so; and the fact that Luke attributes to Jesus the custom of not washing one's hands may be an attempt to project back onto him practices that arose only later on. It is not possible to resolve this question definitively. We should, however, not underestimate the fact that washing one's hands before eating was not a biblical precept.[25]

At Table with His Followers

We have seen that commensality was one of Jesus' favorite ways to establish a profound and intimate contact with other people. Within his own group, he likewise seems to celebrate the most important moments by means of table fellowship.

The Synoptic Gospels tell us that Jesus wished to eat a solemn supper, like the Passover supper, together with his disciples.[26] In particular, Luke strongly underlines this aspiration: "I have eagerly desired to eat this Passover with you."[27] Jesus performed an ancient and formalized rite, and took up two central elements of the ritual supper, the bread and the wine, for a reflection that was particularly his own.[28]

In the narratives of the Last Supper, which speak of the "betrayal" of Judas Iscariot,[29] eating the same food from the same dish is presented as a supreme moment of unity. One of those at table betrayed the very persons with whom he was sharing the food. In Mark, Jesus underlines that the one who was about to betray him was "one who is dipping into the bowl with me,"[30] one of the Twelve, one of those closest to Jesus. John declares that Judas decided to betray Jesus immediately after receiving the "morsel" that Jesus dipped into the bowl and offered him. In the narrative, Jesus seems to want to attract Judas to himself by giving him his own food, and it is in this very moment that the disciple separated himself from him. The food that is now shared takes on a different meaning: it is a metaphor of rebellion and opposition. The supper sets the seal on an intense closeness, but also on a profound disunity. It is presented as a symbolic action in which the creation of unity and the shattering of unity are immediately juxtaposed.

The sharing of food contains the entire symbolic universe and all the potentialities that Jesus bears, because it is intended to annul every difference. But for this very reason—thanks to the power that it unleashes and to the meanings that it possesses—it accelerates the dissension and the decision to break with Jesus. It was probably his followers, after Jesus' death, who reflected on the fact that Judas Iscariot decided to hand him over to his enemies even though he had just shared the Last Supper with him. This scandalized them precisely because they attached such a high meaning to the sharing of food and to the aims that this sharing was meant to attain.

Many scholars maintain that the Gospel narratives have profoundly modified the Last Supper of Jesus under the influence of the ritual commensality that the early communities called the "Eucharist." In these communities, the gathering in which the remembering of Jesus' Last Supper was renewed was central to the process of consolidating the community and forming its identity. The remembering reworked that event, ascribing to it a foundational significance for the identity of the communities in their contemporary context. Nevertheless, this reworking does not eliminate the historical fact that Jesus employed commensality to celebrate solemn moments together with his group.

Besides this, the first testimony to the Last Supper comes from a very ancient text, Paul's First Letter to the Corinthians, which can be dated to the mid-50s of the first century of the Common Era. Paul writes: "I received from the Lord what I also handed on to you, that the Lord Jesus on the night when he was betrayed took a loaf of bread, and when he had given thanks, he broke it" (1 Cor 11:23-24). In this very ancient tradition, the memorial is linked to the fact that Jesus was "handed over." That night was defined as the night on which the "handing over" of Jesus took place. Here, it is not essential to know whether the Last Supper was the Judaic Passover supper as the Gospels of Mark, Luke, and Matthew think, or a supper before Passover as the Gospel of John seems to think. What counts is the customary employment by Jesus of the communal meal as the setting for celebrating decisively important events and for imparting his teaching.

We have other narratives where Jesus eats with the disciples, but none of these attains the levels of profundity and the symbolic weight of the Last Supper. Mark's Jesus (1:29-31) eats without any solemnity in the house of Simon and Andrew, together with two other disciples, James and John. He is served by Peter's mother-in-law, whom he has just healed.[31] In Matthew, Jesus appears to be inside a house that served as a base at that time: "As he sat at dinner in the house, many tax collectors and sinners came and were sitting with him and his disciples." He gives hospitality even to persons of dubious morality, inviting them to eat with him and his disciples. The phrase "tax collectors and sinners" (Matt 9:9-13) designates persons who are wicked[32] on account of their professional work and are irrevocably subject to condemnation. The Pharisees find this habitual closeness of Jesus to sinners problematic, and they ask his followers: "Why does your teacher eat with tax collectors and sinners?" The historicity of Jesus' habitual commensality with transgressors of the Law seems undeniable. He justifies his behavior by his desire to invite them to change their lives. Here too, commensality becomes the context in which he hands on his message more directly and effectively.

At Table with Friends

Let us look again at the episode in Luke 10:38-42 in which a woman named Martha offered Jesus hospitality in her house. This may involve a meal, since her sister Mary sat at Jesus' feet and listened "to his word." It is therefore probable that Luke imagines her sitting on the straw mat or couch on which he was "reclining" while eating. The Gospel of John (12:1-8) seems to know a different version: Jesus was a guest at Bethany (and not in an anonymous village as in Luke 10) in the house of a friend, Lazarus. One of his two sisters, Martha, served, while the other, Mary, anointed Jesus with perfumed oil. In both versions, we find personal friends of Jesus, or at any rate sympathizers, who are very different from the Pharisees mentioned above. But he seems to have the same desire to teach friends or persons who are close to him in the domestic environment where they carry out completely indispensable household tasks.

Scenes of commensality in which Jesus is anointed by a woman, similar to the scene in John 12:1-8, are also found in Mark (14:3-9/Matt 26:6-13) and in Luke (7:36-50).[33] All these narratives apparently refer to the same episode, but they report it in differing ways. For our present purposes, the most interesting point is that in Mark, Jesus was "reclining" as the guest at a meal in the house of Simon the leper in Bethany. During the meal, a woman with an alabaster vase drew near and anointed him. In Luke (7:36), Jesus was invited by a Pharisee named Simon, and "reclined" to eat. A "sinful woman" of that town (not to be identified with Mary of Magdala, who is never presented in such terms in the Gospels) bathed the feet of Jesus with her tears and then dried them with her hair. Jesus rebuked Simon for not having received him in a worthy manner: he failed to perform the acts of welcoming a guest, that is, washing his feet, giving him the kiss of welcome, and offering him perfume. Accordingly, this scene clearly shows not only the status of the guest and the welcome to which he was entitled but also the fact that a meal was always an occasion for expressing judgments and opinions, as well as dissensions and more or less veiled accusations. In general, the meal gave the householder the opportunity to "stage" the event on the basis of his own lifestyle and his own ideas. The judgments expressed in Luke's narrative show that the Pharisees and Jesus evaluated things very differently: their verdict was that the woman was a sinner, but he pardoned her. The Pharisees gave vent to their incredulity with regard to Jesus' behavior, but the woman believed in him.

Another important example is the scene in John (2:11) that depicts a meal in the village of Cana. Here, Jesus was a participant in a festal moment in the midst of people who led the same type of life as he, namely, the life of a villager. It is a wedding feast, and Jesus seems to be very welcome as a *guest*, along with his mother, his brothers, and his disciples.

We may well have doubts about the historicity of this event, given the symbolic significance that the evangelist attributes to the episode. But the scenario of the narrative is historically plausible. It presents Jesus and his disciples in the position of guests at a social occasion that emphasizes the ties and hierarchies of the village families. It is interesting that John presents the first of Jesus' miraculous "signs," the changing of water into wine, here. The rites and the symbols John describes are typical of a banquet: the wine that is served and the water prepared for purifying ablutions before the meal (according to the customs of some Judean groups). In other words, John too takes up the scenes of commensality as an occasion for Jesus to teach and hand on his message. Indeed, in the Fourth Gospel the entire narrative of Jesus' activity is intentionally placed in the brackets formed by this first meal, which is the inaugural public act of Jesus, and the Last Supper.[34] Convivial scenes also appear in chap. 21 of John, which was added in the final redaction. This becomes the concluding solemn act of the life that Jesus leads in common with his followers. The shared meal is the most appropriate symbol to express this life.

MIRACLES TO FEED THE HUNGRY:
THE SIGN OF ABUNDANCE

In Mark's Gospel, Jesus' attentiveness to the people who follow him also finds expression in an active concern to satisfy their hunger. The narrative first presents five thousand persons, then subsequently four thousand, who have no means of support. They are attracted by Jesus and remain with him. They are hungry, but they seem to have no idea what to do. Instead of dispersing, they wait. Jesus performed the functions of a host: he shared with those present the little he had, making it increase enormously and distributing it generously. The narrative does not describe a banquet or a convivial gathering of the community. It speaks of the need to help thousands of people and to supply them with food out in the open countryside. These miracle stories depict an ideal of extreme abundance for those who are in need, as we see from the fact that a huge quantity of loaves and fishes remain even after all have eaten their fill. And the fact that thousands are present shows how great is the celebrity and the power of Jesus.

The narrative of the miraculous event emphasizes the disproportion between the human and the superhuman, and between life and death. The enormous quantity of food that is given to help those who are hungry underlines how essential food is to human life: abundance guarantees that life will continue but scarcity puts life at risk. Jesus' action here is an immensely powerful statement that lends added strength to the content of his message and shows what his own expectations were. The supreme ideal in Jesus' eyes seems to be that anyone who is in distress should be able to have his needs supplied through the work of God. The question of righting the imbalances in society is absent.[35]

The miraculous aspect has led many scholars to doubt the historicity of this scene and to read the stories of the multiplication of food as something created by the followers of Jesus after his death in order to construct an "idealized" image. Consequently, these miraculous narratives should be "analyzed as components of the literary motifs of the Gospel narratives,"[36] not as aspects of the historical Jesus. We are forced to hypothesize, however, that these narratives did not appear out of thin air and that something extraordinary did take place. It is, of course, true that those who transmitted the stories were not present; they could not relate something they themselves experienced directly.[37] All they related is second-hand information that they could not verify. Nevertheless, the fact remains that the authors of the Gospels regard commensality and the abundance of food as a symbol that we cannot dispense with if we want to understand the practice of life of Jesus in its totality.

Eating Together in the Parables

Eating together is a central element in a number of famous parables that give us an idea of what Jesus himself probably thought about commensality. In one Lukan parable (16:19-31), the banquet is a crude but highly dramatic image that draws a contrast between a rich man "who feasted sumptuously every day" and a poor man "at his gate who longed to satisfy his hunger with what fell from the rich man's table." In the story Jesus told, the tables are turned in the next world: "The poor man died and was carried away by the angels to be with Abraham. The rich man also died and was buried. In Hades, where he was being tormented, he looked up and saw Abraham far away with Lazarus by his side."[38] In this parable, the act of eating and satisfying one's hunger separates the rich man and Lazarus. The function of the act of eating in this parable is to shed a realistic light on a social division. Jesus found this division so utterly intolerable that he made *eating* the reason why the rich man is condemned to suffer the torments of Hades. The rich man is not blamed for his wealth, but for eating alone. He excluded the poor and did not share his food with them. This parable looks authentic because it accords with the message of Jesus or finds a coherent scenario in it. It must be read against the backdrop of the saying about the impossibility for rich persons to enter the kingdom of God (Mark 10:25) and of the beatitude "Blessed are you who are poor, for yours is the kingdom of God" (Luke 6:20).

Similarly, in another parable (Luke 17:7-10), eating appears as the indication of a state of affairs that demands and receives implicit disapproval on the part of Jesus. There can be no doubt that this passage denounces the practice of requiring slaves, on their return from working in the fields, to prepare food for their masters and to wait on them at table—and only then are they themselves allowed to eat. Jesus turns an implacable eye on the cruelty and harshness of the master's conduct and on the insurmountable social barriers. Once again, it is the act of eating that makes the imbalance completely clear and that consolidates the lack of social unity. This parable too looks authentic. It accords well with Jesus' action at the Last Supper, when he dressed like a slave to wash the disciples' feet (as John relates)[39] or pronounced the saying recorded by Luke in this context of commensality: "I am among you as one who serves" (22:27).

As we have mentioned, the parable of the banquet is transmitted to us in three different versions in Luke, Thomas, and Matthew (Luke 14:15-24; *Gospel of Thomas* 64; Matt 22:1-14). Exegetical analysis shows that the version closest to that spoken by Jesus is certainly not that of Matthew, but that of Luke and Thomas.[40] A householder organized a supper and invited persons who were his social equals—as we see from their activities, which are prominent and customary in the life of a village. They were involved in looking after their own households and managing their domestic business. This scene, where the heads of households eat together, sheds an interesting light on what Jesus may have thought about the distribution of goods and about the practice of alliances and social relationships among the members of one particular social group. The story also contains pointers about the customs that had to be followed in issuing or receiving an invitation and about the symbolic impact these customs had in terms of status and of participation in cultural life.

Matthew's version takes us into a completely different context of exchanges and invitations. We are now far removed from the original parable of Jesus and from his understanding of what sharing food meant. But precisely because Matthew presents a version of Jesus' words that is not historically reliable, his text shows us how the evangelist himself understood the ritual meal that was practiced by some groups of Jesus' followers around the 80s of the first century C.E. In particular, there are two points that distinguish Matthew's version. After the king's servants have gathered everyone they found on the streets, to take the places of the destined guests who had declared that they could not come, the banquet hall fills up. It seems to be a vast hall that accommodates many people, "both good and bad" (Matt 22:10). In Luke, the householder commands that "the poor, the crippled, the blind, and the lame" be brought in (14:21). Matthew has changed the context, thereby altering the human and social meaning that Jesus probably wished to emphasize into an ethical meaning: "good and bad" are moral categories that do not indicate differences in status, discriminations, or social imbalances. This may mean that Matthew has taken a parable that referred realistically to a social division and transformed it into a story that alludes to communities of a period later than Jesus. He changed the theme of the unjust inequality between the rich and the poor, which was a source of great suffering, into an ecclesiological theme. According to Matthew, the community of Jesus' followers must address the good news to everyone, even to the "bad," in order to welcome them and convert them. The king's wedding feast for his son—the very model of a solemn meal taken at table—is thus the central symbol of what the community is. However, Matthew, who may be worried about the situation of the community in his own days, then goes on to underline that the king expelled from the banquet anyone who was not wearing a "wedding robe" (probably a sign of the fact that the conversion has taken place).[41] But the idea that those without a wedding robe and sinners who deserved reproach must be expelled from the common table is precisely what Jesus did not accept. This solution is foreign to Jesus' way of thinking and to his egalitarian habits. Matthew seems very remote from Jesus here: now, a practice of gathering together to eat in one particular way has become the symbol of a conventional religious attitude.

In the core of the original parable, we can glimpse some typical elements of convivial practice: the invitation to a great dinner, the expectation on the part of the host that he will meet his guests, the refusal by some of those invited to take part, the change in the invitation, and the participation by new guests. The interplay of many ideological elements enlivens the narrative. On the lips of Jesus, they become a metaphor that functions as an incentive to attach greater weight to the egalitarian aspects of his message.

In the three parables we have looked at, Jesus takes up various aspects of what it means to eat together. He sees this as the clearest and most dramatic manifestation of the relationships that are typical of his milieu. When people eat together, they display unambiguously the *real* relationships between persons and between social strata. Jesus' gaze is penetrating and realistic. The rich hold their banquets without the slightest concern for the hungry beggars; the masters tell their slaves, who are exhausted from work, to wait on them at table; the heads of prosperous households tend to invite their social equals but do not issue any invitation to the poor, the blind, the crippled, and the lame. But the imminent judgment of God will fall on all these persons—and this demands a conversion and a radical change in the way they practice commensality. The way of eating together that Jesus proposed thus becomes the expression of new relationships, both between individuals and between social strata in the households.

The Symbolic Complexity of Conviviality

In the scenes of conviviality, including those in the parables, we have encountered a great variety of persons, of groups, and of social strata: men and women, heads of households, slaves, sick persons, poor persons, sinners, tax collectors, Pharisees, kings. The locations vary: people may eat in palaces and sumptuous houses, or in modest dwellings, or simply at some place along the road or in the fields. The table is Jesus' preferred place for teaching, and here he criticizes conduct and attitudes that are revealed precisely in the act of eating together. The meals taken in common function as a metaphor for the way Jesus calls into question the relationships and the values that many people appreciate. He comes into contact with the greatest variety of persons precisely when they are united by sharing food. This facilitates his unique mode of communicating and of revolutionizing reality. At the same time, it also uncovers the dissent of those who do not agree with his practice.

It is above all the Pharisees and the disciples of John the Baptizer who attack Jesus' way of practicing commensality (cf. Mark 7:1-5). They ask him to explain the difference between his position and that of John: "Why do John's disciples and the disciples of the Pharisees fast, but your disciples do not fast?" (Mark 2:18-20; Luke 5:33-35; Matt 9:14-17). The answer that Mark, Luke, and Matthew put on the lips of Jesus (Mark 2:19-20; Luke 5:34-35; Matt 9:15; cf. John 3:29) was probably not uttered by him on this occasion; nevertheless, it contains a reflection on fasting and feasting. Here, Jesus recalls the solemn festal situation of a wedding, where the presence of the bridegroom determines the manner in which the banquet is celebrated: "You cannot make wedding guests fast while the bridegroom is with them, can you? The days will come when the bridegroom will be taken away from them, and then they will fast in those days" (Luke 5:34-35). François Bovon rightly comments that although Jesus regards the present time as the wedding day, he does not identify himself directly with "the bridegroom." The allegorical interpretation that sees Jesus as the bridegroom is the work of the evangelists.[42] Jesus himself associates the time of the wedding feast with face-to-face encounters and with the creation of new relationships between human beings—not with the time of fasting and asceticism.

A further complication is that although eating and abstaining from eating, satisfying one's hunger and fasting, are opposite forms of action, both of these are codified and efficacious, since both actions recognize the value of food as a factor that distinguishes, that imposes obligations, or that excludes. For Jesus, fasting was not the preferential form of social integration. He did not actually disavow fasting, nor did he institute it as an important religious sign or testimony. The form of social integration he preferred was to receive food from other people in contexts where people worked together and gathered together in households.

In view of the reciprocal nature of commensality, where one receives something in return for what one gives, we must ask what Jesus thought he was giving in return for the food he received. It is likely that he thought he was offering the promise of participation in the imminent "banquet" in the kingdom of God (of which we shall speak below) and of the abundance of food this kingdom would soon offer to all those who entered it.

To what extent is it true to say that Jesus regarded the sharing of food as a high form, perhaps even the highest form, of human socialization? It seems that Jesus—at least the Jesus of Luke and Matthew—regarded eating together as a necessary practice, which, however, was open to a variety of interpretations. And Jesus warned against potential misunderstandings in this area. He was aware that people said about the Baptizer, who fasted: "He has a demon!" And he knew that "the Son of Man" was accused of being "a glutton and a drunkard, a friend of tax collectors and sinners" (Luke 7:33-34; Matt 11:18-19). This saying, which is unparalleled in the tradition of the words of Jesus, shows that he felt that people were defining him on the basis of his specific attitude to food and his manner of eating. Some found this laudable, while others found it reprehensible.

This accusation entails a further aspect, namely, that Jesus habitually ate in bad company.[43] The sharing of food becomes the sign of an unacceptable openness. What interests Q (on which Luke and Matthew depend) is the charge that Jesus was "a glutton and a drunkard" and "a friend [*philos*] of tax collectors." The second element in this accusation is regarded as more serious, since the definition of Jesus as a friend of such persons means disqualifying him and completely blackening his reputation.[44] It means quite simply that Jesus is an immoral person.[45] Obviously, Jesus' practice of commensality involved more than the encounters with sinners and tax collectors. But the fact that these accusations were made gives us a glimpse of his adversaries' opinions about Jesus and the people with whom he mingled every day.

We can only formulate hypotheses about what Jesus actually intended. He saw eating together as an occasion for coming close to people and sharing their life. He may well have regarded commensality as the strongest form of social gathering. It seems that commensality played the most fundamental role in the "construction of the human person."[46] In other words, it was more important even than the gatherings in the synagogue and the Temple. Jesus regarded eating as the principal context for inclusion rather than exclusion. It is here that the poorest persons and the so-called sinners must be given their place.

As we have seen, it is above all Luke who insists on the necessity of including the poor and of inviting them to eat in one's own home (Luke 14:13). In the parable of the banquet, it is only Luke who speaks of inviting "the poor, the crippled, the blind, and the lame" (14:21). He is also the only evangelist who relates the parable of the rich man who held great banquets while the poor Lazarus stood outside his gate and begged (16:19-31). However, there is no scene from real life in which we see Jesus eating with the poor or serving them at table. It is, of course, true that many poor persons were probably present in the two episodes of the multiplication of food that Mark transmits (Mark 6:33-44; 8:1-9), but this is not a central feature of these narratives. It is *Luke* who brings out a radical aspect of the life of Jesus that the other evangelists move into the background. We may ask whether he has projected onto Jesus an ideal that we find elsewhere, for example, in the Acts of the Apostles, as characteristic of the first community of disciples in Jerusalem.

Jesus seemed to want to organize gatherings at table in such a way that they express the overturning of the established order that was taking place. This is because he awaited the imminent arrival of the justice of the kingdom of God. And he proposed his alternative in people's houses and in the places where they habitually gathered, since it was here that the strongest expressions of private and public fellowship could be made. He put forward a new kind of regulation that could be followed in the private households that he regarded as the centers of social construction.

What Jesus was proposing can be grasped most clearly when we look at the structural antithesis between the one who "reclines" to eat and the one who serves him. The rupture or fault line runs between being served and serving. We have seen that the evangelists depict Jesus as fully aware that it was normal in the society of his day for a slave to work all day long and then to prepare food for his master; only after this was he allowed to eat (Luke 17:7-8). This "normality" is a deviant normality, and Jesus refused to accept it. At the Last Supper (though only in Luke), Jesus asked: "Who is greater, the one who is at the table or the one who serves? Is it not the one at the table? But I am among you as one who serves" (22:27). These words find confirmation when he washed his disciples' feet at the Last Supper, as related by John (13:1-17).

The historicity of this scene is supported by the consideration that it can scarcely have been invented either by John, who pays little attention to social distinctions, or by the communities of Jesus' disciples after his death. These communities created their own customs. Over the course of time, they gave the widows the task of washing feet, turning this into a service that these women were obliged to perform for "the saints" (1 Tim 5:10). John's Jesus intended to overturn the existing order of such actions. Indeed, he instituted this revolution as a foundational characteristic of his own Supper. Jesus, the Lord and master, put on the garments of a slave and performed the action that was typical of slaves: he cleaned other people's feet.[47]

Paul finds it intolerable that social inequalities are manifested during the ritual supper: the rich ate while the poor who were present suffered hunger (1 Cor 11:20-22). He does not seem to find it necessary to institute a rite that would manifest the inversion of roles—we find this only in the narratives of Luke and John. All that Paul does is to denounce the situation in Corinth where unjust discrimination persists in the rite of the common supper that commemorates Jesus. He emphasizes not the inversion, but the necessity of equality and inclusion. He does not justify his criticism by referring to Jesus' behavior or by recalling the practice of life or the words of Jesus. At most, Paul's affirmations may indicate that the courageous and binding ideal of Jesus remained alive in him, even if in a somewhat attenuated form.

We find it difficult to deny that Jesus himself created a special rite within the shared supper. After his death, this was given the name *eucharistia*. The strongest argument in favor of this position is the fact that the most ancient text that attributes this institution to Jesus comes from Paul, who maintains that he is handing on the words of Jesus as he has received them: "For I received from the Lord what I also handed on to you, that the Lord Jesus on the night when he was betrayed took a loaf of bread, and when he had given thanks, he broke it and said, 'This is my body that is for you. Do this in remembrance of me.' In the same way he took the cup also, after supper, saying, 'This cup is the new covenant in my blood. Do this, as often as you drink it, in remembrance of me'" (1 Cor 11:23-25). The remembrance of Jesus is expressed in a repetition of the essential act of taking food together with all others.

The fact that Mark (14:22), followed by Matthew (26:26), does not relate the words of Jesus, "Do this in remembrance of me," which Paul (followed by Luke) relates, is certainly significant. It is also significant that the *Didache* does not relate any words of Jesus when it specifies the words that are to be uttered in the "Eucharist."[48] We do indeed find in John too a command to repeat an action performed by Jesus at the Last Supper, but this has nothing to do with eating the bread and drinking the wine. After washing the disciples' feet at an exceptional point in the Supper, that is, during the meal rather than at the beginning,[49] Jesus commanded them to repeat the same act in the future: "If I, your lord and teacher, have washed your feet, you also ought to wash one another's feet. For I have set you an example, that you also should do as I have done to you" (John 13:14-15). But for John too, the convivial rite that surrounds the action of washing the feet and acts as its backdrop is the setting chosen by Jesus to transmit the central nucleus of his teaching.

It is difficult to use these silences as an argument that the eucharistic rite is a later creation by the communities of Jesus' disciples. On the contrary, Jesus' insistence on conviviality and on the need to understand this in an unusual manner, as well as the fact that conviviality signals the imminence of events that were hoped for (the "kingdom of God"), lend plausibility to the adoption of the Eucharist as the central ritual action. It may well be that the groups practiced it in very different ways, but the various forms need not necessarily have been incompatible.

The importance Jesus attributed to commensality is perfectly understandable as the expression of his resolve to seek direct encounters with the people in the villages and to enter their homes. It was a consequence of his lack of interest in other places, such as the centers of political power, and of his decision not to organize a school to teach his disciples in a fixed place. Besides this, the way in which he gathered and included people influenced the way in which he exercised authority over them. The act of eating together creates reciprocal trust and credibility. It aims at satisfying hunger in every sense of the word, and offers the essential basis for every human project. Although he himself was an uprooted person, this act of sharing food allowed Jesus to create customs among the people he met and guaranteed that links would be maintained in a lifestyle that was difficult and highly insecure.

The Future Banquet

Eating together is a metaphorical expression of the future kingdom of God, which has the common table at its very center.[50] In Matthew, Jesus declares: "I tell you, many will come from east and west and will eat with Abraham and Isaac and Jacob in the kingdom of heaven" (8:11).[51] Luke relates that at the Last Supper, Jesus declares that he will drink "the fruit of the vine" anew in the kingdom of God (22:18). Obviously, the kingdom of God is a future hope, not something that can be described in detail. At most, allusions help one to picture it, and the language of eating and drinking has become the metaphorical instrument to depict and grasp this unknown reality. The table in the kingdom of God seems above all to be the recompense promised to those who "have stood by" Jesus in his "trials": "I confer on you . . . a kingdom, so that you may eat and drink at my table in my kingdom, and you will sit on thrones judging the twelve tribes of Israel."[52]

Was this only a metaphor, or did Jesus envisage a "kingdom of God" in which people would literally eat and drink? Was the practice of eating together only the preferred means for the communication of the message, or was this practice itself the message? Some scholars have seen the saying in which he speaks of all those who will come from east and west to recline at table with Abraham, Isaac, and Jacob as a metaphor rather than as the expectation of a splendid banquet.[53] But it is not impossible that Jesus had a genuine banquet in mind, since at the resurrection Abraham, Isaac, and Jacob too would be able to assume a genuine body and eat in a physical manner.

The collection of sayings of Jesus known as the "Beatitudes" (Luke 6:20-23 and Matt 5:3-11; cf. *Gospel of Thomas* 54, 68, 69) has come down to us in two different forms, a short form with four sayings transmitted by Luke and a longer form with eight sayings transmitted by Matthew. These most likely go back to a list of four sayings contained in the source known as Q, three of which are most probably authentic words of Jesus.[54] These make it very clear that the kingdom of God that Jesus had in mind was not a heavenly, immaterial reality: "Blessed are you who are poor, for yours is the kingdom of God"; "Blessed are you who are hungry now, for you will be filled"; "Blessed are you who weep now, for you will laugh" (Luke 6:20, 21a, and 21b). To laugh, to eat one's fill, and to possess the kingdom are hopes that will be realized in a renewed earthly world. Likewise, the beatitude about the meek expresses the idea of an earthly kingdom of God: "Blessed are the meek, for they shall inherit the earth" (Matt 5:5).[55] In Matthew's perspective, this may refer to the Land of Israel.

Enormous numbers of Jesus' followers in the first and second centuries envisaged a kingdom of God or of the Messiah on earth that would be inaugurated very soon.[56] One witness to this expectation is the Revelation of John, which speaks of a period of a thousand years (Rev 20:3-7; 21:1-4, 10, 23-27; 22:1-5). The Ebionites expected a millenarian kingdom, as did Cerinthus, who is mentioned in a number of early Christian sources. Justin, writing around the middle of the second century, believes in a period of "a thousand years in a Jerusalem rebuilt" on earth,[57] although he is aware that other Christians disagree with this idea.[58] Irenaeus, at the end of the second century, is a convinced millenarian. He records an oral tradition in which Jesus speaks of a material kingdom characterized by rich resources of food: "The Lord taught about those times and said, 'The days will come in which vines will bear ten thousand branches, each branch ten thousand twigs, each twig ten thousand clusters, each cluster ten thousand grapes, and each grape when pressed will yield twenty-five measures of wine.... Similarly, each grain of wheat will yield ten pounds of fine flour, bright and pure; and the other fruit, seeds, and herbs will be proportionately productive according to their nature, while all the animals that feed on these products of the soil will live in peace and agreement one with another, yielding complete subjection to human beings.'"[59] It is only in the first years of the third century that a spiritualizing interpretation of every aspect of Jesus' preaching about the kingdom of God begins to be predominant.

Let us sum up. In the context of eating together, Jesus transmits his message in a more intimate manner, but he also behaves in a way that turns upside-down the habitual religious and social customs of commensality. He revolutionizes the practice of eating together through his reversal of hierarchies, his attention to the position of slaves and of women, his inclusion of the poor and the marginalized, and his closeness to transgressors.

The sharing of food, which is in itself an important dimension of human life, is integrated into a system of extraordinary realities: in the vision of Jesus, an abundant and exceptional meal overturns the order of everyday things. Thanks to its exceptional character, such an occasion can be the manifestation of the divine intervention that renews the order of things and guarantees a more satisfying lifestyle. The shared meal becomes the symbol of the future kingdom of God, which seems to be imagined as an earthly world in which a miraculous abundance reigns.

The abundance shows that a reversal has taken place: there is an exit route from uncertainties, injustices, and sufferings. It is obvious that every shared meal contains the dream or the evocation of abundance, and the participants inevitably reflect on how this abundance might become a reality, even if it is as yet absent or remote.

Jesus chose as the highest example of the encounter between human beings a commensality that includes everyone—not a collaboration in family life, the marriage union, or the study of Torah. When friends, rich and poor, righteous and unrighteous eat together, this teaches people what the kingdom of God on earth will be. This is why Jesus taught about the kingdom in the context of a shared meal. And this is why his instruction about the kingdom of God is in some sense an instruction about how people should eat together.

5

JESUS LEAVES HOME AND IS MADE AT HOME WITH OTHERS

Without a House of His Own— in the Houses of Others

Jesus has left his house and work, but he regularly frequents the domestic settings and the houses of other persons. What is the logic behind this dialectic between detachment from a house and the request to enter a house?[1]

We shall see below that Jesus demanded that the itinerant disciples completely abandon their own world. Despite this, however, he does not in any way belittle the importance of the household.[2] Indeed, we see on various occasions that he attributes a positive function to it. He often displays his intention of strengthening the ties that unite the members of a family unit. In one instance, his compassion for a widowed mother led him to restore to life a boy who had just died (Luke 7:11-17);[3] since she had no husband, she would be left destitute. On another occasion (Mark 5:1-20/Luke 8:26-39/Matt 8:28-34), he healed a man who was "possessed by an unclean spirit," and when the man asked to be allowed to follow Jesus and "to be with him," he ordered him to return to his home.

Jesus shared the life of the houses in which he stayed for a time. He was welcomed into the house of Simon and Andrew (Mark 1:29),[4] the house of Martha (Luke 10:38), and the house of Zacchaeus (Luke 19:5-9). He charged the disciples to look for lodging for him in the villages that he was about to visit (Luke 9:52). In short, he showed an attitude toward kinship contexts that oscillated between detachment and sharing their life. These two ways of relating to houses are not contradictory, since each has a precise object.

At this point, let us paint a concrete backdrop for the figure of Jesus by reflecting on the consequences of relationships of this kind. To be without a dwelling and goods means being weak, since one is a stranger to, or remote from, the cohesive network of kinship and the protection offered by a domestic environment—things that are basic to the security of every individual. At the same time, however, it also means freedom from the bonds and the requirements of kinship and the domestic environment. It means having in one's own self a strength that one can rely on in a variety of situations.

In any culture, but particularly in the culture of Jesus, the kinship organization is a system of life in which individuals bound by ties of blood and of matrimony participate in the common management of goods and resources.[5] Every kinship grouping constitutes a primary structural form with regard both to the individual and to the collective, both to the living and to the dead. It forms the basis of identity,[6] but it can also be the context in which individual members undertake autonomous or divergent initiatives. This means that the kinship grouping is no stranger to internal division, conflict, and abandonment.

What we find in first-century Israel is not the family as this is commonly understood,[7] but a more articulated nucleus that includes persons who live together and share a lifestyle and material goods. They earn their living together and occupy a position in the world.[8] The Greek noun appropriate to this reality is *oikos*,[9] which indicates a system of coherent relationships and bonds in terms of kinship, work, and territory. The anthropological term "household"[10] corresponds very well to this.

The space of domesticity[11] may include persons who are not linked by kinship. It can involve a large group covering more than two generations. The survival and the continuity of this group depend on the maintenance of links that have different goals (biological ties, voluntary ties, economic links, or emotional bonds). Above all, the existence of a household is based on shared work and consumption, and on powers and roles that also unite non-relatives and clients in one and the same localized productive system. The head of the household[12] is the authority, and not only in kinship relationships. He is the administrator of the properties and the manager of the various activities on which the household is based, as well as its judge. It is he who regulates the relationships and the collective perspectives of the household.

In the milieu of Jesus, the *oikos* was structured by an ideal monogenetic principle. It was constructed around the head of the household, especially around his function of guaranteeing social and biological reproduction.[13] He could be a father, that is, one who had begotten children, but this need not always be the case. For particular needs, other intermediary or collateral figures could take the role of the head who bore responsibility for the affairs of the household. Nevertheless, the "father's seed" remained the absolute marker of patrilineal descent and of the rights exercised within the paternal family group. Women entered this descent cognatically (that is, through their relation to the male descendants as wives, sisters, or daughters); they had specific roles that gave them their identity, in relation to specific rights.[14]

The domestic group sought to realize a number of goals, and there were great differences from one household to another, thanks to the various ways of understanding descent and its practical consequences, the relationship between husband and wife, parents and children, the succession from one generation to another, and the means of production and distribution. When we look at the households, therefore, we are examining a network of relationships that often vary from house to house, and that needs to be made explicit in each individual case. Although it may be difficult to uncover with certainty the networks and structures of kinship and household, this is one of the most effective ways of gaining access to the everyday world in which Jesus lived.

The Variety of Houses: Styles and Relationships

In the course of the Synoptic Gospels, we encounter a great variety of houses[15] in which people's domestic life is located. Let us attempt a schematic classification. We can imagine very grand houses in some of the parables; and the houses of Levi and Zacchaeus may belong to this category. It is more normal to find medium-sized and small houses in the narratives that speak of the activities of Jesus and his disciples. Archaeological research into the houses and the forms of the family in the Land of Israel in the first century has uncovered a variety of situations that do not always fit easily into established categories: we have villas, large dwellings, houses with a courtyard, medium-sized houses, small houses, and houses situated in blocks of buildings with multiple dwellings, the so-called *insulae*. It is not impossible to locate the individual scenes in the Gospels in one or other of these types of dwelling.[16]

According to John Crossan and Jonathan Reed,[17] if we wish to reconstruct the domestic milieus and the local relationships in which Jesus was immersed, we should reflect on the specific situation of Capernaum, a place that can give us a closer picture of the reality of his life. The households of Capernaum reflect the life of fishers and rural farmers. Archaeological excavations have shown that the dwellings there were not comparable to those of the cities, either in the materials used in their construction or in their size. No inscriptions or architectural forms have been discovered that suggest the existence of dwellings or civic buildings comparable to those of Sepphoris or Tiberias, nor have refined or luxury ceramics come to light. This means that domestic life must have been somewhat simple, confined to the essentials. The houses that Jesus customarily visited were, therefore, those of people lower on the social scale; if we want to picture them, we cannot think exclusively in terms of the dwellings mentioned in some of the parables. These more modest houses were the center of social existence and of the customary techniques of exchange and hospitality. The life of the village households is not only introverted. Often, such households are the ultimate stratum to be reached by the political processes of the external world or the last to resist such processes. The external world influences the village in various ways, since it is centered on the *polis*, of which the village is a satellite. At the point of overlapping between these two levels—kinship-local on the one hand and political-external on the other—we find the houses that form a backdrop to Jesus.

In the world of the first century, the link between *oikos* and *polis* is frequently realized through patron–client relationships.[18] Although these relationships are often rooted in the *polis*, they are to some extent constructed on the basis of the network of villages and of the production in the *oikoi*. A patron who normally lives in the city has clients in villages who receive political protection and economic favors from him. In the patron–client relationship, individuals who belong to different milieus—including heads of households—are linked by reciprocal relationships that envisage a consistent range of collaborations and alliances governed either by custom or by legal ties.[19] Patronage was a central element of the Roman cultural experience and formed a vital part of the conscious ideology of the Romans, of the way they saw themselves, of what their world was and what it ought to be.[20] It is difficult to say to what extent the life of the *oikoi* in their relations with the *polis*[21]—at least where this involved matters of some importance— was determined by the patron–client relationship. At any rate, we must ask how far Jesus took into account, or was himself conditioned by, the system of asymmetrical and differentiated relationships that are characteristic of patronage when he visited the houses of acquaintances and supporters.[22]

We know that in some settings that resemble the social situation of the Land of Israel at the time of Jesus, it was not easy for patronage to function at every level of society. Monetization and grave indebtedness may have made it less possible for the poor strata to benefit from this system,[23] since those who are too poor are not useful clients, and, in turn, patrons do not have sufficient wealth to maintain the relationship. In such a situation, in the absence of the patron–client relationship, other social forms may have met the needs of the *oikos*, with a completely different impact on the domestic group.

We have already seen that Jesus avoided cities. In the small centers he visited, there may have been persons who were dependent on patrons who were living in urban milieus. It is no longer possible to estimate their number, but they doubtless existed. Jesus, however, did not conform to the idea of a necessary relationship between the *oikos* and the *polis*. He shows that he distrusts systems of reciprocal compensation, and solidarity between the city and the countryside generated by self-interest. His objective was not to link households and the political powers in the cities by means of a patron–client relationship.

The parable of the prodigal son shows how Jesus saw the relationships between the rural households and the city. He had a positive view of the father and head of the household, whom the parable locates in a village far away from the city.[24] We see a conflict between the city, regarded as a dangerous place, and the village, envisaged as a safe refuge. The city (perhaps Hellenized) seems to exercise an attraction on a member of the younger generation. The parable condemns this attraction, and, in fact, the story of the younger son in the city ends in ruin. But the parable also expresses a negative verdict on the attitude of the elder son, who displays a defensive attachment to the domestic nucleus that prevents him from approving of his brother's return. The parable intends to present a model of cohesion whereby the dramas are all resolved: the traditional household ought to open its doors unconditionally, even to those who make a mess of their lives, those who have threatened its existence, or those who want to detach themselves from it. The head of the household has an irreplaceable function: it is he who guarantees the prosperity and the continuity of the resources and of the values that unite the group. Jesus does not seem to want to promote the economic and political potential of the households nor to motivate them to an integration into a system of relations dominated by the towns.

A Group without a Place of Its Own

We know little about the domestic environment from which Jesus came, in the sense of a productive group that earned its living through its own work. We know that he was situated in Nazareth (Mark 6:1; Luke 4:16; Matt 13:54), that he had a mother and father, brothers and sisters (Mark 6:3; 3:32; cf. Luke 4:22; John 6:42), and that his trade was perhaps that of a carpenter (Mark 6:3; Matt 13:55). The point is not to localize Jesus in one specific *oikos* but to explore the position this had in his mental map and how it influenced his public activity and his preaching. We start from the presupposition that there existed a domestic world, with all its practical and ideal aspects, in which he was formed and which he subsequently abandoned for reasons that we do not know. If his trade was that of a carpenter, an artisan and builder, it is probable that he was following the trade of his father here, since it was normal in the world of artisans for a son to inherit his father's work. Workers of this kind could be independent, and they could travel a great deal because of their work; but we must grasp the *kind* of mobility that this involved. The fact that the artisan had to move to places where houses were to be built or repaired outside their own village, and even far away from the village, and that they were therefore obliged to be absent for more or less lengthy periods, does not mean that they lacked a fixed abode. They returned to their own homes after the work was finished. Jesus may indeed have carried out work of this kind, but it is obvious that his life and his way of seeing the world included other scenarios in addition to the domestic environment in which he grew up.

During his itinerant preaching, households become one of the social points from which he could have direct knowledge of persons and their relationships. His contact with the domestic sphere put him at the very center of important and absorbing activities. As we have said, the village *oikoi* were also centers of production, with olive presses, wine presses, and ovens for making utensils and producing pottery.[25] Jesus was perfectly well aware that the social and economic life revolved entirely around the household.

Nevertheless, Jesus did not choose an *oikos* as the social base of his own activity. He did not take kinship as his starting point.[26] Instead, he established a form of grouping that was not localized and that gathered disparate persons with various motivations: the discipleship group.[27] The important point in this group is personal adherence to the message of the leader, not family origin, "professional" or productive qualification, or wealth. This means that a group of disciples was formed through the adherence of individuals, and in this sense it belongs to the broader concept of a "voluntary association."[28] This type of association, which can take a great variety of forms, is born of the free encounter between subjects or between categories of individuals and between their projects and aspirations. We know that discipleship is an organizational segment that unites a group of persons who meet together[29] in order to learn doctrines and modes of life but are also motivated by needs that can be satisfied by the strategic ability of the master.

One distinctive characteristic of the group of Jesus' disciples is that they are "interstitial." This term designates a body that lacks a defined social position and is therefore obliged to take its place in those spaces and occasions that remain "empty" because they are not occupied by institutions. For example, an interval of time is interstitial when it is not occupied by work or by other necessary physical activities. A physical space is interstitial if it does not belong to households or to specific proprietors. Interstitiality is always temporary. An interstitial existence does not entail settling definitively in spaces that are assigned to one, nor does it intend to exercise functions that are recognized in society.

Jesus, an itinerant without goods, takes his place in already-existing contexts in the situations he encounters. He does not have a stable base of his own. He does not occupy an independent local or institutional "site" of his own. This means that he is in constant need of recognition and legitimation. When they were confronted by Jesus' itinerant group, people probably wondered whether or not to receive them: ought their attitude to be positive or negative? Whatever is not institutional demands an adherence that by definition requires an innovative judgment. It mobilizes people's ability to evaluate and to make decisions. In other words, when a voluntary social form appears on the scene, it demands that people evaluate it and make up their minds about it.

The identity of the members of the discipleship group is constructed in a completely different manner from that of the members of the *oikos*. We could say that while the household is the non-voluntary organizational level that is able to guarantee the exercise of the "idea of relationship,"[30] not all the relationships of an individual are limited to the *oikos*. The voluntary association, from the patron–client relation to discipleship, comes into being precisely in order to meet needs that the households and the administrative, political, and religious institutions do not satisfy. Of its very nature, therefore, the voluntary association tends to be in tension with the *oikos*. We should not, however, posit an absolute antithesis between the *oikos* and discipleship, because in some instances the social goals of the two forms can be coordinated, thus avoiding conflict. At the same time, this dialectical relationship implies a number of discontinuities, because it assigns social roles, both external and internal, to those who belong to the two social forms. The construction and the negotiation of identity meanings[31] are constant processes, and they become ever more highly articulated and differentiated in response to the strains that come from the outside.[32] In the case of Jesus' movement, the impetus to modify the identity of the *oikos* does not come from inside the *oikos* itself: when the discipleship group makes contact with the household, it poses a challenge that unleashes reactions and new motivations.

In the village households, Jesus' group presents the appearance of an unforeseen form of organization that enters into the domestic sphere in an anomalous and unusual manner. It is an interstitial reality that fills certain spaces around and between the households. This dialectical relationship between discipleship and households can throw light on much of Jesus' activity.[33] Accordingly, our analysis will concentrate on the relationship between the household (not merely on kinship) as a source of identity and of functions that are acquired and perpetuated, and the discipleship group, which is understood as the outcome of voluntary adherence and as a form of aggregation that did not previously exist.

THE INDIVIDUAL CALL

Jesus' summons to follow him seems never to be addressed to a household as a whole, but only to single individuals. This call often creates conflicts between these individuals and the household from which they come, since this milieu may think that the result of the itinerant life is to weaken the strength of the group and thus reduce its cohesion by taking away one of its members.

In the ancient world, it was normal for one who wished to follow a master to make himself independent of his own household. The distance from one's original milieu could vary, since the master–disciple relationship took various forms. For example, although the communities of Pharisees (*ḥaburôt*) and the rabbinical schools were well integrated into the structure of society, the decision to join one of these could provoke conflicts with a person's family.[34]

It is clear that the decision to join an itinerant and marginal life, full of discomfort, could cause a family conflict and lead to painful adjustments for the disciple. At the same time, however, this conflict also leads to the construction of a social subject with an independent identity that tends to be rather strong. Is it Jesus who creates this possibility,[35] or does he address only those individuals who are already in a social condition that makes it possible for them to make a decision of such importance? We believe that it is precisely the detachment of Jesus and his disciples from the family nucleus and from material possessions that leads to a kind of behavior that is centered on the individual and that broadens the possibilities of choice available to this individual. The fact that the self-affirmation of the individual takes place by means of a conflict shows the innovative power that Jesus' movement brought to social behavior and to its inherent logic. Some scholars have suggested that this freedom of choice was a prerogative of the upper classes,[36] as represented for example by Flavius Josephus, who wanted to experience the various religious forms in order then to choose freely the one he believed to be best: "I would be able to choose the best, if I had experienced them all" (*Vita* 10).[37]

The milieu in which Jesus moved was very different from that of the priestly aristocracy. This means that our primary interest cannot be in the upper classes that we meet in the texts. Rather, we must take account of a more varied social situation: the addressees of Jesus' preaching are to be found in different strata of the population. Some moments have a tremendous transformative impact that offers individuals from various social strata the possibility of making dynamic choices that are much more difficult to realize in times of stagnation and conformity. During the lifetime of Jesus, the Land of Israel was going through one of these moments of dynamism and instability, where Romanization was only one factor. This situation prompted a variety of political–religious responses. Individuals felt the need to find solutions for their own households and to evaluate the divergent religious proposals. We are convinced that earliest Christianity was born at a moment in which, within the context of the household, the construction of strong individual personalities was possible.[38]

The Adult Generation Abandons Home

What were the social features of the persons who accepted the call to abandon their own households in order to follow Jesus? The conditions laid down for those who became members of his entourage, and what this meant in practice, are spelled out unequivocally in a number of passages in the Synoptic Gospels: "Sell your possessions, and give alms" (Luke 12:33), and "None of you can become my disciple if you do not give up all your possessions" (Luke 14:33). In other texts, it is the disciples who underline the radicalism of their adherence to Jesus: "Look, we have left everything and followed you" (Mark 10:28; Matt 19:27; Luke 18:28-30). In some passages, Jesus demands that his followers "hate" their parents (Luke 14:26; Matt 10:37-38), and he describes the dramatic conflict that breaks out in a family when one of its members decides to abandon the house and follow him (Luke 12:52-53; Matt 10:35-36; *Gospel of Thomas* 16).

The Synoptic Gospels also show the behavior of some persons whom Jesus invites to follow him, such as Simon and Andrew, James and John (Mark 1:16-20; Matt 4:18-22; Luke 5:1-11); Levi (Mark 2:13-17; Luke 5:27-32; Matt 9:9-13); a scribe or a man who is not identified more precisely;[39] the rich man, who, however, draws back (Mark 10:17-22; Luke 18:18-23; Matt 19:16-22); and those who volunteer to join him.[40] In some instances, we know nothing about how specific persons came to be his followers. These include the women mentioned by Luke (Joanna, Mary of Magdala, Susanna, and others unnamed: Luke 8:1-3; cf. Mark 15:40-41). Taken together, these narratives offer us a great deal of information about the social backgrounds and identities of the disciples.

The ways in which individuals join Jesus, the goals they pursue, and the consequences this entails—all this sheds light on the vast spectrum of social and cultural differences in the group of those who were attracted to him. Their characters were far from homogeneous, but these very differences bear witness to a decisive point: they were united by the decision to come to him in a relationship that was personal, not mediated by third parties. The common element seems to be the acceptance by all the disciples of an alternative life. They have accepted Jesus as their leader and established a personal relationship with him.

In the Synoptic Gospels, Jesus never issued a call in a house but only on the roads and in the places where people work. As we have seen, Mark relates how Jesus called some future disciples while they were mending their nets on the shore of the lake; according to Luke, he called them while they were fishing. And Levi was "sitting at the tax booth." Nevertheless, these persons clearly had close ties to their households, since they almost immediately took Jesus into their dwellings. Simon and Andrew had the same work and lived in the same house (according to Mark 1:29). The same appears to be the case with James and John, who worked with their father: we glimpse a household with Zebedee at its head. The fact that Jesus chose his disciples in the places where they worked suggests that he was looking for people with experience, people able to relate to both old and young persons.

When we look at situations in which several generations are present—fathers, adult sons or daughters, and the children of the latter—an examination of the intergenerational relationships tells us more about the social situation of those who abandon their houses in order to follow Jesus. The persons who appear in the Gospel narratives belong to three generations: the elderly, the adults, and the young, or adolescents and children.[41] In our opinion, none of the disciples belongs to the generation of the elderly, and none to the generation of the young; none of the disciples is a child. Jesus' dealings are with adults. The presence of Simon's mother-in-law makes it obvious that he is an adult; she appears to belong to the preceding generation (Mark 1:29-31; Luke 4:38-39; Matt 8:14-15). When Jesus took James and John away from their work, it is clear that they were the intermediate generation between their father Zebedee and any children they may have (Mark 1:16-20; Luke 5:10-11; Matt 4:18-22). The generational situation is clear, because Mark writes that their father was working with other adults, fishers who received wages. In this case, the father, who belongs to the older generation, did not become a disciple. Indeed, he did not seem to react to the appearance of Jesus on the scene. Jesus did not call him: he preferred Zebedee's sons. And Zebedee had nothing to say. He had no role in this scene, and he remained where he was.

According to a saying in Luke, "Whoever comes to me and does not hate father and mother, wife and children, brothers and sisters, yes, and even life itself, cannot be my disciple" (14:26), the ideal disciple seems to possess unequivocal characteristics. He is a man with father and mother, wife and children, brothers and sisters. Here, Luke presupposes a large *oikos* that can contain a large number of relatives. Since the ideal disciple has both parents and children, he is imagined as belonging to the intermediate generation. The decisive role is played not by the father who heads the household, but by the married man, who is surrounded by brothers, sisters, a wife, and children. Matthew's version seems to confirm this situation: "Whoever loves father or mother more than me is not worthy of me; and whoever loves son or daughter more than me is not worthy of me" (10:37-38). This text describes the situation more precisely, because it shows that the one who follows Jesus may equally be a son or a father. The fact that he is related first to the older generation and then to the younger generation establishes definitively that the disciple belongs to the intermediate level.

This finds further confirmation in the concrete instances where people abandoned their homes.[42] As we have seen, in Luke's version Peter said to Jesus: "Look, we have left our homes and followed you." Jesus replied: "Truly I tell you, there is no one who has left house or wife or brothers or parents or children, for the sake of the kingdom of God, who will not get back very much more in this age, and in the age to come eternal life" (Luke 18:26-30; Mark 10:28-30; Matt 19:27-29). The order of these renunciations (house, wife, brothers, parents, and children) shows that in Luke, the one who abandons the others is a man situated between the higher level of his parents and the lower level of his own children. The text envisages an action taken by a member of the intermediate generation.

One of Jesus' sayings (Luke 9:59-60; Matt 8:21-22) presents the relationship between the generations even more emblematically. It seems that the father, the guiding figure at the head of the *oikos,* has just died. He was the supreme authority in the household to which his son was linked. The attention of the narrative is concentrated on the son, a figure who represents the generation tied to duties and tasks. Now that the father has died, it is he who will succeed him in the guidance of the household. Jesus demands that he detach himself absolutely from the totality of the household—and this means that he will not even go to "bury" the father who has just died. Exegetes have often underlined the theological aspect of this demand, in which Jesus required the violation of the fundamental biblical norm that one must honor one's father, and they have asked what authority or self-consciousness on Jesus' part could legitimate such a requirement.[43] But to read the passage in this way overlooks the consequences for the relationships in the household if the son were to obey Jesus' call.

Let us reflect a little on this story. The logic of the household is based on mediation, on alliances, and on a chain of recompenses for what the individual member does, and the only way to extricate oneself from this logic is to shatter it completely. Jesus requires that the painful abandonment of the household from which a person comes must be total and instantaneous, and there is no going back on this decision.[44] It is painful to neglect to bury one's father or not to ensure that this is carried out, but this is not qualitatively different from every other detachment from one's own home. Jesus demands instantaneous and immediate detachment. The man must ignore every aspect of household business and mediations if this is what prevents him from following Jesus. No excuse for procrastination is acceptable.

In other texts, it is unclear whether the disciples belong to the older generation or to the intermediate, adult generation, although we find the second hypothesis more plausible. For example, there is generational uncertainty regarding a group of women who follow Jesus with his other adherents: Mary of Magdala, Joanna, Susanna, Mary the mother of James the younger, and other women whose names are not given by Mark and Matthew. Luke tells us that some of them (whom he mentions by name) were well-off and supported Jesus' group with their own private means. But it does not seem possible to define any of them clearly in terms of generational criteria (Luke 8:1-3; cf. Mark 15:40-41; Matt 27:55-56), although the fact that they were able to dispose freely of their own property suggests that they belonged either to the intermediate generation or to the prosperous elderly generation. Luke states that Joanna was the wife of Herod's administrator, but we can neither affirm nor exclude the possibility that she was an elderly woman with adult sons.

The same uncertainty applies to other cases that we have met. We hear nothing of the ancestry, descendants, or collateral relatives of Levi (Luke 5:27; Mark 2:13-15; Matt 9:9-10); not even his wife is mentioned. His father is not mentioned, and we cannot say with certainty that Levi himself belongs to the intermediate generation. The same is true of the "rich" man whom Jesus invited to follow him (Mark 10:17-22; Luke 18:18-23; Matt 19:16-22). This narrative helps us to complete the picture of the social identity of those "invited" to follow Jesus: the fact that he can dispose of his goods may mean that he belongs to the category of householders. But we are not told to what generation he belongs. Only Matthew says that he is "young"—in an addition that does not belong to the older narrative (Matt 19:22). Nor are we told anything about the age of the disciples to whom Jesus addresses radical calls to follow him (Luke 9:57-62).

The episode of the widow's son at Nain (Luke 7:11-17) is illuminating. It seems that neither the mother nor the son is a disciple of Jesus. The young man does not express any desire to follow him, nor does Jesus ask him to do so—perhaps because he is still very young. This confirms that the followers were not chosen from among those who are very young. Instead, Jesus prefers autonomous adult men. The exclusion of the younger generation emphasizes the position and the consolidated identity of the intermediate and older generations.

All these narratives concentrate our attention on one particular social trait. Despite the lack of precise information about the individuals, we can say that the adults who appear in these stories appear to be able to make strategic choices: to stay or to go, to make use of their own goods or to renounce these, to submit to the risk of itinerancy or to refuse this risk. The persons whom Jesus detached from their households had a free or critical attitude vis-à-vis their own social milieu. They probably belonged to the same generation as Jesus himself. They were vigorous, mature persons, people who could be counted on. When Jesus says, "I will make you fish for people," he is telling them that their strengths and abilities will be put at the service of an immensely important task. They will attract people and bring them together, and they can bring into this new experience the energies and abilities they have already demonstrated in their organization of the work of fishing.[45]

Jesus' words "None of you can become my disciple if you do not give up all your possessions"[46] suggest that he was addressing proprietors, not penniless persons. One who sells must have the power to do so. The total abandonment of one's goods (not only of money) shows that the disciple was envisaged as possessing goods and as willing and free to dispose of these goods at present or in the future. It is possible that a son who was not autonomous at present could ask his father to give him his inheritance (as in the parable of the "prodigal son")[47] and would then sell this. In this situation, he was not a householder, because he depended on others in order to obtain now what would be his inheritance.

Since Jesus says that the ideal disciple must "hate" his parents (Luke 14:26), it appears that most of the itinerant disciples were not householders. Hatred of one's father implies that he is the authority that directs the house, not one member on an equal footing with everyone else. One revolts against the powerful or against superiors, not against the weak or those on the same level as oneself. We may therefore conclude that in order to start out on his path, the ideal disciple must sell all that belongs to him; this sometimes requires the consent of the father or the head of the household. We cannot, however, wholly exclude the possibility that the members of the intermediate generation had possessions of their own, and that they could sell these without asking for any authorization.

How extensive were the possessions that these persons had to sell in order to follow Jesus? There may be a hint in the houses in which they lived. Levi's dwelling is certainly a large house with slaves, while Simon's house seems small or medium-sized. The same modest format underlies the disciples' affirmation that they have abandoned everything (Mark 10:28-30), where it appears that the houses they have left were rather small (though nothing suggests that they were poor). Obviously, the situation varies from case to case.

Our hypothesis is that the disciples were seldom responsible for a household group. Rather, they were members of a household headed by their father or another older man. They may or may not have been married; they may have been men or women; and they appear to enjoy a certain freedom to dispose of their goods.

Conflicts among the Members of a Household

Conflicts should not be thought of solely as instruments of destruction or as forms of sheer aggression. A conflict is an encounter between different forces that promote evolutions and aggregations of various kinds.[48] As Georg Simmel said more than a century ago, a conflict is a process that seeks to repair the dualism that divides people, and is a path toward reconciling divisions and seeking unity.[49] In our present context, various aspects of Jesus' actions can be explained by the idea that the one who provokes a conflict seeks an ultimate social recomposition. The conflictual impact that Jesus had on households can shed light on the meaning of his itinerant lifestyle, of his eating together with other people, and of the way in which he entered people's houses.

The Gospels do not tell us about any conflict between the disciples and the households from which they came, but they do relate an obvious clash between Jesus and his family, when his mother and his brothers came to him. They were worried by his activity, which they regarded as excessive. As we have seen, it is in this context that Mark locates Jesus' words "Whoever does the will of God is my brother and sister and mother" (Mark 3:35). This scene implies that some time has passed since Jesus left his family and his work, but we have no information about the date of this separation. Nor do we know if it was traumatic. But almost all the references to his family have a conflictual aspect, or at least imply a conflict.

Jesus' conflictual position is obvious in the saying "Whoever comes to me and does not hate father and mother, wife and children, brothers and sisters, yes, and even life itself, cannot be my disciple" (Luke 14:26). Such words seem to have a wider reference than the question of discipleship: they could be taken as the paradigm of his entire personal experience.

The synoptic tradition sees this climate of misunderstanding and incomprehension as extending beyond the circle of Jesus' relatives to include the people of his village as well. In one story, Jesus' preaching in the synagogue at Nazareth met with reactions of suspicion and downright hostility. Faced with this attitude on the part of his fellow townspeople, Jesus declared: "A prophet is not without honor, except in his own hometown, and among his own kin, and in his own house."[50] Jesus saw himself as rejected by his own milieu and even by his own family. The Gospels do not tell us that as soon as he arrived in Nazareth, he visited his own dwelling or his closest relatives. His only interest seems to be in meeting the people who were in the synagogue. Luke goes so far as to write that Jesus' fellow townspeople attempted to kill him (4:29). When Mark has Jesus say that a prophet is not welcomed "in his own hometown," nor by "his own kin, and in his own house," he wants the reader to understand that not even his own household offered Jesus help. And this means that Jesus experienced extreme rejection there. Mark introduces the hostility of Jesus' family members because he wants to show the solitude of Jesus as he faced this dramatic and insurmountable difficulty.

The saying about the prophet in his hometown (which we also find in the *Gospel of Thomas* 31) is very concise, but there can be no doubt about its meaning. It shows the total rejection of Jesus: his own peasant milieu (according to Mark) and his own family have not taken him seriously, and have therefore refused to honor Jesus as a prophet. Many have been infected by this suspicion and rejection, even those who would have been his most natural allies.

The conflicts are one thing; the categories that frame the conflicts and make them explicit are another. Jesus himself presents a "theory" about conflicts in an extensive summary of the clashes that can occur. It is his arrival on the scene and his radical preaching that create the conflicts in households. In Luke, he states: "From now on five in one *oikos* will be divided, three against two and two against three; they will be divided father against son and son against father, mother against daughter and daughter against mother, mother-in-law against her daughter-in-law and daughter-in-law against her mother-in-law" (Luke 12:52-53; Matt 10:34-36). Interestingly, this list presents six different categories of relationship. Matthew lists only five and gives a different version: "For I have come to set a man against his father, and a daughter against her mother, and a daughter-in-law against her mother-in-law; and one's foes will be members of one's own household" (10:35-36). In this passage, the "man" is the son of the head of the household. The *Gospel of Thomas* 16 has still another version: "For there will be five in a house: three will be against two, and two against three. The father against the son, and the son against the father—and they will stand solitary."

In these three passages, the conflict caused within the domestic group is set out plainly. Only one of the three oppositions is between men: father against son, or son against father. Two oppositions occur between four female categories: mother/daughter and mother-in-law/daughter-in-law (Luke 12:53). The conflict breaches a first ideal unity between father and son, a second ideal unity between mother and daughter, and a third ideal unity between mother-in-law and daughter-in-law.[51] The generational structure implied is that of an *oikos* where a kinship group of two generations live and clash: the generation of the parents and that of the married son. Since this is the most complete and inclusive kinship model that we find in the Synoptic Gospels, it functions as a point of reference and classification for the relationships throughout the household that are caused by the activity and the preaching of Jesus.

Following the polarized picture in Luke of a conflict of "three against two" in an *oikos* of five persons, we can envisage a model in which the "two" are the parents, who are opposed to the younger generational group (son, daughter, and daughter-in-law). The mother is the only one to whom two roles are attributed, as mother and as mother-in-law. It is, however, symptomatic that the parents do not appear as a pair of opponents, nor are they ever described as husband and wife.[52] Similarly, the son and the daughter are never described as brother and sister, and the daughter-in-law is never called the wife of the son. This means that the text makes a selection of the roles and positions that it wishes to present. The conjugal and collateral links are not of primary importance.

The main accent lies on the generational relationships, and the links and oppositions are described in terms of a vertical dimension. The conflict is no mere incident: it is embedded in the structural logic of the development of the household and seems to be portrayed here as the certain effect of the "division" that Jesus says he has come to bring. We may perhaps say that his preaching disunites and "dislodges" persons who, thanks to the cycles of life itself, are already on the path that leads to separation and to the inevitable succession of one generation after another. It is indeed certain that there will be a parting of the ways between the generations; Jesus comes to bring this about, or to accelerate its realization.

As we have said, the conflict is between the parents on the one hand and their son and daughter and daughter-in-law on the other. Two points must be underlined here. According to Luke, the disciples who leave their homes to follow Jesus may be not only sons but also daughters and even daughters-in-law. In the case of Joanna the wife of Chuza (Luke 8:1-3), the evangelist seems to think that married women can leave their own husbands in order to follow Jesus. Luke depicts a conflict between two generations, not within one and the same generation, when he speaks of "three against two" as if the three were acting in consonance against the two. He does not speak of a conflict between one person and four others; it is only in such a case that we could say with certainty that each single member of the household, on becoming a disciple of Jesus, separates from the other four or becomes their enemy. This is how Matthew sees things: he concludes with the words, "and one's foes will be members of one's own household" (10:36). Matthew, who is remote in time from the itinerancy of Jesus, sees the conflict not as the result of the opposition between two generations, nor as the result of separating from the rest of the family, but as the disagreement in a household between one member who is a believer and the others who are not.

The Lukan text with which we started contains a theoretical diagram of the conflict that is generated when one member of the household wants to share the itinerant life of Jesus, and we believe that this text is extremely important. We should note that, in Luke, it is the father who is mentioned first, while in Matthew it is the "man." Matthew's final comment sums up everything from the point of view of this one person. He generalizes by concentrating the hostility of all the family members against the potential disciple: the entire household is against him. In the *Gospel of Thomas,* the clash within the *oikos* pits two persons against three, but the only opposition mentioned explicitly is that between son and father. The saying concludes with the affirmation that they will be alone, the one against the other.[53]

If these three texts, Luke, Matthew, and Thomas, independently employ in different ways this saying of Jesus about the conflict between five members of an *oikos,* this means that the problem played a significant role in the earlier tradition behind these Gospels. The saying does not, in fact, tell us anything about the generation to which the disciples belonged; it speaks of a hypothetical situation of two opposing groups. It does not tell us which generation de facto followed Jesus. It could be speaking of the departure from a house of the father and mother, who have clashed with their son, their daughter, and their daughter-in-law— or of the departure of the younger members, who have clashed with their parents. But in our opinion, both Matthew and Luke read the saying in the light of what the intermediate generation does.[54]

Luke's text about "hating" the members of one's family seems to imply a radical criticism of the normal intergenerational relationships in the household. It shows that the conflict is inevitable. Following

Jesus necessarily entails a breach and a disregard for normal household duties, namely, getting married and taking care of one's fields and one's animals (as we see in the parable of the banquet, which Luke relates immediately before the saying about "hating," 14:18-20). This saying implies a critical distance vis-à-vis a fundamental kinship line, that of consanguinity in three generations. Those who are to be "hated" are bound to one another by strong ties and by emotional bonds from which it is hard to detach oneself: obviously, it is harder to separate from one's relatives than from other members of the household. Luke could have proposed only hatred of work or of the possession of goods—in other words, hatred of one's own social position. Instead, his accent is on the relatives in three generations.

We can draw important distinctions within Jesus' movement between the itinerant followers and those supporters who remain in their own homes and continue their normal activities. As we have said, this clear-cut distinction must be nuanced by taking account of sympathizers, of followers who were somewhat unsure or undeclared, and of persons who asked questions about Jesus, either out of interest or out of suspicion. The network of relationships allows us to glimpse the coexistence of dynamics and situations with a whole spectrum of nuances.

In this section, we have seen how the itinerant disciples were obliged to separate from their households. We shall now look at the texts that speak of those who welcomed Jesus' group while remaining in their own houses.[55]

Jesus instructed his disciples to stay overnight in the villages through which they passed, lodging with those who were willing to offer them generous hospitality (Luke 10:5-7; Matt 10:12-13). This presupposes that the head of the domestic group—one of whose roles is to decide whether to welcome strangers into his home—receives them and charges the entire *oikos* to exercise the functions of hospitality. The relationship of the *oikos* to the itinerants in terms of support, but also in terms of the identities of both groups and of their expectations, is expressed in the way in which hospitality was practiced. Accordingly, we must ask whether an anthropological reading of the texts sheds any light on the function of the head of the household that welcomes the disciples, and on the consequences of this hospitality. In other words, what social mechanisms are mobilized, and what does this lead to?

We can summarize the basic situation in a few words. The grand Hellenistic-Roman houses had some places that were public and other, more private places for the servants, the slaves, and those persons who were attached to the household in various ways but did not take part in its shared activities. There were masculine and feminine places that created a specific geography within the house. A guest was admitted to some spaces and refused admittance to others, on the basis of criteria of kinship, of the management of the household, of the relationships between the members of the household, of its political functions, etc. The fact that Jesus and his followers were welcomed into people's houses does not mean that they were automatically associated or identified with the kinship structures of those who opened their doors to them. Kinship and family are not the only context in which a house can be used.

When Jesus asked for hospitality, he was looking not only for a place to sleep but also for a place to gather his followers and anyone who wanted to meet him or approach him. He also used the house as a place for teaching (Mark 7:17-23) and for contact with persons or clients who did not live in the house. In this way, the householder was involved in something much more complex than a simple offer of food and lodging to travelers.

The head of the household could serve Jesus in a variety of ways, by giving him a symbolically important position or by openly offering him the role of master, preacher, or friend. Various forms of reciprocal attention and mutual benefit were mobilized during the time Jesus spent in other people's houses. But the situation that arose for those whom he met was complex. Those who actively offered Jesus recognition and a space for his activity listened to him, paid attention to him, and received a message; but not all the members of the household who were involved in the gestures of hospitality had access to his teaching. Not all of them were directly interested in what he had to say, or were attracted by his teaching. And not all of them were free to listen to him. It was easier for family members or friends to be present for at least part of his instruction, but other members or frequenters of the house were probably excluded from it. The Gospel texts note the important differences created here. It suffices to recall the case of Martha, who worked while Jesus was teaching in her house. Her words to Jesus about her sister Mary shed light on how hospitality could be offered in a house where friends and sympathizers of various kinds came together (Luke 10:38). In other instances, Jesus' entrance into other people's houses was much less significant. According to the Synoptic Gospels, Jesus celebrated the Passover supper in a *triclinium*, but the owner of the house seems not to have any direct contact with him.[56] We must dismiss the idea that Jesus' visits to people's houses led to outcomes that were automatic, homogeneous, or foreseeable.

Let us return to the highly significant words of Jesus when he sent out the Twelve: "Whatever house you enter, stay there, and leave from there" (Luke 9:4; Mark 6:10; Matt 10:11). Luke and Matthew both write that the disciples are to announce peace to the house they enter, and that they are to "remain" there if they are welcomed (Matt 10:11-13). The itinerant disciples must accept the "sedentary" disciples who continue to live in their own households, and must accept the hospitality these persons offer them. "To enter" (*eiserchomai*) and "to leave" (*exerchomai*) are verbs of movement; the verb "to remain" (*menein*) indicates here a temporary pause between the two movements. This was a brief "stay," a visit that was neither rapid nor excessively prolonged. Jesus forbade them to go from house to house. They were to remain in one house in order in one sense to belong to it and to launch a new project in it. The disciples, like Jesus himself, seem remote from public milieus, since they led a life in contact with domestic milieus, with people's work, and with families. But they were not organized in accordance with the usual structures of religious movements or groups: they did not follow anything resembling a "conventual" life based on precisely formulated principles. Jesus does not seem to have wished to change the existence of the houses he visited by obliging them to adopt forms of behavior that he had instituted or institutionalized. He did not bring any moral code, rules that his hosts must accept, or norms that they must obey. He proclaimed to the household that the eschatological kingdom was close at hand and invited them to conversion, then left them and continued to move from place to place.

Jesus saw the disciples as "laborers" for the harvest of God (Luke 10:2), and as workers they were entitled to a reward (Luke 10:7). He demanded this recompense for his followers; but the households were free either to welcome them or to refuse them admittance.[57] When he asked the households for their collaboration, this was not a casual request, but was part of a deliberate project. Jesus did not select the houses in which his group was to stay on the basis of their conformity to a standard of morality, of their observance of the Law, or of their adherence to specific precepts of his movement: he made no distinctions. Indeed, he told the disciples to eat whatever was set before them,[58] and therefore without posing conditions about respecting dietary rules. He respected the customs of those who opened their doors to him. In this case, Matthew's Gospel does not accurately reflect the historical situation of Jesus, since it states that the houses must be "worthy" to receive the disciples. The requirement to avoid a blemish on one's reputation by entering houses that were not respectable probably reflects the situation many decades after Jesus, when his followers were already organized in small communities and were obliged to behave correctly. The rigor and the fervor of the earliest days were now a thing of the past, and they needed to be reminded of the importance of a "worthy" lifestyle.[59]

It was normal for travelers in the Land of Israel in the first century to receive hospitality in the course of their journeys. On this point, Jesus and his followers are in complete harmony with their milieu. Various requests for hospitality were addressed to the heads of households, and they were normally required to give a positive answer. This hospitality was however understood more as a practice of reciprocal aid than as pure generosity on the part of those who lived in the house and made their domestic resources available. Although hospitality was widely practiced, it could be refused because of the difficulties that are always entailed by dealings with those who are "different." The refusal to cooperate with strangers is one way to protect oneself and one's property. Support networks operate in a context of security, where people are not afraid that the hospitality they offer may cause them to suffer harm. For this reason, those who present a material risk to the household are refused admittance.[60] Hospitality is offered to friends, but it is refused to those who are of a different religion, to foreigners, and those of whom one is afraid. A Lukan parable (11:5-8) tells of a man who welcomes into his house at midnight a friend who is on a journey, and then goes to his neighbors in the middle of the night in quest of food for the guest. But it was more difficult for foreigners to find a welcome. Luke (9:52-55) relates that a Samaritan village refuses to receive Jesus and his followers, because they are Judeans and thus do not belong to the same religious world.

Jesus was aware that those whom he sent out might encounter hostility, and he warned them beforehand. They must ask for hospitality free of charge. They were not to take with them a purse, or a bag, or sandals. They had no weapons to tackle any problems that arose: "Go on your way. See, I am sending you out like lambs into the midst of wolves" (Luke 10:3-4). The itinerants were invited to take a docile and dependent attitude that symbolized the unpretentious service they were called to give. At the same time, Jesus told the disciples to perform a gesture of rejection against the villages that did not receive them: they were to wipe the dust off their sandals[61] as a sign of distance from those who refused to shoulder the burden of welcoming them.

Jesus certainly reflected on the very various ways in which hospitality was practiced in his land; we see this in the parable of the banquet, which describes—and denounces—a realistic situation.[62] Those who are invited refuse to take part in the banquet because it clashes with the activity of their own *oikos*. The *oikos* appears as an introverted world that promotes its own prosperity and autonomy and is interested primarily in its own affairs: buying fields and cattle, and occasions of great importance such as weddings.[63] The guests calculate the potential value of their material interests and matrimonial alliances. When they all refuse the invitation,[64] the host in the parable orders his slave to invite destitute persons (Luke 14:21). In effect, this parable suggests that banquets ought to be employed to receive those who are outside the structure of reciprocal recompense, of competition, and of redistribution. This was unthinkable for those who accepted the strategy of social climbing that was normally pursued by the individual households.

We find another expression of Jesus' unusual attitude in the parable of the poor Lazarus at the gate of the rich man. Lazarus is hungry, but he is not allowed to enter, because this rich man does not practice the hospitality to the poor that was recommended in the parable of the banquet. The ordinary system of hospitality is not extended to destitute persons who cannot reciprocate. This example shows the nuances of hospitality: it can be requested, presupposed, or suggested. It can be a matter of obligation. Or it can simply be ignored.

In Jesus' vision, the heads of households should open the doors of their dwellings to those in need, instead of withdrawing from such persons. Luke relates the encounter between Jesus and Zacchaeus, the chief tax collector. Jesus told him: "I must stay at your *oikos* today" (Luke 19:5). Zacchaeus, a rich householder, opened his home to Jesus, welcomed him and gave him support; but he did not abandon his habitual way of life and his professional work to become an itinerant. All that he did was to convert to a more honest and just lifestyle. He declared: "Look, half of my possessions, Lord, I will give to the poor; and if I have defrauded anyone of anything, I will pay back four times as much" (19:8). The Lukan Jesus lent his support to the function of the householder, which is not to be denied or belittled. He confirmed this function by inviting Zacchaeus to change his lifestyle, not to abandon his dwelling and his work. Jesus' religious ideal demands a redistribution or a sharing of goods, not the destruction of family networks.

It is only the itinerant followers who were able to sell everything. Those who remained in their own houses, like Zacchaeus, were asked to reshape their lives. This accords with the picture of a movement that was based both on the detachment of its more active members from the *oikoi* and on the hospitality that the *oikoi* offered to these persons.

An Interstitial Strategy

These reflections allow us to construct a more complete picture of the relationship between the itinerant followers and the households.

Jesus wanted to strengthen a practice of hospitality that was widespread in his culture, but was threatened by attitudes that gave priority to the interests of the household. He denounced the mechanism of giving and receiving among the heads of households, since this usually excluded the social strata that lacked goods or social positions that could be exchanged. Jesus believed that these poor classes could benefit both from his itinerant disciples (who were to sell everything and give the proceeds to the poor) and from his sedentary followers (who were to open their houses and give a part of their goods to the destitute). This insistence on the "request for hospitality" seems to be part of Jesus' project of socio-religious transformation. On the one hand, he demanded significant changes of behavior on the part of the households, and he turned their system upside-down. The houses must practice hospitality even toward those who were incapable of repaying this. In other words, their hospitality must not be dictated only by the prospect of gaining some advantage through a more or less equal repayment in the future.[65] Jesus demanded hospitality, but he did not promise an alliance between social classes and groups. He detached the act of giving from the certainty of gaining a benefit and the expectation of a future recompense. At the same time, this motivation applied to the itinerants too. Jesus required his followers to travel without any private means of support, because it must be clear to those who received them that they would never be able to give anything in exchange—neither hospitality nor material goods nor political protection nor social integration. They were now destitute, deracinated, and interstitial. Jesus demanded that the itinerant disciples abandon their homes and sell their goods because this was the only way to prevent them from becoming instruments of an alliance between their own household and the household that received them. They were poor, but not beggars. They had no financial prospects, and were thus less able to enter relationships that bound them to the houses they visited; nor would these households press them to do so.

We should not forget that one indirect (though perhaps also intended) effect of entering people's houses is that Jesus and his followers enter into the life of the villages and take part to some extent in this life. We have seen that Jesus had no wish to play a role on the public stage offered by the cities. He stood secure on the stage offered by smaller or marginal settlements. He did not always frequent the grand houses; instead, he was present in the small households. It is only in Jerusalem that he would change his strategy.

The hospitality requested by his movement is not a simple mechanism whereby the poverty of the itinerants would be compensated by the wealth of those who receive them. It is not practiced with a view to establishing a general social equilibrium, nor does it seek to resolve the problem of the poorer strata of society. Rather, the mechanism of hospitality seeks to combine "detachment" from one's family milieu with the introduction into much larger milieus. The hospitality creates links with all those who adhere to what Jesus is doing, and makes it possible for his movement both to free itself from traditional social relationships and to reach large sectors of the population.

The fact that Jesus, or some itinerant preachers, lived temporarily in a house transformed the movement's internal life and its social relationships. A whole variety of people came into this house. All these persons, who in some way or other accepted the message of Jesus or were seeking him, transformed the house into a space crowded with people and full of movement. Thanks to the presence of Jesus, the domestic space became accessible to persons who would never otherwise have been admitted to it. Relationships that were previously unimaginable became possible.[66] The house was transformed from a private place that excluded others into an open space that included them.

Jesus never made hospitality an occasion for allowing himself to be integrated in a stable manner into a household or a village. He passed through the houses. He brought the extraverted and intersecting principles of his movement into the introverted logic of the household. He did not settle down into domesticity, into the structures of production and consumption, or into the routines of mutual assistance in the household.

The interstitial nature of the movement can be seen in the subtle and pervasive religious dissemination that often took place in the houses and domestic spaces where Jesus was a guest. The movement did not create alternative social forms to those that already existed, nor did it seek to overturn institutional and religious mechanisms. Instead, it aimed to transform the basic social relationships and points of reference—domestic life, the spheres of intimate relationships—in which everyone lived. The interstitiality that saturates spaces disseminates and transforms, creating a new kind of link between houses and establishing unforeseen homogeneities.

Jesus worked in a situation in which the poorer social strata were not able to utilize the mechanisms of patronage. It is irrelevant whether or not he was familiar with the social system of patronage.⁶⁷ He appears to have been living in one of the crisis situations described by Andrew Wallace-Hadrill, where the relationships between patron and client are gravely weakened. Halvor Moxnes correctly observes that the rich in the Gospel of Luke do not want to behave like patrons: "they are portrayed as unwilling to show such generosity as one should rightly expect" from patrons.⁶⁸ Jesus' requirement that the itinerant disciples give away their possessions without asking for any recompense and that the others offer a hospitality that falls outside the mechanism of reciprocal exchange undermines the very basis of the patronal relationship and makes it useless. We believe that Jesus did not actually intend to transform the patronal system. For one thing, he had other objectives; and for another, it is virtually impossible to eliminate this mechanism of power. We believe that Jesus was inspired by the Jubilee in the book of Leviticus to envisage another social model, that of the restoration of equality.⁶⁹ The transformation of the *oikos* that Jesus proposed is a step toward the regeneration of the whole community of Israel.

Jesus wanted to shatter the mechanisms that imprisoned the world he encountered in a whole series of ruptures and divisions—between cities and country villages, between the rich and the poor, between the hungry and the satiated, between the sick and the healthy, between the violent and the meek, between women and men, and between Judeans and non-Judeans. He relied on households as places where he could modify and annul such distances between people. In this way, he brought peace to the divided parties, acting on a different level and bringing people together in such a way that the division could be healed.

Hospitality thus became the symbol of his project. It had to be practiced in such a way that the house was no longer a place that sanctioned social inequality, the alliance between the powerful and the rich, and the dependent status of the poor. On the contrary, it had to become the place where the excluded were included and all shared in the renewed world.

6

JESUS AND HIS BODY

The Place of Corporality

The human body, an essential and inescapable element of life, is at the center of surprising shifts of emphasis and reworkings in the course of history. The cultural meaning of the body is the result of the convergence of a physical-biological system and a project that is generated by the cultural alchemies applied to this system. The body is closely linked to culture, and it becomes the resonance of culture or the place where culture makes its voice heard. It is difficult to recognize this link if we take a naturalistic view as our starting point, regarding the body only as a reproductive biological organism rather than as the subject of inescapable relationships. The fact is that human beings are bodies subject to cultural codifications. Human bodily data offer us one of the first points of access to a culture (understood in the sense of meanings that are transmitted and of instruments used to express these meanings). It is the body that keeps institutions and cultural practices alive.

The body is a fundamental, inalienable material for every individual. Every aspect of human existence, whether concrete or abstract, is rooted in corporality. A number of anthropological theories have been formulated in this sense. Marcel Mauss sees the body as the largest "instrument" of the human being;[1] Mary Douglas sees it as a "natural symbol";[2] the studies of Margaret M. Lock and Nancy Scheper-Hughes see it as a "mindful body."[3]

In their study of the various aspects of the body, anthropologists and historians classify attitudes, powers, inclinations, or deficiencies of *individual* persons. Their work first deconstructs and then reassembles the bodily material. The result of their analysis is the production of "another body" that does not always integrally restore the bodily reality. There is sometimes a considerable distance between the two bodies, the real body and the outcome of anthropological analysis. The general rule that every thematization is the fruit of a discourse that is formulated and constructed by an interpreter applies also to the body. Scholars "read" the body on the basis of intellectual motivations that are linked to different personal, political, cultural, and contemporary situations. The hypotheses and theories to which this situation leads may be heterogeneous, or even contradictory,[4] but they provide knowledge and insights that can be combined with the outcome of other analyses—and this, after all, is how human knowledge works.

The body interacts closely with the systems of meaning and the intellectual processes of the milieu of which it forms a part, and this interaction is even more obvious in the field of religion. The body must be understood, not as a simple reality that is illuminated or ennobled by the religious element but as one of the components to which the religious life owes its consistency. Religions are constructed and perpetuated in the body: they are bodily. In keeping with the structures of meaning that are proper to each culture, the mechanisms of the power of religion become concrete precisely in interventions in the body.

Corporality plays an important role in the construction of the relationship between real beings and imaginary or transcendent beings that is expressed in the process whereby life is sacralized. In religious contexts, various characteristics of the body are utilized in order to define centrally important points of human thinking and action. They serve to define duties and tasks, to set limits to these, to impose them, or to withhold them. On both the individual and the collective level, a large number of religious roles are granted or refused on the basis of differences of gender,[5] of age, or of membership in one particular ethnic group.

Our starting point, therefore, is that religion always needs to express itself in a bodily manner and that the body has the ability to give appropriate expression to religious reality. The body incarnates supremely religious functions in the frontier that it creates between one individual and another, in its power to confer individuality, and in its ability to activate the presence of each person.[6]

Anthropological research brings to light the differences and the specific characteristics of human corporality in various cultures. It often devotes considerable space to exceptional or extraordinary behavior (such as trances, the consumption of particular substances, mystical-ecstatic tremors, songs, exhausting dances, and so on) in the belief that these make it possible to understand more completely the specific character of a religious practice or belief. Anthropologists pay particular attention to cases of bodily anomalies or the infringement of physical borders.⁷ This is because the various cultures respond to the dangers to which the body is exposed, or to its deficiencies, by mobilizing mechanisms (by means of exclusion, isolation, deformations, and so on)⁸ that reveal central aspects of their religious systems.

When we speak of corporality in ancient religions—in the present instance, in the Judaism in which Jesus was born—we cannot always clear up the obscurity and the contradictions that are due to the distance in time and situation between today's reader and the ancient texts. Here too, therefore, we must attempt to immerse ourselves in the culture of Jesus' time, prescinding from doctrines that were elaborated in subsequent centuries. Above all, we must not project onto him the mind-body dualism that is typical of one tendency in ancient and modern philosophy, as if this was something that could be taken for granted. Such a distinction was indeed widespread in certain social groups, above all in the Hellenized upper classes; but these were intellectual minorities. In the Synoptic Gospels, the Greek noun *psychē* ("soul") does not indicate the soul as a spiritual and immortal substance separate from the body, but the life of the person in its entirety.⁹ In Judaic culture, a human being's identity is linked to his or her bodily nature and to physical membership in a people. And with regard to life beyond this earth, we should not forget that resurrection concerns not the immortality of the soul but the revivification of the body.

Our principal interest is in the bodily practice of Jesus. In the earliest Christian texts, the bodily images that we encounter are often fleeting and indirect, but they are very helpful toward an understanding of Jesus' behavior. The first questions we ask are rather simple. What can we know about the bodily dimension or the functions of bodies? How is Jesus described in his corporality? And is there anything in the texts that gives us a glimpse of the ideas he had about his own body?

Bodies Procreate: Jesus' Genealogical Position

Bodies give life to or procreate other bodies. According to the Gospels, however, Jesus does not procreate. One salient characteristic of his life is that he did not have children of his own. He did not take on the father's role. His whole life is conditioned by this lack of descendants.

Jesus, however, belongs to a genealogical lineage. In the Gospels of Matthew and Luke, he is presented within and by means of an extremely important descent. His genealogical lineage is portrayed in a conceptual framework that values the continuity and the perpetuation of an uninterrupted chain of masculine generations. In the Judaic culture of his

Jesus and His Body

time, many regarded the human body as an instrument to be used for the total construction of the people of Israel. From Abraham onward, all his descendants have procreated and have brought forth in their successive generations a bodily reality that is structured and is conceptually cohesive. The individual body is not in the least irrelevant or neutral with regard to the totality of bodies: it has a specific dimension in the transgenerational chain. For Matthew and Luke, Jesus too shares this position. At the same time, however, he appears to suspend it, precisely because he does not marry and does not beget children.

Let us begin with the *incipit* of Matthew's Gospel, since it closely represents the Judaic conception of genealogical corporality. The first words of any written text are always revelatory. They introduce the theme and set the tone for the discourse that follows. Matthew opens his text with a title: "Book of the birth [*genēsis*][10] of Jesus the Messiah, the son of David, the son of Abraham" (1:1).[11] This "book" records all the meanings of physical birth.

In order to grasp more precisely the originality of this *incipit*, it suffices to recall that the Gospel of Mark begins simply with the baptism of Jesus by John and the Gospel of Luke by setting the historical and political framework for the story, while John demonstrates the supernatural origin of Jesus as the incarnate Logos. Matthew introduces Jesus as the outcome of a collective and transgenerational physical story. He refers to the dimension of a body that is generated by other bodies, which in turn were generated by other bodies, and so on back to Abraham.

For Matthew, the body is a physical entity in which a uniform dimension, or same reality, is made present in time and is repeated in the individuals. The first section of Matthew juxtaposes and connects the personages of Judean history within the inescapable bonds of begetting and being born. The only thing mentioned here is the relationship that binds the generations in an uninterrupted succession. Thirty-eight times he repeats the key verb "begat" (*egennēsen*), which denotes the procreation of a human being, thereby expressing the absolutely essential character and the continuity of a vital act. When he writes, "Abraham begat Isaac, and Isaac begat Jacob, and Jacob begat Judah and his brothers" (1:2), Matthew is referring to specific persons identified by their individual names. They become the ancestors and the founders of the identity of Jesus. At the close of the genealogy, Matthew writes, "All the generations from Abraham to David are fourteen generations; and from David to the deportation to Babylon, fourteen generations; and from the deportation to Babylon to the Messiah, fourteen generations" (1:17). This is how he concludes this human story of fathers and sons in a fixed and unalterable framework that is not only genealogical but also chronological and historical.

The generations linked by this biological process lead to a final outcome. In Matthew's text, the goal of one generation after another is Jesus. The Judaic world that Matthew has in mind is constituted by one single physical descent from the seed of Abraham. This explains the centrality of the act of begetting by men.[12] In some instances, this male presence is accompanied by the mothers (Tamar, Rahab, Ruth, the wife of Uriah, and Mary). The mention of these women has given rise to many questions.[13] The point that interests us here is that they are all mentioned to reinforce the idea of the continuity from one generation to another. According to Matthew, Jesus is legitimated by his descent from Abraham and from David, and this legitimacy is transmitted to him by Joseph, who is a descendant of David, although this happens through his wife, Mary—who is probably also thought to be of the Davidic line, since she is married to one of his descendants: "Jacob begat Joseph the husband of Mary, of whom Jesus was born, who is called the Messiah" (Matt 1:16).

This is an apologetic text that takes into consideration only the Judean people and traces the path through the generations toward a final exalted birth. In the chain of Jesus' predecessors, after fourteen generations, Abraham's body becomes physically present in the body of David and politically and territorially concrete in his kingdom. After a further fourteen generations, the people of Israel are deported to Babylon. Jesus belongs to the physical lineage of Abraham and David. His body is born at the moment when another territorial and political expansion of the body of his ancestors is to take place, the messianic kingdom of Israel. The chain of generations is valuable because it is based on the materiality of the flesh, as recorded in a memorable list of indisputable acts of procreation.

Matthew's text highlights the most basic bodily powers. His text expresses the perpetuity of an initial patrimony, but also the universal human ability to make progress in life. As so often in Judaic culture, Matthew lacks any purely conceptual definition. The philosophical and political significance is expressed only through the memory of the continuous procreative action. The evangelist affirms not only that Jesus is endowed with a body in which the body of Abraham and of David is made present, but also that Jesus is located at a moment in which the royal and territorial expectations that have always existed are realized physically in his body.

Jesus and His Body 133

A map of the generations is not proof of any historical reality; its function is to exalt the origin of individuals who are *the origin* of other individuals who in turn are *the origin* of yet other individuals in one single unity. We could say that for Matthew, the background to which Jesus belongs is constituted by a people whose collective bodily existence has been reconstructed in his genealogy. This people can be represented by means of ciphers with a symbolic and numerological meaning: three units of fourteen procreative stages. According to calculations that were widespread in various religious groups at that time, this meant that Jesus was situated at the beginning of the final period of human history.[14] The Matthean calculation points to the beginning of the final age and can also be thematized in terms of lives that were "replicated" and indissolubly linked to a "culmination." Those who enter into this genealogical map retain their own physical individuality, but the identities that they possess are in one sense indivisible. The subjects are mentioned here not because of their individual characteristics but because they have physically reproduced their own condition in other subjects. And they are presented only as part of the generational chain that unites them to the world of their ancestors.

In Matthew, this process of mapping offers a way to "dwell" in the world and to have a role in the history of human beings. The collective Judean body has a corresponding political and territorial destiny in the history of humanity. Without this body, Jesus would lack historical concreteness and identity, and he would be incompatible with the Judaic religious milieu as a whole. As the final outcome of so many generations, he takes on a historical and eschatological role with regard to the Judean people.

The Gospel of Luke likewise presents a genealogy of Jesus (3:23-28), but it has a very different function from that of Matthew.[15] In Luke, Jesus' identity is not constituted by the collective Judean genealogical body. Luke has his own individual way of looking at the many individuals who precede Jesus. He begins not with Jesus' birth but with the beginning of his public activity: "Jesus was about thirty years old when he began his work." Luke immediately adds: "He was the son (as was thought) of Joseph son of Heli, son of Matthat ... ," and presents a patrilineal genealogical series that shows Jesus' descent from Adam. Luke declares his disagreement with the common view that Jesus was the son of Joseph, and although the physical dimension that links him to Joseph's ancestors is not lacking, the verb "procreate" is never employed in this text. The numerous genitives, representing the seventy-six generations behind Joseph, show that the continuity passes from one man to the next. But at the close of the genealogy Adam is said to be "of God." The seventy-seventh generation, represented by Jesus, is the moment when his public activity begins, immediately after the baptism administered by John.

Luke's genealogical story works backward in order to reach the most ancient starting point possible, namely, Adam—or rather, God himself (Luke 3:38). It expresses a perspective that broadens out to become universal, as it goes back toward the first man and his father, the Creator. Jesus is linked to the very beginnings of the human era by a chain that culminates in the figure of Adam. In this way, he takes his place in a physical nexus that involves every human being. Luke's intention here is not only to present a map of the Judean people culminating in Jesus; he does not limit his vision to the seed of Abraham, but includes the Judaic descent of Jesus in a genealogical system that embraces the whole of humanity.

Matthew and Luke interpret Jesus' bodily descent differently, in the light of the knowledge and the positions taken by the groups of his followers several decades after his death. They do not reflect the personal thinking of Jesus, nor the consciousness that he may have had of his own self and of his world. And besides this, they tell us nothing about his physical appearance.

When His Contemporaries Looked at Jesus, What Did They See?

The Gospels have little to say about the physical figure of Jesus. They give us no description, and seem uninterested in his height, the color of his hair or his eyes, or the timbre of his voice.[16] We never hear anything about his physical aspect as he walks along the roads and visits people's houses. This is an indicator of how those who composed the narratives thought. Their silence about the outward appearance of Jesus is due not only to the fact that none of the evangelists had ever seen him but also to a sensitivity with regard to Jesus' corporality, which is different from our own perception. We must, therefore, look for the indications or signals that tell us something about how they saw and perceived him. The recognition of this obscurity and this difference should make us cautious about drawing conclusions, but it certainly allows us to call into question the way in which the physical appearance of Jesus has been perceived both on a more popular level and among scholars.

Jesus and His Body

Although there is uncertainty about the historical reliability of many of the physical actions and postures that the Gospels attribute to Jesus, our analysis requires us to center our investigations on his body. This will allow us to penetrate his individual history more deeply and will give us concrete information about his person, even if we are not be able to have a complete picture of his physical appearance.

Every body is imagined and represented by specific cultural systems that place varying emphases on the outward appearance, on the functioning of the body, and on the centrality of the physical dimension. When we conjure up the picture of individual persons, our mental processes construct them in relation to what their bodies show or make visible. On the basis of the garments that cover them or the objects that they bear on their bodies, we think of them as elegant or as untidy, as modest or as shameless. The body of Jesus was inevitably the object of reflection of this kind by his contemporaries. They were able to see on his body things we cannot know—or that perhaps would not have told *us* very much. Nevertheless, if we read the Gospels closely, we can sometimes recognize interesting details.

First of all, the only parts of Jesus' body that were visible were his face, his hands, and his feet—although it is difficult to be sure about even as much as this, since we do not know whether his feet were usually shod or his head usually covered. And it is possible that this varied, depending on circumstances.

Second, the body of Jesus appears in the Gospels as the "destination" of the actions and thoughts of other persons. Although the texts tell us little about what his contemporaries saw of the physical figure of Jesus, and their information is often only indirect, they do allow us to glimpse what people in some first-century milieus thought about this body.

People saw Jesus on the streets, in the town squares, and in the fields. He seems not to carry anything with him as he moves around. There are no signals of his status, although it is highly likely that his garments presented the signs of a man who respected the religious norms. Some texts indicate that Jesus wore on his cloak the fringe or tassel (*tzitzit* or *kanaf*) prescribed by biblical law (Num 15:38-39; Deut 22:12).[17] In a saying attributed to him by Matthew (23:5), he accused the Pharisees of wanting to lengthen their fringes. It follows that while he himself accepted the duty of wearing them, he insisted that this be done without ostentation.[18] The way in which Jesus used his own body gave those who saw him the message that it was good to respect the biblical law,[19] but it is highly significant that when Jesus wanted to hand on in private a more intense message to his disciples (who see him every day), the cloak with its fringes was no longer sufficient (better: it is not of use). Chapter 13 of the Gospel of John, which we shall discuss below, tells us that Jesus took off his cloak, then took a linen towel and tied it over his tunic: he put on the clothing habitually worn by slaves. In the eyes of his disciples, the way he dressed here is the physical depiction of a slave.[20] Through his traditional mantle with the fringes, through his criticism of the Pharisees, and through putting on the garments of a slave, Jesus shows his awareness of the communicative aspect and the functionality of a person's clothing and of physical appearance in general.

Like most men, Jesus probably wore the tunic (*chitōn*) under his mantle or cloak (*himation*).[21] This is confirmed by his words in Luke: "From anyone who takes away your coat do not withhold even your shirt."[22] He did not wear sumptuous or unusual garments. The account in the Gospel of John about the soldiers who cast lots for his garments is very dubious from a historical point of view, because the intention of the evangelist was to show that they were doing something that was prophesied by Ps 22:19: "They divided my clothes among themselves, and for my clothing they cast lots."[23] John writes: "When the soldiers had crucified Jesus, they took his clothes and divided them into four parts, one for each soldier. They also took his tunic; now the tunic was seamless, woven in one piece from the top. So they said to one another, 'Let us not tear it, but cast lots for it to see who will get it'" (19:23). John appears to think that the tunic was more valuable than the cloak. This would mean that the Johannine Jesus was a man who wore well-made garments of good quality.

What image did the body of Jesus, clothed in a tunic and cloak, transmit to his contemporaries as he moved from village to village? Some of the details that emerge from the texts may be insignificant, but others may have been typical of Jesus alone.

Although he is in constant movement, Jesus seems not to protect his body with the garments worn by travelers. As we have said, we do not know whether he wore sandals or covered his head. He probably had no bag or baggage, or objects of any kind. The very explicit order to his disciples not to carry a bag, extra garments, or a store of food surely illustrates his own lifestyle: he must have applied to himself what he demanded of the others. His behavior was austere, with a limited use even of the most necessary goods. He relied on the support and hospitality of other people (and certainly on divine help) for his own sustenance. His criticism of those who lengthened their fringes probably means that they were not conspicuous on his own cloak but were of the appropriate length. If it is true that his tunic was of good quality, this means that he did not want to make a show of poverty or shabbiness. He did not wish to wear garments that would proclaim him to be a traveler in difficulty or would underline his radical marginality. He did not want to be different in any way from the people among whom he moved.

Jesus offered the following reflection on everyday needs: "I tell you, do not worry about your life, what you will eat, or about your body, what you will wear. For life is more than food, and the body more than clothing" (Luke 12:22-23). He placed food and clothing on the same level, and affirmed that attaching importance to one's physical well-being could lead to a distortion of one's existence. The primary concern in this saying, however, is in fact the defense of one's physical life. Jesus did not neglect food and clothing, either for himself or for others; all he did was to recommend that one search for the authentic meaning of food and clothing. His aspiration was that people should expect to be clothed like "the lilies of the field" that are clothed by the generosity of God in a splendor even greater than that of Solomon (Luke 12:27-28): "But if God so clothes the grass of the field, which is alive today and tomorrow is thrown into the oven, how much more will he clothe you—you of little faith!"

In some of the sayings attributed to him, we find affirmations that show us something of how those who observed him continuously thought about him. The texts also reveal the thinking of Jesus—of an everyday Jesus who pressed his companions and the people close to him, and who wanted to minimize their concerns about the body. He wanted people to have food and prosperity, but above all, he wanted to combat the lack of trust in the God who provides food and clothing.

We ought not to forget the human and social dimension of these intentions that are attributed to Jesus in a milieu that certainly had urgent needs. His criticism of those unduly concerned about clothing is a criticism of the ostentatious and discriminating function that clothing can have in one's relationship to other persons. Garments are means of inclusion and exclusion, and they cannot have escaped Jesus' notice. When he reduced their value, his intention was to free his followers from the enticements and the compulsions of self-affirmation. If the appearance of the disciples was obviously rich or poor, those who saw them would associate them with one specific social level, whether high or low. In this way, they would no longer be free to act independently.

All four Gospels that were to become canonical tell us that after his arrest, Jesus was clothed in a particular garment. His normal appearance was altered and made unnatural. Mark (15:17) relates that the soldiers to whom Pilate handed him over "clothed him in a purple cloak," and that after mocking him by calling him the king of the Judeans, "they stripped him of the purple cloak and put his own clothes on him" (15:20). Matthew relates that the soldiers clothed him in "a scarlet robe" (27:28). It is important to note that it was the soldiers who attacked the prisoner, insulting him and striking him in a scene of cruel humiliation. The body of Jesus was exposed to their eyes and was examined during a lengthy scene of clothing and stripping. His body underwent an alteration. It was the object of other people's actions.

The scene in Luke is completely different. Only this evangelist relates a face-to-face encounter between Jesus and Herod, in the presence of scribes and priests (23:8-12).[24] It may be the austerity of Jesus' body that provoked fury and bitterness. This is how Luke describes the encounter: "Herod with his soldiers treated him with contempt and mocked him; then he put a splendid robe on him, and sent him back to Pilate." This act established a friendship between Herod and Pilate (23:12). Luke thus retains the presence of the soldiers, which he found in Mark's narrative, but he has added Herod, giving him a function as protagonist and linking him closely to Pilate. The soldiers who insulted Jesus remain on stage, but they were not the soldiers of Pilate, and they played no autonomous role. Besides this, the scene of clothing is located at a different point in the story. Luke does not tell us that Jesus was stripped of his own clothes. The "splendid" garment that was put on him was neither a purple cloak nor a scarlet robe. The scene before Herod looks like an intermezzo before the conclusion of the face-to-face encounter with Pilate.

The Gospel of John does not tell us that Jesus was first stripped of his clothes. As in Mark, it was Pilate's soldiers who clothed Jesus in a purple cloak. This is the only Gospel that underlines the public character of this disguisement. The body of Jesus was exposed to the people in an ironically "regal" manner. The purple cloak and the crown of thorns are symbols employed to present to the public a deformed image of Jesus. They make his state of abasement, degradation, and defeat indisputable.

The garment that was placed on Jesus—with details that differ in the four narratives—shows his body as something that defines his person. The people are offered eloquent and totally altered images of the physical person of Jesus: he was clothed like a soldier (the scarlet robe in Matthew), or he was clothed sumptuously but without the signs of rank (the elegant robe in Luke), or else he was clothed perhaps as a king or a high dignitary (the purple cloak in Mark and John). The expensive garment that Herod put on him, falsifying his external appearance, was meant to annul the socio-religious role that Jesus had gradually taken on. It made his body ridiculous, in order to send him back to Pilate as a weak and inoffensive man (Luke 23:11). The entire performance is a powerful means of affecting the opinion people had of Jesus, in order to make ineffective what he was and what he did. The body of Jesus was exposed and rendered obviously ridiculous in order to besmirch his reputation and to diminish his prestige among the people and the authorities themselves.

At the moment of his crucifixion, Jesus was stripped of his clothes, and from then on appeared even more exposed and weakened. It was in this state that they bound him to the cross. This naked and crucified body cancelled the preceding images. In the consciousness of those who were present and in the collective memory, the image that Jesus wanted to give of his body during his encounters with the population of the villages was now denied and extinguished.

Other Looks, Other Appearances

Some of the actions of Jesus himself and of those who observed him allow us to see how others looked at him and to come closer to the physical reality of Jesus, as this was perceived by his contemporaries.

As we have seen, the narratives tell us frequently, in varying degrees of directness, that Jesus ate and drank. We must, however, ask how he rested, how he got up, how he prayed, how he wept, and so on. Whatever may be said about the historicity of the individual instances, the Gospels agree in ascribing to him the habits of a normal human being. For example, he fell asleep in the boat (Mark 4:38). According to the Judaic custom, he prostrated himself on the ground to pray.[25] When he learned that Lazarus had died, he wept; this may of course be a lamentation that is part of the customary ritual procedure, but such procedures can certainly lead to genuine tears. He lifted his eyes up to heaven when he prayed before raising Lazarus from the dead (John 11:41) and in the lengthy prayer on his last evening (John 17:1). When the Passover drew near, he rode on a donkey, a means of transport used by Mediterranean people. This typified the way that Jesus lived among the people in the real world. He maintained an obstinate silence and did not utter a single word at critical moments (Matt 26:62) when he was interrogated after his arrest. Various persons—for example, Peter and Mary of Magdala—embraced and bathed his feet (and cf. John 11:32). When he was arrested, chains were put on him and pulled tight; many persons "laid hands on him" (Mark 14:46; Matt 26:50). Some began to spit in his face (Mark 14:63; Matt 26:67) and strike him (Matt 26:68).

According to John, Jesus spit on the earth and made a paste of the mud with which to heal a blind man: "He spread the mud on the man's eyes, saying to him, 'Go, wash in the pool of Siloam' [. . .]. Then he went and washed and came back able to see" (9:6-7). Although Jesus had just declared that he was "the light of the world," he performed a bodily action and did not limit himself to words. The communication between two bodies, between Jesus and the blind man, took place through bodily and material instruments.

The physical relationship of Jesus to the earth, to the ground, is interesting here. Once again, it is John who tells us that during the dramatic scene of the woman accused of adultery, Jesus "bent down and wrote with his finger on the ground" (8:6, 8).[26] We do not know what Jesus wrote. The interesting point here is that touching the ground, placing one's hands on the soil, is something done by ordinary people such as farmers. It shows the close relationship to the earth on the part of those who live in the countryside among the fields where they work.

The Gospels strategically highlight a number of sayings that show the importance Jesus attached to what people do with their faces. Above all, we see his condemnation of those who altered their facial features theatrically in order to get other people to admire them. We read in Matthew: "Whenever you fast, do not look dismal, like the hypocrites"—it would be better to translate *hypokritai* as "those who put themselves on the stage, those who want to make a public display of themselves"—"for they disfigure their faces so as to show others that they are fasting. . . . But when you fast, put oil on your head and wash your face, so that your fasting may not be seen by others" (6:16-17). Jesus declared that the only one who should see that a person is fasting is God, "your Father who is in secret" (6:18). Matthew's Jesus was extremely attentive here to the influence that persons can exercise by the way they modify their facial features; he was so profoundly aware of this function of the face that he refers to the practice of actors on the stage. The noun *hypokritēs*, "actor," speaks of one who plays a role on stage, and Matthew employs it frequently (6:2, 5 and chap. 23). The importance that Jesus attaches to the modification of one's facial expression is also shown in his counsel that one should wash and adorn one's face, so that no one will realize that one is practicing abstinence from food. In both these instances, therefore, there is a simulation, an intentional modification of the face.

The Body Is Taken Prisoner

After he was arrested, the physical relationship between Jesus and the persons encountered during his travels from place to place came to an end. No matter what he or others may have expected, it was no longer possible for him to move around: in the eyes of his contemporaries, the body of Jesus was now the possession of the authorities. He lost his liberty. His mobility and his whole lifestyle were deliberately annihilated. We see many institutional subjects moving around him. The members of the Sanhedrin, the high priest, Pilate, Herod, the soldiers and the guards, and the servants of the priests occupy the space and dominate both Jesus and those around him. Suddenly, they burst onto the stage with their authority, which they exercise physically. Political supremacy and physical constraint take hold of Jesus and immobilize him.

The arrest sets in motion bodies and subjects with changed relationships. Jesus is now separated from his followers; Judas has joined the armed group that arrests Jesus, the unnamed persons (perhaps soldiers) who bring him from place to place. Next, the religious and political authorities intervene, interrogating Jesus and condemning him. Finally, there are those who lead him to his execution.[27] The radical change in the relationships between individuals and groups is translated into bodily actions and is symbolically represented in the night, in the darkness, when an armed group seizes Jesus. His body is docile. He hands himself over, putting himself into the hands of those who have come to bind him: all the narratives agree on this point. Only one of his followers takes hold of a sword and wounds the "slave" of the high priest.[28] This physical action ends the confrontation between the two groups.

There are other physical interventions that Jesus must suffer. Just before his arrest, he told his disciples that he was "deeply grieved, even to death." He threw himself on the ground and prayed (Mark 14:32-35; Matt 26:36-38). He received Judas's kiss and was seized and led off. He was handed over to Pilate (Mark 15:1). He was clothed in mockery and crowned with thorns, and they took him away to crucify him (Mark 15:16-20). He was given vinegar to drink in a sponge on a stick (Mark 15:36/Matt 27:28/Luke 23:36). He cried out in a loud voice and breathed his last (Luke 23:46; Mark 15:37/Matt 27:50). Mark adds that Pilate was surprised to learn that Jesus was already dead; but when he was assured that this was the case, he gave permission to take down the corpse from the cross.[29] Joseph of Arimathea did so. He then wrapped it in a linen cloth and laid it "in a tomb that had been hewn out of the rock" (Mark 15:45).

According to Luke, the cross was laid on Jesus' shoulders and was subsequently carried by Simon of Cyrene (23:26). The people stood and watched (23:35a); it was only the "leaders" and the soldiers that mocked him (23:35b-36). Mark (15:29-31), followed by Matthew (27:38-43), writes that the passers-by also insulted Jesus, along with the chief priests and the scribes (Matthew adds: "and elders"); neither Mark nor Matthew mentions the soldiers. Mark writes that the two men who were crucified alongside Jesus also insulted him, but Luke corrects this by stating that one of the two defended him (Luke 23:39-43). Luke agrees with Mark that Joseph of Arimathea "went to Pilate and asked for the body of Jesus" (Mark 15:42-44; Luke 23:50; Matt 27:57-61). The passion narratives present a sequence that continually alternates between those who do something and those who look on.

After relating the kiss of Judas, Matthew lists a number of actions that concern the immobilization of Jesus' body. Jesus was bound (Matt 27:2/Mark 15:1), and this is how he was brought before the governor. Jesus did not reply; he gave no expression to what he felt, nor did he satisfy the curiosity of those who interrogated him. In addition to the crown of thorns, he received a reed in his right hand (Matt 27:29). Matthew is the only evangelist who writes that before Jesus refused to drink the wine mixed with gall, he performed the very eloquent gesture of raising the drink to his lips: "but when he tasted it, he would not drink it" (27:34). As in Mark, Jesus "cried again with a loud voice and breathed his last" (Matt 27:50). Pilate orders that the body of Jesus be given to Joseph, and it is laid in the new tomb (Matt 27:57-61).

The nature and the significance of this drama are represented in substance by the physical treatment that Jesus underwent: violent, cruel, and contemptuous actions, but also compassionate actions. This means that the active role of the body of Jesus is less important, and very little space indeed is left for the description of Jesus' feelings and emotions in relation to his physical pain and his fear of dying.

This majestic complex of representations of the body of Jesus during his arrest, his passion, and his death is so impressive that in later memory it replaced the image of the "historical" body of Jesus. We see as early as the Letters of Paul, in the fifties of the first century, that the prevalent picture of Jesus is that of the crucified man: "For Judeans demand signs and Greeks desire wisdom, but we proclaim Christ crucified, a stumbling block to Judeans and foolishness to Gentiles" (1 Cor 1:22-23). The two pictures of his body—the body humiliated in mockery and torture and the body on the cross—had the effect desired by the political authorities. The picture of Jesus among the people of his land was in effect cancelled out by the sheer power of the degrading treatment to which he was exposed from his arrest to his crucifixion.

From our point of view, we note that there are assuredly many conceptions of the body implicit in the passion narratives, and that these play an essential role in the attempt to reconstruct a historical picture of the body of Jesus. This applies equally to the texts that narrate the apparitions of his risen body. The Gospel narratives and other early Christian texts claim that Jesus returned to life after his death and that his body appeared to the disciples over a certain period of time.[30] These narratives have given readers in later generations a picture of Jesus that turns the picture of the humiliated body upside-down. The defeat of Jesus was perceived above all as a physical destruction, the annihilation of his person. The reaction to this defeat likewise assumed a bodily form: Jesus overcame the humiliating destruction because his body rose from the dead. He won a bodily victory. In the early Christian texts, we find a variety of perceptions and understandings of the risen body of Jesus. The important point is that his risen body became the basis for the understanding both of the nature of his humiliated and executed body and of the nature of the same human body when it was alive before the passion.

Christian iconography in later centuries has witnessed the alternation of two pictures of the body of Jesus, that of the risen Jesus (or Christ as Pantocrator) and that of the crucified Jesus. He has been depicted either in the state of humiliation or, on the contrary, as a body that was exalted and clothed in glory, in the fullness of his rehabilitation. The picture of the body of Jesus in its normal conditions seems to have been eliminated by the pictures of the passion and the resurrection, which were widespread and predominant in subsequent memory.

An Inclusive Subject: The Crowd

The crowd often occupied physically the spaces in which the events of Jesus' life took place. It is a subject that was present *en masse* at Jesus' healings and at his discourses, so that his concrete existence was interwoven with that of many other individuals of flesh and blood who were uprooted and distant from their own houses.[31]

In this section, we shall investigate how Jesus was physically involved in the embrace of the crowds that followed him. What happened when numerous persons came together in a gathering of this kind, and tried to get as close as possible to Jesus?

The Gospels contain no descriptions of the countryside or of natural places. It is the people who create the milieu, the physical atmosphere, and the landscape itself. The narratives tell us that many people came to Jesus and surrounded him in a material sense. Jesus won them over as he talked to them, and they stayed with him. On many occasions, the narratives depict Jesus in the thick of people who will not let him go.[32] It is this reciprocal tension that makes the crowds active and participating subjects. The crowd does not exist before it encounters Jesus. It is his presence, or his passing through a village, that calls the crowd together. The crowd intensifies the significance of what Jesus is doing. His great discourses[33] presuppose a gathering of numerous persons who seek in him a master whom they can trust. As a crowd, they then take on the role of protagonists.

The scenes dominated by large crowds do not exclude the possibility of individual encounters at close quarters. Such encounters help to make more concrete the faces and the bodies that made up a large part of the reality of Jesus' world. For example, a man "with an unclean spirit," whom Jesus healed (Mark 1:23), reached him in a synagogue that was apparently full of people who were attracted by his person. Very impressive encounters took place on the roads, where normally a multitude of persons were on the move. At Mark 10:17-21, as Jesus was setting out on a journey, a man[34] ran up to him and knelt before him. This physical act of kneeling communicates in a dramatic manner the meaning of the encounter: the gesture of the kneeling body before the standing figure of Jesus expresses the devotion of this person. Two individuals face one another in a moment of extreme tension. The two faces are close to each other, and the two men can speak. In this bodily encounter, Jesus looked into the eyes of his interlocutor and "loved" him. Mark's narrative thus underlines the intention to communicate with the eyes, and this is followed by a request. Jesus felt the desire to have this man in his company: "Go, sell what you own ... then come, follow me" (Mark 10:21). He wanted to establish a stable connection to the man, and demanded that he change his life.

Similarly, in another passage, it is the bodily actions that show how individuals enter into a relationship with Jesus. The encounter with a foreigner, a Syro-Phoenician woman, is depicted by means of a bodily gesture: "She came and bowed down at his feet."[35] The action of this woman who bowed down to the ground was intended to gain the healing of her daughter, and she succeeded in this.

In some instances, unusual bodily gestures are highlighted. An exceptional case is the woman who, without uttering one single word, entered the house of a Pharisee during a banquet, looked for Jesus, and occupied an unaccustomed space "behind him at his feet." She wept at his feet and bathed them in her tears. Then, in absolute silence, she dried his feet with her hair and anointed them with a perfumed oil (Luke 7:36-50). All that the narrative mentions is the gestures and the locations of the bodies.[36] It is the body that transmits and regulates the messages. The sequence of physical actions demonstrates the nature and the role of the bodies. We should note that those present were disconcerted by the fact that a sinner like this should touch Jesus. This scene shows clearly that a profound relationship to Jesus implies contact with his physical person, even if this infringes the social customs.

On another occasion, a deaf man who "was scarcely able to speak"[37] was presented to Jesus in the midst of a crowd. Jesus took him aside "in private" (Mark 7:32). Here, a direct encounter with Jesus entails a separation from the crowd.[38] Jesus touched the sick man, put his fingers into his ears, and touched his tongue with his own saliva. The relationship between these two persons is bodily. Jesus then lifted his eyes to heaven. His body experienced a strong and anomalous sensation that is expressed by the verb *stenazō*, "to sigh powerfully."[39] Finally, he gave a command: "Be opened!" Clearly, Jesus' corporality was appealed to by those who are depicted in the Gospels as his interlocutors. And he wanted to enter into direct contact with bodies, with sickness. He demonstrated physically what he intended to do. The milieu that sought him out and that determined what he did was the milieu of the human faces and voices that brought their needs to him.

There are many typical scenes of crowd movements. Many persons follow him literally. Mark tells us that wherever Jesus went, the sick were brought out onto the public squares so that they could touch him (Mark 6:56/Matt 14:36). For the people, touching Jesus meant being in his space, annulling the distance and separation, and taking hold physically of something that was his. In the Gospel texts, touching is seen as the greatest point of communication with Jesus. Mark relates that even children were brought to him in order that he might "touch" them (10:13) and that they might be united to him in this way. The aim of the crowds was contact with Jesus.

One fundamental implication of this gathering of the crowds around Jesus is often a distance from their own homes and villages. This is how the people come to be with Jesus on the mountains or in unaccustomed locations around the lake. This creates a liminal situation, a condition of socio-religious alteration. People tend to move out into unusual regions in order to get to know a teacher and to affirm their belief in his projects.

When they move into the places where Jesus is, they think that they will acquire strength and find what they lack. This leads to new knowledge and new memories.[40]

From the perspective of the narrative structure, it is extremely important to note that without the description of the gatherings of the crowds, we would not know the significance and the power of Jesus' presence. It is because these masses of people move from one place to another that we can perceive the power of Jesus and of his body. And when we consider the effort that this involves for many people as they move to unknown places in order to get close to him, we realize the discomforts and the needs that motivate them. Above all, we grasp the expectations and the tensions felt by so many of those who put their trust in Jesus.

There are gaps in our information about the relationship between Jesus and the crowds, about their closeness to him and the physical pressure they put on him. We do not know exactly the dimensions, the provenance, or the expectations of these crowds. Mark speaks in one passage of five thousand persons, and in another passage of four thousand (6:33-44 and 8:1-9); numbers are never given elsewhere. The powerful public impact made by Jesus is undeniable, but it is not quantifiable. A single explanation will not suffice, since the crowds were drawn to Jesus by a variety of contingent factors and hopes. On occasion, these gatherings went beyond the intentions or the decisions of Jesus himself, forcing him to act and perhaps to assume the role of healer, exorcist, and worker of miracles.

According to the Gospels, Jesus is bodily present among people in a variety of situations. The encounters often take place on the road, and sometimes he appears overwhelmed by the physical needs of his followers, by their hunger, their weariness, or their inability to stay awake. Jesus brings together bodies, situations, and projects, each time in different ways.[41] Those who take part in the multiplication of the loaves and fishes are not the same as those who hear the Sermon on the Mount. The physical reality of Jesus has a dominant role in defining the religious world that spontaneously comes into existence around him in various places.

Jesus did not establish any specific, fixed place where people could come together to form a new religious model or system. In his encounters with the crowd, we see the mental borders and the territorial extension of his movement, the map of his activity. People gathered in various places and then dispersed: there was no distinct and stable group that always moved around with Jesus. The crowd did not create a pressure group or a defensive movement, and Jesus had no intention of using the crowd to his own advantage. He did not organize the crowd in such a way as to guarantee the continuity of his activity. He quickly escaped from the crowd and bid them farewell. What happens after Jesus took his leave is not attributable to any directive on his part.

This makes it clear that Jesus was not moving around with crowds of "people" of his own with a defined identity.[42] Many followed him to Jerusalem and thronged around him in the city, but they were absent when he was arrested. The people did nothing when he was taken prisoner; there were no mass movements in his defense. The crowds in the city were present only at some of the phases that preceded the execution, and the reports of their attitude do not agree. In Mark, the crowds derided Jesus,[43] but in Luke, they sympathized with him.[44] In Matthew, the crowds appeared hostile—at least, those who demanded that Pilate put him to death (27:25).

Although Jesus deliberately sought out the people, the physical pressure of the crowds that he did not endure for any length of time made him desire only brief contacts. After an encounter, as we have seen, he manifested the need to continue his preaching elsewhere. The trajectory of the crowds converged on Jesus, but it diverged from the trajectory that Jesus followed. The people flocked around him in their attempt to take hold of him and prevent him from leaving, but he showed that he was a man on the move, continuously searching.

Anthropological-historical analysis seeks to uncover the social dynamics that are unleashed and to see what happens to the religious leader who is accompanied by huge crowds. The real Jesus absorbs the reality of the crowds and is profoundly marked by it. His stature can be seen in the way in which he lives in the world together with an immense number of other persons.[45] Jesus can be described on the basis of what the masses are looking for in him, of how they move toward him, and of the hopes they place in him. People run from all directions, they flock to him, they enter houses in order to get a glimpse of him. Essentially, they want to touch him (Mark 1:32-33; 2:13; 3:7-8; 5:21; 6:32; 6:54-56; 9:14; etc.). The phenomenon of Jesus cannot be understood without this powerful relationship that is established by touching him—even if only fleetingly. It is a relationship made up of profound and concrete needs that cannot be reduced to abstract ideological or theological expectations.

At his death, however, Jesus was without the people. They observed and commented, but did not act. The anonymous crowds disappeared immediately afterward. We have no way of knowing whether these same individuals had earlier contributed to the spread of the religious movement that found its inspiration in Jesus. The only certain fact is that the crowds that had been close to him were silent and vanished into the shadow, into invisibility, for as long as the general disorientation lasts. Later, other groups would come into existence, but without the presence of Jesus, the wonder worker whom people could touch. To "follow" him meant something else now, and led to a different kind of life. The body he once had has disappeared from the streets and the villages.

The Body in Danger

Precisely because it could be touched physically, the body of Jesus was exposed to danger. We have spoken above of flight and concealment: Jesus wanted not only to reach the people, but also to escape from them. Mark writes on two occasions that because of the crowd that surrounded him, Jesus and the disciples "could not even eat" (3:20 and 6:31). It is not easy to live under such uncomfortable conditions, after preaching in the open air or while being crushed by the crowd. Jesus was continuously exposed to fatigue, discomfort, and danger.

According to the Gospel narratives, however, the risk of which Jesus seemed to be most aware was the risk of being killed. He was physically vulnerable and thought that his life was in danger. He sensed that his opponents wanted to "destroy" him, to "kill" him (Mark 3:6; 11:18). This preoccupation may have generated the saying in which he invites his followers not to seek to save their own lives but to lose them for his sake.[46] Mark locates these words in the context of one of Jesus' three predictions of his passion. Quite apart from the theological question that plays a central role in this prediction, the Markan Jesus appears conscious of his own weakness and of the risk he incurs by going into Jerusalem, since that will make it possible for those who have the power to harm him, to find him. In John, Jesus is presented as continually exposed to death. For example, he asks explicitly: "Why are you looking for an opportunity to kill me?" (7:19), and he frequently takes refuge in flight. This emphasis in the Gospel of John is probably a development of a passage in the Gospel of Mark where Jesus heals a man in the synagogue on a Sabbath day, and the Pharisees and Herodians thereafter plot to kill him (Mark 3:6-7). Immediately after this, Mark relates that Jesus withdraws with his disciples to a place near the lake.[47]

It may well be that the picture of Jesus fleeing to escape the danger of death is not historical. His story concludes with his execution, and it is possible that all the preceding events are reread and interpreted in the light of this; accordingly, it is perfectly possible that premonitions of the end have been projected back onto his life. But we should not quickly dismiss the hypothesis that Jesus was realistically afraid of being exposed to a violent death. It is probable that, like every human being, Jesus knew that the project of his life must be realized through his own body. Accordingly, he protected it where he could, keeping it safe from capture and death, and endeavoring to escape before he was attacked anew. This is a rational defense technique that aims to avoid total defeat and physical destruction. Self-defense becomes meaningless only when a person has a false self-image.

The hypothesis that Jesus was afraid of being killed must be evaluated in terms of the historical context and the cultural imagination of the world in which he lived. In times of uprisings and repressions, religious leaders with a mass following that may be hostile to the dominant powers face a high risk of death. Herod, a client-king of the Romans, "succeeded in keeping the country under control, but only with unusual repression."[48] The period of Pontius Pilate's government was characterized by revolts and disorders with messianic movements, attacks by brigands, theocratic tensions, prophets, and innovators.[49]

We have already said that Luke relates that Jesus is informed about a recent act of repression by Pilate, who had executed a number of Galileans who had offered sacrifices in the Temple in Jerusalem and had then probably staged an uprising. Jesus reacted as follows to the story of these Galileans who were moved by religious ardor: "Do you think that because these Galileans suffered in this way they were worse sinners than all other Galileans? No, I tell you; but unless you repent, you will all perish as they did. Or those eighteen who were killed when the tower of Siloam fell on them—do you think that they were worse offenders than all the others living in Jerusalem? No, I tell you; but unless you repent, you will all perish just as they did" (Luke 13:2-5). Jesus regarded these deaths, whether ordered by Pilate or caused by the collapse of a tower, as the symbol of a situation in which violent death could occur at any moment. It seems difficult to doubt the historicity of these words of Jesus, because, as we have already said, they refer to particular historical circumstances and do not contain any elements that would tend to confirm the vision or the theology of the groups that existed after his death. Indeed, they reflect a vision of the "end" that is similar to the vision attributed to John the Baptizer.

As anthropological studies of catastrophes suggest, Jesus' eschatological vision was based on the perception of risk. He believed that sinners would very soon be punished, because the cosmic catastrophe from

The Body of Jesus and the Healings

One important point is that all the Gospel narratives attribute to Jesus the power to heal.[51] This ability is the background or the paradigmatic structure on which the relationships between the body of Jesus and the bodies of other persons are often constructed. However, a clear explanation of Jesus' powers is not supplied by the thaumaturgic paradigm on its own, that is, by the assertion that Jesus was a person endowed with the power to accomplish extraordinary deeds. In general, thaumaturgic abilities are not obvious per se, but remain hidden. It is easier, however, to understand such abilities in the context of a discourse that employs the metaphor of the "power" (*dynamis*) inherent in the body or the metaphor of the exorcist, who "expels" demons. People recognized that the body of Jesus had the ability to heal and to liberate. When the Gospels speak of miraculous healings, they give a certain amount of space to his gestures, which are always sober and restrained. We do not find the grandiose scenarios or the complex ceremonies that sometimes accompany prodigies of healing; what we are told is that Jesus was accustomed to lay on hands, to touch, and to use his own saliva.[52] In the Gospel of Mark,[53] similar and repetitive narrative frameworks are employed to speak of those who seek healing or the liberation of their bodies: "All who had diseases pressed upon him to touch him" (3:10); "And all who touched him [or: his cloak] were healed" (6:56; cf. Matt 14:36). Sometimes people throng around him and nearly crush him in the hope of finding help, because "he had healed many." We have spoken above of the bodily actions with which Jesus healed a man who was deaf and dumb (Mark 7:32-33). He used different actions when he healed Simon's mother-in-law, who was ill with a fever: "He came and took her by the hand and lifted her up. Then the fever left her, and she began to serve them" (Mark 1:31).

On all these occasions, the central point is the physical contact with Jesus' body. There are also healings "at a distance" where he heals the body of a person who is distant, as in the case of the centurion's servant (Matt 8:5-13; Luke 7:1-11). Sometimes, Jesus healed with a command, that is, with his will alone. However, the fact that the Gospels speak of healings without direct contact should not obscure the large number of cases in which the body of Jesus is the physical instrument of the healing.

The exorcisms in which Jesus drove out the negative spirits without touching the bodies of those possessed cannot be seen independently of the metaphorical explanations of the power of the body and of the exorcistic action. The power over the spirits, which Jesus attributed in one instance to prayer (Mark 9:29), implies that the exorcist has dominion over his own body.[54] And this brings us back to the specific corporality of Jesus, which is at the center of the miracle stories.

Some episodes make it clear how Jesus performed the healings. The Synoptic Gospels relate how he was involved in one healing only by means of his corporality, quite apart from any intention of his own (Mark 5:23-31; Matt 19:18-26; Luke 8:40-56). A woman suffering from hemorrhages has heard about Jesus, "and she came up behind him in the crowd and touched his cloak. . . . Immediately aware that power [*dynamis*] had gone forth from him, Jesus turned about in the crowd and said, 'Who touched my clothes?' And his disciples said to him, 'You see the crowd pressing in on you; how can you say, "Who touched me?"'" (Mark 5:23-31; cf. Luke 8:45). This scene makes it abundantly clear that the body of Jesus was thought capable of unleashing and communicating a special energy that was contained in his physical dimension.[55] We find the same idea in Luke's Gospel, where Jesus says: "I noticed that power had gone out from me" (8:46). This episode was presented by Mark as a typical example of what happened when people thronged around Jesus; and Luke states on another occasion that "All in the crowd were trying to touch him, for power came out from him and healed all of them" (6:19). Let us repeat that the decisive element is the use of touch. The words "Who touched me?" show clearly that the evangelists held that Jesus' body possessed healing power. Unless it is reached physically, it does not unleash its effects upon others. In other words, Jesus was not only a charismatic preacher, but a man who brought about prodigious transmissions of power from one body to another.

Luke, however, insists that Jesus voluntarily touched the bodies he wanted to heal. In the case of the leper, "he stretched out his hand and touched him" (5:13); and he intentionally touched the bier of the dead boy (7:14). Similarly, he touched the wounded ear of the high priest's servant, thus allowing his own power to reach another body (22:51). Here, the metaphors of power and of the flowing forth of power from the body are combined.

In these narratives, the real body of Jesus is in some way hidden and as it were turned into a metaphor by his healing power; its presence in these stories is almost implicit. Some people seek to touch the body of Jesus in the hope of a transfer of thaumaturgic energy. Touching implies a systemic continuity between two bodies that have different endowments but belong to each other by virtue of their substantial contiguity. The connection is established, and the identification or conjunction between them that is envisaged by the relationship between curing and healing takes place. The power that dwells in the body of the thaumaturge is transmitted to the weak and imperfect body and cancels its imperfection. Here, the body heals by contact.

The Gospels seem to explain bodily healings by physical contact and exorcisms in different ways. In exorcism the alienation caused by the illness is overcome by expelling the impure spirit that has made the person ill.[56] The same applies to adorcism, the invocation of a good spirit that is to descend into a person's body. In the bodily healings, on the contrary, there is a physical power or energy (of a supernatural kind) that is communicated to the imperfect body and restores it to the state of wholeness. In both cases the explanation uses the metaphor of transferring a power. We can see elementary physiological codifications in this metaphor of the body that receives and transmits; this metaphor generates a repertoire of bodily actions that are intended to restore abilities and well-being to the body after a dysfunctional period. Those who go to Jesus are not asking for medicines or for some particular ritual. All they want is to connect their own body to the body of Jesus.

How far is this image of the body of Jesus in the Synoptic Gospels historical? At the close of his study of the miracle traditions in the Gospel of Mark, Barry Blackburn concludes that this tradition does not depend on groups of followers of Jesus from a Hellenistic milieu who projected onto him at a late date the image of the so-called *theios anēr*. Rather, the roots are to be found in the most ancient Judean tradition in the Land of Israel, passed on by the historical disciples who were present at Jesus' healings. But does the image that the first disciples had of him correspond to the historical reality of Jesus?

The extreme complexity of this question is well illustrated by the episode in which a transformation or transfiguration took place in Jesus' body without any apparent voluntary act on his part (Mark 9:1-17; Luke 9:28-36; Matt 17:1-9). Jesus ascended a mountain accompanied by only three disciples, Peter, James, and John, whom he had chosen to be initiated into a remarkable experience.[57] On the peak of the mountain, Jesus encountered Moses and Elijah,[58] who came from the supernatural world and appeared to him when Jesus has already been transformed: "He was transfigured . . . and his clothes became dazzling white" (as Mark and Matthew write). Matthew and Luke also speak of the splendor of his face. Matthew writes: "His face shone like the sun," while Luke states: "The appearance of his face changed."⁵⁹ Luke's text does not speak specifically of the "face" but of "the appearance [*eidos*] of the face [*prosōpon*]," probably in order to emphasize that his facial expression changed; the other physical features seem to remain unaltered. Luke avoids the term "metamorphosis," since what happens to Jesus here is not the same as the phenomena of bodily transformation that were spoken of in the classical world.⁶⁰

The Gospels thus display a further quality of the body of Jesus: the fact that it (or at least, its face) is capable of transfiguration. This adds a sense of mystery and exceptionality to his person. It is certainly not irrelevant to note that the evangelists speak explicitly of his face, since it is this that gives individuality to the physical body. Similarly, it is not by chance that they mention his garments, since these give a visible form to the bodily features of Jesus. Taken together, the changed face and the splendid garments bestow an unequivocal individuality on his entire person; Jesus is, therefore, described by means of changes to his body.⁶¹ In Mark, a total metamorphosis takes place, but in Luke it is only the face that changes (perhaps because Jesus is seen here in an attitude of prayer).

In their accounts of the transfiguration of Jesus, the Gospels do not speak about his interior attitude but only about his body. The change of appearance does not seem to be due to an emotional impulse, nor is it linked to mental states such as desire, fear, joy, or irritation. The power that takes hold of the body of Jesus is manifested only in the splendor of his body, but it is not clear whether this comes from an internal or an external light. The two prophetic figures are mysteriously oriented to the body of Jesus. During the entire episode of the transfiguration, he remains an earthly being with recognizable physical features. He continues to be the Jesus whom the disciples know. He is silent and listens to what the two prophets say. At the close, he himself speaks to the disciples, consoling them and giving them courage. His gestures and his outward appearance confirm that he is alive. In the view of the evangelists, what is perhaps the most extraordinary event in the life of Jesus, his physical contact with the supernatural world, is manifested completely in his body.

With the exception of the miracles and the transfiguration, the authors of the Gospels never say that the body of Jesus presents an unusual appearance. It does not experience heavenly journeys, nor does it possess ubiquity. In general, it behaves normally. It is true that at the beginning of his public life, Jesus is in the desert and is tempted by Satan. He is transported to the pinnacle of the Temple, and then to a very high mountain. But according to the Gospels of Mark, Luke, and Matthew, it is Satan, not Jesus' own body, that does all this.

The presumed normality of Jesus' body is, however, negated by the episode in which he walked on the water of the Sea of Galilee. The scenery is the lake with its surrounding countryside, as so often in the Gospels. The disciples cross the lake in a boat, and it is now that the supernatural powers of Jesus are revealed in the form of an extreme physical lightness: "When evening came, the boat was out on the sea, and he was alone on the land. When he saw that they were straining at the oars against an adverse wind, he came towards them early in the morning, walking on the sea. He intended to pass them by. . . . But immediately he spoke to them and said, 'Take heart, it is I; do not be afraid'" (Mark 6:47-50).

The thaumaturgic power of Jesus, the splendor of the transfiguration, and the ability to walk on the water are interconnected elements that form one single picture. Nevertheless, they do not eliminate the perception that Jesus has a normal body. They do not communicate the idea that his body is different or remote from that of human beings.

We believe that we are right in saying that both Jesus and the people who seek him perceive his body as the principal place where his experience has its origin and the place where his fate is manifested and unfolds. It is a normal body, but freed of the preoccupation with food and clothing and with social appearances. At the same time, this body is absolutely unique, because it is full of a thaumaturgic, radiant, purifying *dynamis*. The political authorities understand this well, and their strategy is to attack the body of Jesus, degrading its public image and putting an end to its human work. The outcome is completely clear: it was in the risen body that his followers saw his victory.

Through the way he lived and through the message he communicated, all that Jesus did was to invite people to seek God. But the people, attracted by the power of his body, sought his extraordinary person. The people were in search of him.

7

JESUS AND EMOTION

Feelings and Desires

How Do We Get to Know the Inner Life of Jesus?

Our intention in this chapter is not to answer the question Jesus puts to his disciples "Who do people say that I am?" nor the question "Who did Jesus himself think he was?" We want to find out something about Jesus' feelings, about his reactions to the situation of his people and his land. In short, we want to learn something about his inner life.

Getting to know the most intimate aspects of a person is always an extremely arduous task, even in the case of our own contemporaries. In the case of Jesus, the task is made more complicated by the fact that (as we have mentioned several times) the available documents relate the life story of Jesus many decades afterward, on the basis of written and oral testimony from his followers or from persons who had contact with them. We have many times recalled that it is not possible to verify historically the circumstances of time and place in which Jesus delivered his discourses or performed his most memorable actions. To reconstruct the way in which Jesus perceived his own experiences, therefore, does not seem possible. The only correct and safe approach is to reformulate the question as follows: What did the evangelists think about the emotions and feelings of Jesus? This question has often been overlooked by exegetes, but it is both legitimate and highly useful.

The Cultural Meanings of Emotions

In order to understand better how the Gospels interpreted the interior life of Jesus, it is essential to grasp the nature of feelings and emotions in a particular context of meanings and values, and how influential they are both in the construction of a person's identity and in relationships among individuals.

There have been many discussions of the meaning of the word "emotion."[1] Here, we take into consideration not only the emotions and feelings, but also the will, the aspirations, and conscious longings—the entire complex of interior states of mind and reactions. The theoretical basis of our analysis is a type of anthropological research that regards personal and intimate emotions as generated by relationships between subjects.[2]

The interior life of an individual is a reaction both to the stimuli that come from the external environment and to the person's relationship to this environment. Desires and feelings are generated by these relationships, or are dependent on them. In order to explore such feelings, therefore, we must begin by studying models of interaction between individuals in all the variety of their concrete contexts.[3] And since emotions and feelings are always expressed visibly, reflection on them must take account of their bodily manifestations in looks, sounds, gestures, and movements. The emotions transpose the individual into a dimension involving the body that is altered and sometimes disturbing. The emotions construct intimate and deep perceptions that manifest themselves in corporality.[4] Various cultures identify different points within the body as the seat and origin of emotional attitudes. It is only secondarily and in a complementary manner that the emotions belong to the realm of thinking.

In every culture, relationships between individuals generate actions and reactions with emotional outcomes that can be perceived and interpreted. But the perception and interpretation of these emotional states (for example, suffering or comfort) necessarily presuppose shared patterns of behavior. The emotions are not simply congenital biological facts. They are cultural products and constructions that give expression to a strong desire for recognition and belonging. Franz Boas argues that they are the outcome of the form taken by our social life and by the history of the group to which we belong.[5] The emotional state can be induced by moral or religious conventions, whether freely chosen or imposed by others. It can be elaborated in sophisticated ways so as to become uncontrollable, or, on the contrary, it can be controlled or denied by ideas about personal decorum, good manners, aesthetic requirements, or taboos. The emotions in the depths of the person can be covered over and reined in by rigid or repressive customs that alter individual needs. In every culture, the positive or negative connotation

Jesus and Emotion

of the various emotions and the consequent models of expression alert us to the presence of symbolic worlds full of light and shade, and imply a bodily condition that is infinitely variable.[6] The archipelago of emotional phenomena is so vast that no generalization is acceptable.[7]

It is on the basis of these reflections that we look at the specific modes of expression employed by Jesus, to see how the evangelists envisage his internal reactions to the situations he encountered.[8]

Jesus' itinerant lifestyle uprooted him from customary relationships to his own household and to those of other persons, and he met many people in situations in which the normal rules governing relationships were modified. This permitted a variety of inner reactions both in Jesus and in others. If we look at the specific situations in which Jesus displayed anger or compassion, this may allow us to grasp how he evaluated the world in which he lived. It will show us what he would have liked to change, and what he wanted his followers to learn with regard to feelings and longings.

We cannot limit our investigation to those passages in which the evangelists explicitly attribute feelings and emotions to Jesus. More commonly, his reaction is manifested through his actions. For example, the fig tree that bears no fruit was immediately cursed, but we are not told anything about the emotional reaction that led Jesus to utter the words: "May no one ever eat fruit from you again!" (Mark 11:14). And when Jesus said about Judas, "Woe to the man by whom the Son of Man is betrayed!" (Luke 22:22), we may legitimately suppose that the curse was generated by an interior emotion that is not mentioned by the evangelists. On another occasion, Jesus remained serene when his opponents set a trap for him. He merely asked, "Why are you putting me to the test?" (Mark 12:15). In fact, control over one's emotions follows a behavioral codex that varies from one culture to another. A greater or lesser abnormality in a person's conduct within one particular social model is an indirect means of expressing feelings that are molded and imposed by a specific culture. In this way, even where feelings are not mentioned explicitly, a text may in fact be attributing feelings to Jesus by describing a gesture on his part.

Jesus' Compassion

Mark's Gospel relates an occasion when many people gathered together but had nothing to eat. Jesus called his disciples and told them: "I have compassion [*splanchnizomai*] for the crowd, because they have been with me now for three days and have nothing to eat. If I send them away hungry to their homes, they will faint on the way—and some of them have come from a great distance" (8:1-3). Jesus revealed his state of mind in unequivocal terms: he felt compassion. But the word "compassion" is not a good rendering of the Greek verb that Mark employs. The noun *splanchnon* designates the bowels, which were regarded as the origin of feelings and emotions. It evokes the center of human corporality, which is the vital source of interior emotions. The verb *splanchnizomai* is employed to express the intensity of the states of mind that are envisaged as profound upheavals within the body. The mentality that we encounter here involves a high degree of embodiment of emotional states. The body is the expressive subject of these emotions, not merely a "container" for them.

Jesus' compassion is communicated by the words he addressed to the disciples in a tense situation of human need. He feared for the crowd, who were exposed to danger, and he sought to help them. Mark 8:2-3 gives no authorial description of Jesus' feelings. Jesus' compassion, generated by his awareness that so many people were in great need, was affirmed explicitly by his own words. Here, "compassion" is a feeling that presupposes both an intense sympathy and a desire to act. Jesus feared that the people might die, and he acted to satisfy the hunger of those who had been faithfully following him "now for three days."

There is a further element in this narrative: when he expressed his sympathy with a crowd in difficulty, Jesus communicated his own feelings to his disciples in order to urge them to act. He made them aware of what they ought to do. Mark uses the verb *splanchnizomai* to define an "upheaval" in Jesus that generated his action. This verb shows us how Mark envisaged the intimate motivations of Jesus.[9] Here is the point: if behavior is to be changed, there must be a prior change in a person's interior attitude and in his or her way of reacting to situations.

This attempt by Jesus to involve the disciples displays a fundamental mechanism of instruction and of the transmission of teaching. Jesus showed and taught the interior reactions that ought to be cultivated and stimulated in relation to the crowds. He endeavored to arouse those feelings that would lead to good conduct. As we shall see, he also endeavored to check those feelings that have reprehensible consequences. In other words, Jesus not only sheds light on his own inner life. He reveals his emotion in order to get others to share it and to take an active attitude toward other people.

In the episode of the leper, related at Mark 1:40-44, Jesus' decision to heal was prompted by a feeling of compassion. The narrative is not reduced to Jesus' words. He seemed so deeply shaken by his emotion that he stretched out his hand and touched the sick man—the interior feeling of pity is revealed by his body. The exchange of words with the sick man revealed something of their states of mind. The sick man longed for healing, but he honored the rules governing respect and appropriate conduct, and said only, "If you wish" (1:40). Jesus replied: "I do wish [*thelō*]." The dialogue plays on the verb "to wish/long for" (*thelō*) and underlines the interior emotion and intention. The leper appealed to Jesus, and we see from his gesture of touching the sick man that Jesus was moved. We are far removed here from automatic miracle working.[10] Mark underlines the fact that Jesus' emotions have a concrete outcome: the need to give help to others.

Anxiety and Sadness

The Gospels of Mark and Matthew present various emotions and internal experiences of Jesus in the scene in the Garden of Olives. He prayed in an alarming situation, immediately after the Last Supper. After they had eaten, discussed with one another, and sung hymns, the followers of Jesus were isolated and a prey to anxiety. They were aware of the danger that threatened. Jesus predicted that they "will all be scandalized" (Mark 14:27); the verb *skandalizomai* means literally "to be taken in a trap." Peter vigorously protested against Jesus' prediction (14:29) and declared that he was ready to die with him rather than deny him (14:31); his companions said the same. In this scene, Jesus is the absolute protagonist: it is he who gave the commands, who made the decisions, who explained, and who then prayed. He told his disciples to take their places in the Garden of Olives: "Sit here while I pray" (14:32). He showed his concern for them and revealed his knowledge of their state of mind. He did not ask them to pray; all they were to do was to wait while he tackled the situation alone. While he was going to pray, he decided (apparently on the spur of the moment) to take three of his disciples with him. At this point, his emotions became intense: "He took with him Peter and James and John, and began to be distressed [*ekthambeō*] and agitated [*adēmoneō*]" (14:33). *Ekthambeō* designates the state of alarm, of being taken by surprise, overwhelmed, or terrified. It indicates a profound change that may be due to an unforeseen event or to uncertainty about what is going to happen. In early Christian literature, this verb was used only by Mark. In another passage (9:15), the crowd was upset, excited, when Jesus appeared unexpectedly. They were taken aback when they saw the one for whom they had been waiting so long. Similarly, the women who entered Jesus' tomb were deeply moved when they saw a young man sitting there (16:5). Mark employs a similar verb, *thambeō*, to express the state of anxiety and concern of Jesus' followers in view of the difficult situation that awaited them in Jerusalem (10:32) and to express the amazement and astonishment of those who witnessed the exorcism performed by Jesus in the synagogue (1:27). The *Gospel of Thomas* attributes to Jesus a saying that sheds light on the various phases of the spiritual life: "Jesus says: The one who seeks should not cease seeking until he finds, and when he finds, he will be astounded, and when he is astounded, he will reign, and when he will reign he will rest."[11] The verb employed to express "amazement" (if this fragmentary text is interpreted correctly) is *thambeō*.[12] The same saying is found in the *Gospel of the Hebrews*, which however employs the verb *thaumazō* ("to be astonished").[13] The striking point in this teaching is that "amazement" is not evaluated negatively: it is simply one phase of spiritual progress, a stage that must be left behind in order to finally attain the interior peace expressed by the verb "to rest" (*anapauomai*). This saying, which is transmitted by two very different Gospel traditions, makes it likely that Jesus taught his disciples about how to react emotionally to various situations in life. He would have shown them how he understood the emotions and helped them to employ their own emotions in order to attain the higher levels of the interior life.

Let us return to the scene in the Garden of Olives. In the presence of his three followers, Jesus declared: "I am deeply grieved, even to death; remain here, and keep awake" (Mark 14:34). Jesus did not communicate his sadness to all his disciples and that he felt mortally wounded by it, but only to those whom he had chosen to share this experience. The exhortation to "keep awake" underlines his distress and shows that he is aware that this moment is crucial. It is now that he throws himself on the ground and prays (14:35). At that period, Judeans practiced prostration only in the strictly personal prayer in which they brought their individual lives before God. They stood together with others for the obligatory and institutional prayer for the needs of the whole community. The individual ritual action implies a situation of interior agitation, anxiety, and sadness. On this occasion, Jesus decided to pray in a particularly intense and individual manner. The evangelists describe not only the emotional state of Jesus, but the situation that prompted this state and the response that he chose to make to it, namely, prayer.

Matthew seems not to like the verb *ekthambeō*, "to be moved deeply," which he found in Mark's text. He prefers *lypeomai* (Matt 26:37), which means "to be saddened, to experience pain, to be afflicted." The difference between the two Gospel narratives is the subtle but relevant distinction between the state of agitation (in Mark) and the feeling of pain and sadness (in Matthew). Both evangelists emphasize that Jesus was tense, and they agree in employing the verb *adēmoneō*, which means "to be anxious." It is possible that Matthew wanted to avoid the verb *ekthambeō* because of its implicit nuances. It suggests agitation and uncertainty in the face of something unknown, something surprising; but Matthew prefers "sadness," because this feeling presupposes that Jesus knew what made him sad—and this in turn means that he was not taken by surprise.

Indignation and Anger

Another situation in which we see Jesus' emotions is the episode in which he met a group of children. He embraced them and blessed them, and he rebuked his own disciples when they tried to prevent this direct contact.[14] Taking children in one's arms entails more than just looking at them or talking to them. This gesture is much more powerful and communicative, since it clearly reveals a person's emotional state. The people wanted Jesus to welcome their children by means of a physical gesture of contact that would transmit his beneficent power, and this is what he did. The children were not in fact sick, so they did not need to be freed from illnesses: presumably, the parents wanted Jesus to embrace them in order that the power they attributed to him might be transmitted to the children, or that this power might protect them and keep them healthy. Like Mark, Matthew does not speak of healings here. All he says is that Jesus "lays on hands." This is a formal gesture signifying protection, rather than an act of welcoming the children.

The interesting point here is that Jesus' followers rebuked the adults and tried to stop them from bringing their children to him. They probably wanted to protect Jesus (cf. Mark 3:30), but he reacted with an outburst of indignation when he "saw" this behavior (Mark 10:14). The Gospels affirm in other words that in certain circumstances Jesus could not bear any interference by others (not even by his own disciples) that would distort the meaning of what he was doing. His indignation was caused by the obstacles that they were putting in the way of his action, and by their inability to understand it. Here too, Jesus' reaction to a situation—namely, his instruction about the importance of children in the kingdom of God—was generated by an interior emotion.

It is important to note that Mark underlines Jesus' indignation, while Luke and Matthew avoid mentioning it.[15] In Mark, the emotional reactions of Jesus emphasize the importance of what he must do. They shed light on his person and on the goals of his activity.[16] Jesus' activity on behalf of other people was generated by his interior state.

The Power of Silence

There are various degrees of silence, and it has various outcomes. Sometimes silence is suffered passively, and at other times it has an "active" dimension, when people fall ostentatiously silent. Silence can also be experienced as a threat, as something to be feared. As David Le Breton has written, the desire for silence reveals the search for peace, for a favorable place in which one can settle down. Loud noise is the mortal enemy of the moral attitude that is manifested in this longing for silence.[17] Silence allows us to reflect on our own intentions and to concentrate on the decisions that are to be taken. Both keeping silent and measuring out the words one says involve wisdom.

Mark's narrative gives a particular emphasis to Jesus' silence during his trial. An anthropology of silence can help us understand the feelings that Mark attributes to Jesus here. Le Breton writes that "silence is a path that leads to one's own self" and "heightens one's awareness of being alive." It underlines a moment of "emptying" that allows one to rediscover one's inner unity and to make difficult decisions.

Jesus is silent in order to come to rest in himself. His silent body is an eloquent challenge to those who accuse him and interrogate him. He is silent and offers no explanation before the Sanhedrin when false and discordant testimonies pile up against him (Mark 14:56-59). He defends himself by retreating within himself. This reaction provoked the high priest to move into the center of the assembly and interrogate him in person: "Have you no answer?" (14:60). "But he was silent and did not answer" (Mark 14:61; Matt 26:63). Mark does not think that Jesus lacked all emotions at this point, or that he did not know what to reply. Mark sees this silence as a deliberate choice: Jesus does not wish to communicate his own feelings or reasonings. And silence is often motivated by the conviction that one ought really to be talking about completely different things.

This emotionally rich scene paints a powerful picture of Jesus as an authoritative figure who is completely enclosed in silence. Here, keeping silent means taking a stance and giving an answer. Silence allows Jesus to escape the clutches of others. They cannot influence him in any way, since he makes it impossible for anyone to manipulate his words. It is he who controls and dominates the situation and prepares to utter the final and decisive words. His silence simply ignores the tendentious accusations and creates the conditions for his final answer to the high priest, when he will declare that he is the Messiah (Mark 14:62). His silence allows Jesus to express all the emotional richness of his affirmation: "I am; and you will see the Son of Man seated at the right hand of the Power, and coming with the clouds of heaven" (Mark 14:62). If Jesus had gotten involved in a debate with his untrustworthy enemies, his last words would certainly not have had the same significance and power. It is possible that when Mark highlights the transition from silence to speaking, he also intends to highlight a change in the tension within Jesus himself,[18] who moves from docile endurance to the prophetical impetus.

The Problems Involved in Leave Taking

Every human relationship is an intermezzo between drawing near and parting, between a meeting and a farewell. The wealth of personal emotions involved in a parting makes it particularly interesting. Jesus often had to take leave of the crowds, and the evangelists sometimes agree in placing a special emphasis on this moment of parting. The agreement of the tradition may make it possible to get back to the authentic attitude of Jesus.

His meetings with people often take place in a way that breaks with the usual customs: a sick man is let down through a hole in the roof; a woman of ill repute draws near to Jesus in a house that she had never entered before; a huge crowd gathers out in the open fields, and so on. These encounters may be brief and transitory, but they are very intense; and this leads us to ask what emotions were generated when Jesus took leave of the crowds. The beginning of a relationship brings the hope of a change, of something out of the ordinary run of things; but the parting breaks off these expectations, since it implies that one is sent back to the normality that was briefly interrupted, back into a time when nothing new can be expected. Although a door may remain open, the parting puts an end (sometimes painful, sometimes undesired) to a pleasant situation. After a moment of intense closeness and getting to know one another, the parting leaves a profound mark on those who have met.

Taking leave puts an end to being together. Is it possible that Jesus felt some strong emotion when he parted from the crowds? Can we reconstruct what Jesus felt when the fluid group of individuals who were interested in him went their separate ways after he had taken leave of them? And can we reconstruct what the crowd felt?

In some cases, Jesus met a person and wanted to keep him with him; in other cases, he sent away people who would have liked to stay with him. The moment of separation was sometimes acutely unpleasant.

The crowds who flocked together were composed of persons who followed converging paths on one occasion or for a certain period, but then went their separate ways. When Jesus took leave of them after a more or less lengthy encounter, they reacted emotionally both to this parting and to the return to normal life in their own domestic environment. This process influences the feelings of Jesus too. As we have seen, his primary reaction when he takes leave of the people is compassion. Those who cannot follow Jesus in his radically itinerant lifestyle must be sent back to their own homes. This is the moment in which suffering, compassion, courage, or patient endurance may visibly emerge.

Is it conceivable that Jesus intended to return to meet once again the people from whom he had taken leave? It seems unlikely that this was his intention, or that he suggested that he would visit the place again. It is much more probable that he believed that he had done what was necessary and that he had to move on to another place—and this is exactly what the Gospels tell us.

In the episode of the distribution of the loaves and fishes, Mark emphasizes both the moment when Jesus welcomed the crowd and the moment when he sent them away. A crowd of people who had left their own homes, an unstructured gathering, came to Jesus. Mark relates that Jesus saw their lack of organization and arranged them in groups (6:39-40). He took leave of them in two phases (6:45-46). First of all, Jesus sent the disciples away, making them get into the boat and cross to the other shore ahead of him. This suggests that the disciples did not want to leave him alone, where he may be at the mercy of the crowd. Once he was left alone, Jesus sent the crowd away (the verb used here is *apolyō*) and took his leave of them (the verb used here is *apotassō*, "to depart, bid farewell"). These two verbs express the two directions of the parting of the ways: in a quite literal sense, Jesus and the crowd went in opposite directions. The people returned to where they came from, while Jesus followed his own path and ascended the mountain to pray. Mark does not give a full description of Jesus' leave taking; no parting words are recorded. Matthew writes only that Jesus sent the crowd away; he did not speak of the leave taking as such.[19] It is possible that John knew Mark's narrative and that he attributed a particular significance to the fact that it was Jesus who departed from the crowd, rather than the crowd that left Jesus. John writes that Jesus withdrew—indeed, that he fled—from the crowd who wanted to make him king (John 6:15).

At any rate, Mark's narrative, which Matthew takes over, insists that he wanted to be alone when he took leave of the crowd, and this indicates a closer relationship between Jesus and the people than one might at first suppose. No one dictates what Jesus must do here. It is he who initiated the contact and who closed it, and the power of his personality was at the center of the leave taking. At crucial moments, he chose to be alone when he gave full expression to what he felt about the people.

In other episodes in the Gospels, Jesus takes leave of individuals. The emphasis here is on the transformation of their existence by the encounter with Jesus, and the narratives implicitly let the reader understand the personal emotions of those involved.

We find one instance of this personal leave taking in Luke, when Jesus healed a man possessed by demons. He wanted to remain with Jesus, but he was told: "Return to your home, and declare how much God has done for you" (Luke 8:39). Not content with freeing him from his state of possession, Jesus restored him with a new hope to a normal situation, to the home where he could live at last, now that he was cured. Luke also underlines that after Jesus has cured a man suffering from dropsy, he "sent him away" (14:4). For Luke, as for Mark, every encounter on Jesus' part concludes with a leave taking, a formal act of sending a person away.

A feeling of deep pity is expressed in Matthew's parable of the king who feels compassion for the sad fate of an insolvent debtor. Although he could have forced the man to work to repay his debt, "out of pity for him, the lord of that slave let him go him and forgave him the debt" (18:27). The element of pity and its meaning are well expressed by the words "let him go": the man was allowed to retain his liberty. Could this parable reflect the feelings of Jesus himself? The story certainly affirms that the king's compassion has brought about a "conversion" in him, making him see the situation in a new light. And this compassion has an important consequence: a man was set free; he was allowed to go.

When Jesus meets people, the final moment of the encounter can have one of two consequences, either the decision to join Jesus and follow him or to return to one's own home. The feelings and expectations kindled by the moment of parting may vary, but they are always significant. In some meetings with individuals, Jesus seems to express an attitude of reserve, since he does not want his miracles to cause a commotion. His primary desire is that those whom he has healed or instructed should return to their homes in good health or in a condition of trust. After their encounter with Jesus, who has brought about healing and conversion, they will not only experience being separated from him. They will also feel strengthened by their hope in the kingdom of God. It is not impossible that these moments of separation are the very first context that generated the hope that Christ would return, a hope that has such deep roots in the earliest Christian faith and in the liturgy celebrated by Jesus' followers after his death (1 Cor 16:22; Rev 22:20).

WILL, DESIRE, DECISION

The "will," in the sense of a desire for a goal that one wishes to attain, is expressed in the Gospels by the verb *thelō*.[20] The verb *boulomai*, which designates the "will" in the sense of a decision that one takes, is used less frequently with regard to Jesus (cf. Matt 11:27; Luke 10:22). But we should not insist too much on these linguistic distinctions. What counts are the concrete episodes that the Gospels describe and the personal relationships that they depict. Our hypothesis is that it is possible to identify a number of nuances of the longing or will of Jesus.

Some passages relate Jesus' desire to avoid the drama of a violent death, as when he prays: "Remove this cup from me" (Luke 22:42). He immediately, however, subordinates his own aspirations to the will of God: "Yet, not my will but yours be done." His personal desire is expressed and then immediately disavowed. Indeed, the expression of his personal will serves only to emphasize his renunciation. The entire episode is based on the awareness by Mark, Luke, and Matthew that it is possible for the longing or will of Jesus to differ from that of God. The dramatic quality of the scene depends on the implicit contrast between Jesus and God, which is resolved in a sublime manner when Jesus submits to the supreme value, namely, to the decision of God.

The center of the narrative thus consists of two opposed wills. The synoptic evangelists think that Jesus initially envisaged a different outcome, and this fact is extraordinarily important for their interpretation of the life of Jesus. The words of his prayer presuppose that he thought that an outcome other than his arrest and death was possible. According to Mark, echoed by Luke and Matthew, Jesus says: "Father, for you all things are possible; remove this cup from me."[21] He seems to hope that the divine omnipotence can open up other paths for him, and he entrusts his last dramatic hopes to the infinite possibilities of God.

Nevertheless, Jesus is firmly resolved to accept the ineluctability of the will of God. "*As* you want" (Matt 26:39) and "what you want" (Mark 14:36) constitute the boundary within which Jesus' emotions find expression.[22] The words Jesus speaks look like a rhetorical device on the part of the evangelists, intended to exalt the divine element and illuminate the fruitfulness of Jesus' response: he regards the divine will as perfect and as necessary, no matter what this will may be. The Gospels do not imagine Jesus making any alternative suggestion of his own—God alone can determine if any other outcome is in fact possible. The only aspiration on the part of Jesus is that God may remove the "cup" from him, but only if this would not thwart the divine plans.

In the three Synoptic Gospels, this episode clearly assumes that although Jesus wishes for a different outcome, he in fact knows in advance what is to happen to him.[23] The disconcerting power of this scene derives from the idea that Jesus already knows perfectly well that God has made a decision that runs contrary to his own desires, and this disturbs him and prompts him to pray. The Gospels think that it is useful to express this drama in words of prayer.

John's conception of the desire and the will of Jesus seems far remote from that of Mark, Luke, and Matthew. John has eliminated the scene in the Garden of Olives. Jesus does not address any request to God on his own behalf on the eve of the dramatic final act, and there is no trace of any opposition to what awaits him or of any preoccupation about his fate. The will of Jesus is always that of the Father. He cannot desire anything that will not happen, because he knows beforehand what will take place. For John, therefore, there is no place in Jesus for any desires that do not agree with those of God. He presents a completely different type of prayer to God, while Jesus is still in the building where the Last Supper has just been eaten. The Johannine Jesus does not pray for himself. He prays that, in the future, his followers may come to where he will be, in the same "glory" that he possesses. This request expresses a desire on his part: "I desire (*thelō*) that those also, whom you have given me, may be with me where I am, to see my glory, which you have given me" (John 17:24). And this will certainly happen, because the desire of Jesus is the perfect expression of the desire of God.

Unlike John, the other evangelists sometimes portray Jesus' disappointment or discontent when the opposition of others thwarts the realization of his desires. The synoptic evangelists see a distance between what Jesus wants and what actually occurs. One example is the words he addressed to Jerusalem: "How often have I desired [*ethelēsa*] to gather your children together . . . but you were not willing!" (Luke 13:34; Matt 27:37). Jesus' expectation or desire was not fulfilled, and he regretted this setback.

On one occasion, related only by Luke, the disciples James and John wanted to know whether Jesus intended to punish a Samaritan village that was unwilling to receive them: "Lord, do you want [*theleis*] us to command fire to come from heaven and consume them?"[24] This question presupposes that the disciples wondered about Jesus' deep feelings and intentions. James and John appear to be suggesting that Jesus follow a religious model in which those who behave badly are punished through the use of a prophet's supernatural power. The narrative indicates that the disciples were aware that Jesus acted on the basis of a desire that they often failed to comprehend. Jesus was a man whose actions were generated by ideas that were hidden from the others and were hard to grasp. His followers would have liked to get to know these ideas, but they found it difficult to penetrate the inner life of Jesus.

In another episode related by Mark, Luke, and Matthew, Jesus wondered about the thoughts and judgments of other people. He wanted to know what people thought he was, and how they assessed the meaning of his presence among them: "Who do people say that I am?" (Mark 8:27). Jesus put the same question to his disciples. When Peter replied, "You are the Messiah," Jesus revealed his desire that this disciples' conviction should not be communicated to others. This passage shows that Jesus wondered about thoughts and intentions that he did not know (Matt 16:13; Luke 9:18). It is difficult to be sure whether Jesus' question expresses a genuine desire, and whether the evangelists believed he was in fact ignorant of what other people thought about him; one can argue in favor of either hypothesis. It is conceivable that Jesus merely pretended not to know, in order to lead his disciples to find the right answer. It is also possible that the entire scene is a narrative expedient, intended to show that the people did not understand who Jesus really was, and that only the disciples (and especially Peter) were able to grasp this. Another possibility is that the narrative is constructed in such a way that the declaration of Peter, "You are the Messiah," is addressed both to Jesus and to the other disciples. In Matthew, Peter's confession is a revelation that God has granted him. In Luke, it is prepared by Jesus' prayer. Here, Jesus is genuinely looking for information that concerns his own person.

"I HAVE COME IN ORDER TO . . .":
JESUS EXPRESSES HIS DESIRE AND HIS INTERIOR PASSION

Two sayings of Jesus show us what Luke thought about Jesus' feelings with regard to his own person and his destiny. These words undeniably communicate an absolute certainty about his task and a firm desire to carry it out, but at the same time they also express expectancy, anguish, hope, and urgency. Jesus declared: "I came to bring fire to the earth, and how I wish it were already kindled! I have a baptism with which to be baptized, and what stress I am under until it is completed!"[25] Luke's Jesus states what he regarded as his task and the conception that he had of himself when he expressed the desire that his project may be realized quickly and completely. At the same time, however, he expressed his awareness that this had not yet happened. This saying illustrates a discontinuity between project and reality. Jesus anxiously awaits the realization, and this expectation kindles and unleashes his passionate eagerness for what is to come. Similarly, the core of the words recorded in the *Gospel of Thomas*—"I have cast fire upon the world, and see, I am guarding it until it blazes"[26]—is the hope of a future and rapid realization that no one will be able to overlook.

A second saying—"What stress I am under until it is completed!"—expresses Jesus' inner torment as he awaits his "baptism," that is, the difficult trial he must undergo. This seems to weigh down upon him and make him afraid. His words "until it is completed!" show that he is awaiting the trial that will be dramatic and inevitable. It may be something Jesus wants, or it may be something that goes against his expectations—this is not clear, since even a serious and difficult trial may be something he wishes. The Gospels thus describe Jesus' emotions with regard to his task and his mission as an ardent desire, but also as a feeling of oppression and fear.

Let us sum up. Emotions are a basic ingredient of the life of Jesus. He gets involved with persons and situations in the human world. He displays both sympathy and severity, sometimes yielding to his own feelings and sometimes resisting them.[27] Jesus is profoundly marked by all that is human, by all human emotions.

The principal emotions of Jesus that we see in the Gospels are compassion, indignation, and a passionate desire. All these emotional states drive him forward to carry out his project of transformation and of struggle, in order to eliminate from society everything that presents an obstacle to the imminent arrival of the kingdom of God. Jesus appears to have tried to inculcate in his disciples his own feelings and his own internal reaction when confronted by the presence of evil.

Conclusion

THE CONCRETE REALITY OF A RADICAL LIFE

If we are to understand Jesus, we must begin with his lifestyle in continuous movement, with the way in which he communicated with other people, and with the nature of the social grouping he created in order to spread his message. We are convinced that a primarily theological reading of the career of Jesus empties it of much of its power and its meaning. Unlike those who are interested exclusively in Jesus' words and his religious ideas, our key in reading from the outset has been his person in his concrete relationship to the places and the people of his land. The effect of his actions depended on his encounter with the ordinary people, most of whom lived in the villages. Those whom he gathered around him and who followed him constantly were not chosen for their exceptional qualities or for their religious stature. Often, they belonged to active and rising social strata. These individuals moved freely around with Jesus, and, after his death, they scattered in various directions. Sometimes they met people and incorporated them into his movement; sometimes they themselves were assimilated and disappeared. The driving force that connected Jesus' followers to him was their desire to meet him and the attraction that he exercised on them.

In our "excavations" of the life of Jesus, we have combined traditional analyses (historical, philological, and archaeological) with less conventional hypotheses of an anthropological character, because what we are facing is a world of personal face-to-face encounters, a world that is significant precisely because it is precarious, exposed to danger, and made up of persons who tend to be marginal and have specific difficulties. We have not spoken of a Jesus who would lack all ties to the world, of an innovator who "imported" a project from outside. Jesus was solidly rooted in the complexity of daily happenings. He was weighed down by the real burdens of his own historical period.

The Concrete Reality of a Radical Life

Jesus was a Judean who remained alien to the aspirations and lifestyles introduced by Romanization. Faced with the cultural power of Rome, he appealed to the most intimate and strongest element of his own culture, that is, to the idea of the absolute power of the Judaic God and to the necessity that God reign by taking possession of the whole earth. Nothing could be more distant from Jesus than an attempt to integrate the peasant villagers into the urban life of the powerful or to secure for them a position in the structures of Roman dominion. It was by means of a change of life within individual households in the small towns and villages that his people would soon enter into the millenarian era of prosperity and messianic peace with all other peoples. The most fertile soil on which his preaching fell was, in fact, the hope for the kingdom of God, which would fight against injustice and eliminate it. Jesus took on the urgent task of announcing the imminence of this cosmic event of regeneration—no matter what this might cost him personally, and no matter what the outcome of his preaching might be. It was urgent to warn people and get them to change their lives so that they might gain the right to enter the future kingdom.

Jesus endeavored to get people to bring about in the reality of their lives the ideals of liberation and regeneration that are envisaged in the utopia of the Jubilee in the book of Leviticus. He strove with all his power to bring about this expectation. "Forgive us our debts as we too have forgiven our debtors" is the synthesis of his life's practice and his message. People are summoned to forgive one another and to accept God's pardon before the arrival of his royal dominion. What are the salient points of this project?

Jesus' public life began with a radical personal choice that departed from what had been the custom of his life up to that point. He abandoned everything. He chose an uncertain itinerant existence without roots. He broke the bonds to his own milieu, and he asked a similar detachment of his closest disciples. Jesus' choice was mature and would last irreversibly until his death. In his eyes, this was not simply a personal path from which he could not turn back but a strategy of enormous proportions.

The groups that grew up around him accepted his invitation to say no to family, work, and property, while at the same time finding a place in village houses, in the domestic network both in the countryside and in the small rural centers. The creative and transformative capacity of Jesus lies in the relationship—which is dialectic, but certainly not totally conflictual—between the group of disciples and the kinship groups. The constant uncertainty and the voluntary uprootedness in which Jesus lived allowed him to introduce unusual and indeed revolutionary ways of life into the domestic environment.

Jesus entered many houses. He asked for hospitality and he spent time there. He did not envisage any stable center or organized institutional form for the group of his disciples, who did not enjoy guarantees or protection from any religious authority. The group of disciples constituted an interstitial social form in other people's dwellings, where they mingled with the populace without either distinguishing themselves from others or imposing themselves on others. This group penetrated the consolidated structures. Jesus wanted to lead people to transform their houses into places of welcome that were open to the poor. In this way, the people of Israel would return to the equality they had at their origin.

This lifestyle made him strong and weak at one and the same time. Without any stable points of reference, he was essentially a fragile man, exposed to external forces. But it was precisely the radicalism of the life he had undertaken that allowed him to trust in God and to hope for the beginning of a new world.

Jesus addressed all those who were Judeans. In order to do so, he traveled far and wide through his land, sustained by his trust in his project. Jesus wanted to speak to all the people of Israel, in order to communicate what he knew and what he wanted to happen very soon. He accepted the conditions of life of the ordinary people. But he wanted to do more than proclaim words. He shared with others and was involved in their lives. And he paid a heavy price in his own person.

Jesus concentrated on the Land of Israel, to which he felt he belonged. For him, this territory was not identical with the territorial divisions laid down by the Romans; he went beyond the borders to seek those who were scattered or far away. The region through which he traveled is defined, above all, by real individuals. Jesus was not a local religious leader who would limit his activity to Galilee. He wanted a face-to-face relationship with people wherever they were, even in Judea.

In his indefatigable wanderings, all that Jesus had to rely on was his own strength. Having abandoned everything, he carried nothing with him—not even a bag. This state of lacking goods and protection was the root and foundation on which he built his entire existence. His renunciation of certainty made him independent of every link based on money, family, or work. All that he had was what he himself was able to do. His authenticity consisted of having nothing and possessing only his own self. All that Jesus had was his own body, a body exposed to dangers and to needs, like every human body. But although others perceived his

The Concrete Reality of a Radical Life

body as exactly the same as their own, *his* body lacked all protection. As the story unfolded, the body of Jesus was threatened and hunted down, and finally succumbed to the power of the authorities. The texts may be fragmentary and opaque, but we can affirm that the historical reality of Jesus is tangible and visible in these elements of solitude and deprivation.

Whenever Jesus spoke or preached, something happened. People became a part of his physical world. The preaching coincided with a transformation that transcended the projects of those who accepted his practice of life and his words. Every word that he spoke drove to the center or pushed to the margins. His words either united people around him or created resistance. He embodied the dynamics of life. Ultimately, he was defeated by a complex group of factors that accumulated against him. It was Jesus himself who had set these factors in motion, but he was not able to control them.

When he moved around, Jesus had very precise plans. He did not want to go along the principal roads nor to meet the cities or contact the urban population. He may have sensed that the city dwellers would basically be deaf to what he had to tell them, because their energies were tied up in the struggle for supremacy and power. The aspirations and hopes of the urban groups were presumably oriented toward the success and the affirmation that the Romanization in the cities promised them. Jesus' proclamation was diametrically opposed to such hopes of success, and he himself rejected all such aspirations. He did not seek to gain a good position, and he had no access either to the higher levels of the religious elite or to a role where he would exercise political authority.

From time to time, Jesus separated himself from everyone else. After spending so much time with the crowds and after so many urgent encounters day after day, he needed to pause and to get away from the world around him. After speaking with so many people, he felt the need to withdraw from the external pressure and to find his own center in an internal space of his own. He sought solitude in order to pray, to cultivate a direct relationship with God.

This habit of praying alone reveals an extremely important dimension of his identity. Although he sought a relationship with everyone, he was at the same time essentially a solitary man, because he was independent and autonomous. He found all the support he needed in an appeal to the supernatural—and only to the supernatural. It was this practice of invoking God and surrendering himself unconditionally to God that sustained him and was at the root of his solitary personal life.

Because he isolated himself and withdrew so often, the disciples knew only a part of what he was and what he had done. They remained ignorant of many of his experiences; other experiences were communicated only to those closest to him. A part of his life remained buried in a secrecy that no one has ever penetrated.

One of the aspects destined to remain obscure is the physical image of Jesus. The texts allow us to know what he did and the relationships he established with other people, but they do not describe his appearance. The fact remains that people wanted to have contact with his body in order to be healed. The physical pressure of the crowds, which is amply recorded in the Gospels, underlines the value of the corporal activity of Jesus, his concrete corporality. His body, which worked miracles, determined the perception of other people and even of his own disciples. His body conditioned all his relationships and formed the background to the events that defeated him. The body of Jesus was the goal toward which people moved. The desire to be with him was translated into the need to touch him.

People sought out his body because it was endowed with extraordinary power: it was able to heal sickness and exorcise demons. Jesus regarded these abilities as the advent of the rule of God in the world. People were surprised and astounded by this exceptional power. Those who met him were convinced that his body had an extraordinary and unique quality. We see this in the three disciples who were present at the mysterious event of the transfiguration, or in those who related that his body defied gravity and crossed the Sea of Galilee in a miraculous manner. This news spread, and whole groups of people demanded extraordinary and prodigious actions on his part.

It is above all toward the end of his life that the body of Jesus underwent events of exaltation and of devotion, but also of rejection and destruction, that remained indelibly imprinted on the memory of his followers. Many things happened to his body—it was hunted down and found; it was touched and imprisoned. It was acclaimed with hosannas and it was mocked. Finally, it was tortured and destroyed. After his death, his companions contrasted the glorious body of the resurrection with the body that had been crucified by the Romans. Others heard nothing of it and remained disappointed at what had happened.

Jesus demanded personal conversion. His objective was the lost sheep of the house of Israel. He was engaged personally to further this project of salvation, which entailed a dialogue and a confrontation that entered into the interior life of each person. He manifested the power of conviction by creating parables that shed light on the person's life or by looking directly into the eyes of each interlocutor. This personal relationship with Jesus was open to everyone. There were no exclusive privileges here—not even in favor of the poor, although they were his main concern. If there was a privileged group, it was the group of those who deviated from social and religious norms whom he invited to conversion.

Jesus took part in the ceremonial and religious life of his milieu. He rejected neither the Temple nor the sacrifices, but he developed other religious forms of his own within the overarching context of Judaic practice. Formal ritual played a limited role for him. Human action and way of life were much more important. His actions ignored the danger of rigid religious precepts, and he succeeded in reaching and gathering together all kinds of persons. The most important act from a symbolic point of view was eating together. In Jesus' egalitarian and innovative vision for society, sharing a meal was an especially favorable situation for the communication of his message. When he ate with others, he denounced the condition of the slaves, the domestic service that prevented women from hearing his message, and the social marginalization of the poor.

During one supper, he turned the customary social roles upside down by performing the revolutionary gesture of washing the feet of his followers. The "banquet" was the symbolic picture of the kingdom of God. But eating or drinking wine together in the expectation of the imminent kingdom had not only a metaphorical meaning: people would literally eat and drink in the kingdom, since Jesus imagined a future world of material abundance (this, at any rate, was the conviction of a majority of his followers in the first two centuries after his death). God would at last intervene to bring wealth and justice and to regenerate the world in accordance with equality.

Jesus did not, however, offer an account of how the kingdom of God would be set up. He invited people to wait. He put all his trust in the inner transformation and in acts of reparation on the part of Israel. He did nothing to influence the authorities, nor did he attempt in any way to influence or to take political power. Such ideas were foreign to his activities. It is true that the Roman reaction to him and their decision to eliminate him were political, but their assessment of him did not understand his real intentions. Jesus did not attempt to control the outcome of his activity. The Gospels of Mark, Luke, and Matthew hold that he finally accepted that this outcome would be his death and that he interpreted it as an unquestionable decision that God had taken. This is why he submitted to his death.

Jesus took enormous risks. Emotions were inevitable components of his life. Our hypothesis is that the (meta-)language of the emotions can disclose something of his interior life. The Synoptic Gospels speak above all of his compassion. They show us something of the control he exercised over his feelings, and the anger that could break out. The evangelists' attention to his emotions probably lies behind a model that has deeply influenced later religious cultures. It seems that Jesus taught his disciples to imitate his own emotions, especially compassion, to inculcate in them exemplary moral behavior. We can also find traces of his most intimate thinking in the sayings attributed to him by the *Gospel of the Hebrews* and the *Gospel of Thomas*, which present his teaching on the various phases of the spiritual life (amazement, interior peace, self-control).

The final picture in the accounts of his prayer in the Garden of Olives reveals the consistent character of his existence. At the close of his life, Jesus was confronted by an irresoluble situation. He had personally accepted the weight of difficulties, of hopes, and expectations. He had placed his hope in God, and he had mobilized forces that could no longer be controlled. At the end of his drama, at the moment of supreme personal tension, we see once again his fidelity to the lifestyle he had embraced. Jesus remained alone, with nothing other than his own strength, face to face with the God whom he continued to obey. He asked for nothing other than what must take place. The final events would be played out before a world that he could not dominate, a world that was essentially remote from him and foreign to him. The man who moved around tirelessly and enjoyed meals with everybody would remain completely alone, immobilized on the wood of a cross.

NOTES

Introduction: On Jesus' Lifestyle

1. Gerd Theissen, *Die Jesusbewegung* (Gütersloh: Gütersloher Verlagshaus, 2004), 11.

2. We use the noun "Judean" or "Judeans" as a translation of the Greek term *Ioudaios* or *Ioudaioi*, which designates the people of Israel who dwell in the Land of Israel or in the diaspora. This term does not designate, therefore, only the inhabitants of one particular region of the Land of Israel (that is, Judea): for example, the Galileans were *Ioudaioi*, and thus "Judeans" following our terminology. Some scholars maintain that *Israēl*, rather than *Ioudaioi*, was the most intimate self-definition (see John H. Elliott, "Jesus the Israelite Was Neither a 'Jew' nor a 'Christian': On Correcting Misleading Nomenclature," *Journal for the Study of the Historical Jesus* 5 [2005]: 119-55), but this can remain a secondary issue in the present context. We use "Judaic" to designate cultural and religious aspects relating to Judeans or Judaism.

3. E. P. Sanders, *Jesus and Judaism* (Philadelphia: Fortress Press, 1985), 11.

4. See Pierre Bourdieu, *Esquisse d'une théorie de la pratique, précédé de trois études d'éthnologie kabyle* (Paris: Seuil, 2000).

5. Adriana Destro, *Antropologia e religioni* (Brescia: Morcelliana, 2005); Talal Asad, "The Construction of Religion as an Anthropological Category," in idem, *Genealogies of Religion* (Baltimore and London: Johns Hopkins University Press, 1993), 27-54.

6. On the history of research see: Albert Schweitzer, *Von Reimarus zu Wrede* (Tübingen: Mohr, 1906); ET: *The Quest of the Historical Jesus* (London: A. & C. Black, 1910); James M. Robinson, *A New Quest of the Historical Jesus* (London: SCM, 1959); Charlotte Allen, *The Human Christ: The Search for the Historical Jesus* (Oxford and New York: Lion-Free Press, 1999); James D. G. Dunn and Scot McKnight, eds., *The Historical Jesus in Recent Research* (Winona Lake, IN: Eisenbrauns, 2005).

7. We have followed the same procedure in Adriana Destro and Mauro Pesce, *Antropologia delle origini cristiane* (4th ed.; Bari and Rome: Laterza, 2008); *Come nasce una religione* (Bari and Rome: Laterza, 2000); *Forme culturali del cristianesimo nascente* (2d ed.; Brescia: Morcelliana, 2008). Cf. also Rodney Needham, "Polithetic Classification," *Man* 3 (1975): 349-69. However, our work also draws on other disciplines, employing the historical reconstruction of the society of that time, as well as historical and philological exegesis, in the light of extensive archaeological, narrative, literary, and religious data.

8. On the theory of the cultural strata implicit in the texts, see Adriana Destro and Mauro Pesce, "Dal testo alla cultura. Antropologia degli scritti protocristiani," *Protestantesimo* 49 (1994): 214-29.

9. For a theory of the "text" and an anthropological interpretation of "texts," see Destro and Pesce, "Dal testo alla cultura," 217-19; and "An Anthropology of Early Christian Texts," in *Religions and Cultures*, ed. Adriana Destro and Mauro Pesce (New York: Global Publications, 2002), 1-26, with additional bibliography.

10. Maurice Halbwachs, *La mémoire collective* (Paris: Presses Universitaires de France, 1939); ET: *The Collective Memory* (New York: Harper & Row, 1980); Marc Augé, *Les formes de l'oubli* (Paris: Editions Payot et Rivages, 1998); ET: *Oblivion* (Minneapolis: University of Minnesota Press, 2004); Jack Goody, *The Power of the Written Tradition* (Washington: Smithsonian, 2000); Aleida Assmann, *Erinnerungsräume* (Munich: Beck, 1999).

11. Alain Le Boulluec, *La notion d'hérésie dans la littérature grecque: IIe-IIIe siècles*, 2 vols. (Paris: Etudes Augustiniennes, 1985).

12. Gabriella Aragione, Eric Junod, and Enrico Norelli, eds., *Le Canon du Nouveau Testament* (Geneva: Labor et Fides, 2005).

13. Cf. Mauro Pesce, ed., *Le parole dimenticate di Gesù* (Milan: Lorenzo Valla-Mondadori, 2004), 656-67.

14. Maria Grazia Mara, *Il Vangelo di Pietro* (Bologna: Edizioni Dehoniane, 2002), 7-25; cf. Thomas J. Kraus and Tobias Nicklas, *Das Petrusevangelium und die Petrusapokalypse* (Berlin and New York: Walter de Gruyter, 2004).

15. Mauro Pesce, "Il Vangelo di Giuda, il Vangeli di Giovanni e gli altri vangeli canonici," *Humanitas* 61, nos. 5-6 (2006): 924-30.

16. Jacques Dupont, ed., *La parabola degli invitati al banchetto* (Brescia: Paideia, 1978).

17. John S. Kloppenborg, *The Tenants in the Vineyard* (Tübingen: Mohr Siebeck, 2006), 271-77.

18. There is a primary level in the text made up of those *cultural presuppositions* which the author of the text and the reader he has in mind have in common. The cultural assumptions of this first level are always implicit, but are shared by all the members of the society to which the author belongs. A second textual level incorporates some of the *specific cultural elements* of the social group within which the text is to be used. These elements are always explicitly mentioned in the text. They are common to the author, his addressees, and the environment to which they belong. The third level of a text is where the author expresses his principal, explicit intention. It is at this level that the specific configuration of a religious movement within a religion, of a tendency within a movement, or of a single personality within a particular tendency is revealed. See Destro and Pesce, "An Anthropology of Early Christian Texts," in A. Destro and M. Pesce, eds., *Religions and Cultures* (New York: Global Publications, 2002), 1-26.

19. From a historical point of view, see Carlo Ginzburg, *Il filo e le tracce: Vero, falso, finto* (Milan: Feltrinelli, 2006).

20. The reasonable distance from the past which we judge necessary does not mean that we internalize the contemporary concept of "natural" or "naturalizing." The explanations of the "natural" world, earthly and heavenly, that were current in the first century were profoundly different from our own. The same is true of the political conditions, the social stratification, and the relationships between men and women. Nevertheless, the Gospels and the Letters of Paul, which today are read daily in the churches, often give those who hear them the impression that they are "outside time." If we lack a sufficient awareness of the distance, we end up by interpreting the texts in the light of today's culture, and we lose the possibility of understanding correctly the impact that Jesus had on the culture of his age.

21. Mauro Pesce, "Dalla enciclica biblica di Leone XIII 'Providentissimus Deus' (1893) a quella di Pio XII 'Divino afflante Spiritu' (1943)," in *Cento anni di cammino biblico*, ed. Carlo Maria Martini et al. (Milan: Vita e Pensiero: 1995), 39-100. From the seventeenth century onward, it was thought that historical knowledge, based on a systematic methodology, would be able to bring about understanding among the Christian churches, which were in opposition to one another because of theological principles that were difficult to reconcile. In the second half of the nineteenth century, many theologians recognized that the historical method permitted a reliable knowledge of Christian origins and a common basis of historical data that went beyond theological barriers. Also, a Catholic document such as Pius XII's encyclical *Divino afflante Spiritu* (1943) held that historical research could reconstruct correctly the physiognomy of the facts narrated in the biblical documents.

22. Cf. James Clifford and George Marcus, *Writing Culture* (Berkeley: University of California Press, 1986).

23. One example: the First Letter to Timothy (5:10) attributes to the widows the custom of washing the feet of the "saints," but the Gospel of John attributes this to Jesus himself (13:4-17) the action that slaves performed when they washed the feet of guests. This means that there is a discontinuity between the behavior of Jesus and the practice of the early church. If the community memory continued to hand on the narrative of this gesture of Jesus, despite this dissonance, it is probable that the action was actually performed by him. In this case, the criterion of discontinuity favors the historicity of the action and its distinctiveness.

24. Daniel Boyarin, *Borderlines* (Philadelphia: University of Pennsylvania Press, 2004), 8-13 and 205.

1. Jesus on His Landscape

1. See Adriana Destro and Mauro Pesce, *Antropologia delle origini cristiane* (4th ed.; Bari and Rome: Laterza, 2008), 9-11.

2. In the present chapter, we often draw on the theoretical patterns of the anthropology of space elaborated by Tim Ingold, *The Perception of Environment* (London and New York: Routledge, 2000) (here 185-87) and by Marc

Augé, *Le sens des autres* (Paris: Fayard, 1994), 149-72; idem, *Non-Lieux: Introduction à une anthropologie de la surmodernité* (Paris: Le Seuil, 1992); ET: *Non-Places* (London and New York: Verso, 2009).

3. Gaston Bachelard, *La poétique de l'espace* (Paris: PUF, 1957); ET: *The Poetics of Space* (Boston: Beacon, 1994). Tuan Yi-Fu. *Space and Place: The Perspective of Experience* (Minneapolis: University of Minnesota Press, 1977).

4. Peter Gould and Rodney White, *Mental Maps* (2d ed.; Boston: Allen & Unwin, 1986).

5. Michel de Certeau, *L'Invention du quotidien* (Paris: Gallimard, 1980); ET: *The Practice of Everyday Life* (Berkeley: University of California Press, 2002).

6. Augé, *Non-lieux*, 68.

7. Richard A. Horsley, *Galilee: History, Politics, People* (London: Continuum, 1995); idem, "Jésus le galiléen face au nouvel ordre romain," in Daniel Marguerat et al., eds., *Jésus, complements d'enquête* (Paris: Bayard, 2007), 59-69; James F. Strange, "First Century Galilee from Archeology and from the Texts," in Douglas E. Edwards and Christine Thomas McCollough, eds., *Archeology and the Galilee* (Atlanta, GA: Scholars, 1997), 39-48; Jonathan L. Reed, *Archeology and the Galilean Jesus* (Harrisburg, PA: Trinity Press International, 2000); John Dominic Crossan and Jonathan L. Reed, *Excavating Jesus* (San Francisco: HarperSanFrancisco, 2001); Zeev Safrai, *The Economy of Roman Palestine* (London and New York: Routledge, 1994).

8. On the cities of Galilee, see Sean Freyne, "Town and Country Once More: The Case of Roman Galilee," in Edwards and McCollough, eds. *Archeology and the Galilee*, 49-56; E. P. Sanders, *The Historical Figure of Jesus* (Harmondsworth: Penguin, 1996), 105ff.; Gerd Theissen, *Die Jesusbewegung* (Gütersloh: Gütersloher Verlagshaus, 2004), 163-86; John J. Rousseau and Arav Rami, *Jesus and His World* (Minneapolis: Fortress Press, 1995); Paula Fredriksen, *Jesus of Nazareth: King of the Jews* (New York: Vintage Books, 2000) 155-84.

9. Cf. Kenneth G. Holum et al., eds., *King Herod's Dream: Caesarea on the Sea* (New York and London: Horton, 1988).

10. Josephus mentions the "principal road" (*leōphoros*) in *Jewish War* 5.54-58 and the "public road" (*dēmosia*) in 2.228.

11. Israel Roll, "Imperial Roads and Trade Routes beyond the Roman Provinces of Judaea-Palaestina and Arabia. The State of Research," *Tel-Aviv* 32 (2005): esp. 108-9; idem, "The Roman Road System in Judaea," in Lee Israel Levine, ed., *The Jerusalem Cathedra* 3 (Jerusalem and Detroit: Yad Izhak Ben-Zvi Institute and Wayne State University Press, 1983), 136-60; idem, "Roman Roads," in Yoram Tsafrir, Leah Di Segni, and Judith Green, eds., *Tabula Imperii Romani, Judaea Palestina* (Jerusalem: Israeli Academy of Sciences and Humanities, 1994), 21-22; idem, "Roads and Transportation in the Holy Land in the Early Christian and Byzantine Times," in *Akten des XII. Internationalen Kongresses für christliche Archäologie* (Jahrbuch für Antike und Christentum, supplementary vol. 20; Münster: Aschendorff, 1995), 1166-70; Amos Kloner, "Stepped Roads in Roman Palestine," *Aram* 8 (1996): 111-17; Moshe Fischer,

1. Jesus on His Landscape 181

Benjamin Isaac, and Israel Roll, "Roman Roads in Judaea II. The Jaffa-Jerusalem Roads," *Biblical Archaeologist* 50, no. 4 (1996): 244-45.

12. Safrai, *The Economy*; Dennis Duling, "The Jesus Movement and Social Network Analysis. Part I: The Spatial Network," *Biblical Theology Bulletin* 29 (1999): 156-75; idem, "The Jesus Movement and Network Analysis," in Wolfgang Stegemann, Bruce J. Malina, and Gerd Theissen, eds., *The Social Setting of Jesus and the Gospels* (Minneapolis: Fortress Press, 2002), 301-32; David A. Dorsey, *The Roads and Highways of Ancient Israel* (Baltimore and London: Johns Hopkins University Press, 1991).

13. Duling, "The Jesus Movement," 164-69.

14. Strange, "First Century Galilee," 41-42.

15. John Dominic Crossan, *The Historical Jesus: The Life of a Mediterranean Jewish Peasant* (San Francisco: HarperSanFrancisco, 1991), 18.

16. Eric M. Meyers, "The Cultural Settings of Galilee: The Case of Regionalism and Early Judaism," *Aufstieg und Niedergang der römischen Welt* II 19 (1999): 686-702; later published as Eric M. Meyers and James F. Strange, *Archeology, the Rabbis, and Early Christianity: The Social and Historical Setting of Palestinian Judaism and Christianity* (Nashville, TN: Abingdon, 1981), here 143.

17. In addition to the classic study by Karl Ludwig Schmidt, *Der Rahmen der Geschichte Jesu* (Darmstadt: Wissenschaftliche Buchgesellschaft, 1919), see also a work that has not been much used by exegetes: Maurice Halbwachs, *La topographie légendaire des évangiles en Terre Sainte*, édition préparée par Marie Jaisson (Paris: PUF, 2008). On the historical memory, see Paul Connerton, *How Societies Remember* (Cambridge: Cambridge University Press, 1989).

18. Halbwachs, *La topographie*, 124.

19. Topographically, a village is first and foremost an aggregation of dwellings. In terms of the structure of the territory, it is a unit of settlement with varying degrees of intensity of habitation and different organizations (Gabriel Le Bras, *L'Eglise et le village* [Paris: Flammarion, 1976]). On villages in classical antiquity, see Sabine Fourrier, "Villages, villes, ethniques," in *Identités croisées en un milieu méditerranéen: le cas de Cypre (antiquité-moyen âge)* (Mont-Saint-Aignan: Université de Rouen, 2006), 101-9; Peter Richardson, "Khirbet Qana (and Other Villages) as a Context for Jesus," in James H. Charlesworth, ed., *Jesus and Archeology* (Grand Rapids: Eerdmans, 2006), 120-44; Gershon Edelstein, Ianir Milevski, and Sarah Aurant, *The Rephaim Valley Project: Villages, Terraces, and Stone Mounds. Excavations at Manahat, 1987-1989* (Jerusalem: Israel Antiquity Authority, 1998); Richard A. Horsley, "Archeology and the Villages of Upper Galilee: A Dialogue with Archeologists," *Bulletin of the American Schools of Oriental Research* 297 (1995): 5-16.

20. Mark tells us that Jesus moved around through "villages, towns, and countryside" (*eis kōmas, poleis, agrous*, 6:56), but he also speaks of village-cities (*kōmopoleis*), which may have been independent villages or market towns. In Mark, the countryside too seems to be thought of in terms of an inhabited center.

21. Adriana Destro, ed., *Antropologia dei flussi globali* (Rome: Carocci, 2006), 7-9.

182 *1. Jesus on His Landscape*

22. Lellia Cracco Ruggini, "La città imperiale," in E. Gabba and A. Schiavone, eds., *Storia di Roma*. 4: *Caratteri e morfologie* (Turin: Einaudi, 1989), 201-7.

23. Luke has a tendency to apply the word *polis* to settlements that were certainly not cities, such as Capernaum, Chorazin, Nain, and Nazareth. In some cases, *polis* defines what John (cf. Luke 2:4/John 7:2) or Mark (Luke 9:10/Mark 8:23) calls *kōmē*, a "village." However, the use of these terms in Matthew and Luke can be misleading: the authors of these two Gospels are urban men who assimilate the situation of Jesus too much to their own situation.

24. Q is a very ancient collection of sayings of Jesus, which no longer survives. It permits us to get behind the Gospels and come closer to Jesus himself. The principal reason why many exegetes hypothesize the existence of this collection is that Matthew and Luke share many sayings of Jesus that are not found in Mark and that display a close literary relationship. For a demonstration of the existence of Q, see John S. Kloppenborg, *The Formation of Q* (Philadelphia: Fortress Press, 1987); idem, *Excavating Q* (Minneapolis: Fortress Press, 2000), 12-38; James M. Robinson, P. Hoffmann, and John S. Kloppenborg, eds., *The Critical Edition of Q* (Minneapolis and Louvain: Fortress Press and Peeters, 2000); Enrico Norelli, in Claudio Moreschini and Enrico Norelli, *Early Christian Greek and Latin Literature*. 1: *From Paul to the Age of Constantine* (Peabody, MA: Hendrickson, 2005) (Ital. orig., *Storia della letteratura cristiana antica greca e latina*. 1: *Da Paolo all'età costantiniana* [Brescia: Morcelliana, 1995], 68-95).

25. This small town underwent development in the second century as a consequence of the revolt of Bar Kokhba, and is described later in the Hebrew text of the Tosefta (third century C.E.) as a middle-sized city (*Makkoth* 3.8). It was located ca. five kilometers to the north of Capernaum. The synagogue uncovered by Zev Yeivin's excavations dates from the fourth century (Zev Yeivin, "Ancient Chorazin Comes Back to Life," *Biblical Archeological Review* 13, no. 5 [1987]: 22-36); Robert W. Smith, "Chorazin," *Anchor Bible Dictionary* 1 (1992): 911-12.

26. For Mark, Bethsaida is a village (*kōmē*). Josephus relates that Herod Philip changed it into a city named Julias in honor of the daughter of Augustus (or possibly in honor of the mother of Tiberius: Jerome Murphy-O'Connor, *The Holy Land: An Oxford Archaeological Guide* [5th ed.; Oxford: Oxford University Press, 2008], 228). He erected important buildings there and increased its population (Josephus, *Jewish Antiquities* 18.2.1 §28). Politically, the city belonged to Gaulanitis. See James F. Strange, "Bethsaida," *Anchor Bible Dictionary* 1 (1991): 692-93. On the textual problems of Mark 8:22, 26, and the interpretation of the episode (which is attested only by Mark, and is omitted by Matthew and Luke), see Camille Focant, *L'Évangile selon Marc* (Paris: Cerf, 2004), 309-13.

27. If this is correct, Jesus would not be stating that he has worked miracles inside the cities of Chorazin and Bethsaida; he would simply be referring to his rejection in a region where he had worked. The contrast between these two areas may have been created by the redaction of Q, expressing the geographical-religious map of Q rather than that of Jesus himself. Tyre and Sidon, however,

1. Jesus on His Landscape 183

may be the personifications of the Gentiles as such rather than territories that Jesus had visited: see Joel 3:4; Zech 9:2; 2 Esdras 1:11.

28. Matthew and Mark speak only of a deserted place near the Sea of Galilee (Matt 14:13; Mark 6:32; cf. also John 6:1). For Matthew, Mark, and Luke, this was an area surrounded only by villages (*kōmai*) and fields (*agroi*): Luke 9:12; Mark 6:36; Matt 14:15.

29. Reed, *Archeology*, discusses the estimates, which vary from 1,000 to 25,000 inhabitants, and argues against the excessive figures; see also Kloppenborg, *Excavating Q*, 214-15.

30. See Virgilio C. Corbo, "Capernaum," *Anchor Bible Dictionary* 1 (1991): 866-69; Vasilios Tzaferis, ed., *Excavations at Capernaum* 1 (Winona Lake, IN: Eisenbrauns, 1989); Reed, *Archeology*, 139-69, esp. 166-69.

31. See Reed, *Archeology*, 169.

32. See also J. Andrew Overman, "Jesus of Galilee and the Historical Peasant," in Edwards and McCollough, *Archeology and the Galilee*, 67-73.

33. Robert Redfield, *The Little Community and Peasant Society and Culture* (Chicago: University of Chicago Press, 1989); Eric R. Wolf, *Peasants* (Englewood Cliffs, NJ: Prentice Hall, 1966); John W. Cole and Eric R. Wolf, *The Hidden Frontier: Ecology and Ethnicity in an Alpine Valley* (Berkeley: University of California Press, 1999).

34. As happened at Capernaum, according to Matt 9:9 and 17:24, and possibly at Jericho (cf. Luke 19:2).

35. See E. P. Sanders, *The Historical Figure of Jesus* (Harmondsworth: Penguin, 1996), 106.

36. Horsley, *Galilee*, Part 3; see also Douglas E. Oakman, "The Countryside in Luke-Acts," in Jerome Neyrey, ed., *The Social World of Luke-Acts* (Peabody, MA: Hendrickson, 1991), 151-73.

37. Cf. Augé, *Non-Lieux*, 62-66.

38. Cf. Matt 4:15, "the road by the sea" (see Duling, "The Jesus Movement," 166). *Hodos* is used in Matthew in the normal physical meaning of "road": 8:28; 21:19; 13:14-19; 22:9. According to some commentators (cf. Joachim Gnilka, *Das Matthäusevangelium* [Herders theologischer Kommentar zum Neuen Testament I/2; Freiburg i.Br.: Herder, 1988], ad loc.), the command "Do not go onto the road of the Gentiles" derives from those followers of Jesus who did not wish to extend the proclamation of the Gospel to those who were not Judeans; and the fact that at some point in time someone did in fact want to extend the proclamation to non-Judeans shows that *Jesus* limited his activity to Judeans alone. This saying belongs to Jesus' commands to the disciples. We have four different versions of these commands (Mark 6:7-13; Luke 9:2-6; Luke 10:1-12; Matt 10:5-15) and a fragment in Paul (1 Cor 9:4-6, 14). Luke has two versions because one is dependent on Mark and the other on Q. A comparison with Luke 10:1-12 shows that Matthew too is dependent on Q. But it is only Matthew (not Luke) who relates the prohibition of taking the roads used by non-Judeans and of entering the city of the Samaritans. Did Matthew add this prohibition to Q, or did Luke eliminate it? Luke 9:52-56 relates that the disciples enter a Samaritan village "to

make ready" a lodging for Jesus, but the Samaritans reject them. This means that Luke is aware that the question of whether or not to enter places where the Samaritans lived was a problem for the movement of Jesus. It is highly probable that Luke has eliminated the prohibition by Jesus, because he wanted to underline the necessity of openness toward the Samaritans. In short, arguments can be presented in favor of both theses. According to John, Jesus spends two days in a Samaritan village (John 4:40), and many Samaritans come to faith in him.

39. Amy-Jill Levine, *The Social and Ethnic Dimension of Matthean Salvation History* (New York: Edwin Mellen, 1998), 52.

40. Roll, "Imperial Roads," 108-9.

41. Many other historians and exegetes agree with us in locating Jesus in this manner, for example, E. P. Sanders (*The Historical Figure of Jesus*). Theissen (*Die Jesusbewegung*, 139ff.) has attempted to classify the Judaic socio-religious "renewal" movements on the basis of the milieus that they influenced: the desert, the mountains, and the densely populated rural districts. He rightly locates Jesus in the last of these.

42. On the extent of the Land of Israel in the various epochs and in the conceptions of various Judaic texts, see Philip Alexander, "Geography and the Bible: Early Jewish Geography," *Anchor Bible Dictionary* 2 (1992): 977-88; Rachel Havrelock, "The Two Maps of Israel's Land," *Journal of Biblical Literature* 126 (2007): 649-67.

43. For the northern border envisioned by Josephus and the rabbinical literature see the map published by Raphael Frankel, Nimrod Getzov, Mordechai Aviam, and Avi Degani, *Settlement Dynamics and Regional Diversity in Ancient Upper Galilee: Archeological Survey of Upper Galilee* (Jerusalem: Israel Antiquities Authority, 2001), 110-13 (map on p. 112). See also Sean Freyne, *Jesus: A Jewish Galilean: A New Reading of the Jesus-Story* (New York: T & T Clark 2006), 78.

44. It seems strange that in order to go toward the Sea of Galilee, he should first pass by way of Sidon, which is to the north of Tyre, and that he should pass by way of the lake to arrive at the center of the Decapolis, to the southeast of the lake itself; but this is not "absurd" (*contra* Focant, *L'Évangile selon Marc*, 290), since Jesus wanted to get across a very vast territory, and he followed the itineraries dictated by circumstances. In reality, we know nothing about this particular journey by Jesus. See Sanders, *The Historical Figure of Jesus*, 105.

45. Cf. Focant, *L'Évangile selon Marc*, 290.

46. Sanders, *The Historical Figure of Jesus*, 105.

47. *Jewish War* 2.477-479 and *Jewish Antiquities* 17.324. Philo mentions a strong Judean presence in "Phoenicia, Syria, and especially that part which is known as Coele-Syria" (*Legatio ad Gaium*, 281).

48. Frankel et al., *Settlement Dynamics*, 153, and map 4.2 on p. 112.

49. In the Acts of the Apostles, the disciples ask Jesus whether this is the time when he will "restore" (*apokathistaneis*) the kingdom of Israel (1:6).

50. The assignment to Herod Philip of the territory of Gaulanitis, Trachonitis, Batanaea, and Panias introduced a border *within* Galilee between his domain and the Galilean domain of Herod Antipas.

1. *Jesus on His Landscape* 185

51. The titles of the following two books underline the Galilean identity of Jesus: Giuseppe Barbaglio, *Gesù ebreo di Galilea: Indagine storica* (Bologna: Edizioni Dehoniane, 2002), and Sean Freyne, *Jesus: A Jewish Galilean* (London and New York: T&T Clark, 2006). See also Eric M. Meyers, "Jesus and His Galilean Context," in Edwards and McCollough, eds., *Archeology and the Galilee*, 57-66.

52. Frankel et al., *Settlement Dynamics*, 141-42.

53. The corrections with regard to times and places that Luke makes to Mark's account do not substantially modify the Markan framework, with the exception of his mention of Jesus' preaching in Judea (Sanders, *The Historical Figure of Jesus*, 105). In Matthew, the disciples are sent to preach "in *all* the cities of Israel" (10:23; cf. Crossan and Reed, *Excavating Jesus*, 125), and the "cities" that Jesus visits in Matt 11:1 may not be exclusively Galilean cities. Jesus' visit to the regions of Tyre and Sidon is retained in Matthew.

54. It has been observed that Luke frequently fails to give any precise information about the topography of the events of Jesus' life (see Octave Merlier, *Itinéraires de Jésus et chronologie dans le quatrième évangile* [Athens: Institut français, 1961], 8). It is possible that in the course of his efforts to acquire information Luke became convinced that it was no longer possible to know exactly where many episodes had taken place.

55. Merlier, *Itinéraires de Jésus*, 8.

56. John 4:2 specifies that Jesus himself did not baptize, but only his disciples.

57. This is the third time that Jesus is in Judea, if we include as the first time his baptism by John.

58. John mentions in 4:2 an initial period in which Jesus and his followers baptize together with John the Baptizer. He may perhaps imagine that this place was one of the bases that Jesus preferred. It is at any rate significant that Jesus in this case does not return to Galilee, which thus seems not to have been his place of reference.

59. This question is debated. See Sean Freyne, "Locality and Doctrine. Mark and John Revisited," in F. van Segbroeck et al., eds., *The Four Gospels 1992* (Louvain: Louvain University Press, 1992), 1889-1900; Laurence M. Willis, *The Quest of the Historical Jesus* (London and New York: Routledge, 1997).

60. Maria Luisa Rigato, *Giovanni: L'enigma, il presbitero, il culto* (Bologna: Edizioni Dehoniane, 2007).

61. See Ekkehard Stegemann and Wolfgang Stegemann, *Urchristliche Sozialgeschichte* (Stuttgart: Kohlhammer, 1997); ET: *The Jesus Movement* (Minneapolis: Fortress Press, 2001), 306ff.

62. The Gospel of John dedicates chaps. 13-14 to the Last Supper (on the exclusion of chaps. 15-17 from the Last Supper, see Adriana Destro and Mauro Pesce, *Come nasce una religione* [Bari and Rome: Laterza, 2000], 65-84). The synoptics give it much less space.

63. John S. Kloppenborg, "Dating Theodotos (CJ II 1404)," *Journal of Jewish Studies* 51 (2000): 243-80. Other scholars had maintained that there were no

synagogues in the Land of Israel in the first century, but Kloppenborg argues that the term "*synagōgē* was used of buildings not only in Egypt and Cyrenaica but also in early Roman Palestine" (277). This means that Horsley is incorrect to assert that the "synagogues" of which the Synoptic Gospels speak were assemblies that were often held in the open air (*Galilee*, Part 3).

64. Cf. Luke 4:15-28; 4:33-38. Luke 4:44 tells us that Jesus preached in the synagogues of *Judea*, but Luke does not mention this when Jesus speaks to Pilate in chap. 23. This silence is strange, since the Gospel of John seems to have Jesus say that the synagogues in which he preached were in Judea: cf. John 18:20; 6:6; 13:10.

65. Destro, ed., *Antropologia dei flussi globali*; Arjun Appadurai, ed., *Globalization* (Durham, NC: Duke University Press, 2000); Ulf Hannerz, *Transnational Connections* (London and New York: Routledge, 1996).

66. Theissen, *Die Jesusbewegung*, 161.

67. Sean Freyne, *Galilee from Alexander the Great to Hadrian, 323 B.C.E. to 135 C.E.* (Edinburgh: T&T Clark, 2000); idem, *Galilee, Jesus and the Gospels* (Minneapolis: Augsburg, 1988); idem, "Herodian Economics in Galilee: Searching for a Suitable Model," in Philip F. Esler, ed., *Modelling Early Christianity* (London: Routledge, 1995), 23-46; Richard A. Horsley and John S. Hanson, *Bandits, Prophets, and Messiahs* (London: Continuum, 2000); Horsley, *Galilee*.

68. On Sepphoris, see James F. Strange, "Six Campaigns at Sepphoris: The University of South Florida Excavations, 1983-1989," in Lee Levine, ed., *Galilee in Late Antiquity* (New York and Jerusalem: Jewish Theological Seminary of America, 1992), 339-55; Eric M. Meyers, Ehud Netzer, and Carol L. Meyers, *Sepphoris* (Winona Lake, IN: Eisenbrauns, 1992); Ehud Netzer and Zeev Weiss, *Sepphoris* (Jerusalem: Israel Exploration Society, 1994); James F. Strange, "Sepphoris," *Anchor Bible Dictionary* 5 (1992).

69. See James F. Strange, "Tiberias," *Anchor Bible Dictionary* 6 (1992): 547-49.

70. Mark Chancey, *Greco-Roman Culture and the Galilee of Jesus* (Cambridge: Cambridge University Press, 2008), 83.

71. Horsley, "Jésus le galiléen," 62.

72. Rami Arav and Richard A. Freund, eds., *Bethsaida: A City by the North Shore of the Sea of Galilee* (3 vols.; Kirksville, MO: Truman State University Press, 1995, 1999, 2004).

73. We do not know for certain the extent to which Greek was spoken in the cities of Sepphoris and Tiberias at the time of Jesus. On the basis of the limited numbers of Greek inscriptions, it has been suggested that the Herods initiated the process of introducing the Greek language into the cities, and that this developed in the second century (Chancey, *Greco-Roman Culture*, 122-65).

74. Horsley, "Jésus le galiléen," 63.

75. Horsley and Hanson, *Bandits*, 38, 66; Jean-Pierre Lémonon, *Ponce Pilate* (Paris: Les Editions de l'Atelier, 2007 [1st ed. 1981]).

76. Chancey, *Greco-Roman Culture*, 56.

77. Horsley, *Galilee*, Part 3.

1. Jesus on His Landscape

78. Theissen, *Die Jesusbewegung,* 162.

79. Some have hypothesized that he went there to work as a carpenter, and others that his language presupposes knowledge of the theater that had been erected there (R. Batey, "Jesus and the Theatre," *New Testament Studies* 30 [1984]: 563-74), but this has been contested by Zeev Weiss and Ehud Netzer, "Architectural Development of Sepphoris during the Roman and Byzantine Periods," in Edwards and McCollough, eds., *Archeology and the Galilee,* 118 and 122: the theater was not built before the last years of the first century and the beginning of the second.

80. Theissen, *Die Jesusbewegung,* 182ff., with the sources cited there.

81. Theissen, *Die Jesusbewegung.* He argues on the basis of evidence from 1 Maccabees, Josephus, and rabbinic texts.

82. Cf. Halbwachs, *La topographie.* Cf. the mechanism of memory in the Ciceronian oration according to Ann Vasaly, *Representations: Images of the World in Ciceronian Oratory* (Berkeley: University of California Press, 1993), 39.

83. We have a fragment in a small Oxyrhynchus papyrus, P.Oxy. 840. On this, see François Bovon, "Fragment Oxyrhynchus 840. Fragment of a Lost Gospel, Witness of an Early Christian Controversy over Purity," *Journal of Biblical Literature* 119 (2000): 725-28; Michael J. Kruger, *The Gospel of the Savior: An Analysis of P. Oxy. 840 and Its Place in the Gospel Traditions of Early Christianity* (Leiden: Brill, 2005); Mauro Pesce, ed., *Le parole dimenticate di Gesù* (Milan: Lorenzo Valla-Mondadori, 2004), 620-23.

84. Only Matt 21:12 speaks of an ass. The term *pōlos,* which Mark and Luke employ, could also mean a "horse."

85. These are the following: the triumphal entrance; the lament over Jerusalem (not found in Mark); the expulsion of the merchants; the cursing of the fig tree; the debate about the authority of Jesus; the parable of the tenants in the vineyard (Matthew presents other parables as well); the debate about God and Caesar; the debate about the resurrection; the question about the most important commandment (not found in Luke); the discussion about the Messiah as son of David; the invectives against the scribes and Pharisees (introduced by Matthew; Luke has a very brief passage on this theme); the widow's offering in the Temple (not found in Matthew); the eschatological discourse; the woman who anoints Jesus while he is at table in Bethany (which is not found in Luke in this context but is present in John).

86. The historicity of this attitude can be demonstrated on the basis of two sources, Mark and Luke. Luke specifies that the disciples whom Jesus sends are Peter and John, and this detail can only be based on a special Lukan source independent of Mark. The story contains one element, namely, the man who transports a water jar, and this episode may have been committed to memory precisely because of its singular character. Matthew 26:18 says nothing about the sending of the two disciples and the man who carries the water jar. See François Bovon, *L'Évangile selon saint Luc (Lc 15,1—19,27)* (Geneva: Labor et Fides, 2001).

87. John S. Kloppenborg, *The Tenants in the Vineyard* (Tübingen: Mohr Siebeck, 2006), 271-77.

88. This episode is attested by only one independent source. Its authenticity is supported by the fact that the context is an inseparable part of the narrative and cannot have been introduced by the evangelist.

89. Although this parable is transmitted only by Luke, it certainly goes back to Jesus, because it is consistent with Jesus' avoidance of the cities and with the central nucleus of Jesus' idea about forgiveness. The parables seem to be the literary genre that best expresses the originality of Jesus. The synoptic comparison (where this is possible) shows that Luke is often more faithful than Matthew in reporting the parables.

90. Ernst Bammel and C. F. D. Moule, eds., *Jesus and the Politics of His Day* (Cambridge: Cambridge University Press, 1984); Richard A. Horsley, *Jesus and Empire* (Minneapolis: Fortress Press, 2003).

91. Chancey, *Greco-Roman Culture*, 52.

2. Jesus on Foot

1. Every book published about Jesus in the last three decades, especially in the aftermath of the studies by Gerd Theissen in the 1960s, emphasizes that he was an itinerant preacher. See also Mauro Pesce, "Discepolato gesuano e discepolato rabbinico. Problemi e prospettive della comparazione," *Aufstieg und Niedergang der römischen Welt* II 25/1 (Berlin: Walter de Gruyter 1982), 351-89. But Max Weber had already pointed to the differentiation between closer followers and followers who provided support as one of the fundamental structures of the groups that form around great religious leaders: "If his prophecy is successful, the prophet succeeds in winning permanent helpers . . . who have a purely personal relationship to him. . . . Moreover, in addition to these permanent helpers, who are active co-workers with the prophet in his mission and who generally also possess some charismatic qualifications, there is a circle of followers comprising those who support him with lodging, money, and services and who expect to obtain their salvation through his mission" (*Wirtschaft und Gesellschaft* [Tübingen: Mohr 1922]; quoted from the ET, *Economy and Society* [Berkeley: University of California Press, 1978], 452). We feel somewhat reluctant to use the term "itinerancy," because this abstract noun could lead to the idea that Jesus chose a religious lifestyle that was considered virtuous per se (like chastity or poverty in mediaeval and modern religious orders).

2. We do not want to "apply" to Jesus' experience Augé's concept of "non-place," since that would not shed light on the question we are investigating here.

3. In *Non-Lieux*, Augé elaborates the distinction drawn by Michel de Certeau in *L'Invention du quotidien* between place and space, between the "place," as an ensemble of elements that coexist in a certain space, and the "space," as the animation of these elements that is brought about by mobility. He argues that those who move transform the road, defined geometrically as a *place* of urban life, into a *space*.

2. Jesus on Foot

4. The rejection that Jesus suffers in his own village, at Nazareth (Mark 6:1-6/Matt 13:53-58), is also comprehensible because he disregards the relational networks that his fellow villagers expect him to respect.

5. Matthew modifies this picture slightly because, for him, Jesus' continuous moving around has lost some of its historical significance. He mentions that Jesus abandons Nazareth and seems to think that Capernaum is the place of his residence (in 4:12, he employs the verb *katoikein*, which means "to reside," as we also see from Matt 2:23), as if this was the base for all Jesus' movements in Galilee. Another indication that Matthew thinks along these lines is the fact that Jesus pays the Temple tax at Capernaum (cf. 17:24); the house mentioned in Matt 17:25 and 9:10, 28 seems to be his base (Ulrich Luz maintains that it is not clear which house this is: Ulrich Luz, *Das Evangelium nach Matthäus. 2. Teilband. Mt 8-14* [Zurich: Benzinger Verlag, 1985], ad loc.). Whether it be the house of Jesus himself or of other persons, Matthew presents it to us as a dwelling where Jesus is at ease with his disciples, at least for the purpose of eating, and where he can extend hospitality to others (cf. also Matt 13:1, 34). Matthew 9:1 calls Capernaum "his city." This means that Matthew weakens the meaning of an uninterrupted moving around on the part of Jesus and partly modifies the idea of an itinerancy without a base. This picture in Matthew, however, is not in conformity with the historical behavior of Jesus.

6. Luke 10:5-7; Mark 6:10-11; cf. John Dominic Crossan and Jonathan L. Reed, *Excavating Jesus* (San Francisco: HarperSanFrancisco, 2001), 125.

7. James F. Strange, "First Century Galilee from Archeology and the Texts," in Douglas E. Edwards and Christine Thomas McCollough, eds., *Archeology and the* Galilee (Atlanta, GA: Scholars, 1997), 42.

8. Simon C. Mimouni has emphasized this point: "Les imposteurs dans les communautés chrétiennes des Ier-IIe siècles," *Annali di Storia dell'Esegesi* 27 (2010) 255-64.

9. Georges Hubert de Radkowski, *Anthropologie de l'habiter. Vers le nomadisme* (Paris: PUF, 2002), 82.

10. "These galli do not seem to have had a fixed organization, but were wandering groups, with song and music": Halvor Moxnes, *Putting Jesus in His Place* (Louisville and London: Westminster John Knox Press, 2003), 79.

11. Ibid., 67.

12. See Marc Augé, *Non-Lieux: Introduction à une anthropologie de la surmodernité* (Paris: Seuil, 1992).

13. Mark 13:33-37/Matt 25:13-15. The parable of Luke (Luke 19:12-14, 27; cf. Luke 12:38-40) is very different from that of Mark 13:33-37.

14. The scenes in these parables depict high social strata: it is these persons who travel. We should, however, not exclude the possibility that members of the lower strata of society could likewise travel for reasons of necessity (for example, funerals, religious duties, work as craftsmen, farm labor).

15. Strange, "First Century Galilee," 41-42.

16. Daniel Hervieu-Léger, *La religion en mouvement: Le pèlerin et le converti* (Paris: Flammarion, 1999); Alphonse Dupront, *Du Sacré, croisades et*

pèlerinages: Images et langages (Paris: Gallimard, 1987); Victor Turner and Edith Turner, *Image and Pilgrimage in Christian Culture* (New York: Columbia University Press, 1995); Shemuel Safrai, *Wallfahrt im Zeitalter des zweiten Tempels* (Neukirchen-Vluyn: Neukirchener Verlag, 1981).

17. To some extent, John 4:21-25 seems to attribute to Jesus criticism of the idea of pilgrimage.

18. Cf. Hervieu-Léger, *La religion en mouvement*.

19. The same necessity is seen at the time of Jubilee: cf. Lev 25:9 and Mauro Pesce, "La remissione dei peccati nell'escatologia di Gesù," *Annali di Storia dell'Esegesi* 16 (1999): 45-76.

20. "And lest he himself be interpreted as simply the new broker of a new God, he moved on constantly, settling down neither at Nazareth nor at Capernaum. He was neither broker nor mediator but, somewhat paradoxically, the announcer that neither should exist between humanity and divinity or between humanity and itself. Miracle and parable, healing and eating were calculated to force individuals into unmediated physical and spiritual contact with one another. he announced, in other words, the brokerless kingdom of God": John Dominic Crossan, *The Historical Jesus: The Life of a Mediterranean Jewish Peasant* (San Francisco: HarperSanFrancisco, 1991), 422.

21. The Johannine contrast between adoring God in a localized temple (the goal of what modern language calls the "pilgrimage") and adoring God in one's own self through the Spirit does not reflect either the historical itinerancy of Jesus or his central interest, and strips away every territorial dimension from Jesus' itinerancy.

22. We take Mark as our example: "Jesus went about among the villages teaching. He called the twelve and began to send them out two by two" (6:6); "When they had crossed over, they came to land at Gennesaret" (6:53); "and getting into the boat again [where the disciples were], he went across to the other side" (8:13-14); "They came to Bethsaida" (8:22). Jesus converses with his disciples as he walks with them: "Jesus went on with his disciples to the villages of Caesarea Philippi, and on the way he asked his disciples..." (8:27); "They went on from there and passed through Galilee. He did not want anyone to know it" (9:30); "Then they came to Capernaum; and when he was in the house he asked them: 'What were you arguing about on the way?'" (9:33); "He left that place and went to the region of Judea and beyond the Jordan," and it seems that the disciples were present (10:1, 10): "They were on the road, going up to Jerusalem, and Jesus was walking ahead of them; they were amazed, and those who followed were afraid" (10:32); "They came to Jericho. As he and his disciples and a large crowd were leaving Jericho..." (10:46); "When they were approaching Jerusalem, at Bethphage and Bethany, near the Mount of Olives, he sent two of his disciples..." (11:1). The scene does not change during his movements in Jerusalem: "Then he entered Jerusalem and went into the Temple; and when he had looked around at everything, as it was already late, he went out to Bethany with the twelve" (11:11); "Then they came to Jerusalem. And he entered the Temple and began to drive out those who were selling..." (11:15); "And when evening

came, Jesus and his disciples went out of the city" (11:19); "In the morning as they passed by, they saw the fig tree withered away to its roots" (11:20); "Again they came to Jerusalem . . ." (11:27); "As he came out of the Temple, one of his disciples said to him . . ." (13:1); "When it was evening he came with the twelve" to the place prepared for the Passover (14:17).

23. Jacques Le Goff, *Pour un autre moyen âge* (Paris: Gallimard, 1977).
24. "Jesus departed with his disciples to the sea": Mark 3:7.
25. When we speak of *prayer* here, we should think of the *personal* prayer that the studies by J. Heineman have carefully distinguished from the institutional, collective, and public Judaic prayer.
26. Frequently, the silence imposed by Jesus in the Gospel of Mark has been explained on exclusively theological and religious grounds in the wake of the celebrated essay by Wilhelm Wrede, *Das Messiasgeheimnis in den Evangelien* (Göttingen, 1901; ET: *The Messianic Secret* [Cambridge: Lutterworth, 1987]). Scholars have spoken of a "messianic secret" (see also Giorgio Jossa, *Dal Messia al Cristo* [Brescia: Paideia, 2000]), but we must surely begin by looking at the structure of itinerancy as the context in which Jesus develops his techniques of withdrawal and silence.
27. It is possible that some interpretations of Jesus, such as those we find in the Gospels of Thomas and John, have developed in the light of this kind of experience on Jesus' part.
28. More than a century ago, Albert Schweitzer underlined the need of solitude as a characteristic trait of Jesus, but he did not understand that this was a recurrent solitude with an essential function, a solitude born of the structure of Jesus' itinerancy. Schweitzer imagined that Jesus wanted to be "alone with the disciples" as a strategy "to carry out what he already had in mind" (*Das Messianitäts- und Leidensgeheimnis: Eine Skizze des Lebens Jesu* [Tübingen: Mohr, 1901]; quoted from the ET: *The Mystery of the Kingdom of God* [New York: Dodd, Mead, 1914], 175, 179; often reprinted). Furthermore, he proposed the insufficiently founded hypothesis that Jesus spent a long period, fall and winter, alone with his disciples in a "heathen territory" (*The Mystery*, 253).

3. Jesus Face to Face

1. A tendency to underestimate the role played by the persons whom Jesus met is already at work in the Gospels, given that their primary aim is to highlight the extraordinary figure of Jesus.
2. On the methodological level, it would be necessary to give a complete list of the individual examples, but space does not allow this. We limit ourselves to the Gospel of Mark, where we find an extraordinary succession of very varied persons: Simon, Andrew, James, and John (1:16-20); persons in the synagogue at Capernaum (1:21-28); a man in the same synagogue who is possessed by a demon (1:23); Simon's mother-in-law in her house (1:30); sick persons and demoniacs (1:32-34); the entire city (1:33); a leper (1:40-45); a paralytic accompanied by four persons (2:3-12); scribes who are present at the healing of the

paralytic (2:6); Levi at the tax house (2:13); many tax collectors and sinners in Levi's house (2:15); disciples of John and disciples of the Pharisees who are fasting (2:18); Pharisees (2:23); a man with a withered hand in the synagogue (3:1-5); people who come from the surrounding regions (3:8-9); the Twelve: Simon Peter, James and John the sons of Zebedee, Andrew, Philip, Bartholomew, Matthew, Thomas, James the son of Alphaeus, Thaddaeus, Simon the Cananaean, Judas Iscariot (3:16-18); those around Jesus (3:21); scribes (3:22); his mother, brothers (and sisters) (3:31-32); disciples ("those around him") and the Twelve (4:10); a demoniac (5:1); Jairus, one of the rulers of the synagogue (5:21-24, 35-43); a woman with a flow of blood (5:25-34); a list of brothers and sisters of Jesus (James, Joses, Judas, Simon, and the unnamed sisters) (6:3); the Twelve (6:7); the Twelve, sent out to preach (6:30); the crowd of five thousand (6:33); Pharisees and scribes (7:1); the Syro-Phoenician woman (7:25-30); a deaf and mute man in the region of the Decapolis (6:31-37); the crowd of four thousand persons (8:1-9); Pharisees (8:11); the blind man at Bethsaida (8:22); Peter (8:29, 32-33); Peter, James, and John (9:1-10); disciples with scribes (9:14-15); a mute child possessed by a demon (9:17-27); the Twelve (9:35); John, who asks Jesus about an exorcist (9:38); Pharisees (10:2); children (10:13); a rich man (10:17-22); James and John (10:35-40); blind Bartimaeus at Jericho (10:46-52); people in the Temple, money changers and sellers of doves (11:15-16); chief priests, scribes, and elders (members of the Sanhedrin) (11:27); Pharisees and Herodians (12:13-17); Sadducees (12:18-27); a scribe (12:28); Peter, James, and Andrew (13:1-27); Simon the leper (14:3); the woman with the vase of perfume (14:3-9); Judas Iscariot (14:10); the Twelve at the Last Supper (14:17-26); Judas (14:43); the young man wearing a linen garment (14:51); the high priest, elders, and scribes (14:53-64); slaves (14:65); Pilate (15:1-15); the crowd that demands the release of Barabbas (15:8-14); soldiers (15:16-20); Simon of Cyrene (15:21-22); passers-by who insult Jesus, priests, and scribes (15:29-32); one of those present with a sponge soaked in vinegar (15:36); a centurion (15:39); some women, Mary, Mary the mother of James and Joses, Salome, and many others (15:40-41); Joseph of Arimathea (15:43); Pilate (15:44); Mary of Magdala and Mary the mother of James (15:47); Mary of Magdala, Mary the mother of James, and Salome (16:1); Mary of Magdala (16:9); the Eleven (16:14).

3. Gerd Theissen, *Die Jesusbewegung* (Gütersloh: Gütersloher Verlagshaus, 2004), 146; cf. 141-51.

4. Mark 1:2-11; Matt 3:1-12; Luke 3:1-22; John 1:29-36; *Gospel of the Nazarenes* 1 (in Jerome, *Against the Pelagians* 3.2.1); *Gospel of the Ebionites* (in Epiphanius, *Panarion* 30.13.6-8); *Gospel of the Hebrews* (in Jerome, *Commentary on Isaiah* 11.1).

5. On John the Baptizer, see Joan Taylor, *John the Baptist within Second Temple Judaism: A Historical Study* (London: SPCK, 1997); Edmondo Lupieri, *Giovanni Battista fra storia e leggenda* (Brescia: Paideia, 1988); Mauro Pesce, "Gesù e il sacrificio ebraico," *Annali di Storia dell' Esegesi* 18 (2001): 146-51.

6. Josephus speaks of this in his so-called autobiography, written toward the end of the first century C.E. (*Vita* 1.1).

3. Jesus Face to Face

7. "In the wilderness" (according to Mark 1:4); "into all the region around the Jordan" (according to Luke 3:3).

8. John Dominic Crossan, *Jesus: A Revolutionary Biography* (San Francisco: HarperSan Francisco, 1994), 51.

9. Josephus, *Jewish Antiquities* 18.117; Mauro Pesce, "La remissione dei peccati nell'escatologia di Gesù," *Annali di Storia dell'Esegesi* 16 (1999): 45-76; on the baptism of John the Baptizer, see Edmondo Lupieri, *Giovanni Battista nelle traditioni sinottiche* (Brescia: Paideia, 1988), 27 and 74; idem, *Giovanni Battista fra storia e leggenda*, 31-36, 60-61, 119-31; Richard E. DeMaris, "The Baptism of Jesus: A Ritual-Critical Approach," in Wolfgang Stegemann, Bruce J. Malina, and Gerd Theissen, eds., *The Social Setting of Jesus and the Gospels* (Minneapolis: Fortress Press, 2002), 137-57.

10. Roger T. Beckwith, "The Year of the Messiah," in *Calendar and Chronology, Jewish and Christian* (Leiden: Brill, 2001), 217-75.

11. *Gospel of the Nazarenes*, quoted by Jerome, *Against the Pelagians* 3.2.1.

12. Josephus writes that the immersion aimed at "the purity of the body" (*Jewish Antiquities* 18.117).

13. On John's diet, see James A. Kelhoffer, *The Diet of John the Baptist: "Locusts and Wild Honey" in Synoptic and Patristic Interpretation* (Tübingen: Mohr Siebeck, 2005); Edmondo Lupieri, "La purità impura," *Henoch* 7 (1985): 15-43.

14. In Luke, however, the picture of the Baptizer resembles that of an itinerant preacher, since we read that he "went into all the region around the Jordan" (Luke 3:3).

15. Luke 7:17-23; Matt 11:26. It is probable that both Luke and Matthew have taken this episode from the source of sayings of Jesus known to scholars as "Q."

16. See Gerd Theissen and Annette Merz, *Der historische Jesus: Ein Lehrbuch* (3rd ed.; Göttingen: Vandenhoeck & Ruprecht, 2001); ET: *The Historical Jesus: A Comprehensive Guide* (London: SCM, 1998), 146.

17. This is shown by some words of Jesus (Matt 23:15) and by the extreme mobility of Paul even before he belonged to the Judean group of believers in Jesus. Paul moves between Jerusalem, Damascus, and Arabia. See Jacob Neusner and Bruce Chilton, eds., *In Search of the Historical Pharisees* (Waco, TX: Baylor University Press, 2006).

18. See Adriana Destro and Mauro Pesce, "Fathers and Householders in Jesus' Movement: The Perspective of the Gospel of Luke," *Biblical Interpretation* 11 (2003): 211-38.

19. Families of fishers could form cooperatives and work on contracts. They could display an organizational capacity that went beyond the limits of their own families, making use of salaried workers and helpers. Craftsmen worked for the fishermen, constructing anchors, boats, and baskets to hold the fish. The fish were processed, conserved, and distributed by wholesale merchants throughout the rest of the Land of Israel and the Mediterranean region. Merchants and producers supplied salt, wine, oil, and amphoras to the boats (see K. C. Hanson and Douglas E. Oakman, *Palestine in the Time of Jesus* [Minneapolis: Fortress Press,

1998], 107-9). On the system of fishing in the Sea of Galilee, see K. C. Hanson, "The Galilean Fishing Economy and the Jesus Tradition," *Biblical Theology Bulletin* 27 (1997): 99-111.

20. James F. Strange, "First Century Galilee from Archeology and from the Texts," in Douglas E. Edwards and Christine Thomas McCollough, eds., *Archeology and the Galilee* (Atlanta, GA: Scholars, 1997), 39-42.

21. "As they were going along the road, someone said to him, 'I will follow you wherever you go.' And Jesus said to him, 'Foxes have holes, and birds of the air have nests; but the Son of Man has nowhere to lay his head.' To another he said, 'Follow me.' But he said, 'Lord, let me first go and bury my father.' But Jesus said to him, 'Let the dead bury their dead; but as for you, go and proclaim the kingdom of God.' Another said, 'I will follow you, Lord; but let me first say farewell to those at my home.' Jesus said to him, 'No one who puts a hand to the plow and looks back is fit for the kingdom of God.'"

22. Adriana Destro and Mauro Pesce, "Seguire un maestro," in G. Filoramo, ed., *Maestro e discepolo* (Brescia: Morcelliana, 2002), 141-58; Adriana Destro and Mauro Pesce, *Come nasce una religione* (Bari and Rome: Laterza, 2000), 32-40.

23. Diogenes Laertius, 7.1-2.

24. This is one explanation of the liberty and variety in the transmission of the deeds and words of Jesus.

25. Gerd Theissen, *Studien zur Soziologie des Urchristentums* (Tübingen: Mohr Siebeck, 1989).

26. See Martin Hengel, *Nachfolge und Charisma* (Berlin: Töpelmann, 1968); ET: *The Charismatic Leader and His Followers* (Eugene, OR: Wipf & Stock, 2005).

27. Theissen, *Die Jesusbewegung*, chap. 1.

28. A description of these adherents only in terms of their membership in particular social strata is inadequate, because they differ in their localization, their relationships, and their mobility, and these factors have to be taken into consideration in addition to their status as peasants, craftsmen, or wealthy persons. Cf. Theissen, *Soziologie des Urchristentums*.

29. Theissen, *Die Jesusbewegung*, chap. 1.

30. Many recent studies have highlighted the tendency of the Gospels to keep silent about the role played by women in Jesus' movement and to reduce this to secondary and subordinate functions. See below notes 31, 32, 67, 68, 71 and Chapter 5, notes 14 and 51.

31. Ramsay MacMullen, "Women in Public in the Roman Empire," *Historia* 29 (1980): 208-18; Jane F. Gardner, *Women in Roman Law and Society* (Bloomington: Indiana University Press, 1986); Sarah B. Pomeroy, ed., *Women's History and Ancient History* (Chapel Hill, NC, and London: University of North Carolina Press, 1991); Ross Shephard Kraemer, *Her Share of the Blessings* (New York and Oxford: Oxford University Press, 1992).

32. Jan N. Bremmer, "Why Did Early Christianity Attract Upper-Class Women?" in Antoon A. R. Bastiaensen and Antonius Hilhorst, eds., *Fructus*

centesimus (Dordrecht: Kluwer, 1989), 35-47; Judith M. Lieu, "The Attraction of Women in/to early Judaism and Christianity," *JSNT* 72 (1998): 5-22.

33. Destro and Pesce, "Fathers and Householders," 215.

34. Kraemer, *Her Share of the Blessings*, 139.

35. This ritual structure is present in Mark, too, although it is not emphasized as clearly as in Luke. This may mean that Luke has projected onto Jesus a ritual pattern of his own.

36. Frederick Barth's anthropological reflection on groups (*Ethnic Groups and Boundaries* [Prospect Heights, IL: Waveland Press 1969], 10-11) regards the following factors as important for the work of analysis: (a) the permanent character or the decline of a group; (b) the values and goals that are shared within the group; (c) the existence of systems of communication and exchange; and (d) distinctive traits vis-à-vis the outside, and the recognition of this kind of distinctiveness.

37. Many lists of the Twelve existed in the early church; see the recent translation by François Dolbeau of the Greco-Syrian list and of the list attributed to Epiphanius of Salamis, in Pierre Geoltrain and Jean-Daniel Kaestli, eds., *Écrits Apocryphes Chrétiens* 2 (Paris: Gallimard, 2005), 453-80.

38. Theissen, *Die Jesusbewegung*, 35, following Dennis Duling, "The Jesus Movement and Social Network Analysis. Part I: The Spatial Network," *Biblical Theology Bulletin* 29 (1999).

39. In Matthew and Luke, but not in Mark.

40. See W. Klassen, *Judas: Betrayer or Friend of Jesus* (London: SCM, 1996).

41. Destro and Pesce, "Seguire un maestro," 142-45.

42. However, they preach only after spending a certain period of time with him: see Mark 6:7; Luke 9:1-2; and perhaps Matt 10:1.

43. This saying probably comes from the Q source. The fact that the institution of the Twelve disappeared very soon after the death of Jesus shows that the saying about the twelve thrones belongs to that part of the tradition that was less influenced by the earliest churches.

44. Luke 22:29-30. Matt 19:28 speaks instead of *palingenēsis*. It is important to remember that the number twelve has a symbolic value and could be interpreted as a reference to the twelve tribes of Israel, as the saying in Matt 19:28 affirms. Also, the function of judge definitely belongs to the Son of Man, who will come at the end of the world. The choice of the Twelve thus seems to imply that Jesus intends to be the judge of the whole people of Israel, together with his disciples, at the inauguration of the kingdom.

45. The *imminence* of the kingdom of God is presupposed by the discussions about the commanding role that each of the Twelve is to play in it (Mark 10:35-42; Luke 22:24).

46. See Mary Douglas, "Cultural Bias" (Occasional Paper of the Royal Anthropological Institute of Great Britain and Ireland 35; London: Royal Anthropological Institute, 1978), reprinted in *In the Active Voice* (London: Routledge & Kegan Paul, 1982), 7.

47. François Bovon, *L'Évangile selon saint Luc (1,1-9,50)*. Vol. 1 (Geneva: Labor et Fides, 2007), ad loc. Hans Klein (*Das Lukasevangelium* [Göttingen: Vandenhoeck & Ruprecht, 2006], 375) suggests that "if the Twelve are to be compared to the twelve patriarchs, the seventy should be seen as an allusion to the administrative officials of Israel," on the model of Num 11:16, 24 where the seventy elders are Moses' collaborators. Besides this, the Sanhedrin was made up of seventy members (Mishnah, tractate *Sanhedrin* 1.6). Josephus appointed seventy elders for the administration of Galilee during the revolt (*Jewish War* 2.220; 5.270f.), and the Zealots did the same in Jerusalem (*Jewish War* 4.334f.). At Alexandria, there were seventy elders. Finally, the *Book of Enoch* speaks of seventy shepherds (*1 Enoch* 89:59; cf. Klein, *Das Lukasevangelium*, ad loc.).

48. We accept the thesis that the "brothers" of Jesus are his brothers by blood. No canonical text that speaks of the brothers of Jesus tells us that these were not the sons of Mary and Joseph; if this had been a sensitive issue, it would have been natural to clear up the doubts. The early Christian testimonies often present the brothers of Jesus with his mother in such a way that she appears to be truly their mother (*Gospel of the Nazarenes*; cf. Jerome, *Against the Pelagians* 3.2.1; John 2:11-12; Mark 6:3; Acts 1:14). Daniel Marguerat ("Jésus et ses frères," in Daniel Marguerat et al., eds., *Jésus, complements d'enquête* [Paris: Bayard, 2007], 142-49) has recalled that in the second century Tertullian and Hegesippus spoke of genuine brothers of Jesus, while the *Protevangelium of James* spread the theory that the brothers of Jesus were the sons of Joseph from an earlier marriage. It was only in the fourth century that Jerome introduced the opinion that there was no clear distinction drawn in Hebrew between "brothers" and "cousins." The Catholic exegete John P. Meier dismisses the claim that the noun *adelphos* ("brother") is regularly used in the Greek New Testament for what we call "cousins" (*A Marginal Jew: Rethinking the Historical Jesus* [4 vols.; New York: Doubleday, 1991], 1:324-29). There is only one text in the Septuagint that can be adduced in support of Jerome's hypothesis: 1 Chron 23:22. We find a much more conservative Catholic thesis than that of Meier in Josef Blinzler, *Die Brüder und Schwestern Jesu* (2d ed.; SBS 21; Stuttgart: Katholisches Bibelwerk, 1967).

49. See Acts 12:17 and 15:19, where it appears that the supreme authority to whom people have recourse in Jerusalem is James.

50. This tradition is followed by Hegesippus, quoted by Eusebius, *Historia ecclesiastica* 4.22.4.

51. Mark 6:3; cf. Matt 13:55-56; John 6:42. Luke 4:16-30 omits this passage.

52. Images of Jesus' family gradually emerged over the centuries. Some are limited to the depiction of the mother with child, or of the young Jesus with his mother and often with his father. This is how the so-called Holy Family was constructed. Unlike the Gospel of Mark, therefore, the best-known iconography suggests that the domestic milieu of Jesus contained only three types of persons (father, mother, and Jesus): the father is inserted, and the brothers and sisters are eliminated. The sisters are mentioned only in Mark 6:3; the other evangelists omit them. The elimination of the brothers and sisters excises one element

3. Jesus Face to Face 197

from the historical figure of Jesus, while the presence of the father reinforces the pattern of parents and children, on which the domestic milieu is based. The combination of these two factors has "canonized" one exclusive type of family, which does not agree with the type we find in the Gospels.

53. This saying certainly goes back to Jesus himself, because it assumes that it is possible to do the will of God without any intervention by the grace of God or without any christological help. It is transmitted by Mark 3:31-35; Matt 12:46-50; Luke 8:19-21; *Gospel of Thomas* 99; *Gospel of the Hebrews*, quoted by Epiphanius, *Panarion* 30.14.5; and by the unknown Gospel that may be used in *2 Clement* 9:11 (on these two last texts, see Mauro Pesce, ed., *Le parole dimenticate di Gesù* [Milan: Lorenzo Valla-Mondadori, 2004], 643-44; 609). Matthew has modified Mark, changing "the will of God" to "the will of my Father." He moves away from the original words of Jesus in order to maintain his own christological viewpoint and to underline that the only criterion of kinship in religious matters is dependence on the "father" who is God (see Joachim Gnilka, *Das Matthäusevangelium* [Herders theologischer Kommentar zum Neuen Testament I/2; Freiburg i.Br.: Herder, 1988], ad loc.).

54. The expression "out of his mind" would be so grave on the lips of disciples, friends, or relatives of Jesus that some scholars have suggested that Mark is speaking not of Jesus but of the crowd, that is, "It has gone mad." See Camille Focant, *L'Évangile selon Marc* (Paris: Cerf, 2004), 151-53.

55. François Vouga, *Geschichte des frühen Christentums* (Stuttgart: UTB, 1994), highlights the tendency of the itinerant preachers, after the death of Jesus, to take a hostile attitude to his family.

56. See Adriana Destro and Mauro Pesce, "Kinship, Discipleship, and Movement," *Biblical Interpretation* 3 (1995): 266-84; Adriana Destro and Mauro Pesce, *Antropologia delle origini cristiane* (4th ed.; Bari and Rome: Laterza, 2008), 68-72.

57. Francis J. Moloney attempts to avoid the contrast between the position of Jesus and that of his brothers by maintaining that his brothers "asked him to leave Galilee for Judea but not to be in Jerusalem for the feast" (*The Gospel of John* [Collegeville, MN: Liturgical, 1998], 237).

58. "When they had entered the city, they went to the room upstairs where they were staying, Peter, and John, and James, and Andrew, Philip and Thomas, Bartholomew and Matthew, James son of Alphaeus, and Simon the Zealot, and Judas son of James. All these were constantly devoting themselves to prayer, together with certain women, including Mary the mother of Jesus, as well as his brothers" (Acts 1:13-14).

59. Richard Bauckham, "James and the Jerusalem Community," in O. Skarsaune and R. Hvalik, eds., *Jewish Believers in Jesus* (Peabody, MA: Hendrickson, 2007), 55-95.

60. According to Jerome, *Vir. Ill.* 2. ET: J. K. Elliott, *The Apocryphal New Testament* (Oxford: Clarendon, 1993), 9-10.

61. Translation by A. F. J. Klijn, *Jewish-Christian Gospel Tradition* (Leiden: Brill, 1992) 80.

62. Crossan asks why the execution of James should have led to the deposition of Ananus after a mere three months in office. "James must have had powerful, important and politically organized friends in Jerusalem," even before the death of Jesus (*Jesus: A Revolutionary Biography*, 152).

63. Bauckham represents a widely held view when he suggests that James would only gradually have assumed the pre-eminent position that he seems to have in Acts 15, and that he certainly has in Acts 21 ("James," 67).

64. On friendship from a sociological perspective, see Shmuel N. Eisenstadt and Luis Roniger, *Patrons, Clients and Friends* (Cambridge: Cambridge University Press, 1984), 21.

65. John 15:13-15. We should, however, note that John takes a very positive view of the function of the slave (cf. Destro and Pesce, *Come nasce una religione*, 51-59). See also A. Destro and M. Pesce, "The Colour of Words. An Analysis of the Gospel of John. From 'Social Death' to Freedom in the Household," in P. Arzt-Grabner and Christina M. Kreinecker, eds., *Light from the East: Papyrologische Kommentare zum Neuen Testament* (Wiesbaden: Harrassowitz, 2010), 27-46.

66. John 13:23; 19:26; 21:20. The Gospel of Mark also seems to assume that Jesus chooses the disciples because he loves them (Mark 10:21).

67. John 12:3. See Margaret M. Beirne, *Women and Men in the Fourth Gospel* (London: Sheffield Academic Press, 2003/Edinburgh: T&T Clark, 2004).

68. See the article by Kathleen E. Corley, "Were the Women around Jesus Really Prostitutes?" in *Women in the Context of Greco-Roman Meals* (Society of Biblical Literature 1989 Seminar Papers; Atlanta: Scholars, 1989), 487-521. She notes that the Gospel tradition nowhere affirms explicitly that Jesus was well known as one who ate with prostitutes (519); the only evidence in favor of this idea is Matt 21:31, where Jesus says that "tax collectors and prostitutes" will enter the kingdom of heaven before the others. The Greco-Roman image of the symposium, however, envisages the presence of women, some (but not most) of whom were courtesans and sometimes also prostitutes. The influence of this image on the Gospel tradition makes no distinction between the movement of Jesus and the customs of Greco-Roman society (519-21).

69. Luke 10:38-42. See Carolyn Osiek and David Balch, *Families in the New Testament World: Households and House Churches* (Louisville: Westminster John Knox, 1997), 140-44.

70. The fact that the Gospel of John too speaks of Martha and Mary, although in completely different terms, shows that despite the contradictory information given by the two Gospels, these women had an important place in early Christian memory. They may have been sedentary followers of Jesus.

71. On the activity of women in the so-called house churches, see Carolyn Osiek and Margaret Y. MacDonald, *A Woman's Place: House Churches in Earliest Christianity* (Minneapolis: Augsburg Fortress Press, 2005), 17ff. See also A. Destro and M.Pesce, "Dal gruppo interstiziale di Gesù alla *ekklēsia*:

3. Jesus Face to Face 199

mutamenti nel ruolo delle donne," *Annali di Storia dell'Esegesi* 27, no. 2 (2010) 3-21.

72. Mark 7:24-30/Matt 15:21-28. On Matthew's version, see Amy-Jill Levine, *The Social and Ethnic Dimension of Matthean Salvation History* (New York: Edwin Mellen, 1998), 131-64.

73. The episode of the Samaritan woman at the well is probably a theological creation of the Gospel of John, and we can omit it here. Its symbolic elements are much stronger than its realistic traits.

74. Gerd Theissen, *Urchristliche Wundergeschichten* (Gütersloh: Mohn, 1998); Theissen and Merz, *Der historische Jesus*; Graham H. Twelftree, *Jesus the Exorcist* (Tübingen: Mohr, 1993); Clinton Wahlen, *Jesus and the Impurity of Spirits in the Synoptic Gospels* (Tübingen: Mohr Siebeck, 2004); Barry Blackburn, *Theios Anēr and the Markan Miracle Traditions* (Tübingen: Mohr, 1991); Meier, *A Marginal Jew*, vol. 2; Santiago Guijarro, "The Politics of Exorcism," in Wolfgang Stegemann, Bruce J. Malina, and Gerd Theissen, eds., *The Social Setting of Jesus and the Gospels* (Minneapolis: Fortress Press, 2002), 159-74.

75. In the parable of the Good Samaritan, Jesus says that the Levite and the priest do not stop to help the wounded man, but this cannot really be read as a criticism of the priesthood as an institution.

76. Pesce, "Il Vangelo di Giovanni e le fasi giudaiche del giovannismo," in G. Filoramo e C. Gianotto (a cura di), *Verus Israel: Nuove prospettive sul giudeocristianesimo. Atti del Colloquio di Torino (4-5 novembre 1999)* (Brescia: Paideia 2001), 55-58.

77. For a debate on the historicity of the passion narratives, see John Dominic Crossan, *Who Killed Jesus?* (San Francisco: HarperSanFrancisco, 1996); Raymond E. Brown, *The Death of the Messiah* (2 vols.; New York: Doubleday, 1999); Ellis Rivkin, *What Crucified Jesus?* (New York: UAHC, 1997), 1-77.

78. See, for example, Ekkehard Stegemann and Wolfgang Stegemann, *Urchristliche Sozialgeschichte* (Stuttgart: Kohlhammer, 1997); ET: *The Jesus Movement* (Minneapolis: Fortress Press, 2001).

79. According to some manuscripts, Jesus used the language of fishers and declared that it is easier for a hawser (*kamilos* in Greek) to pass through the eye of a needle. The copyists then replaced *kamilos* with the almost identical noun *kamēlos*, which is pronounced in the same way, but means "camel."

80. Luke 6:24. In Matthew, this discourse is pronounced on a mountain.

81. See Maria Luisa Rigato, *Giovanni: L'enigma, il presbitero, il culto* (Bologna: Edizioni Dehoniane, 2007).

82. See Levine, *Social and Ethnic Dimension*, 1-57.

83. Gnilka, *Matthäusevangelium*, ad loc. See his remarks on the difficult theological question that divides Catholics and Protestants.

84. We prefer not to discuss here the difficult question of the relationship between orality and writing as instruments employed in communication.

85. Filoramo, ed., *Maestro e discepolo*, 7-10.

4. Jesus at Table: Eating Together

1. Claude Lévi-Strauss, *Le cru et le cuit* (Paris: Plon, 1964); Mary Douglas, "Deciphering a Meal," *Daedalus* 101 (1972): 61-81; Jack Goody, *Cooking, Cuisine and Class: A Study in Comparative Sociology* (Cambridge: Cambridge University Press, 1982); Aïda Kanafani-Zahar, Séverine Matthieu, and Sophie Nizard, eds., *A croire et à manger: Religions et alimentation* (Paris: L'Harmattan, 2007); cf. also Max Weber, *Economy and Society*. II (Los Angeles: University of California Press, 1978), 434-35.

2. We recall the celebrated tripartite structure of Marcel Mauss (giving, receiving, giving back) primarily because of the idea of a *process* that this implies. No gift is made in one single instant, in such a way that the action would be suddenly over. Cf. Marcel Mauss, "Essai sur le don. Forme et raison de l'échange dans les sociétés archaïques," published as volume 2 of *Année Sociologique* (1923-1924).

3. When a host receives a prominent person in his house, he invites the leading representatives of his own milieu in order to demonstrate to the powerful guest the network of support and clientship on which he can rely. The guest is rewarded for his willingness to come to the house by being included within this network.

4. Maurice Godelier, *L'énigme du don* (Paris: Fayard, 1996), 7-16.

5. Dennis E. Smith, *From Symposium to Eucharist: The Banquet in the Early Christian World* (Minneapolis: Fortress Press, 2003), 13-172.

6. Carolyn Osiek and David Balch, *Families in the New Testament World: Households and House Churches* (Louisville: Westminster John Knox, 1997), 193-214 (at 210-214), single out the *refrigerium* and the *agapē* in relation to early Christianity, and more specifically to the Eucharist.

7. Smith, *From Symposium to Eucharist*, 82-132.

8. Max Weber, *Economy and Society*, 434.

9. Cf. Matt 10:10. According to John Dominic Crossan and Jonathan L. Reed (*Excavating Jesus* [San Francisco: HarperSanFrancisco, 2001]), 125, Jesus' followers are dependent for food and lodging on the domestic groups that they visit, but they do not receive alms. The hospitality and the food they receive are not a genuine salary but are a metaphorical "recompense." There is no doubt about the historicity of the saying "The laborer is worthy of his hire," given the dependence of Matthew and Luke on Q and the independent testimony in 1 Cor 9:14; Jas 5:4; *Didache* 13.1-2. See Mauro Pesce, ed., *Le parole dimenticate di Gesù* (Milan: Lorenzo Valla-Mondadori, 2004), 504.

10. Actually the Gospels do not say that Jesus was "sitting at table," but that he was "reclining" (see, e.g., Luke 22:14; John 13:12). See Adriana Destro and Mauro Pesce, *Come nasce una religione: Antropologia e esegesi del Vangelo di Giovanni* (Bari and Rome: Laterza, 2000).

11. Mark 14:17-31; Matt 26:30-35; Luke 22:14, 21-34; John 13:1—14:31. The Last Supper can be seen from a variety of perspectives, namely, in terms of the

4. Jesus at Table: Eating Together

place where it is held or of the preparations required. In the Gospel of John, more strongly than in other texts, it is seen as a convivial rite that presents remarkable and indeed anomalous features with regard to current customs—for example, the washing of the feet, which comes at a point in the narrative that contradicts ancient customs of hospitality and convivial meals. See Adriana Destro and Mauro Pesce, *Come nasce una religione* (Bari and Rome: Laterza, 2000), 48-59.

12. Luke 17:7-10. Cf. Luke 11:5-7, which relates the parable of the friend who comes at night.

13. Matt 8:11; Luke 13:29; Mark 14:25. Cf. Norman Perrin, *Rediscovering the Teaching of Jesus* (London: SCM, 1967), 161-64.

14. See Smith, *From Symposium to Eucharist*, 238-39.

15. Ibid., 224.

16. See ibid., 223.

17. Since Luke seems particularly fond of the verb *paratēreomai* ("to observe"), this may be an indication that the entire narrative is his creation. This, however, is not certain, since an author can rewrite in his own fashion a story that he has taken over from others, introducing into it his own preferrred vocabulary.

18. The fact that Luke repeats the question "Is it lawful on the sabbath . . . ?," which is also found in Luke 6:9 (where it depends on Mark 3:4), suggests that he has constructed this scene. However, the episode of healing (Luke 14:2-6) does not form part of the following commensal scene.

19. See Rinaldo Fabris, "La parabola degli invitati alla cena. Analisi redazionale di Lc. 14,16-24," in Jacques Dupont, ed., *La parabola degli invitati al banchetto* (Brescia: Paideia, 1978), 128-41; E. Spring Steele, "Luke 11:37-54: A Modified Hellenistic Symposium?" *JBL* 103 (1984) 379-94.

20. Ezio Pellizer, "Della zuffa simpotica," in Massimo Vetta, ed., *Poesia e simposio nella Grecia antica: Guida storica e critica* (Rome and Bari: Laterza, 1983), 31-41.

21. Many scenes show Jesus eating on the road. In Mark 11:12-13, he looks for fruit on a fig tree; the disciples bring a loaf with them (Mark 8:14) or pluck ears of grain (Mark 2:23); they go into a village to buy food that they will then eat on their own (John 4:8). Some of these stories will be analyzed below.

22. Commentators rightly ask what the "yeast" of the Pharisees and of Herod is, and how it could have influenced the disciples (see Camille Focant, *L'Évangile selon Marc* [Paris: Cerf, 2004], 304-8). The "yeast" has often been linked to the bread that the disciples have with them on the boat, or to the bread in the preceding miracle story. We would emphasize the sharing of food. This provides the occasion for Jesus to teach, and he takes up the theme of the leavened bread, which is a typical element of eating together. The focus on bread in Jesus' teaching reappears later in the words he speaks at the Last Supper. Focant recalls that Paul too speaks of "yeast," of the bread of the Passover, and of Christ as "our Passover" in 1 Cor 5:6-8.

23. Our affirmation of the historicity of this fundamental aspect of the life of Jesus is based on the following considerations. We begin with an observation that cannot be denied, namely, that Jesus needed to eat. Logically speaking, it is probable that he needed to eat along the road. In the social imagination in which Mark presented the practice of life of Jesus, it was normal that he looked for food everywhere he went.

24. Mark 7:1-23/Matt 15:1-20. It is strange that Luke has omitted this story.

25. Roger P. Booth, *Jesus and the Laws of Purity: Tradition History and Legal History in Mark 7* (Sheffield: JSOT, 1985), 155-87; Adriana Destro and Mauro Pesce, "La normatività del Levitico: Interpretazioni ebraiche e protocristiane," *Annali di Storia dell'Esegesi* 13 (1996): 15-37.

26. Smith, *From Symposium to Eucharist,* 225, doubts whether the Last Supper of Jesus was a Passover supper. He argues that "those who support the historicity of the tradition in Mark often interpret Jesus' last meal with his disciples as a Passover meal. This thesis has not stood up to scrutiny however. For example, there is very little relationship to a Passover meal in the Last Supper text at all, other than introductory reference (Mark 14:12-16), and that is clearly Mark's creation. Thus, even if Jesus did celebrate a Passover meal with his disciples as his last meal, we do not have a clear reminiscence of such a meal in the description we now have."

27. Luke 22:15-16. The *Gospel of the Ebionites* (Epiphanius, *Panarion* 30.22.4) appears to assume this Lukan formulation when it places the following words on the lips of Jesus: "I have no desire to eat the flesh of this Paschal Lamb with you" (trans. J. K. Elliott, *The Apocryphal New Testament* [Oxford: Clarendon, 1993], 15); Pesce, *Le parole dimenticate,* 610.

28. The narrative of the Last Supper is transmitted by several sources: Paul in 1 Cor 11:23-26; Mark 14:22-25; Matt 26:25-29; Luke 22:15-20; John 13:1-20 (where, however, the command to repeat it concerns the gesture of washing the feet of the others, not the gestures and the words connected with the bread and the wine); *Didache* 9.1-5 (where there is no mention of any gesture or word of Jesus).

29. For a thorough study of Judas, see W. Klassen, *Judas: Betrayer or Friend of Jesus* (London: SCM, 1996).

30. Mark 14:20. Luke has the following: "But see, the one who betrays me is with me, and his hand is on the table" (22:21). Matthew has a similar formulation: "The one who has dipped his hand into the bowl with me will betray me" (26:23).

31. On this occasion, we are not told that Jesus taught during the meal, as often happened.

32. See Crossan and Reed, *Excavating Jesus,* 119. They argue that this term does not designate "sinners" who repent: "It means the deliberately, continuously, and obstinately wicked. The term 'tax collectors' or 'toll collectors' indicates those who collaborate with the local or imperial oppressors and/or operate with excessive force, bribery, or corruption."

4. Jesus at Table: Eating Together 203

33. Joël Delobel, "L'onction par la pécheresse: La composition littéraire de Lc., VII,36-50," *Ephemerides Theologiae Lovanienses* 42 (1966): 415-75.

34. Obviously, this is then followed by the final part of the narrative—the arrest, the death, and the resurrection—which we cannot examine in detail here.

35. The Gospels of Luke and John do not relate the second multiplication of food, perhaps because these evangelists regarded Mark's narrative in chap. 8 (paralleled in Matt 15:32-39) as a narrative repetition that could be ignored.

36. See Smith, *From Symposium to Eucharist*, 223.

37. On the debate about the historicity of the miraculous deeds of Jesus, cf. Gerd Theissen and Annette Merz, *Der historische Jesus: Ein Lehrbuch* (3rd ed.; Göttingen: Vandenhoeck & Ruprecht, 2001), §10; John P. Meier, *A Marginal Jew: Rethinking the Historical Jesus* (4 vols.; New York: Doubleday, 1991-2009), vol. 2.

38. Luke 16:22-23. On Luke 16:19-31 as a whole, see Bovon, *Évangile selon saint Luc*. Vol. 2 (Geneva: Labor et Fides, 1991), ad loc.

39. John 13:4-16. On the historicity of this action, see chap. 6 below.

40. On this parable, see Dupont, ed., *La parabola degli invitati*, and Mauro Pesce, "Ricostruzione dell'archetipo letterario comune a Mt 22,1-10 e Lc 14,15-24," in Dupont, ed., *La parabola degli invitati*, 167-236.

41. Giuseppe Barbaglio, "La parabola del banchetto di nozze nella versione di Matteo," in Dupont, ed., *La parabola degli invitati*, 91-96; Joachim Gnilka, *Das Matthäusevangelium* (Herders theologischer Kommentar zum Neuen Testament I/2; Freiburg i.Br.: Herder, 1992), vol. 2, ad loc.

42. Bovon, *Évangile selon saint Luc*, vol. 1 (Geneva: Labor et Fides, 1991), ad loc.; cf. Gnilka, *Matthäusevangelium*, vol. 2, ad loc. Gnilka likewise underlines the christological interpretation superimposed by Matthew; cf. also Focant, *L'Évangile selon Marc*, 124.

43. Cf. Crossan and Reed, *Excavating Jesus*, 116.

44. Ibid., 119.

45. On this saying, see Howard Clark Kee, "Jesus: A Glutton and Drunkard," *New Testament Studies* 42 (1996): 347-93, reprinted in Bruce Chilton and Craig A. Evans, eds., *Authenticating the Word of Jesus* (Leiden: Brill, 1999), 311-32.

46. The concept of the "construction of the human person" is based on an anthropology that sees the individual as born into a culture and entering from the very first moments of his or her existence into a process of development and improvement that is guaranteed by the cultural milieu. See Claude Calame and Mondher Kilani, eds., *La fabrication de l'humain dans les cultures et en anthropologie* (Lausanne: Payot, 1999); Francesco Remotti, *Forme di umanità* (Milan: Bruno Mondadori, 2002).

47. See Destro and Pesce, *Come nasce una religione*, 51-54; Mauro Pesce, "La lavanda dei piedi Gv 13,1-20, il 'Romanzo di Esopo' e i 'Saturnalia' di Macrobio," *Biblica* 80 (1999): 240-49.

48. *Didache* 9:1. Since the command by Jesus to repeat the act of breaking the bread and drinking the wine is found in Paul (taken over by Luke), but not in Mark and Matthew, some scholars find it difficult to affirm the historicity of this command (see Smith, *From Symposium to Eucharist*, 227).

49. Destro and Pesce, *Come nasce una religione*, 48-51.

50. The act of "eating and drinking" in common should not be too quickly interpreted as an anticipation of the kingdom of God. The way in which Jesus wants to change the rules about the sharing of food does not anticipate such realities. Jesus' behavior does indeed seek to overturn the disorder and injustice that hold sway in the present age, but this will be realized to the full only in the kingdom of God.

51. Cf. Luke 13:28-29: "There will be weeping and gnashing of teeth when you see Abraham and Isaac and Jacob and all the prophets in the kingdom of God, and you yourselves thrown out. Then people will come from east and west, from north and south, and will eat in the kingdom of God."

52. Luke 22:29-30. The idea that one will eat and drink is also found in Luke 14:15: "Blessed is anyone who will eat bread in the kingdom of God!"

53. These critics argue that a physical banquet with dead persons would be impossible.

54. Jacques Dupont, *Les béatitudes* (3 vols.; Paris: Etudes Bibliques, 1969-1973).

55. However, this text comes from Ps 35:11 in the Septuagint version and therefore may not be an authentic saying of Jesus. See also *Didache* 3:7.

56. Carlo Nardi, *Il millenarismo: Testi dei secoli I e II* (Fiesole: Nardini, 1995).

57. Justin, *Dialogue with Trypho* 80.5. See Philippe Bobichon, *Justin Martyr: Dialogue avec Tryphon. Edition critique, traduction, commentaire* (2 vols.; Fribourg: Academic Press Fribourg, 2003), 965-68.

58. Justin, *Dialogue* 80.1-5; 81.1-4.

58. Irenaeus, *Adv. Haer.* 5.33.3 (trans. Elliott, *Apocryphal New Testament*, 29-30, slightly modernized here).

5. Jesus Leaves Home and Is Made at Home with Others

1. In *Forme culturali del cristianesimo nascente* (2d ed.; Brescia: Morcelliana, 2008), 67-97, we looked only at the Gospel of Luke. In the present book, we concentrate more on the historical figure of Jesus, his strategy, the "interstitial" nature of his movement, and the unified logic of his utopia.

2. On the domestic sphere, see Jack Goody, *Production and Reproduction* (Cambridge: Cambridge University Press, 1977). For the classical anthropological literature on family ties and the reproduction of the households, organization and production, see, for example, Jack Goody and Stanley J. Tambiah, *Bridewealth and Dowry* (Cambridge: Cambridge University Press, 1974);

Claude Meillassoux, *Femmes, greniers et capitaux* (Paris: Maspero, 1975); ET: *Maidens, Meals and Money* (Cambridge: Cambridge University Press, 1981).

3. See Bovon, *L'Évangile selon saint Luc*. Vol. 1 (Geneva: Labor et Fides, 1991), ad loc.

4. In Luke 4:38 and Matt 8:14, the house belongs to Simon alone.

5. On the formal instruments employed in kinship analysis, see Leonardo Piasere and Piergiorgio Solinas, *Le culture della parentela e l'esogamia perfetta* (Rome: CISU, 1998); Rodney Needham, "Remarques sur l'analyse de la parenté," in Rodney Needham, ed., *La parenté en question* (Paris: Seuil, 1977), 103-31; Roger M. Keesing, *Kingroups and Social Structure* (New York: Holt Rinehart Winston, 1975).

6. The elementary or nuclear family of two successive generations is the basic reproductive nucleus of every kinship system. Historically speaking, it is not the dominant structure, nor is it the only background against which it is meaningful to speak of family structures. See Jack Goody, *The Development of the Family and Marriage in Europe* (Cambridge: Cambridge University Press, 1983); David I. Kertzer and Richard P. Saller, eds., *The Family in Italy from Antiquity to the Present* (New Haven: Yale University Press, 1991); David I. Kertzer and Marzio Barbagli, eds., *Family Life in Early Modern Times, 1500-1789* (New Haven: Yale University Press, 2001). This concept of the elementary family is not automatically applicable to the ancient world.

7. Halvor Moxnes notes that there is no term in Greek or in Latin that corresponds to our noun "family." We find instead *oikonomia*, that is, the administration of a "household" (H. Moxnes, ed., *Constructing Early Christian Families: Family as Social Reality and Metaphor* [London and New York: Routledge, 1997], 20, with a reference to Moses I. Finley, *The Ancient Economy* [London: Chatto & Windus, 1973], 17-21). The Latin noun *familia* corresponds substantially to the Greek *oikos* and to the anthropological concept of the domestic nucleus ("household"). The Latin *familia* corresponds to an enlarged grouping, and its meaning is not univocal. Jane F. Gardner and Thomas Wiedemann, *The Roman Household* (London and New York: Routledge, 1991), 3-4, specify some of the principal meanings of *familia*: "a certain body of persons, defined either by a strict legal bond between the persons themselves or in a general sense of people joined by a looser relationship of kinship," "slaves," and "several persons who all descend by blood from a single remembered source." In Columella, *De re rustica* 1.5.7, *res familiaris* indicates the *villa* as property.

8. It is impossible to cite here the vast American and European scholarly literature on families and households: see Meyer Fortes, "Introduction," in Jack Goody, ed., *The Developmental Cycle in Domestic Groups* (Cambridge: Cambridge University Press, 1971); Jack Goody, *The Oriental, the Ancient, the Primitive* (Cambridge: Cambridge University Press, 1990); John H. Elliott, "Temple versus Household in Luke-Acts," in Jerome H. Neyrey, ed., *The Social World of Luke-Acts* (Peabody, MA: Hendrickson, 1991), 211-40; Suzanne Dixon, *The Roman Family* (Baltimore and London: Johns Hopkins University Press, 1992); Richard P. Saller, *Patriarchy, Property and Death in the Roman Family*

(Cambridge: Cambridge University Press, 1994); Santiago Guijarro, "The Family in First-Century Galilee," in Moxnes, ed. *Constructing Early Christian Families*, 42-65; Sarah B. Pomeroy, *Families in Classical and Hellenistic Greece* (Oxford: Clarendon, 1997); Adriana Destro, "Pensare la famiglia. Percorsi e problemi," in Adriana Destro, ed., *Famiglia islamica* (Bologna: Pàtron, 1998), 9-28; Jan Willen van Henten and Athalya Brenner, eds., *Families and Family Relations as Represented in Early Judaisms and Early Christianities: Texts and Fictions* (Leiden: Deo, 2000); Geoffrey S. Nathan, *The Family in Late Antiquity* (London: Routledge, 2000).

9. On the term *oikos/oikia*, see David G. Horrell, "From *adelphoi* to *oikos theou*: Social Transformation in Pauline Christianity," *Journal of Biblical Literature* 120 (2001): 293-311.

10. Some scholars draw a distinction between "domestic nucleus" and "household" (Gérard Lencoud, "Groupe domestique," in *Dictionnaire de l'éthnologie et de l'anthropologie* [Paris: PUF, 2000], 313), but, in general, anthropologists tend to emphasize that living together and sharing resources and work are elements that characterize both these concepts.

11. "Domesticity" is a relational space that is watched over and protected with a view to the maintenance and the defense of the *oikos*. As we shall see below, it represents the roles to which members of a household are linked.

12. In the Latin world, this figure is often designated by the term *pater familias*.

13. The acts that prepare the conjugal union (contracts, feasts, transactions) are the task of the men, and especially of the head of the household. The father supervises every detail of the conduct of the marriages contracted by the members of the domestic group. This group thus gives him a qualified symbolic role.

14. K. C. Hanson and Douglas E. Oakman, *Palestine in the Time of Jesus* (Minneapolis: Fortress Press, 1998), 30-31; W. Cotter, "Women's Authority Roles in Paul's Churches: Countercultural or Conventional?" *Novum Testamentum* 36 (1994): 350-72; Judith Wegner, *Chattel or Person: The Status of Women in the Mishnah* (New York and Oxford: Oxford University Press, 1988); Carolyn Osiek and Margaret Y. MacDonald, *A Woman's Place: House Churches in Earliest Christianity* (Minneapolis: Augsburg Fortress Press, 2005), 144-244; David Balch and Carolyn Osiek, eds., *Early Christian Families in Context* (Grand Rapids: Eerdmans, 2003), 111-84.

15. Santiago Guijarro, "La familia en la Galilea del siglo primero," *Estudios Bíblicos* 53 (1995): 461-68; Pieter J. J. Botha, "Houses in the World of Jesus," *Neotestamentica* 32 (1998): 37-74; Carolyn Osiek and David Balch, *Families in the New Testament World: Households and House Churches* (Louisville: Westminster John Knox, 1997), 5-36; Andrew Wallace-Hadrill, "Domus and Insulae in Rome: Families and Household," in Balch and Osiek, eds., *Early Christian Families*, 3-18; Monika Trümper, "Material and Social Environment of Greco-Roman Households in the East," in Balch and Osiek, eds., *Early Christian Families*, 19-43; Eric M. Meyers, "The Problems of Gendered Space in Syro-Palestinian Domestic Architecture: The Case of Roman-Period Galilee," in Balch and Osiek, eds.,

Early Christian Families, 44-69; John Dominic Crossan and Jonathan L. Reed, *Excavating Jesus* (San Francisco: HarperSanFrancisco, 2001), 83-85, 103-12, 202-7; Isabella Baldini Lippolis, *La domus tardoantica: forme e rappresentazioni dello spazio domestico* (Imola: University Press Bologna, 2001).

16. See Destro and Pesce, *Le forme culturali del cristianesimo nascente*, 91. (a) We have an example of a villa in the case of the householder who has an *oikonomos* (Luke 16:1-8), and perhaps also in the parable of the banquet (Luke 14:15-24). (b) Large dwellings are represented by the house of the rich man who fails to see the poor Lazarus (Luke 16:19-21), by the house of Levi, who is able to host a "large" banquet (Luke 5:29), and by the house of Zacchaeus (Luke 19:2-10). The houses of the two Pharisees who invite Jesus (Luke 11:37 and 14:1, 7) may also belong here. (c) A spacious house with a courtyard is found in the parable of the prodigal son (Luke 15:11-32). It is possible that other houses opened onto the same courtyard. (d) Medium-sized houses: perhaps that of Simon, who has no slaves, and that of the little *oikodespotēs* who probably has only one slave to carry out all the tasks (Luke 17:7-9). (e) Small houses: the house of Martha (Luke 10:38-42) and the house in Emmaus (24:28-29), where the narrative does not speak of slaves. (f) Houses in an *insula*: it is possible that Luke envisages adjacent houses in the parable of the man who receives a friend by night (Luke 11:5-8) and goes to a neighbor to ask for food (11:5).

17. See Crossan and Reed, *Excavating Jesus*, 81-87, and the sources on which they draw.

18. Richard Saller's definition of patronage: "First, it involves the reciprocal exchange of goods and services. Secondly, to distinguish it from a commercial transaction in the marketplace, the relationship must be a personal one of some duration. Thirdly, it must be asymmetrical, in the sense that the two parts are of unequal status and offer different kinds of goods and services in the exchange—a quality which sets patronage off from friendship between equals" ("Patronage and Friendship in Early Imperial Rome," in A. Wallace-Hadrill, ed., *Patronage in Ancient Society* [London and New York: Routledge, 1990], 49).

19. Saller emphasizes that in the Imperial period, the *patronus-cliens* relationship does have a "technical" meaning, but it does not have a formal legal status. Nothing prevented a Roman from having more than one *patronus*. The vast spectrum of links between men of differing status included links between elderly aristocrats and young men (ibid., 60).

20. See Andrew Wallace-Hadrill, "Patronage in Roman Society: From Republic to Empire," in A. Wallace-Hadrill, ed., *Patronage in Ancient Society*, 65.

21. Since Luke has a tendency to apply the term *polis* to settlements that were certainly not cities (see chap. 1 above, n. 23), he also tends to locate the action and the words of Jesus within the relationship between *oikos* and *polis* (see also Ekkehard Stegemann and Wolfgang Stegemann, *Urchristliche Sozialgeschichte* (Stuttgart: Kohlhammer, 1997), Part III).

22. According to Andrew Wallace-Hadrill, patronage could "provide a connection between the centre of power and the peripheries which the centre

sought to control. From the point of view of the society, patronage represented a flexible method of integration and simultaneously of social control. . . . From the point of view of the individual patron, the ability to persuade others of his power to secure access to benefits was the basis of social credibility" ("Patronage in Roman Society," 85).

23. Wallace-Hadrill mentions three situations in which the function of patronage is weakened. This happens above all when the poor are "too numerous to enter into significant personal" relationships, or when crises occur as a result of debt. The greater the weakness and poverty of the lower classes, the less interesting and fruitful are the patronage relationships. A second case concerns the distribution of land and grain, as with the Gracchi at Rome. A third case would occur when the "relationship of dependence and protection" is monetized ("Patronage in Roman Society," 70-71).

24. Cf. Luke 15:15, where the parable relates that an urban dweller (*politēs*) sends the dissolute son to work in his fields outside the city.

25. James F. Strange, "First Century Galilee from Archeology and from the Texts," in Douglas E. Edwards and Christine Thomas McCollough, eds., *Archeology and the Galilee* (Atlanta, GA: Scholars, 1997), 41-42. See, for example, the house of the wine merchant in Bethsaida. There may also have been tanneries, for example, near Bethsaida: see Richard A. Freund, "The Tannery of Bethsaida," in Rami Arav and Richard A. Freund, eds., *Bethsaida: A City by the North Shore of the Sea of Galilee* (3 vols.; Kirksville, MO: Truman State University Press, 1995, 1999, 2004), 233-48. These businesses did not necessarily have a family base. See Peter Richardson, "Khirbet Qana (and Other Villages) as a Context for Jesus," in James H. Charlesworth, ed., *Jesus and Archeology* (Grand Rapids: Eerdmans, 2006), 120-44.

26. Van Henten and Brenner, *Families and Family Relations*, 188. Van Henten underlines the importance, alongside the "family," of "three other models": a holy community, a group of philosophers of a particular type (the *hairesis*), and the Christians considered as a single people (ibid., 188-90).

27. Adriana Destro and Mauro Pesce, *Come nasce una religione* (Bari and Rome: Laterza, 2000), 25-39; Adriana Destro and Mauro Pesce, "Seguire un maestro," in G. Filoramo, ed., *Maestro e discepolo* (Brescia: Morcelliana, 2002), 142-45; Destro and Pesce, *Forme culturali*, 13-48, esp. 21-31.

28. See John S. Kloppenborg and Stephen G. Wilson, eds., *Voluntary Associations in the Ancient World* (London: Routledge, 1996).

29. See Destro and Pesce, *Come nasce una religione*, 28-39.

30. On the terminology relating to identity, see François Laplantine, *Le métissage* (en collaboration avec A. Nouss) (Paris: Flammarion, 1997); *Je, nous et les autres* (Paris: Le Pommier, 2006); Ulf Hannerz, *Cultural Complexity* (New York: Columbia University Press, 1993).

31. See Hannerz, *Cultural Complexity*.

32. See Zygmunt Bauman (with Keith Tester), *Conversations with Zygmunt Bauman* (Cambridge: Cambridge University Press, 2001).

33. See Destro and Pesce, *Forme culturali*, 67-87.

5. Jesus Leaves Home and Is Made at Home with Others

34. See Pesce, "Discepolato gesuano e discepolato rabbinico. Problemi e prospettive della comparazione," *Aufstieg und Niedergang der römischen Welt II. Prinzipat 25/1* (Berlin/New York Walter de Gruyter, 1982), 351-89, 383 n. 108.

35. See, for example, Leonid Mihajlovic Batkin, *L'idea di individualità nel Rinascimento italiano* (Bari: Laterza, 1992); Michael Foucault, *Technologies of the Self: A Seminar with Michel Foucault*, ed. Luther H. Martin, Huck Gutman, and Patrick H. Hutton (Amherst: University of Massachusetts Press, 1988); Philippe Lejeune and Catherine Viollet, eds., *Genèses du "Je"* (Paris: CNRS Editions, 2000).

36. On the urban elites and individual choices, see Richard Rohrbaugh, "Ethnocentrism and Historical Questions about Jesus," in Wolfgang Stegemann, Bruce J. Malina, and Gerd Theissen, eds., *The Social Setting of Jesus and the Gospels* (Minneapolis: Fortress Press, 2002), 33-39.

37. For Josephus, the ideal was that decisions be determined not by membership in a family or a group but by the personal choice that is possible only because many things are on offer and accessible (at least to certain social strata). See Destro and Pesce, *Le forme culturali*, 77-78.

38. Adriana Destro and Mauro Pesce, "Identità collettiva e identità personale nel cristianesimo paolino e giovanneo," *I quaderni del ramo d'oro* 2 (1998): 33-64. See Martin Hengel, *Nachfolge und Charisma* (Berlin: Töpelmann, 1968), who argues that Jesus' call to follow him is valid only for the individual.

39. For Luke 9:57-58 he is simply a man; for Matt 8:18-20 he is a "scribe."

40. Like the two unnamed individuals in Luke 9:59-60 and 9:61-62.

41. Destro and Pesce, *Forme culturali*, 78-81.

42. Luke 18:28-29/Mark 10:28-30/Matt 19:27-29. See Santiago Guijarro, *Fidelidades en conflicto. La ruptura con la familia por causa del discipulado y de la misión en la tradición sinóptica* (Salamanca: Universidad Pontificia de Salamanca, 1998), 206-7.

43. See, for example, Hengel, *Nachfolge und Charisma*.

44. Every renunciation is linked dramatically to the time at which it is undertaken. "If not now, then when?" is a saying attributed to Hillel, a master of the preceding generation. Jesus knows that if the breach with the *oikos* does not take place "now," it will never take place. We disagree with Hengel (*Nachfolge und Charisma*) that this text intends to demonstrate the superiority of Jesus to the commandment to honor one's father and mother. Rather, what is at stake is the need to cut off in a radical manner the relationships with the household, which would otherwise continue to put a restraining bridle on the disciple. If the disciple puts off responding to the call, he has de facto created a hierarchy of values, since he has not accepted the primacy of the lifestyle of Jesus.

45. In other passages too, Jesus defines the work of the itinerant preacher in language drawn from the world of work or of wages, for example, the world of the agricultural workers who are needed for the harvest. See Luke 10:2; Matt 9:37-38; Matt 20:1-8.

46. Luke 14:33. Cf. also Luke 12:33, "Sell your possessions and give alms." Although this saying, which is found only in Luke, is not addressed explicitly

only to the disciples who must follow Jesus, this is probably the case. See Halvor Moxnes, *The Economy of the Kingdom* (Philadelphia: Fortress Press, 1988), 66-68.

47. It is well known that the parables are not always a safe source of information about daily social practice or about social structures. Nevertheless, an exact comparison with the sources that inform us about daily life, such as the papyrus documents (see John S. Kloppenborg, *The Tenants in the Vineyard* [Tübingen: Mohr Siebeck, 2006], 355-87, on viticulture), confirms the realism of many of the elements contained in the parables.

48. See Adriana Destro and Mauro Pesce, "Die zentrale Rolle des Konflikts in Verkündigung und Handeln Jesu," in Gabriella Gelardini and Peter Schmid, eds., *Theoriebildung im christlich-jüdischen Dialog* (Stuttgart: Kohlhammer, 2003), 131-49; Adriana Destro, *Antropologia e religioni* (Brescia: Morcelliana, 2005), 211-13.

49. Georg Simmel, *Soziologie: Unterschungen über die Formen der Vergesellschaftung* (Leipzig: Dunker & Humblot, 1908), 213, 216, 218. On the theory of conflicts, see also Louis Kriesberg, *The Sociology of Social Conflicts* (Englewood Cliffs, NJ: Prentice-Hall, 1973); Louis Kriesberg, *Social Conflicts* (Englewood Cliffs, NJ: Prentice-Hall, 1982); Louis Kriesberg, *Constructive Conflicts* (Lanham, MD: Rowman & Littlefield, 1998). See also Adriana Destro and Mauro Pesce, "Die zentrale Rolle des Konflikts in Verkündigung und Handeln Jesu," in Gabriella Gelardini, ed., *Theoriebildung im christlich-jüdischen Dialog* (Stuttgart: Kohlhammer, 2003), 1. 3-5.

50. Mark 6:4; Luke 4:24; Matt 13:57; and cf. John 4:44 (which locates these words in a completely different context).

51. It is symptomatic that the conflict does not regard husband and wife, or father and mother. See John Dominic Crossan, *The Historical Jesus: The Life of a Mediterranean Jewish Peasant* (San Francisco: HarperSanFrancisco, 1991), 300. It is the mention of a wife who originally belongs to another family—the daughter-in-law, who comes from outside—that shows that this text is speaking of a household based on an extended and inclusive family. The mention of the daughter-in-law confirms the impression that these households are patricentric and that the line of descent is masculine. On the movement of the productive and reproductive women between households and groups the anthropological literature is particularly extended. See Goody, *Production and Reproduction*; Meillassoux, *Femmes, greniers et capitaux*; Claude Lévi-Strauss, *Les structures élémentaires de la parenté* (Paris: PUF, 1949); ET: *The Elementary Structures of Kinship* (Oxford: Taylor & Francis, 1969).

52. See Destro and Pesce, "Fathers and Householders," 211-38; Crossan, *The Historical Jesus*, 300ff.

53. Luke, Matthew, and the *Gospel of Thomas* employ and rework a saying of Jesus transmitted by the earlier tradition. This evoked two parts of a verse in Micah (7:6): "The son treats the father with contempt, the daughter rises up against her mother, the daughter-in-law against her mother-in-law; your enemies are members of your own household." The idea of a conflict between

the discipleship movement and the *oikos* is, however, completely absent from Micah.

54. We may wonder whether the departure of the intermediate generation from the household, which Jesus desires, is the fruit of an intergenerational conflict that was endemic in Judean society at that time. In the parable of the prodigal son (Luke 15:11-32), which we have discussed above, we have a picture of a conflict between the father and a son, and between the younger and the elder sons. Jesus condemns this conflict, which ends in a disastrous defeat for the elder son. See Destro and Pesce, *Forme culturali,* 87. On intergenerational conflict in the ancient world, see Stephen Bertman, ed., *The Conflict of Generations in Ancient Greece and Rome* (Amsterdam: Grüner, 1976); Oscar Fuà, "Da Cicerone a Seneca," in Umberto Mattioli, ed., *Senectus* vol. 2 (Bologna: Pàtron, 1995), 202-6.

55. The Gospel of Luke gives us particularly abundant information on this point: (1) Jesus teaches in a house (5:17); (2) the centurion (7:1-10); (3) the conflict between Jesus and his mother and brothers (8:19); (4) a man is healed and sent back to his *oikos* (8:39); (5) the head of the synagogue (8:49-56); (6) the Twelve are instructed to ask for hospitality in people's houses (9:4); (7) a *neaniskos* is given back to his father (9:42); (8) a Samaritan village refuses to offer hospitality (9:52-55); (9) the Seventy are told to ask for hospitality in people's houses (10:5-10); (10) the *pandocheion* (10:34); (11) Jesus in Martha's house (10:38-42); (12) hospitality toward a friend at midnight (11:5); (13) Jesus in the house of a Pharisee (11:37); (14) again, Jesus in the house of a Pharisee (14:1-24); (15) the places at table (14:8); (16) one should not invite persons who "may invite you in return, and you would be repaid" (14:12); (17) the parable of the banquet (14:15-24); (18) the prodigal son (15:11, 32); (19) the dishonest administrator (16:1-8); (20) the rich man and the poor man (16:19-31); (21) the owner of a small house with only one slave (17:7-9); (22) Jesus in the house of Zacchaeus (19:2-10); (23) hospitality in a house in Emmaus (24:29-30).

56. Although Jesus uses a house for the celebration of the Passover, he seems to occupy only a dining room (*triclinium*), and no other guests or residents in the house take part in the supper (cf. Mark 14:14-15; Luke 22:11-13).

57. This fact is all the more significant when we recall that in many of the villages Jesus visited, inns did not exist—or were in fact unthinkable. Examples are the so-called "inn" (*pandocheion*) of Luke 10:34 or the *katalyma* of Luke 2:7. But although inns certainly did exist, the companions of Jesus normally ignore them. There may have been synagogues with lodging places, as we see from the above-mentioned inscription of Theodotus in a first-century synagogue in Jerusalem. See Lee I. Levine, *Ancient Synagogues Revealed* (Jerusalem: Israel Exploration Society, 1981); L. Michael White, *The Social Origins of Christian Architecture* (2 vols.; Valley Forge, PA: Trinity Press International, 1996, 1997); Destro and Pesce, *Come nasce una religione,* 783-74.

58. The authenticity of this request by Jesus seems historically certain, since we find it in 1 Cor 10:27 ("Eat whatever is set before you") and in the *Gospel of Thomas* 14 ("Eat what they serve you").

59. See Joachim Gnilka, *Das Matthäusevangelium*. 1. Teil. *Kommentar zu Kap. 1,1—13,58* (Herders theologischer Kommentar zum Neuen Testament I/2; Freiburg i.Br.: Herder, 1986), ad loc.

60. Columella, *De re rustica* 1.5.7, suggests that the villa be built not on the road (*in via*), that is, not in places of transit or on routes where many people travel. Persons in transit do not always respect the places that take them in. Columella's text is very important because it implicitly shows that finding lodging in the villages is not a specific practice only of Jesus' group, nor as a custom with a religious meaning.

61. Luke 9:5; 10:10-12. The householders can refuse to offer hospitality; see Adriana Destro and Mauro Pesce, "Codici di ospitalità. Il presbitero, Diotrefe, Gaio, itineranti delle chiese e membri estranei," in L. Padovese, ed., *Atti del IX. Simposio di Efeso su S. Giovanni Apostolo* (Rome: Pontificio Ateneo Antoniano, 2003), 121-35.

62. Luke 14:15-24; Matt 22:1-14; *Gospel of Thomas* 64. The Lukan version is certainly much closer than Matthew's text to the common archetype (see Mauro Pesce, "Ricostruzione dell'archetipo letterario comune a Mt 22,1-10 e Lc 14,15-24").

63. See Luke's version. The *Gospel of Thomas* speaks of the purchase of a field, of preparing a banquet for a friend, and of the collection of debts and taxes.

64. Richard Rohrbaugh, "The Pre-industrial City in Luke-Acts: Urban Social Relations," in Jerome H. Neyrey, ed., *The Social World of Luke-Acts* (Peabody, MA: Hendrickson, 1991), 140-46, illustrates behavioral models in the parable that he regards as typical of "pre-industrial" societies: the double invitation of the guests by the urban elite, and the fact that the social strata who live on the margins of society could not be invited by the elite to enter their spaces.

65. See Halvor Moxnes, "Patron-Client Relations and the New Community in Luke-Acts," in Jerome H. Neyrey, ed., *The Social World of Luke-Acts* (Peabody, MA: Hendrickson, 1991), 264: "Jesus here urges a break with the system of reciprocities in which a gift is always repaid by the recipient." See Elliott, "Temple versus Household," 236-38.

66. This is the explanation of the *prima facie* improbable scene of the prostitute who enters uninvited the house of a Pharisee who has invited Jesus to a meal (Luke 7:37). The presence of Jesus in a house prompted many people to come there. Cf., for example, Mark 1:33; 2:1-2; 3:20.

67. The story of the healing of a centurion's servant (Luke 7:1-10/Matt 8:5-13; cf. also the different version in John 4:46-54) has a strong claim to historical authenticity, since it is transmitted by two different sources, Q and John (see Rudolf Schnackenburg, "Zur Traditionsgeschichte von Joh. 4,46-54," *Biblische Zeitschrift* n.F. 8 [1964]: 58-88; Bovon, *L'Évangile selon saint Luc*. Vol. 1 [Geneva: Labor et Fides, 1991], ad loc.). According to Luke's version, the centurion seems to be a patron who has built the synagogue in Capernaum and who has Judean "friends." The elders of the town act on his behalf as clients. However, the historicity of this element is very much open to debate, although it is, of course,

possible that Matthew has omitted the information about the construction of the synagogue in Capernaum by the centurion, because this did not agree with his view of the relationships with the synagogue, or between Romans and Judeans. See Gnilka, *Das Matthäusevangelium*. 1. Teil (Freiburg i.B: Herder, 1986), ad loc.

68. See Moxnes, "Patron-Client Relations," 255 and 254/257, 264.

69. Our hypothesis is that Jesus was thinking of the equality of the Jubilee described in the book of Leviticus (25:8-55); see Destro and Pesce, "La remissione dei peccati nell'escatologia di Gesù," *Annali di Storia dell'Esegesi* 16 (1999) 56-59. We believe that the ideal of "selling" had deep roots in Judaic culture. We must, however, remember that the insistence on the necessity of detaching oneself from all one's possessions as a condition for following Jesus is found only in Luke, the evangelist who emphasizes most strongly the socio-religious ideal of the Jubilee (see Luke 4:17-19).

6. Jesus and His Body

1. M. Mauss, "Les techniques du corps," *Journal de psychologie normal et pathologique* 32 (1935) 271-93.

2. Mary Douglas, *Natural Symbols* (Harmondsworth: Penguin Books, 1970). For an overview of the discussion about the social order that is expressed by the body and the filters of rigidity and fluidity (a primary concern of Mary Douglas), see Andrew J. Strathern, *Body Thoughts* (Ann Arbor: University of Michigan Press, 1996), 15-16.

3. Nancy Scheper-Hughes and Margaret M. Lock, "The Mindful Body," *Medical Anthropological Quarterly* n.s. 1 (1987): 6-41. For other anthropologies of the body, see Frédéric Duhart, Abdelhakim Charif, and Yannick Le Pape, eds., *Anthropologie historique du corps* (Paris: L'Harmattan, 2005); Françoise Héritier and Margarita Xanthakou, *Corps et affects* (Paris: Odile Jacob, 2004).

4. See Johannes Fabian, *Time and the Other* (New York: Columbia University Press, 1983), 71-79; Fiona Bowie, *The Anthropology of Religion* (Oxford: Blackwell, 2000), 25.

5. Of these, the gender difference is the most disturbing and dramatic. Normally, cultures are very attentive to female diversity. One reason why it is regarded as enigmatic is that it has two possible outcomes. The woman's body produces both that which is the same and that which is different, namely, both the female and the male. See Françoise Héritier, *L'exercice de la parenté* (Paris: Gallimard, 1981).

6. See David Le Breton, *Anthropologie du corps et modernité* (Paris: Presses Universitaires de France, 1990), 23.

7. See Adriana Destro, *Antropologia dei sistemi religiosi* (Bologna: Pàtron, 2002), 81-82.

8. The diversity of ways in which these mechanisms are mobilized reveals an intention to put up a resistance, a more or less rhetorical demand that one's own culture be respected (see Ulf Hannerz, *Cultural Complexity* [New York: Columbia University Press, 1993]).

9. Eduard Schweizer, "*Psyche*. D. Neues Testament," *Theologisches Wörterbuch zum Neuen Testament* 9 (1973): 635-57.

10. *Genēsis* here means "birth" not "genealogy." This is confirmed by Matt 1:18, "The birth [*genēsis*] of Jesus the Messiah took place in this way."

11. On the genealogies, see Leonardo Piasere and Pier Giorgio Solinas, *Le culture della parentela e l'esogamia perfetta* (Rome: CISU, 1998), 203-99. On the genealogy of Jesus in Matthew, see Marshall D. Johnson, *The Purpose of the Biblical Genealogies with Special Reference to the Setting of the Genealogy of Jesus* (2d ed.; Cambridge: Cambridge University Press, 1988); Gnilka, *Das Matthäusevangelium*. 1. Teil, ad loc.; Bovon, *L'Évangile selon saint Luc*. Vol. 1, ad loc.; Amy-Jill Levine, *The Social and Ethnic Dimensions of Matthean Salvation History* (New York: Edwin Mellen, 1998), 59-88.

12. Levine, *Social and Ethnic Dimensions*, 88, maintains that despite the egalitarian impulses that are found in the Gospel of Matthew, its focus remains centered on men.

13. On the questions that have been raised about the morality and the ethnic provenance of these women, see Gnilka, *Das Matthäusevangelium*. 1. Teil, ad loc.

14. The number 50 represents the end. Jesus was situated at the forty-second generation; there were thus still seven more generations to come before the end.

15. See Bovon, *L'Évangile selon saint Luc*. Vol. 1, ad loc.

16. The only exception is the statement in Luke's infancy narrative that tells us that the child Jesus "grew and became strong" (2:40). But this tells us virtually nothing about his physical appearance.

17. According to Luke 8:44/Mark 9:20, a woman touches the fringe of his cloak. In these passages, the evangelists speak of one fringe, while the Bible prescribed four fringes, one at each corner of the garment. In non-Judaic Greek of the first century (Theocritus, Appian, Aelius Aristides, and the Greek magic papyri (see Frederick William Danker, ed., *A Greek-English Lexicon of the New Testament and Other Early Christian Literature* [Chicago: University of Chicago Press, 2000], 564), the noun *kraspedon* ("fringe") is widely used to designate a part of the cloak, without any reference to Judaic religious usages; but in the context of Jesus, it is the Judaic meaning that is central.

18. Matthew 6:1-8 emphasizes an unostentatious practice. According to Gnilka, *Das Matthäusevangelium*. 1. Teil, ad loc., this is a composition by the Matthean school, even if it "undoubtedly breathes the spirit of Jesus."

19. Philip Alexander, "Jewish Law in the Time of Jesus: Towards a Clarification of the Problem," in Barnabas Lindars, ed., *Law and Religion: Essays on the Place of the Law in Israel and Early Christianity* (Cambridge: Cambridge University Press, 1988), 44-58.

20. This is a realistic scene that is not generated by the desire to demonstrate that a presumed biblical prophecy is being fulfilled. The same scene is familiar from texts of the same period such as the Aesop Romance, which employs images and vocabulary similar to those of John. Entering into a relationship with others always implies some particular form of clothing. See Adriana Destro and Mauro Pesce, *Come nasce una religione* (Bari and Rome: Laterza,

2000), 51-54; Mauro Pesce, "La lavanda dei piedi Gv 13,1-20, il 'Romanzo di Esopo' e i 'Saturnalia' di Macrobio," *Biblica* 80 (1999).

21. Mark 5:27 speaks of Jesus' mantle and employs the noun *himation* in the singular. Immediately afterward, the text uses the plural *himatia* to designate not only the cloak but all the garments he wore, that is, the mantle and the tunic. See John 13:4.

22. Luke 6:29. Luke's realism—it is clear that one must first remove the cloak, in order then to be able to remove the tunic—is absent from the parallel passage in Matthew, who actually reverses the order with his typical lack of realism: "And if anyone wants to sue you and take your coat, give your cloak as well" (5:40). *Didache* 1:4 agrees with Luke's logical order, but Justin, *First Apology* 16.1, agrees with that of Matthew.

23. The attempt to demonstrate a theological thesis by means of the presumed fulfillment of a biblical passage, interpreted as a prophecy about the life of Jesus, is historically untenable. What we have here are arguments put forward by the disciples of Jesus after his death.

24. The episode is not found in Mark 15, in Matthew 27, or in John 19; but compare the function of Herod in the *Gospel of Peter*.

25. See, for example, his prayer face-down on the earth in the garden on the Mount of Olives (Mark 14:34/Matt 26:39; Luke 22:41 tells us that he knelt to pray).

26. The episode of the adulteress is missing from many manuscripts of the Gospel of John and seems to be a late insertion. But it has many affinities to the materials used by the Gospels of Mark, Luke, and Matthew.

27. On the arrest in the Gospel of John, see Adriana Destro and Mauro Pesce, "Conflitti e soluzione dei conflitti nel 'Vangelo di Giovanni,'" in L. Padovese, ed., *Atti del X Simposio di Efeso su S. Giovanni Apostolo* (Rome: Pontificio Ateneo Antoniano, 2005), 87-113.

28. Mark 14:27; Matt 26:51; Luke 22:49-50. It is only John 18:10 that identifies this follower as Simon Peter.

29. Mark 15:43-45. In his passion narrative, Mark speaks of the *corpse* of Jesus, not only of his "body."

30. Mark 16:1-8, 9-11, 12-13, 14-18; Luke 24:1-12, 13-35, 36-43; Matt 28:1-11, 16-20; John 20:1—21:23; *Gospel of Peter* 35-77; *Gospel of the Nazarenes* 14 (in Jerome, *De viris illustribus* 16.2-4); *Gospel of the Nazarenes* 15 (in Jerome, Prologue to the *Commentary on Isaiah* 18; *Gospel of the Hebrews* 6 (in Jerome, *De viris illustribus* 2.11-13); 1 Cor 15:4-8.

31. Imagining an individual human body may imply also imagining the home in which it habitually dwells or carries out its activity. It is with reference to this imagined place that a body receives its particular functions.

32. As we have said, it is impossible to be certain about the chronological sequence of Jesus' moves from place to place or about the persons whom he met. We believe, however, that some individual units of tradition, inserted by the evangelists into their narratives, refer to a precise situation, so that we can be certain about the scenario and the types of encounter.

33. The fact that Jesus held lengthy discourses to the crowds may be regarded as historically probable, since the different Gospels agree on this point.

34. Only Matt 19:20 says that he is a young man; Luke 18:18 states only that he is "a ruler." The entire episode is narrated in Mark 10:17-22; Luke 18:18-23; Matt 19:16-22.

35. Mark 7:25. Matt 15:5 corrects Mark by saying that she "prostrated herself" before Jesus. This may also imply that she kissed his feet.

36. As we have seen, Mark 14:3-9, Matt 26:6-13, and John 12:1-8 relate a similar scene. Mark and Matthew tell us that the woman pours the precious ointment on Jesus' head, but they do not say that she is a sinner or that she dries the feet of Jesus with her hair. In John, this woman is not a sinner, but Mary the sister of Lazarus. She pours the precious oil on Jesus' feet and dries them with her hair. In all three cases, we have the recollection of an event that the evangelists have modified in various ways, attributing the action to different women in different houses. The center of the recollection is the extraordinary nature of the woman's actions; only Luke relates these actions with details unknown to the other evangelists.

37. Danker, *A Greek-English Lexicon*, 656.

38. Camille Focant, *L'Évangile selon Marc* (Paris: Cerf, 2004), 291.

39. See Greek Magical Papyri 13.495.

40. Tim Ingold has shown that "dwelling" is inherent to the human being, in the sense that to say "I dwell, you dwell" is identical to "I am, you are." "Dwelling" "encompassed the whole manner in which one lives one's life on the earth" ("Building, Dwelling, Living: How Animals and People Make Themselves at Home in the World," in Tim Ingold, *The Perception of the Environment* [London and New York: Routledge, 2000], 172-88, here 185).

41. This is a significant correction of the classic idea that the framework of the story of Jesus (see Karl L. Schmidt, *Der Rahmen der Geschichte Jesu* [Berlin: Trowitzsch, 1919]) is secondary and entirely the product of redaction. The scenario of the village in preference to that of the city is certainly historical, as is Jesus' gathering of the disciples and the picture of the crowds who come to him. This makes it possible to create a social memory that is linked to particular places.

42. Jesus sometimes appears strongly linked to the crowd; at other times, he appears more strongly linked to his followers. The collective subjects move in different ways. The disciples are not identical to the crowd; at one time, they share the conditions of the crowd and at another time they are separate from it. They physically constitute a group that did not exist previously, and Jesus in his bodily dimension is a part of this group.

43. Mark 15:29/Matt 27:39; see Focant, *L'Évangile selon Marc*, 578.

44. Luke 23:27; but cf. 23:35.

45. Thomas J. Csordas, "Embodiment and Cultural Phenomenology," in Gail Weiss and Honi Haber, eds., *Perspectives on Embodiment* (New York: Routledge, 1999), 143-62; Thomas J. Csordas, ed., *Embodiment and Experience* (Cambridge and New York: Cambridge University Press, 1995); Thomas J. Csordas, *The Sacred Self* (Berkeley: University of California Press, 1994);

6. Jesus and His Body 217

Thomas J. Csordas, *Language, Charisma, and Creativity* (Berkeley: University of California Press, 1997).

46. Mark 8:35. It seems that this is not the original context of this saying, which Luke and Matthew take over from Mark word for word, and which John knows in a different form. This saying was not part of a discourse that alluded to Jesus' death on the cross.

47. John probably regarded this act of isolation as a reaction to the threat of death, and elaborated it amply. In reality, however, Mark 3:7, which speaks of Jesus' withdrawal to the lake, belongs to a subsequent but autonomous literary unit that follows the passage that concludes with the threat to Jesus' life. Accordingly, we are not certain that Mark understood the withdrawal as a way for Jesus to escape the threat. John, however, may have connected the two (since we cannot argue that he read Mark's text in the same way as we read it).

48. Gerd Theissen and Annette Merz, *The Historical Jesus: A Comprehensive Guide* (Minneapolis: Fortress Press, 1998), 141.

49. See Theissen and Merz, *The Historical Jesus*, 141-47.

50. The one who repents will be saved. Only repentance can save a human being from perishing in a violent death. On the anthropology of catastrophes, see Christian Delécraz and Laurie Durussel, eds., *Scénario catastrophe* (Gollion: Infolio, 2007), and Gianluca Ligi, *Nemici invisibili: Antropologia dei disastri* (Rome and Bari: Laterza, 2008).

51. See Barry Blackburn, *Theios Anēr and the Markan Miracle Tradition* (Tübingen: Mohr, 1991); Graham H. Twelftree, *Jesus the Exorcist* (Tübingen: Mohr, 1993); Stevan L. Davies, *Jesus the Healer: Possession, Trance, and the Origins of Christianity* (New York: Continuum, 1995); Clinton Wahlen, *Jesus and the Impurity of Spirits in the Synoptic Gospels* (Tübingen: Mohr Siebeck, 2004); John P. Meier, *A Marginal Jew: Rethinking the Historical Jesus* (4 vols.; New York: Doubleday, 1991-2009), vol. 2. See also Wendy Cotter, *The Miracles of Greco-Roman Antiquity: A Sourcebook* (London: Routledge, 1999); after the publication of our book, Wendy Cotter wrote *The Christ of the Miracle Stories: Portrait through Encounter* (Grand Rapids, MI: Baker Academic Press, 2010).

52. Here, we take into account fifteen cases of miraculous healing narrated by the Gospels: healings of paralytics and physically disabled persons (Mark 2:1-12; John 5:1-9; Mark 3:1-6; Luke 13:10-17; Matt 8:5-13/Luke 7:1-11; John 4:46-54); of blind persons (Mark 10:46-52; Mark 8:22-26; John 9:1-41); of lepers (Mark 1:40-45/Matt 8:1-4/Luke 5:12-16; Luke 17:11-19); and various healings (Mark 1:29-31; Mark 5:24-34/Matt 9:18-26/Luke 8:40-56; Luke 14:1-6; Mark 7:31-37; Luke 22:49-51); see Meier, *A Marginal Jew*, vol. 2. Nine of these healings take place by means of physical contact, sometimes with precise thaumaturgic techniques, and six take place by means of a command from Jesus.

53. Twelftree, *Jesus the Exorcist*; Davies, *Jesus the Healer*.

54. Davies, *Jesus the Healer*.

55. Mark 5:30; Luke 8:46. Matthew 9:20-22 omits Jesus' words about the power that has gone forth from him independently of his own will. For a

discussion of the power transmitted by touch, including in the Hellenistic and Judean milieus, see Blackburn, *Theios Anēr*, 112-17.

56. The Gospel of Mark contains the following episodes of exorcism: 1:21-28 (the demoniac in the synagogue); the demoniac of Gadara (5:1-20); the daughter of the Syro-Phoenician woman (7:24-30); the boy possessed by a mute spirit (9:14-29). To these we should add the exorcisms of a mute demoniac in Matt 9:32-33 and of the mute demoniac in Matt 12:22-23/Luke 11:14. We thus have six cases of exorcism. The controversies about the power through which Jesus drives out the demons (Mark 3:22-27/Matt 12:22-30/Luke 11:14-23); the reply Jesus makes to the disciples of the Baptizer (Luke 7:18-23/Matt 11:2-6); the powers given to the Twelve or to the Seventy to drive out demons (Mark 6:7-12, 30; Matt 10:1-15/Luke 9:1-6; 10:1-11, 17-20); and the reference to the demons that had been driven out of Mary of Magdala (Luke 8:2) are not descriptions of exorcisms but presuppose the exorcistic activity of Jesus and his transmission of this power to his disciples. In the six cases of exorcism, there is no contact between the body of Jesus and the bodies of the possessed. See Meier, *A Marginal Jew*, vol. 2; Twelftree, *Jesus the Exorcist*, 57-129; Davies, *Jesus the Healer*, 90-104.

57. Adriana Destro and Mauro Pesce, "Continuità o discontinuità tra Gesù e i gruppi dei suoi seguaci nelle pratiche culturali di contatto con il soprannaturale?" in Luigi Padovese, ed., *Atti del Nono Simposio Paolino* (Rome: Pontificio Ateneo Antoniano, 2006), 81-98.

58. The latter did not die in the same way as other human beings.

59. The fact that both Matthew and Luke mention Jesus' face, which is not mentioned in Mark, means that we must assume the existence of a common source independent of Mark (unless one wishes to maintain that one of the two Gospels depends on the other).

60. See Blackburn, *Theios Anēr*, 117-20.

61. We do not agree with H. Klein that Luke limits the change to the facial expression and the splendor of Jesus' garments (Hans Klein [*Das Lukasevangelium* [Göttingen: Vandenhoeck & Ruprecht, 2006], 346). F. Bovon takes a different view: he holds that *prosōpon* could indicate not only the face but the entire person (*Évangile selon Saint Luc*, ad loc.).

7. Jesus and Emotion

1. Catherine Lutz and Geoffrey M. White, "The Anthropology of Emotions," *Annual Review of Anthropology* 15 (1986): 409.

2. One of the pioneering studies in the anthropology of the emotions is Jane L. Briggs, *Never in Anger* (Cambridge: Cambridge University Press, 1970), an investigation of the emotional patterns of the Inuit culture. Lutz and White, "Anthropology of Emotions," present the complexity of the positions taken by anthropologists, of the problems involved, and of the currents in the study of the emotions. See also Chiara Pussetti, *Poetica delle emozioni: I Bijagò della Guinea Bissau* (Bari and Rome: Laterza, 2005); Chiara Pussetti, "Introduzione. Discorsi sulle emozioni," *Antropologia* 5 (2005): 5-15; Mary Douglas and Aaron

7. Jesus and Emotion 219

Wildavsky, *Risk and Culture* (Berkeley: University of California Press, 1982); Norbert Elias, *The Civilizing Process* (New York: Urizen, 1939); Robert I. Levy, *Tahitians: Mind and Experience in the Society Islands* (Chicago: University of Chicago Press, 1973); Charles Lindholm, *Generosity and Jealousy: The Swat Pukhtun of Northern Pakistan* (New York: Columbia University Press, 1982); Richard A. Shweder and Robert A. LeVine, *Culture Theory: Essays on Mind, Self, and Emotion* (Cambridge: Cambridge University Press, 1984); Robert R. Desjarlais, *Body and Emotion* (Philadelphia: University of Pennsylvania Press, 1992).

3. Lutz and White, "Anthropology of Emotions," 427.

4. See also Pussetti, *Poetica delle emozioni*, 52.

5. Franz Boas, "The Aims of Ethnology in 1940," in Franz Boas, *Race, Language and Culture* (New York: Free Press, 1988), 635-36.

6. There also exist feelings such as the "sacred terror" of something (this must be distinguished from the terror produced by religious conflicts, about which Bruce Lincoln writes in *Holy Terrors: Thinking about Religion after September 11* (Chicago: University of Chicago Press, 2003). Such feelings are the extreme markers of the identity of specific human groups. Immoderate longings or feelings of envy (even if only presumed) are stigmatized: in terms of the anthropology of culture, we could say that they have received decisive responses and evoked apotropaic actions.

7. For an overview of the emotional situations that affect the personality (especially the feelings of shame and of guilt), see Clifford Geertz, *The Interpretation of Cultures* (New York: Basic Books, 1973), 400-402.

8. Exegetes have devoted little attention to the study of Jesus' emotions. See Benjamin B. Warfield, "The Emotional Life of Our Lord," in Faculty of Princeton Theological Seminary, ed., *Biblical and Theological Studies* (New York: Scribner, 1912), 36-90; Benjamin B. Warfield, *The Person and Work of Christ* (Philadelphia: Presbyterian and Reformed, 1950), 93-145; Benjamin B. Warfield, "Jésus et les emotions," *Hokhma* 58 (1995): 21-49. On a very solid linguistic basis, Stephen Woorwinde, *Jesus's Emotions in the Fourth Gospel: Human or Divine* (London and New York: T&T Clark, 2005), studies the emotions attributed to God and to human beings in the biblical and Judaic literature in order to determine which of the emotions that are ascribed to God are also ascribed to Jesus. He carefully compares the Johannine data with the Synoptic Gospels and other New Testament texts.

9. See also Mark 1:41; 6:34; 9:22.

10. Giancarlo Gaeta, *I Vangeli* (Turin: Einaudi, 2006), ad loc., notes that "Jesus' state of being moved does not belong to the psychological order. This is the reaction of the miracle worker to the illness that he is summoned to heal." This observation, based on Rudolf Pesch, *Das Markusevangelium. 1. Teil* (Freiburg i.B: Herder, 1977), ad loc., is interesting, but there need be no antithesis between a "psychological" aspect and an internal ritual state of mind. From an anthropological perspective, the emotions are culturally codified reactions to social situations, not purely psychological and autonomous aspects.

11. *Gospel of Thomas* 2, following Oxyrhynchus Papyrus 654,5-9; ET: J. K. Elliott, *The Apocryphal New Testament* (Oxford: Clarendon, 1993), 135-36.

12. The Greek text here is lacunose. Cf. the quotation of the same saying in Clement of Alexandria, *Stromata* 5.14.96.3.

13. On this question, see Mauro Pesce, *Le parole dimenticate di Gesù* (Milan: Mondadori, 2004), 695.

14. Mark 10:13-16. See also Matt 19:13-15 and Luke 18:15-17.

15. Mark employs the verb *aganaktein* ("be angry") on two other occasions, not of Jesus, but of the disciples who get angry with James and John (10:41) and are annoyed when a woman pours perfumed oil on Jesus' head (14:4). Mark likes to underline emotional reactions in this way.

16. It is worth asking whether Mark emphasizes Jesus' states of mind only when he is confronted by reprehensible attitudes on the part of the disciples. The point that interests us here, however, is not the incomprehension of the disciples (a theme that many scholars have studied) but rather how Jesus teaches them to react internally to certain situations.

17. For this and the following paragraph, see David Le Breton, "Anthropologie du silence," *Théologiques* 7 (1999): 15; David Le Breton, *Du silence* (Paris: Métailié, 1997).

18. Mark's account of the silence of Jesus may be composed in the light of texts that speak of the silence of Socrates during his trial: see Maximus of Tyre, *Dissertations* 3.7e; Plato in Diogenes Laertius, *Lives of the Philosophers* 3.10; Euripides in Plutarch, *Moralia* 532f. These passages are cited by Danker, ed., *Greek-English Lexicon*, 925, under *siōpō*.

19. Matthew 14:23 employs only the verb *apolyō*, not *apotassō*.

20. This verb is used very frequently: Luke 22:42/Matt 26:39/Mark 14:36; Luke 13:34; Mark 1:41/Matt 8:3/Luke 5:13; Mark 3:13 and 7:24; cf. Mark 9:30; Luke 9:54; Luke 12:49; John 5:21; John 7:1; John 17:24; John 21:22-23.

21. Mark 14:36. Cf. Matt 26:39 ("if it is possible"); Luke 22:42 ("if you are willing").

22. Luke 22:42 posits a simple antithesis between the will of Jesus and the will of God.

23. We should also note that the evangelist Mark places three predictions of the passion on the lips of Jesus (8:31; 9:31; 10:32-33).

24. Luke 9:54. The consuming fire that falls from heaven may be an allusion to the prophetic action of Elijah (2 Kgs 1:9-14).

25. Luke 12:49-50. "The baptism with which I am baptized" (Mark 10:38) is a phrase that contains part of one of the two sayings in Luke.

26. *Gospel of Thomas* 10. Saying 82—"He who is near me is near the fire, and he who is far from me is far from the kingdom"—offers a different interpretation of Jesus' saying, because these words eliminate the distance between Jesus and his project: Jesus does not need to express a wish that the fire may spread, because here the fire is in his own person. Luke seems to reflect more accurately the experience of the historical Jesus.

27. See Unni Wikan, "Beyond the Words: The Power of Resonance," *American Ethnologist* 19, no. 3 (1992): 460-82.

BIBLIOGRAPHY

Alexander, Philip. "Jewish Law in the Time of Jesus: Towards a Clarification of the Problem." In *Law and Religion: Essays on the Place of the Law in Israel and Early Christianity,* edited by Barnabas Lindars. Cambridge: Cambridge University Press, 1988, 44-58.
———. "Geography and the Bible: Early Jewish Geography," *Anchor Bible Dictionary* 2 (1992): 977-88.
Appadurai, Arjun, ed. *Globalization.* Durham, NC: Duke University Press, 2000.
Arav, Rami, and Richard A. Freund, eds. *Bethsaida: A City by the North Shore of the Sea of Galilee.* 3 vols. Kirksville, MO: Truman State University Press, 1995, 1999, 2004.
Augé, Marc. *Le sens des autres.* Paris: Fayard, 1994.
———. *Les formes de l'oubli.* Paris: Editions Payot et Rivages, 1998; ET: *Oblivion.* Minneapolis: University of Minnesota Press, 2004.
———. *Non-Lieux: Introduction à une anthropologie de la surmodernité.* Paris: Le Seuil, 1992. ET: *Non-Places.* London and New York: Verso, 2009.
Bachelard, Gaston. *La poétique de l'espace.* Paris: PUF, 1957. ET: *The Poetics of Space.* Boston: Beacon, 1994.
Balch, David, and Carolyn Osiek, eds. *Early Christian Families in Context.* Grand Rapids: Eerdmans, 2003.
Baldini Lippolis, Isabella. *La domus tardoantica: Forme e rappresentazioni dello spazio domestico.* Imola: University Press Bologna, 2001.
Bammel, Ernst, and C. F. D. Moule, eds. *Jesus and the Politics of His Day.* Cambridge: Cambridge University Press, 1984.
Barbaglio, Giuseppe. "La parabola del banchetto di nozze nella versione di Matteo." In *La parabola degli invitati,* edited by Jacques Dupont. Brescia: Paideia, 1978, 91-96.
———. *Gesù ebreo di Galilea: Indagine storica.* Bologna: Edizioni Dehoniane, 2002.
Barth, Frederick. *Ethnic Groups and Boundaries.* Prospect Heights, IL: Waveland Press 1969.
Batey, R. "Jesus and the Theatre." *New Testament Studies* 30 (1984): 563-74.
Batkin, Leonid Mihajlovic. *L'idea di individualità nel Rinascimento italiano.* Bari: Laterza, 1992.
Bauckham, Richard. "James and the Jerusalem Community." In *Jewish Believers in Jesus,* edited by O. Skarsaune and R. Hvalik. Peabody, MA: Hendrickson, 2007, 55-95.

Bauman, Zygmunt. *Culture as Praxis.* London and Boston: Routledge, 1973.
Bauman, Zygmunt (with Keith Tester). *Conversations with Zygmunt Bauman.* Cambridge: Cambridge University Press, 2001.
Beckwith, Roger T. *Calendar and Chronology, Jewish and Christian.* Leiden: Brill, 2001.
Beirne, Margaret M. *Women and Men in the Fourth Gospel.* London: Sheffield Academic Press, 2003.
Bertman, Stephen, ed. *The Conflict of Generations in Ancient Greece and Rome.* Amsterdam: Grüner, 1976.
Blackburn, Barry. *Theios Anēr and the Markan Miracle Tradition.* Tübingen: Mohr, 1991.
Blinzler, Josef. *Die Brüder und Schwestern Jesu.* 2d ed. SBS 21. Stuttgart: Katholisches Bibelwerk, 1967.
Boas, Franz. *Race, Language and Culture.* New York: Free Press, 1988.
Bobichon, Philippe. *Justin Martyr: Dialogue avec Tryphon. Edition critique, traduction, commentaire.* 2 vols. Fribourg: Academic Press Fribourg, 2003.
Booth, Roger P. *Jesus and the Laws of Purity: Tradition History and Legal History in Mark 7.* Sheffield: JSOT, 1985.
Botha, Pieter J. J. "Houses in the World of Jesus." *Neotestamentica* 32 (1998): 37-74.
Bourdieu, Pierre. *Esquisse d'une théorie de la pratique, précédé de trois études d'éthnologie kabyle.* Paris: Seuil, 2000 (1st ed., Paris: Droz, 1972).
Bovon, François. *L'Evangile selon saint Luc. Lc 1,1—9,50.* Vol. I. Geneva : Labor et Fides, 1991.
———. *L'Evangile selon saint Luc. Lc 9,51—14,35.* Vol. II. Geneva: Labor et Fides, 1996.
———. "Fragment Oxyrhynchus 840. Fragment of a Lost Gospel, Witness of an Early Christian Controversy over Purity." *Journal of Biblical Literature* 119 (2000): 705-28.
———. *L'Evangile selon saint Luc. Lc 15,1—19,27.* Vol. III. Geneva: Labor et Fides, 2001.
Bowie, Fiona. *The Anthropology of Religion.* Oxford: Blackwell, 2000.
Bremmer, Jan N. "Why Did Early Christianity Attract Upper-Class Women?" In *Fructus centesimus,* edited by Antoon A. R. Bastiaensen and Antonius Hilhorst. Dordrecht: Kluwer, 1989, 35-47.
Briggs, Jane L. *Never in Anger.* Cambridge: Cambridge University Press, 1970.
Brown, Raymond E. *The Death of the Messiah.* 2 vols. New York: Doubleday, 1999.
Calame, Claude, and Mondher Kilani, eds. *La fabrication de l'humain dans les cultures et en anthropologie.* Lausanne: Payot, 1999.
Chancey, Mark. *Greco-Roman Culture and the Galilee of Jesus.* Cambridge: Cambridge University Press, 2008.
Cole, John W., and Eric R. Wolf. *The Hidden Frontier: Ecology and Ethnicity in an Alpine Valley.* Berkeley: University of California Press, 1999.

Connerton, Paul. *How Societies Remember.* Cambridge: Cambridge University Press, 1989.
Corbo, Virgilio C. "Capernaum." *Anchor Bible Dictionary* 1 (1991): 866-69.
Corley, Kathleen E. "Were the Women around Jesus Really Prostitutes? Women in the Context of Greco-Roman Meals." *Society of Biblical Literature 1989 Seminar Papers.* Atlanta: Scholars, 1989, 487-521.
Cotter, Wendy. "Women's Authority Roles in Paul's Churches: Countercultural or Conventional?" *Novum Testamentum* 36 (1994): 350-72.
———. "The Collegia and Roman Law: State Restrictions on Voluntary Associations, 64 B.C.E.–200 B.C.E." In *Voluntary Associations in the Graeco-Roman World,* edited by John S. Kloppenborg and Stephen G. Wilson. London: Routledge, 1996, 74-89.
———. *The Miracles of Greco-Roman Antiquity: A Sourcebook.* London: Routledge, 1999.
———. *The Christ of the Miracle Stories: Portrait through Encounter.* Grand Rapids, MI: Baker Academic Press, 2010.
Cracco Ruggini, Lellia. "La città imperiale." In *Storia di Roma. 4: Caratteri e morfologie,* edited by E. Gabba and A. Schiavone. Turin: Einaudi, 1989, 201-66.
Crossan, John Dominic. *The Historical Jesus: The Life of a Mediterranean Jewish Peasant.* San Francisco: HarperSanFrancisco, 1991.
———. *Jesus: A Revolutionary Biography.* San Francisco: HarperSan Francisco, 1994.
———. *Who Killed Jesus?* San Francisco: HarperSanFrancisco, 1996.
Crossan, John Dominic, and Jonathan L. Reed. *Excavating Jesus.* San Francisco: HarperSanFrancisco, 2001.
Csordas, Thomas J. *The Sacred Self.* Berkeley: University of California Press, 1994.
———. *Language, Charisma, and Creativity.* Berkeley: University of California Press, 1997.
———. "Embodiment and Cultural Phenomenology." In *Perspectives on Embodiment,* edited by Gail Weiss and Honi Haber. New York: Routledge, 1999, 143-62.
Csordas, Thomas J., ed. *Embodiment and Experience.* Cambridge and New York: Cambridge University Press, 1995.
Danker, Frederick William, ed. *A Greek-English Lexicon of the New Testament and Other Early Christian Literature.* Chicago: University of Chicago Press, 2000.
Davies, Stevan L. *Jesus the Healer: Possession, Trance, and the Origins of Christianity.* New York: Continuum, 1995.
de Certeau, Michel. *L'Invention du quotidien.* Paris: Gallimard, 1980. ET: *The Practice of Everyday Life.* Berkeley: University of California Press, 2002.
Delécraz, Christian, and Laurie Durussel, eds. *Scénario catastrophe.* Gollion: Infolio, 2007.

Delobel, Joël. "L'onction par la pécheresse: La composition littéraire de Lc., VII, 36-50." *Ephemerides Theologiae Lovanienses* 42 (1966): 415-75.

DeMaris, Richard E. "The Baptism of Jesus: A Ritual-Critical Approach." In *The Social Setting of Jesus and the Gospels*, edited by Wolfgang Stegemann, Bruce J. Malina, and Gerd Theissen. Minneapolis: Fortress Press, 2002, 137-57.

Desjarlais, Robert R. *Body and Emotion*. Philadelphia: University of Pennsylvania Press, 1992.

Destro, Adriana. "Pensare la famiglia. Percorsi e problemi." In *Famiglia islamica*, edited by Adriana Destro. Bologna: Pàtron, 1998, 9-28.

———. *Antropologia dei sistemi religiosi*. Bologna: Pàtron, 2002.

———. *Antropologia e religioni*. Brescia: Morcelliana, 2005.

Destro, Adriana, ed. *Antropologia dei flussi globali*. Rome: Carocci, 2006.

Destro, Adriana, and Mauro Pesce. "Kinship, Discipleship, and Movement. An Anthropological Study of the Gospel of John." *Biblical Interpretation* 3 (1995): 266-84.

———. "La normatività del Levitico: interpretazioni ebraiche e protocristiane." *Annali di Storia dell'Esegesi* 13 no. 1 (1996): 15-37.

———. "Identità collettiva e identità personale nel cristianesimo paolino e giovanneo." *I quaderni del ramo d'oro* 2 (1998): 33-64.

———. "La remissione dei peccati nell'escatologia di Gesù." *Annali di Storia dell'Esegesi* 16 no. 1 (1999): 56-59.

———. *Come nasce una religione: Antropologia e esegesi del Vangelo di Giovanni*. Bari and Rome: Laterza, 2000.

———. "Seguire un maestro. Caratteri e itinerari del gruppo discepolare in Giovanni," in *Maestro e discepolo: Temi e problemi della direzione spirituale tra VI secolo a.C. e VII secolo d.C.*, edited by Giovanni Filoramo. Brescia: Morcelliana, 2002, 141-58.

———. "Fathers and Householders in Jesus' Movement: The Perspective of the Gospel of Luke." *Biblical Interpretation* 11 (2003): 211-38.

———. "Codici di ospitalità. Il presbitero, Diotrefe, Gaio, itineranti delle chiese e membri estranei." In *Atti del IX. Simposio di Efeso su S. Giovanni Apostolo*, edited by Luigi Padovese. Rome: Pontificio Ateneo Antoniano, 2003, 121-35.

———. "Die zentrale Rolle des Konflikts in Verkündigung und Handeln Jesu." In *Theoriebildung im christlich-jüdischen Dialog*, edited by Gabriella Gelardini and Peter Schmid. Stuttgart: Kohlhammer, 2003, 131-49.

———. "Conflitti e soluzione dei conflitti nel Vangelo di Giovanni." In *Atti del X Simposio di Efeso su S. Giovanni Apostolo*, edited by Luigi Padovese. Rome: Pontificio Ateneo Antoniano, 2005, 87-113.

———. "Continuity or Discontinuity between Jesus and Groups of His Followers? Practices of Contact with the Supernatural." In *Jesus and the First Generations of Disciples*, edited by Santiago Guijarro Oporto. Salamanca: Universitad Pontificia de Salamanca, 2006, 53-70.

———. *Antropologia delle origini cristiane*. 4th ed. Bari and Rome: Laterza, 2008.

———. *Forme culturali del cristianesimo nascente*. 2d ed. Brescia: Morcelliana, 2008.

———. "Dal gruppo interstiziale di Gesù alla *ekklēsia*: mutamenti nel ruolo delle donne." *Annali di Storia dell'Esegesi* 27, no. 2 (2010): 3-21.

———. "The Colour of Words. An Analysis of the Gospel of John. From 'Social Death' to Freedom in the Household." In *Light from the East: Papyrologische Kommentare zum Neuen Testament*, edited by Peter Arzt-Grabner and Christina M. Kreinecker. Wiesbaden: Harrassowitz, 2010, 27-46.

Dixon, Suzanne. *The Roman Family*. Baltimore and London: Johns Hopkins University Press, 1992.

Dorsey, David A. *The Roads and Highways of Ancient Israel*. Baltimore and London: Johns Hopkins University Press, 1991.

Douglas, Mary. *Natural Symbols*. Harmondsworth: Penguin Books, 1970.

———. "Deciphering a Meal." *Daedalus* 101 (1972): 61-81.

———. "Cultural Bias." Occasional Paper of the Royal Anthropological Institute of Great Britain and Ireland 35. London: Royal Anthropological Institute, 1978. Reprinted in *In the Active Voice*. London: Routledge & Kegan Paul, 1982.

Douglas, Mary, and Aaron Wildavsky. *Risk and Culture*. Berkeley: University of California Press, 1982.

Duhart, Frédéric, Abdelhakim Charif, and Yannick Le Pape, eds. *Anthropologie historique du corps*. Paris: L'Harmattan, 2005.

Duling, Dennis. "The Jesus Movement and Social Network Analysis. Part I: The Spatial Network." *Biblical Theology Bulletin* 29 (1999): 156-75.

———. "The Jesus Movement and Network Analysis." In *The Social Setting of Jesus and the Gospels*, edited by Wolfgang Stegemann, Bruce J. Malina, and Gerd Theissen. Minneapolis: Fortress Press, 2002, 301-32.

Dupont, Jacques, ed. *La parabola degli invitati al banchetto*. Brescia: Paideia, 1978.

———. *Les béatitudes*. 3 vols. Paris: Etudes Bibliques, 1969-1973.

Dupront, Alphonse. *Du Sacré. Croisades et pèlerinages: Images et langages*. Paris: Gallimard, 1987.

Edelstein, Gershon, Ianir Milevski, and Sarah Aurant. *The Rephaim Valley Project: Villages, Terraces, and Stone Mounds. Excavations at Manahat, 1987-1989*. Jerusalem: Israel Antiquity Authority, 1998.

Edwards, Douglas R., and Christine Thomas McCollough, eds. *Archeology and the Galilee: Texts and Contexts in the Greco-Roman and Byzantine Periods*. Atlanta: Scholars, 1997.

Eisenstadt, Shmuel N., and Luis Roniger. *Patrons, Clients and Friends*. Cambridge: Cambridge University Press, 1984.

Elias, Norbert. *The Civilizing Process*. New York: Urizen, 1939.

Elliott, James Keith. *The Apocryphal New Testament*. Oxford: Clarendon, 1993.

Elliott, John H. "Temple versus Household in Luke-Acts." In *The Social World of Luke-Acts*, edited by Jerome H. Neyrey. Peabody, MA: Hendrickson, 1991, 211-40.

———. "Jesus the Israelite Was Neither a 'Jew' nor 'a Christian': On Correcting Misleading Nomenclature." *Journal for the Study of the Historical Jesus* 5 (2005): 119-55.

Fabian, Johannes. *Time and the Other*. New York: Columbia University Press, 1983.

Fabris, Rinaldo. "La parabola degli invitati alla cena. Analisi redazionale di Lc. 14,16-24." In *La parabola degli invitati al banchetto*, edited by Jacques Dupont. Brescia: Paideia, 1978, 128-41.

Finley, Moses I. *The Ancient Economy*. London: Chatto & Windus, 1973.

Fischer, Moshe, Benjamin Isaac, and Israel Roll. "Roman Roads in Judaea II. The Jaffa-Jerusalem Roads." *Biblical Archaeologist* 50, no. 4 (1996): 244-45.

Focant, Camille. *L'Evangile selon Marc*. Paris: Cerf, 2004.

Fortes, Meyer. "Introduction." In Jack Goody, ed. *The Developmental Cycle in Domestic Groups*. Cambridge: Cambridge University Press, 1971.

Foucault, Michael. *Technologies of the Self: A Seminar with Michel Foucault*, edited by Luther H. Martin, Huck Gutman, and Patrick H. Hutton. Amherst: University of Massachusetts Press, 1988.

Fourrier, Sabine. "Villages, villes, ethniques: La définition identitaire dans les inscriptions chypriotes." In *Identités croisées en un milieu méditerranéen: Le cas de Cypre (Antiquité-Moyen âge)*, edited by Sabine Fourrier and Gilles Grivaud. Mont-Saint-Aignan: Université de Rouen, 2006, 101-9.

Frankel, Raphael, Nimrod Getzov, Mordechai Aviam, and Avi Degani. *Settlement Dynamics and Regional Diversity in Ancient Upper Galilee: Archeological Survey of Upper Galilee*. Jerusalem: Israel Antiquities Authority, 2001.

Fredriksen, Paula. *Jesus of Nazareth: King of the Jews*. New York: Vintage Books, 2000.

———. *From Jesus to Christ: The Origins of the New Testament Images of Christ*. New Haven: Yale University Press, 2000.

Freund, Richard A. "The Tannery of Bethsaida." In *Bethsaida: A City by the North Shore of the Sea of Galilee*. Vol. 3, edited by Rami Arav and Richard A. Freund. Kirksville, MO: Truman State University Press, 2004, 233-52.

Freyne, Sean. *Galilee, Jesus and the Gospels*. Minneapolis: Augsburg, 1988.

———. "Locality and Doctrine. Mark and John Revisited." In *The Four Gospels 1992*. Vol. 3, edited by F. van Segbroeck et al. Louvain: Louvain University Press, 1992, 1889-1900.

———. "Herodian Economics in Galilee: Searching for a Suitable Model." In *Modelling Early Christianity*, edited by Philip F. Esler. London: Routledge, 1995, 23-46.

———. "Town and Country Once More: The Case of Roman Galilee." In *Archeology and the Galilee*, edited by Douglas R. Edwards and Christine Thomas McCollough. Atlanta: Scholars Press, 1997, 49-56.
———. *Galilee from Alexander the Great to Hadrian, 323 B.C.E. to 135 C.E.* Edinburgh: T&T Clark, 2000.
———. *Jesus: A Jewish Galilean*. London and New York: T&T Clark, 2006.
Fuà, Oscar. "Da Cicerone a Seneca." In *Senectus*, vol. 2, edited by Umberto Mattioli. Bologna: Pàtron, 1995, 183-238.
Gaeta, Giancarlo. *I Vangeli*. Turin: Einaudi, 2006.
Gardner, Jane F. *Women in Roman Law and Society*. Bloomington: Indiana University Press, 1986.
Gardner, Jane F., and Thomas Wiedemann. *The Roman Household*. London and New York: Routledge, 1991.
Geertz, Clifford. *The Interpretation of Cultures*. New York: Basic Books, 1977.
Geoltrain, Pierre, and Jean-Daniel Kaestli, eds. *Écrits Apocryphes Chrétiens 2*. Paris: Gallimard, 2005.
Gianotto, Claudio. "Il Vangelo secondo Tommaso e il problema storico di Gesù." In *L'enigma Gesù*, edited by Emanuela Prinzivalli. Rome: Carocci, 2008, 68-93.
Gnilka, Joachim. *Das Matthäusevangelium. 1. Teil. Kommentar zu Kap. 1,1—13,58*. Herders theologischer Kommentar zum Neuen Testament I/1. Freiburg i.Br.: Herder, 1986.
———. *Das Matthäusevangelium. 2 Teil. Kommentar zu Kap. 14,1—28,20*. Herders theologischer Kommentar zum Neuen Testament I/2. Freiburg i.Br.: Herder, 1988.
Godelier, Maurice. *L'énigme du don*. Paris: Fayard, 1996.
Goody, Jack. *Production and Reproduction*. Cambridge: Cambridge University Press, 1977.
———. *Cooking, Cuisine and Class: A Study in Comparative Sociology*. Cambridge: Cambridge University Press, 1982.
———. *The Development of the Family and Marriage in Europe*. Cambridge: Cambridge University Press, 1983.
———. *The Oriental, the Ancient, the Primitive*. Cambridge: Cambridge University Press, 1990.
Goody, Jack, and Stanley J. Tambiah. *Bridewealth and Dowry*. Cambridge: Cambridge University Press, 1974.
Gould, Peter, and Rodney White. *Mental Maps*. 2d ed. Boston: Allen & Unwin, 1986.
Guijarro, Santiago. "La familia en la Galilea del siglo primero." *Estudios Bíblicos* 53 (1995): 461-68.
Guijarro Oporto, Santiago. "The Family in First-Century Galilee." In *Constructing Early Christian Families*, edited by Halvor Moxnes. London and New York: Routledge, 1997, 42-65.

---. *Fidelidades en conflicto: La ruptura con la familia por causa del discipulado y de la misión en la tradición sinóptica.* Salamanca: Universidad Pontificia de Salamanca, 1998.

---. "The Politics of Exorcism." In *The Social Setting of Jesus and the Gospels*, edited by Wolfgang Stegemann, Bruce J. Malina, and Gerd Theissen. Minneapolis: Fortress Press, 2002, 159-74.

Halbwachs, Maurice. *La topographie légendaire des évangiles en Terre Sainte.* Édition préparée par Marie Jaisson. Paris: PUF, 2008 (1st ed., Paris: PUF, 1940).

Hannerz, Ulf. *Cultural Complexity.* New York: Columbia University Press, 1993.

---. *Transnational Connections.* London and New York: Routledge, 1996.

Hanson, K. C. "The Galilean Fishing Economy and the Jesus Tradition." *Biblical Theology Bulletin* 27 (1997): 99-111.

Hanson, K. C., and Douglas E. Oakman. *Palestine in the Time of Jesus.* Minneapolis: Fortress Press, 1998.

Havrelock, Rachel. "The Two Maps of Israel's Land." *Journal of Biblical Literature* 126 (2007): 649-67.

Hengel, Martin. *Nachfolge und Charisma.* Berlin: Töpelmann, 1968. ET: *The Charismatic Leader and His Followers.* Eugene, OR: Wipf & Stock, 2005.

Héritier, Françoise. *L'exercice de la parenté.* Paris: Gallimard, 1981.

Héritier, Françoise, and Margarita Xanthakou. *Corps et affects.* Paris: Odile Jacob, 2004.

Hervieu-Léger, Danièle. *La religion en mouvement: le pèlerin et le converti.* Paris: Flammarion, 1999.

Holum, Kenneth G. et al., eds. *King Herod's Dream: Caesarea on the Sea.* New York and London: Horton, 1988.

Horrell, David G. "From *adelphoi* to *oikos theou*: Social Transformation in Pauline Christianity." *Journal of Biblical Literature* 120 (2001): 293-311.

Horsley Richard A. "Archeology and the Villages of Upper Galilee: A Dialogue with Archeologists." *Bulletin of the American Schools of Oriental Research* 297 (1995): 5-16.

---. *Galilee: History, Politics, People.* London: Continuum, 1995.

---. *Jesus and Empire.* Minneapolis: Fortress Press, 2003.

---. "Jésus le galiléen face au nouvel ordre romain." In *Jésus, complements d'enquête*, edited by Daniel Marguerat et al. Paris: Bayard, 2007, 59-69.

Horsley Richard A., and John S. Hanson, *Bandits, Prophets, and Messiahs.* London: Continuum, 2000.

Hubert de Radkowski, Georges. *Anthropologie de l'habiter: Vers le nomadisme.* Paris: PUF, 2002.

Ingold Tim. *The Perception of Environment.* London and New York: Routledge, 2000.

---. "Building, Dwelling, Living: How Animals and People Make Themselves at Home in the World." In Tim Ingold, *The Perception of the Environment*. London and New York: Routledge, 2000, 172-88.
Johnson, Marshall D. *The Purpose of the Biblical Genealogies with Special Reference to the Setting of the Genealogy of Jesus*. 2d ed. Cambridge: Cambridge University Press, 1988.
Jossa, Giorgio. *Dal Messia al Cristo*. Brescia: Paideia, 2000.
Kanafani-Zahar, Aïda, Séverine Matthieu, and Sophie Nizard, eds. *À croire et à manger: Religions et alimentation*. Paris: L'Harmattan, 2007.
Kee, Howard Clark. "Jesus: A Glutton and Drunkard." *New Testament Studies* 42 (1996): 347-93. Reprinted in *Authenticating the Word of Jesus*, edited by Bruce Chilton and Craig A. Evans. Leiden: Brill, 1999, 311-32.
Keesing, Roger M. *Kingroups and Social Structure*. New York: Holt Rinehart Winston, 1975.
Kelhoffer, James A. *The Diet of John the Baptist: "Locusts and Wild Honey" in Synoptic and Patristic Interpretation*. Tübingen: Mohr Siebeck, 2005.
Kertzer, David I., and Richard P. Saller, eds. *The Family in Italy from Antiquity to the Present*. New Haven: Yale University Press, 1991.
---, and Marzio Barbagli, eds. *Family Life in Early Modern Times, 1500-1789*. New Haven: Yale University Press, 2001.
Klassen, W. *Judas: Betrayer or Friend of Jesus*. London: SCM, 1996.
Klijn, A. F. J. *Jewish-Christian Gospel Tradition*. Leiden: Brill, 1992.
Kloner, Amos. "Stepped Roads in Roman Palestine." *Aram* 8 (1996): 111-17.
Kloppenborg, John S. *The Formation of Q*. Philadelphia: Fortress Press, 1987.
---. *Excavating Q*. Minneapolis: Fortress Press, 2000.
---. "Dating Theodotos (CJ II 1404)." *Journal of Jewish Studies* 51 (2000): 243-80.
---. *The Tenants in the Vineyard*. Tübingen: Mohr Siebeck, 2006.
Kloppenborg, John S., and Stephen G. Wilson, eds. *Voluntary Associations in the Ancient World*. London: Routledge, 1996.
Kraemer, Ross Shephard. *Her Share of the Blessings: Women's Religions among Pagans, Jews, and Christians in the Greco-Roman World*. New York and Oxford: Oxford University Press, 1992.
Kriesberg, Louis. *The Sociology of Social Conflicts*. Englewood Cliffs, NJ: Prentice-Hall, 1973.
---. *Social Conflicts*. Englewood Cliffs, NJ: Prentice-Hall, 1982.
---. *Constructive Conflicts*. Lanham, MD: Rowman & Littlefield, 1998.
Kruger, Michael J. *The Gospel of the Savior: An Analysis of P. Oxy. 840 and Its Place in the Gospel Traditions of Early Christianity*. Leiden: Brill, 2005.
Laplantine, François (en collaboration avec A. Nouss). *Le métissage*. Paris: Flammarion, 1997.
---. *Je, nous et les autres*. Paris: Le Pommier, 2006.
Le Bras, Gabriel. *L'Eglise et le village*. Paris: Flammarion, 1976
Le Breton, David. *Anthropologie du corps et modernité*. Paris: Presses Universitaires de France, 1990.

———. *Du silence*. Paris: Métailié, 1997.
———. "Anthropologie du silence." *Théologiques* 7 (1999): 11-28.
Le Goff, Jacques. *Pour un autre moyen âge*. Paris: Gallimard, 1977.
Lejeune, Philippe, and Catherine Viollet, eds. *Genèses du "Je."* Paris: CNRS Éditions, 2000.
Lémonon, Jean-Pierre. *Ponce Pilate*. Paris: Les Éditions de l'Atelier, 2007 (1st ed., 1981).
Lencoud, Gérard. "Groupe domestique." in *Dictionnaire de l'éthnologie et de l'anthropologie*. Paris: PUF, 2000, 313-15.
Levine, Amy-Jill. *The Social and Ethnic Dimension of Matthean Salvation History*. New York: Edwin Mellen, 1998.
Levine, Lee I. *Ancient Synagogues Revealed*. Jerusalem: Israel Exploration Society, 1981.
Lévi-Strauss, Claude. *Le cru et le cuit*. Paris: Plon, 1964.
Levy, Robert I. *Tahitians: Mind and Experience in the Society Islands*. Chicago: University of Chicago Press, 1973.
Lieu, Judith M. "The Attraction of Women in/to early Judaism and Christianity." *JSNT* 72 (1998): 5-22.
Ligi, Gianluca. *Nemici invisibili: Antropologia dei disastri*. Rome and Bari: Laterza, 2008.
Lincoln, Bruce. *Holy Terrors: Thinking about Religion after September 11*. Chicago: University of Chicago Press, 2003.
Lindholm, Charles. *Generosity and Jealousy: The Swat Pukhtun of Northern Pakistan*. New York: Columbia University Press, 1982.
Lupieri, Edmondo. "La purità impura." *Henoch* 7 (1985): 15-43.
———. *Giovanni Battista fra storia e leggenda*. Brescia: Paideia, 1988.
———. *Giovanni Battista nelle traditioni sinottiche*. Brescia: Paideia, 1988.
Lutz, Catherine, and Geoffrey M. White. "The Anthropology of Emotions." *Annual Review of Anthropology* 15 (1986): 405-36.
Luz, Ulrich. *Das Evangelium nach Matthäus. 2. Teilband. Mt 8-14*. Zurich: Benzinger Verlag, 1985.
MacMullen, Ramsay. "Women in Public in the Roman Empire." *Historia* 29 (1980): 208-18.
Marguerat, Daniel. "Jésus et ses frères." In *Jésus, complements d'enquête*, edited by Daniel Marguerat et al. Paris: Bayard, 2007, 142-49.
Mauss, Marcel. "Essai sur le don. Forme et raison de l'échange dans les sociétés archaïques." Published as volume 2 of *Année Sociologique* (1923-1924).
———. "Les techniques du corps." *Journal de psychologie normal et pathologique* 32 (1935): 271-93.
Meier, John P. *A Marginal Jew: Rethinking the Historical Jesus*. 4 vols. New York: Doubleday, 1991-2009.
Meillassoux, Claude. *Femmes, greniers et capitaux*. Paris: Maspero, 1975. ET: *Maidens, Meal and Money*. Cambridge: Cambridge University Press, 1981.

Merlier, Octave. *Itinéraires de Jésus et chronologie dans le quatrième évangile*. Athens: Institut français, 1961.
Meyers, Eric M. "Jesus and His Galilean Context." In *Archeology and the Galilee*, edited by Douglas R. Edwards and Christine Thomas McCollough. Atlanta: Scholars, 1997, 57-66.
———. "The Cultural Settings of Galilee: The Case of Regionalism and Early Judaism." *ANRW* II 19 (1999): 686-702.
———. "The Problems of Gendered Space in Syro-Palestinian Domestic Architecture: The Case of Roman-Period Galilee." In *Early Christian Families in Context*, edited by David Balch and Carolyn Osiek. Grand Rapids: Eerdmans, 2003, 44-69.
Meyers, Eric M., Ehud Netzer, and Carol L. Meyers. *Sepphoris*. Winona Lake, IN: Eisenbrauns, 1992.
Mimouni, Simon C. "Jésus de Nazareth, de la tradition à l'histoire ou de la tradition à la réalité." In *Le Christianisme des origines à Costantin*, edited by Simon C. Mimouni and Pierre Maraval. Paris: PUF, 2006.
———. "Les imposteurs dans les communautés chrétiennes des Ier-IIe siècles." *Annali di Storia dell'Esegesi* 27 (2010): 255-64.
Moloney Francis J. *The Gospel of John*. Collegeville, MN: Liturgical, 1998.
Moreschini, Claudio, and Enrico Norelli. *Early Christian Greek and Latin Literature*. 1: *From Paul to the Age of Constantine*. Peabody, MA: Hendrickson, 2005. Ital. orig., *Storia della letteratura cristiana antica greca e latina*. 1: *Da Paolo all'età costantiniana*. Brescia: Morcelliana, 1995.
Moxnes, Halvor. *The Economy of the Kingdom*. Philadelphia: Fortress Press, 1988.
———. "Patron-Client Relations and the New Community in Luke-Acts." In *The Social World of Luke-Acts: Models for Interpretation*, edited by Jerome H. Neyrey. Peabody, MA: Hendrickson, 1991, 241-68.
———. *Putting Jesus in His Place*. Louisville, KY: Westminster John Knox, 2003.
Moxnes, Halvor, ed. *Constructing Early Christian Families: Family as Social Reality and Metaphor*. London and New York: Routledge, 1997.
Murphy-O'Connor, Jerome. *The Holy Land: An Oxford Archaeological Guide*. 5th ed. Oxford: Oxford University Press, 2008.
Nardi, Carlo. *Il millenarismo: Testi dei secoli I e II*. Fiesole: Nardini, 1995.
Nathan, Geoffrey S. *The Family in Late Antiquity*. London: Routledge, 2000.
Needham, Rodney. "Remarques sur l'analyse de la parenté." In *La parenté en question*, edited by Rodney Needham. Paris: Seuil, 1977, 103-31.
Netzer, Ehud. *Sepphoris*. Jerusalem: Israel Exploration Society, 1994.
Netzer, Ehud, and Zeev Weiss, "Sepphoris." *Israel Exploration Journal* 43 (1993): 190-96.
Neusner, Jacob, and Bruce Chilton, eds. *In Search of the Historical Pharisees*. Waco, TX: Baylor University Press, 2006.
Norelli, Enrico. "La presenza di Gesù nella letteratura gentile dei primi due secoli." In *Ricerche storicobibliche* 17 (2005): 175-215.

———. "La construction des origines chrétiennes. Quelques étapes aux deux premiers siècles." In *Los comienzos del cristianismo: IV Simposio Internacional del Grupo Europeo de Investigación Interdisciplinar sobre los Orígenes del Cristianismo (G.E.R.I.C.O),* edited by S. Guijarro. Salamanca: Publicaciones Universidad Pontificia 2006, 205-16.

———. "Considerazioni di metodo sull'uso delle fonti per la ricostruzione della figura storica di Gesù." In *L'enigma Gesù: Fonti e metodi della ricerca storica,* edited by Emanuela Prinzivalli. Rome: Carocci 2008, 19-67.

———. "Gesù in frammenti. Testi apocrifi di tipo evangelico conservati in modo frammentario." In *Un altro Gesù? I vangeli apocrifi, il Gesù storico e il cristianesimo delle origini,* edited by Annalisa Guida and Enrico Novelli. Trapani: Il pozzo di Giacobbe, 2009, 39-88.

Oakman, Douglas E. "The Countryside in Luke-Acts." In *The Social World of Luke-Acts,* edited by Jerome H. Neyrey. Peabody, MA: Hendrickson, 1991, 151-73.

Osiek, Carolyn, and David Balch. *Families in the New Testament World: Households and House Churches.* Louisville, KY: Westminster John Knox, 1997.

Osiek, Carolyn, and Margaret Y. MacDonald. *A Woman's Place: House Churches in Earliest Christianity.* Minneapolis: Augsburg Fortress Press, 2005.

Overman, J. Andrew. "Jesus of Galilee and the Historical Peasant." in *Archeology and the Galilee,* edited by Douglas Edwards and Christine Thomas McCollough. Atlanata: Scholars, 1997, 67-73.

Pellizer, Ezio. "Della zuffa simpotica." In *Poesia e simposio nella Grecia antica: Guida storica e critica,* edited by Massimo Vetta. Rome and Bari: Laterza, 1983, 31-41.

Penna, Romano. *I ritratti originali di Gesù Il Cristo: Inizi e sviluppi della cristologia neotestamentaria.* 2 vols. Milan: San Paolo, 1996, 1999.

———. *Gesù di Nazareth: La sua storia. La nostra fede.* Milan: San Paolo, 2011.

Perrin, Norman. *Rediscovering the Teaching of Jesus.* London: SCM, 1967.

Perroni, Marinella. "Lettura femminile ed ermeneutica femminista del NT: Status quaestionis." *Rivista Biblica* 41 (1993): 315–39.

Pesce, Mauro. "Ricostruzione dell'archetipo letterario comune a Mt 22,1-10 e Lc 14,15-24." In *La parabola degli invitati al banchetto,* edited by Jacques Dupont. Brescia: Paideia, 1978, 167-236.

———. "Discepolato gesuano e discepolato rabbinico. Problemi e prospettive della comparazione." *Aufstieg und Niedergang der römischen Welt II. Prinzipat 25/1.* Berlin/New York: de Gruyter, 1982, 351-89.

———. "La lavanda dei piedi Gv 13,1-20, il 'Romanzo di Esopo' e i 'Saturnalia' di Macrobio." *Biblica* 80 (1999): 240-49.

———. "Il Vangelo di Giovanni e le fasi giudaiche del giovannismo." In *Verus Israel: Nuove prospettive sul giudeocristianesimo. Atti del Colloquio di Torino (4-5 novembre 1999),* edited by Giovanni Filoramo and Claudio Gianotto. Brescia: Paideia 2001, 47-67.

———. "Gesù e il sacrifico ebraico." *Annali di Storia dell'Esegesi* 18 no. 1 (2001): 146-51.

———. *Da Gesù al cristianesimo*. Brescia: Morcelliana, 2011.

Pesce, Mauro, ed. *Le parole dimenticate di Gesù*. Milan: Lorenzo Valla-Mondadori, 2004.

Pesch, Rudolf. *Das Markusevangelium. 1 Teil*. Freiburg i.B.: Herder, 1977.

Piasere, Leonardo, and Pier Giorgio Solinas. *Le culture della parentela e l'esogamia perfetta*. Rome: CISU, 1998.

Pomeroy, Sarah B. *Families in Classical and Hellenistic Greece*. Oxford: Clarendon, 1997.

Pomeroy, Sarah B., ed. *Women's History and Ancient History*. Chapel Hill, NC: University of North Carolina Press, 1991.

Pussetti, Chiara. "Introduzione. Discorsi sulle emozioni." *Antropologia* 5 (2005): 5-15.

———. *Poetica delle emozioni: I Bijagò della Guinea Bissau*. Bari and Rome: Laterza, 2005.

Redfield, Robert. *The Little Community and Peasant Society and Culture*. Chicago: University of Chicago Press, 1989.

Reed, Jonathan L. *Archeology and the Galilean Jesus*. Harrisburg, PA: Trinity Press International, 2000.

Remotti, Francesco. *Forme di umanità*. Milan: Bruno Mondadori, 2002.

Ricci, Carla. *Mary Magdalene and Many Others: Women Who Followed Jesus*. Tunbridge Wells: Burns & Oates, 1994.

Richardson, Peter. "Khirbet Qana (and Other Villages) as a Context for Jesus." In *Jesus and Archeology*, edited by James H. Charlesworth. Grand Rapids: Eerdmans, 2006, 120-44.

Rigato, Maria Luisa. *Giovanni: L'enigma, il presbitero, il culto*. Bologna: Edizioni Dehoniane, 2007.

Rivkin, Ellis. *What Crucified Jesus?* New York: UAHC, 1997.

Robinson, James M., P. Hoffmann, and John S. Kloppenborg, eds. *The Critical Edition of Q*. Minneapolis: Fortress Press, 2000.

Rohrbaugh, Richard. "The Pre-industrial City in Luke-Acts: Urban Social Relations." In *The Social World of Luke-Acts*, edited by Jerome H. Neyrey. Peabody, MA: Hendrickson, 1991, 140-46.

———. "Ethnocentrism and Historical Questions about Jesus." In *The Social Setting of Jesus and the Gospel*, edited by Wolfgang Stegemann, Bruce J. Malina, and Gerd Theissen. Minneapolis: Fortress Press, 2002, 33-39.

Roll, Israel. "The Roman Road System in Judaea." In *The Jerusalem Cathedra* 3, edited by Lee Israel Levine. Jerusalem and Detroit: Yad Izhak Ben-Zvi Institute and Wayne State University Press, 1983, 136-60.

———. "Roman Roads." In *Tabula Imperii Romani, Judaea Palestina*, edited by Yoram Tsafrir, Leah Di Segni, and Judith Green. Jerusalem: Israeli Academy of Sciences and Humanities, 1994, 21-22.

———. "Roads and Transportation in the Holy Land in the Early Christian and Byzantine Times." In *Akten des XII. Internationalen Kongresses für christliche Archäologie.* Jahrbuch für Antike und Christentum, supplementary vol. 20. Münster: Aschendorff, 1995, 1166-70.

———. "Imperial Roads and Trade Routes beyond the Roman Provinces of Judaea-Palaestina and Arabia. The State of Research." *Tel-Aviv* 32 (2005): 107-18.

Rousseau, John J., and Arav Rami. *Jesus and His World.* Minneapolis: Fortress Press, 1995.

Safrai, Shemuel. *Wallfahrt im Zeitalter des zweiten Tempels.* Neukirchen-Vluyn: Neukirchener Verlag, 1981.

Safrai, Zeev. *The Economy of Roman Palestine.* London and New York: Routledge, 1994.

Saller, Richard P. "Patronage and Friendship in Early Imperial Rome." In *Patronage in Ancient Society,* edited by A. Wallace-Hadrill. London and New York: Routledge, 1990.

———. *Patriarchy, Property and Death in the Roman Family.* Cambridge: Cambridge University Press, 1994.

Sanders, E. P. *The Historical Figure of Jesus.* Harmondsworth: Penguin, 1996.

Scheper-Hughes, Nancy, and Margaret M. Lock. "The Mindful Body." *Medical Anthropological Quarterly* n.s. 1 (1987): 6-41.

Schmidt, Karl L. *Der Rahmen der Geschichte Jesu.* Berlin: Trowitzsch, 1919. Reprinted, Darmstadt: Wissenschaftliche Buchgesellschaft, 1964.

Schnackenburg, Rudolf. "Zur Traditionsgeschichte von Joh. 4,46-54." *Biblische Zeitschrift* n.F. 8 (1964): 58-88.

Schweitzer, Albert. *Das Messianitäts- und Leidensgeheimnis: Eine Skizze des Lebens Jesu.* Tübingen: Mohr, 1901. ET: *The Mystery of the Kingdom of God.* New York: Dodd, Mead, 1914.

———. *Von Reimarus zu Wrede.* Tübingen: Mohr, 1906. ET: *The Quest of the Historical Jesus.* London: A. & C. Black, 1910.

Schweizer, Eduard. *"Psyche. D. Neues Testament." Theologisches Wörterbuch zum Neuen Testament* 9 (1973): 635-57.

Shweder, Richard A., and Robert A. LeVine, *Culture Theory: Essays on Mind, Self, and Emotion.* Cambridge: Cambridge University Press, 1984.

Simmel, Georg. *Soziologie: Unterschungen über die Formen der Vergesellschaftung.* Leipzig: Dunker & Humblot, 1908.

Smith, Dennis E. *From Symposium to Eucharist: The Banquet in the Early Christian World.* Minneapolis: Fortress Press, 2003.

Smith, Robert W. "Chorazin." *Anchor Bible Dictionary* 1 (1992): 911-12.

Steele, E. Springs. "Luke 11:37-54: A Modified Hellenistic Symposium?" *JBL* 103 (1984): 379-94.

Stegemann, Ekkehard, and Wolfgang Stegemann. *Urchristliche Sozialgeschichte.* Stuttgart: Kohlhammer, 1997. ET: *The Jesus Movement.* Minneapolis: Fortress Press, 2001.

Stegemann, Wolfgang, Bruce J. Malina, and Gerd Theissen, eds. *The Social Setting of Jesus and the Gospels.* Minneapolis: Fortress Press, 2002.

Strange, James F. "Bethsaida." *Anchor Bible Dictionary* 1 (1991): 692-93.

———. "Sepphoris." *Anchor Bible Dictionary* 5 (1992): 1090-93.
———. "Tiberias." *Anchor Bible Dictionary* 6 (1992): 547-49.
———. "Six Campaigns at Sepphoris: The University of South Florida Excavations, 1983-1989." In *Galilee in Late Antiquity*, edited by Lee Levine. New York and Jerusalem: Jewish Theological Seminary of America, 1992, 339-55.
———. "First Century Galilee from Archeology and from the Texts." In *Archeology and the Galilee*, edited by Douglas E. Edwards and Christine Thomas McCollough. Atlanta: Scholars, 1997, 39-48.
Strathern, Andrew J. *Body Thoughts*. Ann Arbor: University of Michigan Press, 1996.
Taylor, Joan. *John the Baptist within Second Temple Judaism: A Historical Study*. London: SPCK, 1997.
Theissen, Gerd. *Studien zur Soziologie des Urchristentums*. Tübingen: Mohr Siebeck, 1989.
———. *Urchristliche Wundergeschichten*. Gütersloh: Mohn, 1998.
———. *Die Jesusbewegung*. Gütersloh: Gütersloher Verlagshaus, 2004.
Theissen, Gerd, and Annette Merz, *Der historische Jesus: Ein Lehrbuch*. 3rd ed. Göttingen: Vandenhoeck & Ruprecht, 2001. ET: *The Historical Jesus: A Comprehensive Guide*. Minneapolis: Fortress Press, 1998.
Trümper, Monika. "Material and Social Environment of Greco-Roman Households in the East." In *Early Christian Families in Context*, edited by David Balch and Carolyn Osiek. Grand Rapids: Eerdmans, 2003, 19-43.
Turner, Victor, and Edith Turner, *Image and Pilgrimage in Christian Culture*. New York: Columbia University Press, 1995.
Twelftree, Graham H. *Jesus the Exorcist*. Tübingen: Mohr, 1993.
Tzaferis, Vasilios, ed. *Excavations at Capernaum* 1. Winona Lake, IN: Eisenbrauns, 1989.
van Henten, Jan Willen, and Athalya Brenner, eds. *Families and Family Relations as Represented in Early Judaisms and Early Christianities: Texts and Fictions*. Leiden: Deo, 2000.
Vasaly, Ann. *Representations: Images of the World in Ciceronian Oratory*. Berkeley: University of California Press, 1993.
Vouga, François. *Geschichte des frühen Christentums*. Stuttgart: UTB, 1994.
Wahlen, Clinton. *Jesus and the Impurity of Spirits in the Synoptic Gospels*. Tübingen: Mohr Siebeck, 2004.
Wallace-Hadrill, Andrew. "Patronage in Roman Society: From Republic to Empire." In *Patronage in Ancient Society*, edited by A. Wallace-Hadrill. London and New York: Routledge, 1989, 63-88.
———. "Domus and Insulae in Rome: Families and Household." In *Early Christian Families in Context*, edited by David Balch and Carolyn Osiek. Grand Rapids: Eerdmans, 2003, 3-18.
Wallace-Hadrill, Andrew, ed. *Patronage in Ancient Society*. London and New York: Routledge, 1989.

Warfield, Benjamin B. "The Emotional Life of Our Lord." In *Biblical and Theological Studies*, edited by members of the faculty of Princeton Theological Seminary. New York: Charles Scribner's Sons, 1912, 36-90.

———. *The Person and Work of Christ*. Philadelphia: Presbyterian and Reformed, 1950.

———. "Jésus et les emotions." *Hokhma* 58 (1995): 21-49.

Weber, Max. *Wirtschaft und Gesellschaft*. Tübingen: Mohr 1922. ET: *Economy and Society. II*. Los Angeles: University of California Press, 1978.

Wegner, Judith. *Chattel or Person: The Status of Women in the Mishnah*. New York and Oxford: Oxford University Press, 1988.

Weiss, Zeev, and Ehud Netzer. "Architectural Development of Sepphoris during the Roman and Byzantine Periods." In *Archeology and the Galilee*, edited by Douglas R. Edwards and Christine Thomas McCollough. Atlanta: Scholars, 117-30.

White, L. Michael. *The Social Origins of Christian Architecture*. 2 vols. Valley Forge, PA: Trinity Press International, 1996, 1997.

Wikan, Unni. "Beyond the Words: The Power of Resonance." *American Ethnologist* 19, no. 3 (1992): 460-82.

Willis, Laurence M. *The Quest of the Historical Jesus*. London and New York: Routledge, 1997.

Wolf, Eric R. *Peasants*. Englewood Cliffs, NJ: Prentice Hall, 1966.

Woorwinde, Stephen. *Jesus's Emotions in the Fourth Gospel: Human or Divine*. London and New York: T&T Clark, 2005.

Wrede, Wilhelm. *Das Messiasgeheimnis in den Evangelien*. Göttingen: Vandenhoeck & Ruprecht, 1901. ET: *The Messianic Secret*. Cambridge: Lutterworth, 1987.

Yeivin, Zev. "Ancient Chorazin Comes Back to Life." *Biblical Archeological Review* 13, no. 5 (1987): 22-36.

Yi-Fu, Tuan. *Space and Place: The Perspective of Experience*. Minneapolis: University of Minnesota Press, 1977.

INDEX OF AUTHORS AND NAMES

Abraham, 82, 91, 99, 131, 132, 134, 204
Adam, 133
Alexander, Philip, 184, 214
Alexander Jannaeus, 12
Ananus, 62
Andrew, 9, 48, 49, 50, 54, 88, 102, 111, 127, 191, 192, 197
Annas, High Priest, 71
Apollonius of Tyana, 30
Appadurai, Arjun, 186
Aragione, Gabriella, 178
Arav, Rami, 180, 186, 208
Asad, Talal, 177
Assmann, Aleida, 178
Augé, Marc, 4, 25, 178, 180, 183, 188, 189
Augustus, 17, 182
Aurant, Sarah, 181
Aviam, Mordechai, 184

Bachelard, Gaston, 180
Balch, David, 80, 198, 200, 206
Baldini Lippolis, Isabella, 207
Bammel, Ernst, 188
Bannus, 43
Barabbas, 71, 192
Barbagli, Marzio, 205
Barbaglio, Giuseppe, 185, 203
Barth, Frederick, 195
Bastiaensen, Antoon A. R. 194
Batkin, Mihajlovic Leonid, 209
Bauckham, Richard, 197, 198
Bauman, Zygmunt, 208

Beckwith, Roger T., 193
Beirne, Margaret M., 198
Bertman, Stephen, 211
Blackburn, Barry, 152, 199, 217, 218
Blinzler, Josef, 196
Bobichon, Philippe, 204
Booth, Roger P., 202
Botha, Pieter J. J., 206
Bovon, François, 57, 95, 187, 196, 203, 205, 212, 214, 218
Bowie, Fiona, 213
Boyarin, Daniel, 179
Bremmer, Jan N., 194
Briggs, Jane L., 218
Brown, Raymond E., 199

Caiaphas, 71
Calame, Claude, 203
Cerinthus, 100
Certeau, Michel de, 180, 188
Chancey, Mark A., 186, 188
Charif, Abdelhakim, 213
Charlesworth, James H., 181, 208
Chilton, Bruce, 193, 203
Chuza, 52, 118
Clifford, James, 179, 219
Clopas, 58
Cole, John W., 183
Connerton, Paul, 181
Corbo, Virgilio C., 183
Corley, Kathleen E., 198
Cotter, Wendy, 206, 217
Cracco Ruggini, Lellia, 7, 182
Crates, 51

Index of Authors and Names

Crossan, John Dominic, 6, 62, 104, 180, 181, 185, 186, 189, 190, 193, 198, 199, 200, 202, 203, 207, 210
Csordas, Thomas J., 216

David, King of Israel, 12, 131, 132
Davies, Stevan L., 217, 218
Degani, Avi, 184
Delécraz, Christian, 217
Delobel, Joël, 203
DeMaris, Richard E., 193
Desjarlais, Robert R., 219
Destro, Adriana, ix, 23, 38, 75, 148, 174, 177-79, 181, 185, 186, 193-195, 197-204, 206-12, 214, 215, 218
Di Segni, Leah, 180
Dixon, Suzanne, 205
Dorsey, David A., 181
Douglas, Mary, 56, 128, 183, 189, 192, 194, 202, 206, 208, 213, 218
Duhart, Frédéric, 213
Duling, Dennis, 181, 183, 195
Dunn, James D. G., 177
Dupont, Jacques, 178, 201, 203, 204
Dupront, Alphonse, 189
Durussel, Laurie, 217

Edelstein, Gershon, 181
Edwards, Douglas E., 180, 183, 185, 187, 189, 194, 208
Eisenstadt, Shmuel N., 198
Elias, Norbert, 219
Elijah, 152, 220
Elliott, James Keith, 196, 197, 202, 204, 219
Elliott, John H., 177, 205, 212
Esler, Philip F., 186
Evans, Craig, 203

Fabian, Johannes, 213
Fabris, Rinaldo, 201
Filoramo, Giovanni, 194, 199, 208
Finley, Moses I., 205
Fischer, Moshe, 180

Focant, Camille, 182, 184, 197, 201, 203, 216
Fortes, Meyer, 205
Foucault, Michel, 209
Fourrier Sabine, 181
Frankel, Raphael, 184
Fredriksen, Paula, 180
Freund, Richard A., 186, 208
Freyne, Sean, 180, 184, 185
Fuà, Oscar, 211

Gabba, Emilio, 182
Gardner, Jane F., 194, 205
Gaeta, Giancarlo, 219
Geertz, Clifford, 219
Gelardini, Gabriella, 210
Geoltrain, Pierre, 195
Getzov, Nimrod, 184
Gianotto, Claudio, 227
Ginzburg, Carlo, 178
Gnilka, Joachim, 73, 183, 197, 199, 203, 212-214
Godelier, Maurice, 79, 200
Goody, Jack, 178, 200, 204, 205, 210
Gould, Peter, 180
Green, Judith, 180
Guijarro Oporto, Santiago, 199, 206, 209

Halbwachs, Maurice, 7, 19, 178, 181, 187
Hannerz, Ulf, 186, 188, 213
Hanson, John S., 186
Hanson, Kenneth C., 193, 194, 206
Havrelock, Rachel, 104
Heli, 133
Hengel, Martin, 194, 209
Héritier, Françoise, 213
Herod Antipas, 23, 46, 52, 64, 71, 85, 114, 138, 139, 141, 184, 186, 201, 215
Herod Philip, 17, 23, 182, 184, 186
Herod the Great, 12, 17, 149
Hervieu-Léger, Danièle, 189, 190
Hilhorst, Antonius, 194
Hoffmann, Paul, 182

Index of Authors and Names

Holum, Kenneth G., 180
Horrell, David, 206
Horsley, Richard A., 17, 180, 181, 183, 186, 188

Ingold, Tim, 3, 179, 216
Irenaeus, 100, 204
Isaac, 82, 99, 131, 181, 204
Isaac, Benjamin, 181

Jacob, 82, 99, 131, 204
Jacob, father of Joseph, 132
James, brother of Jesus, 57, 58, 60, 61, 62, 74, 192, 196, 198
James, son of Alphaeus, 62, 114, 129, 192, 197
James, son of Zebedee, 48, 49, 50, 54, 55, 88, 111, 112, 152, 159, 167, 168, 187, 191, 192, 197, 220
Joanna, wife of Chuza, 52, 111, 114, 118
John, son of Zebedee, 48, 49, 50, 54, 55, 88, 111, 112, 152, 159, 167, 168
John the Baptizer, 14, 42-48, 83, 94, 131, 134, 149, 185, 192, 193
Johnson, Marshall D., 214
Joseph, father of Jesus, 58, 132, 133, 134, 196
Joseph of Arimathea, 51, 64, 65, 141, 142, 192
Josephus, Flavius, 5, 11, 12, 43, 44, 62, 110, 180, 182, 184, 187, 192, 193, 196, 209
Joses, brother of Jesus, 58, 192
Jossa, Giorgio, 191
Judas, brother of Jesus, 58, 192
Judas, son of James, 54, 197
Judas, the zealot 55
Judas Iscariot, 54, 55, 87, 141, 142, 157, 192
Junod, Eric, 178
Justin, xv, xvi, 100, 204, 215

Kaestli, Jean-Daniel, 195
Kanafani-Zahar, Aïda, 200

Keesing, Roger M., 205
Kelhoffer, James A., 193
Kertzer, David I., 205
Kilani, Mondher, 203
Klassen, William, 195, 202
Klein, Hans, 196, 218
Kloner, Amos, 180
Kloppenborg, John S., 15, 21, 178, 182, 183, 185, 186, 188, 208, 210
Kraemer, Ross S., 53, 194, 195
Kraus, Thomas J., 178
Kriesberg, Louis, 210
Kruger, Michael J., 187

Laplantine, François, 208
Lazarus of Bethany, 14, 51, 63, xvi, 89, 139, 216
Lazarus the poor, 91, 96, 124, 207
Le Boulluec, Alain, 178
Le Bras, Gabriel, 181
Le Breton, David, 162, 213, 220
Le Goff, Jacques, 36, 191
Le Pape, Yannick, 213
Lejeune, Philippe, 209
Lémonon, Jean-Pierre, 186
Lencoud, Gérard, 206
Levi, follower of Jesus, xi, 28, 51, 104, 111, 114, 192, 207
Levine, Amy-Jill, 184, 199, 214
Levine, Lee Israel, 180, 186, 211
LeVine, Robert A., 219
Lévi-Strauss, Claude, 200, 210
Levy, Robert I., 219
Lieu, Judith M., 195
Ligi, Gianluca, 217
Lincoln, Bruce, 219
Lindars, Barnabas, 214
Lindholm, Charles, 219
Lock, Margaret M., 128, 213
Lupieri, Edmondo, 192, 193
Lutz, Catherine, 218, 219
Luz, Ulrich, 189

MacDonald, Margaret Y., 198, 206
MacMullen, Ramsey, 194

Malina, Bruce J., 181, 193, 199, 209
Mara, Maria Grazia, 178
Marcus, Gorge, 179
Marguerat, Daniel, 180, 196
Martini, Carlo Maria, 204
Martha, sister of Mary, xi, 51, 63, 66, 89, 121, 198
Mary, mother of James "the less", 66, 114, 192
Mary, mother of Jesus, 58, 132, 192, 196, 197
Mary, sister of Martha, xi, 20, 51, 63, 66, 68, 89, 121, 198, 216
Mary of Magdala, 48, 52, 66, 89, 111, 114, 139, 192, 218
Matthieu, Séverine, 200
Matthias, substitute for Judas Iscariot, 54
Mattioli, Umberto, 211
Mauss, Marcel, 32, 128, 200, 213
Meier, John P., 196, 199, 203, 217, 218
Meillassoux, Claude, 205, 210
Merlier, Octave, 185
Merz, Annette, 193, 199, 203, 217
Meyers, Carol L., 186
Meyers, Eric M., 6, 181, 185, 6, 206
Milevski, Ianir, 181
Mimouni, Simon C., 189
Moloney, Francis J., 197
Moreschini, Claudio, 182
Moshe, 152, 196
Moxnes, Halvor, 30, 127, 189, 205, 206, 210, 212, 213
Murphy-O'Connor, Jerome, 182

Nardi, Carlo, 204
Nathan, Geoffrey S., 206
Nathanael, follower of Jesus, 48
Needham, Rodney, 177, 205
Netzer, Ehud, 186, 187
Neusner, Jacob, 193
Neyrey, Jerome H., 183, 205, 212
Nicklas, Tobias, 178
Nicodemus, 51, 72
Nizard, Sophie, 200
Norelli, Enrico, 178, 182

Oakman, Douglas E., 183, 193, 206
Osiek, Carolyn, 66, 80, 198, 200, 206
Overman, Andrew J., 183

Paul of Tarsus, xii, 62, 74, 88, 97, 98, 142, 179, 183, 193, 201, 202, 204
Pellizer, Ezio, 201
Perrin, Norman, 201
Pesce, Mauro, 177-179, 185, 187, 188, 190, 192-195, 197-204, 207-15, 218, 220
Pesch, Rudolph, 219
Philip, 11, 55, 61
Piasere, Leonardo, 205, 214
Peter (Simon) 9, 28, 48, 49, 50, 54, 55, 73, 74, 88, 102, 111, 113, 139, 152, 159, 168, 187, 191, 192, 197, 205, 207, 215
Pilate, Pontius, 17, 47, 65, 71, 138, 139, 141, 142, 147, 149, 186, 192
Pomeroy, Sara B., 194, 206
Pussetti, Chiara, 218

Radkowski, Georges-Hubert de, 30, 189
Rahab, 132
Rami, Arav, 180, 186, 208
Redfield, Robert, 183
Reed, Jonathan, 9, 104, 142, 180, 183, 185, 186, 189, 200, 202, 203, 207
Remotti, Francesco, 203
Richardson, Peter, 181, 208
Rigato, Maria Luisa, 185, 199
Rivkin, Ellis, 199
Robinson, James M., 177, 182
Rohrbaugh, Richard, 199, 212
Roll, Israel, 180, 181, 184
Roniger, Luis, 198
Rousseau, John J., 180
Ruth, 132

Safrai, Shemuel, 190
Safrai, Zeev, 180, 181

Index of Authors and Names

Saller, Richard P., 205, 207
Salome, 66, 192
Sanders, E. P., xi, 10, 177, 180, 183, 184, 185
Scheper-Hughes, Nancy, 128, 213
Schiavone, Aldo, 182
Schmid, Peter, 210
Schmidt, Karl Ludwig, 181, 216
Schnackenburg, Rudolf, 212
Schweitzer, Albert, 177, 191
Schweizer, Eduard, 214
Shweder, Richard A., 219
Simmel, Georg, 116, 210
Simon, brother of Jesus, 58, 192
Simon the Cananaean, 55, 192
Simon of Cyrene, 142, 192
Simon the leper, 20, 27, 66, 89, 192
Simon Peter (see Peter)
Simon the Pharisee, 89
Simon, son of Clopas, 58
Simon the Zealot, 197
Smith, Dennis E., 80, 82, 83, 200-204
Smith, Robert W., 182
Solinas, Piergiorgio, 205, 214
Solomon, 20, 33, 137
Stegemann, Ekkehard, 185, 199, 207, 209
Stegemann, Wolfgang, 181, 185, 193, 199, 207, 209
Strange, James F., 5, 29, 180, 181, 182, 186, 189, 194, 202, 208
Strathern, Andrew J., 213
Susanna, follower of Jesus 52, 111, 114

Tamar, 132
Tambiah, Stanley J., 204
Taylor, Joan, 192
Thaddaeus, 54, 192
Theissen, Gerd, x, 18, 43, 47, 51, 52, 62, 177, 180, 181, 184, 186-188, 192-195, 199, 203, 209, 217
Theudas, 17
Thomas, 54, 197
Thomas McCollough, Christine, 180, 189, 194, 208
Tiberius, Claudius Nero, 17, 182

Trümper, Monika, 206
Tsafrir, Yoram, 180
Turner, Edith, 190
Turner, Victor, 190
Twelftree, Graham H., 199, 217, 218
Tzaferis, Vasilios, 183

Uriah, 132

Van Henten, Willen, 206, 208
Van Segbroeck, Frans, 185
Vasaly, Ann, 187
Viollet, Catherine, 209
Vouga, François, 197

Wahlen, Clinton, 199, 217
Wallace-Hadrill, Andrew, 126, 206-208
Warfield, Benjamin B., 219
Weber, Max, x, 188, 200
Wegner, Judith, 206
Weiss, Gail, 216
Weiss, Zeev, 186, 187
White, Geoffrey M., 218, 219
White, L. Michel, 211
White, Rodney, 180
Wiedemann, Thomas, 205
Wikan, Unni, 220
Wildavsky, Aaron, 219
Willis, Laurence M., 185
Wilson, Stephen G., 208
Wolf, Eric R., 183
Woorwinde, Stephen, 219
Wrede, William, 191

Xanthakou, Margarita, 213
Xenophon, 51

Yeivin, Zev, 182
Yi-Fu, Tuan, 180

Zechariah, 43
Zacchaeus, follower of Jesus, 72, 85, 102, 104, 124, 207, 211
Zebedee, 48, 49, 54, 66, 112, 192
Zeno, 51

INDEX OF ANCIENT TEXTS

Hebrew Scriptures		**Pseudepigrapha and Josephus**		4:18-22	49, 111, 112
				5:3-11	100
Leviticus				5:5	12
25:8-55	213	*1 Enoch*		5:40	25
25:9	190	89:59	196	6:1-8	240
				6:2-5	140
Numbers		FLAVIUS JOSEPHUS		6:12	xviii
11:16	196	*Jewish Antiquities*		6:16-17	140
11:24	196	18.116	43	6:18	140
15:38-39	135	18.117	44	7:16-20	36
		20.200	62	7:28	69
Deuteronomy				8:5-13	23, 150, 212
22:121	35	*Jewish War*		8:11	99, 204
		2.220	196	8:14-15	112, 205
2 Kings		4.334f	196	8:18-20	209
1:9-14	220	5.270f	196	8:20	28
				8:21-22	113
		Vita		8:22	52
Joel		1	192	8:28-34	102
3:4	183	2	110	8:28	183
				9:1	189
Micah		**New Testament**		9:9-13	111
7:6	210			9:9-10	114
		Matthew		9:10	189
Zechariah		1:16	144	9:14-17	94
9:2	183	2:1-2	73	9:15	95
		2:20-22	12	9:18	22, 67
Psalms		2:23	189	9:20-22	217
22:19	136	3:1-12	192	9:28	189
35:11	204	3:1	43	9:37-38	209
		3:4	43	10:1	195
2 Esdras		3:7-10	44, 46	10:2	54
1:11	183	3:9	44	10:5-15	183
		3:14-15	44, 47	10:5-6	72
1 Chronicles		4:12	189	10:6	52
23:22	196	4:15	183	10:11-13	122

Index of Ancient Texts

10:11	122	19:20	206	27:38-43	142
10:12-13	120	19:22	71, 114	27:39	216
10:23	36, 37, 185	19:27-29	113, 209	27:50	141, 142
10:34	46	19:27	111	27:55-56	66, 144
10:34-36	117	19:28	195	27:57-61	142
10:35-36	111, 117	20:1-2	209	28:1-11	215
10:36	119	21:8	36	28:1	66
10:37-38	111, 112	21:12	81, 187	28:16-20	215
11:12	43	21:19	35, 183	28:19	73
11:18-19	46	21:33-41	21		
11:21	8	21:33	36	Mark	
11:26	193	22:1-14	92, 212	1:2-11	192
11:27	166	22:2-10	81, 203	1:4	44, 193
12:1-8	86	22:9	183	1:6	43
12:46-50	197	22:10	93	1:7	44, 47
12:46	59	23	140	1:14	44, 65
13:14-19	183	23:5	135	1:16-20	49, 11, 112
13:24-28	35	23:15	193	1:16	50
13:31-32	36	23:37	22	1:17	52
13:53-58	189	25:13-15	189	1:21-29	15
13:55-56	196	26:6-13	89, 216	1:23	144
13:57	210	26:6	20	1:27	160
14:2	65	26:7	66	1:29-31	88, 112
14:13	183	26:17-20	20	1:29	28, 102, 111
14:15	183	26:18	187	1:31	150
14:36	145	26:23	202	1:32-33	147
15:1-20	202	26:25-29	202	1:33	212
15:5	216	26:26	18	1:35	9, 38
15:21-28	199	26:29	82	1:36-39	28, 37
15:21	8	26:30-35	200	1:39	15
15:24	72	26:30	20	1:40	37, 159
15:32-39	203	26:36-38	141	1:41	219
15:38	65	26:37	160	1:45	9, 39
16:13	189	26:39	166, 215, 220	2:1-12	69
16:14	43	26:50	40	2:1-2	212
16:16-19	73	26:51	215	2:1	28
16:18	73	26:62	139	2:6	70
17:1-9	152	26:63	162	2:13-17	111
17:13	43	26:67	140	2:13-14	28, 114
17:24-25	189	26:68	140	2:13	147
18:15-17	73	27:25	71, 147	2:18-20	94, 95
18:27	165	27:28	138, 141	2:18	70
19:13-15	220	27:29	142	2:23-27	35, 89, 201
19:16-22	111, 114, 216	27:34	142	2:24	70
19:18-26	151	27:37	167	3:1	15

Mark (continued)		6:39-40	164	10:32	160
3:6-7	38, 148	6:45-46	164	10:35-42	195
3:6	70, 148	6:47-50	154	10:38	220
3:7-8	147	6:54-56	147	10:41	220
3:7	28, 217	6:56	145	10:46	9
3:13	28, 57	7:1-5	94	11:1—14:11	20
3:14-15	53, 69	7:17-23	121, 202	11:8	69
3:17	37, 54	7:24	8, 21, 37, 199	11:11-12	20
3:19-20	29	7:25	216	11:12-13	201
3:20-21	59	7:31	9, 12	11:14	157
3:20	148, 212	7:32-33	150	11:18-19	95, 148
3:21	61	7:32	145	11:27-33	21
3:22	70	8:1-9	96, 146	12:15	157
3:30	161	8:1-3	158	12:28-34	64
3:31-35	59, 61, 197	8:14-21	85	12:39	15
3:35	116	8:14	201	12:41-48	21
4:1	29	8:22-26	9	12:41-44	22, 67, 72
4:14	9	8:22	9	13:3	20
4:35	29	8:27	168	13:33-37	189
4:38	139	8:28	43	14:3-9	89, 216
5:1-20	102	8:31	220	14:3	20, 66
5:17	27	8:35	217	14:4	220
5:21-34	67	9:1-17	152	14:12-17	20
5:21	27, 147	9:1-2	53	14:14-15	211
5:23-31	151	9:2	37	14:17-31	200
5:27	215	9:9-13	88	14:20	202
5:30	217	9:14	147	14:22-25	202
6:1-6	189	9:15	159	14:22	98
6:1	29	9:20	214	14:23	220
6:2	19	9:22	219	14:25	82, 201
6:3	196	9:31	220	14:26	20
6:4	210	9:33	28	14:27	159
6:7-13	183	9:38-40	64	14:29	159
6:7	195	10:1	53	14:31-32	159
6:10-11	189	10:13-16	220	14:32-35	141
6:10	222	10:13	145	14:33	151
6:18	46	10:14	161	14:34	160, 215
6:19	151	10:17-22	111, 114, 144, 216	14:35	160
6:25	43			14:36	141, 166, 220
6:30-32	37	10:21	75, 144	14:46	140
6:32-33	9	10:22	52-71	14:56	59, 162
6:32	147, 183	10:25	72-92	14:60-61	162
6:33-44	96, 146	10:28-30	113, 115, 209	14:62	163
6:34	219	10:28	111	14:63	140
6:36	183	10:32-33	220	15:1	141

Index of Ancient Texts

15:16-20	141	4:44	1, 186	9:5	212
15:17	137	5:1-11	111	9:10-17	9
15:20	138	5:2	49	9:12-14	189
15:29-31	216	5:4-11	49	9:12	195
15:36	141	5:8	50	9:18	168
15:37	141	5:10-11	112	9:19	213
15:40-41	111, 114	5:13	151	9:28-36	152
15:40	64, 66	5:27-32	111	9:52-56	123, 183
15:41	66	5:27	114	9:52	21, 102
15:42-44	142	5:33-35	94, 95	9:54	220
15:43-45	215	6:1-5	86	9:57-62	50
15:43	64	6:13	53	9:57-58	209
15:45	141	6:19	21	9:59-60	113, 209
16	xv	6:20-23	100	9:61-62	209
16:1-8	215	6:20	100	10:1-12	183
16:1	66	6:24-25	46	10:1	57
16:5	160	6:29	215	10:2	122, 209
		7:1-11	150	10:3-4	123
Pseudo-Mark (the		7:1-10	23	10:5-7	120, 189
"Longer Ending")		7:1	212	10:5-6	81
16:9-11	215	7:5	16	10:7	81, 122
16:12-13	215	7:11-17	67, 102, 114	10:10-12	212
16:14-18	215	7:13-14	67	10:11	57
		7:14	151	10:13	8
Luke		7:17-23	193	10:22	167
1:1-4	xvi	7:20	43	10:34	211
2:7	211	7:33-34	46, 95	10:38-42	89
2:40	214	7:33	43	10:42	66
3:1-22	192	7:36-50	65, 89, 145	11:5-8	123, 201
3:2	43	7:36	89	11:27	67
3:3	44, 193	7:37	66, 212	11:28	67
3:7-14	46	8:1-3	52, 72, 111, 114, 118	11:37-54	201
3:16	44, 47			11:37-41	89
3:23-38	133	8:11-21	197	11:43	15
3:38	134	8:26-39	102	12:16-21	35
4:15-28	186	8:39	165	12:22-28	33
4:16-30	196	8:40-56	151	12:22-23	137
4:16	49	8:40-45	67	12:27-28	137
4:17-19	213	8:41	16	12:33	111, 209
4:24	210	8:44	214	12:38-40	189
4:29	117	8:45	151	12:49-51	46, 220
4:33-38	166	8:46	151, 217	12:52-53	111, 117
4:38	49, 112, 205	9:1-2	195	12:53	118
4:42-43	28	9:2-6	183	13:1-3	47
4:43	8	9:4	122	13:2-5	149

Index of Ancient Texts

Luke (continued)		22:7-14	20	2:1-11	59
13:3	xviii	22:11-13	211	2:1-2	59
13:28-29	204	22:14	200	2:11-12	196
13:31	64	22:15-20	202	2:11	90
13:32	23	22:15-16	202	2:12	13, 59
13:29	201	22:18	82, 99	3:1	51, 72
13:34	22, 167	22:21	202	3:22-28	45
14:1-24	64	22:22	157	3:22-24	44, 46
14:2-6	201	22:24	195	3:22	14
14:4	165	22:27	92, 97	3:26-30	44
14:13	96	22:28	53	3:29	95
14:15-24	92, 203, 212	22:29-30	195, 204	3:30	14
14:16-24	81, 201	22:31-34	200	4:1-3	44, 45
14:18-20	120	22:41	215	4:1-2	46
14:21	93, 96, 124	22:42	166, 220	4:8	201
14:23	34	22:49-50	215	4:21-25	190
14:26	111, 112	22:51	151	4:44	210
14:33	111, 209	23:8-12	138	4:46-54	212
15:11-31	23, 211	23:11	139	5:1	14
16:1-8	39	23:26	142	5:18	70
16:19-31	81, 91, 96, 203	23:27	219	6:1	183
		23:29	68	6:6	186
16:22-23	203	23:35	142, 216	6:15	164
17:7-10	2, 201	23:36	141, 142	6:42	196
17:7-8	78, 17	23:39-43	142	6:66	51, 53
18:15-17	220	23:46	141	7:1	37, 70
18:18-23	111, 114, 216	23:49	66	7:2-11	61
		23:50	142	7:10	14, 60
18:18	216	23:55—24:10	66	7:19	70, 148
18:23	72	24:1-2	215	7:20	70
18:26-30	113	24:10	66	7:25	70
18:28-30	111	24:13	35, 215	8:2-11	68
18:28-29	209	24:36-43	215	8:6-8	140
19:2-9	85			8:37	70
19:2	72, 183	John		8:40	70
19:5-9	102	1:15	44	8:59	14, 37
19:5	124	1:26	44	9:1—10:21	14
19:8	124	1:29-36	192	9:6-7	140
19:12	31	1:29-34	44	10:39	14
19:28—22:6	20	1:35-39	48, 50	11:11	63
20:1-8	21	1:35	44	11:32	139
20:46	15	1:36-37	50	11:41	139
21:1-4	21, 67	1:37-39	50	11:53	70
21:1-2	72	1:40	50	11:54	14, 37
21:37	20	1:44	9	12:1-8	89, 216

Index of Ancient Texts

12:1	14	19:1-7	46	*Gospel of Judas*	xvi
12:12-50	20	21:17	196	*Gospel of the Hebrews*	
12:12-19	20				xii, xvi, 61-62,
12:12	20	1 Corinthians			192, 215
12:20-36	20	5:6-8	201	*Gospel of the Nazarenes*	
12:21	9	9:4-6	183		xii, 192, 193,
12:24	35	9:14	183		196, 215
12:36	37	10:27	211	*Gospel of Peter*	xvi,
12:42	51, 65, 72	11:20-22	97		215
12:44-50	20	11:23-25	98, 142,	*Gospel of Thomas*	
13–17	20		202		xii, xvi, 160
13–14	185	11:23-24	88	1	160
13:1—14:31	200	15:4-8	215	2	219
13:1-20	202, 203, 215	15:5	62	10	169, 220
13:1-17	97, 191	15:7	60	12	62
13:4	215	16:22	166	14	211
13:10	136, 186			16	46, 111,
13:12	200	Galatians			117, 119
13:14-15	98	1:19	60	31	117
13:23	198	2:3-16	73	58	100
15–17	185	2:9	60	68	100
15:13-15	198	2:12	60	69	100
17:11	139			64	81, 92, 212
17:24	167	1 Timothy			
18:15	15	5:10	67, 191	*P.Oxy 840*	187
18:20	186				
19:25-27	58, 59	James		*Ascension of Isaiah*	
19:26-27	60	1:27	67		xiii
19:26	198				
20:1—21:23	215	Revelation		*Didache*	xii
21	90	20:3-7	100	1:4	215
21:20	198	21:1-4	100	3:7	204
21:24	15	21:10	100	9:1-5	202
		21:23-27	100		
Acts		22:1-5	100	Eusebius	
1:6	12	22:20	166	*Hist. Eccl.*	
1:14	196			4.22.4	196
1:21-26	54	**Early Christian**			
6:1	67	**Writings**		Irenaeus	
10:1-48	73			*Adv. Haer.*	
12:17	196	"Apocryphal"		5.33.3	204
15:1-29	73	Gospels			
15:5	64			Justin	
15:13	196	*Gospel of the Ebionites*		*1 Apol.* 67	xvi
15:19	196		xii, 192, 202	*Dial* 80.1-5	204

Justin (*continued*)
Dial 103   xvi
Dial 106   xvi

Greek and Latin Writings

Columella
De re rustica
1.5.7   212

Diogenes Laertius
Life of Philosophers
3:10   220
7:1-2   206

Maximus of Tyre
Dissertations 3.7e   220

Plutarch
Moralia
532f   220

INDEX OF SUBJECTS

addressees, of Jesus, 53, 54, 71, 110
anthropology
   of body and corporality, 5, 128, 130, 140-42, 147, 213
   of catastrophes, 217
   of emotions, 155-57, 218-19
   of family and household, 102-4, 204-5
   of food, 7-8, 80, 200
   of identity, 31-32, 88, 103, 109, 203, 208
   of memory, 7, 19
   of mobility and dislocation, 25-29, 188
   of silence, 162
   of space, 3-4, 179-80
   and studies of historical Jesus, xii-xiv
   of texts, xi, xiii, xvii, 3
apparitions, 133. *See also* visions
appearance, of Jesus, 134-39, 152-54, 174. *See also* body
arrest
   of the Baptizer, 45, 46
   of Jesus, 19, 20, 42, 70, 71, 137, 139, 141-43, 147, 178, 203, 215
association, xiii, 48, 52, 73
   voluntary, 80, 108
authorities
   political, 15, 17, 18, 42, 46, 65, 70, 71, 72, 76, 139, 141, 143, 173, 175
   religious, 21, 22, 71

banquet, xvi, 64, 66, 78, 80, 81, 83, 84, 86, 90, 91, 92, 93, 94, 96, 99-102, 120, 123, 124

as paradigm of the Kingdom of God, 82, 95, 99, 175, 204, 207
baptism, 26, 181, 197
   of Jesus, 60, 205
   of John, 56, 143, 205
Bethsaida, 17, 20, 21, 29, 30, 194, 202, 204, 220
blood, 59, 83, 110, 204
   woman suffering from hemorrhages, 80, 163
body, 15, 45, 140-46, 149, 157, 225
   embodiment, 170, 228
   and emotions, 168, 170, 171, 174, 184
   genealogical, 145
   humiliated, in danger, imprisoned, 153-55, 160-61, 185
   of Jesus, 2, 5, 38, 77, 110, 142, 144, 145, 147, 148, 150, 155, 156, 157-58, 160, 164-65, 166, 186
   metamorphosis of, 165-66
   social, 68, 73, 86, 120
borders, 16, 23, 24, 28, 40, 48, 49, 84, 184
   mental, 158
   Roman borders and mental maps of Jesus, 172
brothers, and sisters, 61, 71, 96, 124, 125, 128
   of Jesus, 25, 56, 70, 71, 72, 73, 102, 119, 128, 208, 209
burial, 2, 113
   of Jesus, 65, 66

call, 61, 62, 123, 124, 125
   to abandon, 122
   individual call, 121-22. *See also* detachment

250 Index of Subjects

Capernaum, 21, 25, 28, 30, 39, 40, 61, 71, 72, 117, 194, 201
Chorazin, 8, 182
church, 73-74
   early churches, 52, 57, 64, 82, 83, 88, 179, 195
   house-church, 198, 200, 206
city, 7-8, 11-12, 15, 17-19, 23, 106
   city-states, 5
   contrast betweeen countryside and, 10, 23, 94, 106
   Jesus and, 8-10, 14, 20-23, 25, 105, 173
   See also polis
clothing, 33, 43, 136-38, 154
commensality, 82, 83, 96, 196
   or conviviality, 82, 94, 98
   as practice of Jesus, 83, 85, 87-91, 106, 96, 99, 101
community, 52, 82, 88, 90, 93, 127
   of followers or of disciples, 93, 96
   Johannine, xvii
complexity, cultural, xx, 69, 94, 170, 208, 213
conflict, xi, xii, 22, 79, 110, 116
   between city and village, 10, 21, 23, 106
   within and between households, 34, 57, 103, 109, 111, 116-24, 171, 211
   between Jesus and surrounding society, 38, 76, 117
countryside, 28, 32, 35, 39, 90, 127, 140, 154, 171, 181. *See also* rural areas, land
covenant, 98
cross, xviii, 59, 60, 66, 139, 141, 142, 217
   wood of the, 176
crowd, 17, 58, 67, 76, 83, 85, 143-48, 158, 159, 163-65
   crowds, xii, 65, 69, 71, 147, 173, 174
   movements of, 145
   pressure of, 146-47, 148, 151, 157

crucifixion, 71, 139, 143. *See also* death
cultic space, 21, 22, 48. *See also* ritual
Cynics, 23, 30, 51

death, ix, 91
   of James, 58, 62
   of Jesus, ix, x, xv, xviii, 20, 42, 56, 71, 141-42, 147, 148, 175
   after Jesus' death, 57-58, 60-62, 64, 65, 67, 73-74, 82, 83, 87, 91, 97-98, 134, 149
   of Judas, 54
   of Lazarus, 63
debts, xviii, 171, 208, 212
   indebtedness, 106, 165
Decapolis, 5, 12, 13
demons, 28, 29, 53, 69, 150, 165, 218
   evil/bad spirits, 32, 48, 52, 69, 169
desire, of Jesus, 29, 69, 144, 153, 156, 166, 168
   or will, 166, 168
detachment, from household, work and property, 31, 32, 34, 36, 56, 60, 76, 102, 110, 113, 115, 120, 124, 126, 171, 213
Diaspora, 16, 47, 177
dining room (*triclinium*), 211
discipleship, 107, 108, 109, 116, 210, 211
   itinerant disciples, 52, 72, 102, 115, 120, 122, 125, 127
   mathētai, 50
   See also itinerancy
domesticity, 103, 126, 206
   domestic groups, 26, 34, 40, 104, 106, 118, 120, 206
   of Jesus, 58, 63
   See also households
dynamis, 110, 150, 151, 154. *See also* power of the body

eating, 23, 46, 78-84, 85-86, 87, 89
   Last Supper, 15, 20, 81-83, 87, 88, 90, 92, 97-99, 159, 167, 200

Index of Subjects

in the parables, 91-94
See also banquet, meals
ecology of culture, 3, 4
elites, 8, 17, 56, 173, 209
emotions, of Jesus, xii, 10, 42, 74, 103, 120, 142, 153, 155-69, 176, 218
    anger, 157, 161-62, 176
    compassion, 67, 69, 76, 102, 142, 157-59, 163-66, 169, 176
    indignation, 161-62, 169
    interior life, xii, 155, 156, 160, 174, 176
enemies, of Jesus, 37, 39, 70, 87, 163
    adversaries, 21, 62, 64, 69-71, 76, 96
    opponents, 65, 70, 148, 157
environment, ix, xi, xiii, xviii, 4, 8, 16, 79, 156
    domestic, 28, 31, 57, 89, 103, 107, 164, 172
exorcism, 56, 64, 151, 152, 160, 218. *See also* demons

family, 18, 26, 28, 33, 34, 36, 40, 43, 45, 49-50, 52, 57-62, 68, 102-4, 124, 126, 172
    and discipleship, 109-19
    and friendship, 63, 66
    See also conflict, households
farmer, 105, 140
fasting, 95, 140, 192
fisher, 4, 8, 14, 49, 105, 112
followers, xiii, xix, xx, 4, 27, 34, 35, 48-53, 56-57, 65-66, 77, 83, 86-88, 120-25, 146, 154, 157, 168, 170
    of the Baptizer, 46
    itinerant, 76, 52, 54, 76, 120, 124, 125
    sedentary, 51, 52, 54, 65, 125
    See also disciples
food, 5, 41, 45, 46, 58, 90-93, 95-97, 103, 104, 166
    abstinence from, 152
    abundance of, 112
    feeding, 99, 102, 108-9, 135, 148
    sharing of, 105-8, 110, 111, 113, 212
    See also meals, eating
freedom, x, xi, 27, 103, 110, 116
friends, 20, 62-65, 84, 123
    friendship, 63, 198
    of Jesus, 89-90, 121
    supporters, 62-65, 106, 120
flight, 37-40, 148

Galilee, 4-8, 10, 11-16, 17, 18, 29, 45, 71
    Galilean, xix, 6, 8, 9, 13, 16, 177
generation, 103-4, 106, 110-16, 131-34, 205, 211
    to beget, 104, 131, 132
    genealogy, 131, 133, 134
    intermediate generation, 112-15, 119, 211
    transgenerational, 131

healings, 56, 69, 84, 144, 150-54, 159, 161, 165
heaven, 45, 145, 100, 139
    heavenly journey, 153, 179
Hellenism, xix, 15, 47, 106, 120, 130, 152
    hellenization, 17
honor, 84, 113, 117
hospitality, 16, 26, 34-35, 56, 66-68, 88, 105, 120-27, 136, 172
houses, xi, 66, 73, 102-4, 120-22, 125, 134, 147
    household, 36-37, 39, 102, 103, 102-4, 107-9, 113, 116-24, 125, 126
    householders, 81, 85, 89, 93, 114, 115, 121, 124
    and the individual, 109-10
    types of, 83-85, 94, 104-6, 115, 171-72
    See also domesticity

identity, 10, 16, 26-28, 32, 34, 38, 43, 55, 79, 88, 103, 108-9, 133, 156, 173
institutions, xi, 10, 18, 19, 26, 34-35, 39-40, 43, 45-46, 61, 70, 76, 108, 126, 141, 172
interstitiality, 108, 126
  interstitial, 108-9, 125-27, 172, 204
itinerancy, 32, 35, 37, 39, 115, 119, 188, 191. *See also* disciples/followers, itinerant

Jerusalem, xvi, 5, 8, 13-16, 57-58, 60, 70-72, 126, 147, 149
  attitude of Jesus, 16-24, 60, 167
Judea, xvi, 12-14, 16, 19, 45, 49
  Judean, x, xix, 10, 11-13, 17, 23, 37, 44, 52, 68, 70-73, 123, 132-34, 160, 171, 172

kingdom of God, 34-35, 37, 55-57, 68, 73, 76, 81-82, 95, 99-101, 150, 166, 169, 171, 175
kinship, xiii, 27, 56, 61, 102-4, 105, 107, 109, 118, 121, 171. *See also* family

lake, 5, 13, 111, 146, 154
land, 11, 12, 14, 16, 36, 172
  landscape, 144
  See also territory
Land of Israel, xvi, 5, 7, 12-17, 24, 25, 41, 72, 100, 110, 172, 177
law, 62, 122, 135

man of the village, 7, 10, 19
maps, 3-6, 11
  mental, 3, 4, 8, 16
  mental maps of Jesus, 4, 8, 15, 146
  mental maps of Josephus, 12
  rabbinical mental maps, 12
meals, 80, 81-83, 85, 94, 176. *See also* commensality and conviviality
master, 50, 53, 63, 75, 80, 81, 84, 92, 94, 109

Messiah, 100, 131, 132, 163, 168, 187
memory, xiv-xv, 4, 7, 19, 26, 31, 60, 82, 139, 174
  remembrance, 7, 98
miracles, 9, 14, 27, 90-91, 151-52, 217
  miracle workers/working, 49, 54, 69, 146, 174
mother of Jesus, 13, 44, 58, 59, 60,-62, 66, 90, 116
mobility, 25, 27, 29, 31, 34, 46, 107, 141, 188, 194
  dislocation, xiii, 30, 48
  displacement, 25
  from place to place, 31, 86

Nazareth, 6, 13, 58, 70, 107, 116

oikos, 103, 105, 106, 107-9, 113, 117-20, 124, 127. *See also* domesticity, household

parables, xv, xvi, 35, 71, 81-83, 91-94, 104, 174, 188
  of the banquet, xvi, 64, 92, 96, 120, 123, 124
  of the Good Samaritan, xv, 199
  of the prodigal son, 106, 115
  of the rich man and poor Lazarus, 96, 124
  of the shepherd, 14
  of the tenants in the vineyard, xvii, 21
parents, 59, 104, 111-13, 115, 118-19, 161
  fathers and sons, 131
  See also generation, conflicts
Passover, 19-21, 87-88, 121, 139
patron/client, 105, 106, 108, 127
  patronage, 16, 105-6, 126-27
peasant, 30, 35, 48, 117, 171. *See also* workers, village
Pharisee, 27, 48, 64-66, 70, 83-85, 86, 88, 89, 94, 109, 135, 148

Index of Subjects

pilgrimage, 18, 32-33, 60
polis, 8, 9, 105, 106, 182, 207. *See also* city
poverty, 18, 67, 72, 126, 137
   the poor, 96, 97, 101, 106, 124, 125-27, 137, 172, 175
possession, by spirits, 52, 165
   possessed persons, 29, 69, 102, 151, 165, 218
power
   of the body, x, 132, 146, 150-51, 152, 153, 154, 174
   political, 17, 18, 71, 99, 106, 175
   supernatural, 32, 75, 154, 168
   See also healings
practice of life, xi, 36, 40, 73, 86, 91, 98, 99, 130, 171; *also* style of life, xi, 83
   religious, 22, 44, 79, 129, 160
   social, 4, 36, 210
prayer, 37, 38, 53, 139, 151, 153, 160, 166-68, 176
   Lord's Prayer, xii, xv, xviii
   to pray, 38, 53, 139, 159, 160, 164, 167, 173
preaching, 4, 11, 16, 18, 21, 23, 36-37, 44, 46, 51, 55-57, 73, 100, 118, 173
predictions of the passion, 148, 220
priests, 19, 21, 70, 138, 142
   high priest, 15, 62, 141, 151, 162, 163
prophet, 17, 42, 43, 67, 117, 149, 163, 168
   prophecy, 188, 214, 215
property, 33, 114, 123, 111
purity, 20, 44, 46, 80
   impurity, 80
   washing of hands, 86

relatives. *See* kinship
repentance, 217
   to repent, xviii, 8, 47, 149
resurrection, 99, 130, 143, 174, 187
revelation, 38, 44, 54, 168

ritual, xix, 44, 53, 68, 80, 87, 93, 97, 98, 139, 152, 160, 175
   rite, 18, 20, 44, 87, 90, 97, 98, 201
roads, 5-6, 11, 111, 144, 156, 173
   the road of the Gentiles, 11, 72, 183
   Roman, 5, 11, 180
   routes and paths, 5, 6, 29
Romanization, 7, 17, 18, 23, 24, 110, 171, 173
   the Romans, x, 8, 11, 12, 15, 16, 23, 49, 70, 72, 105, 172, 174
rural areas, 6, 9, 10, 17, 171
   and the city, 106
   as Jesus' place of action, 6, 18, 24, 35

Sabbath, 70, 84, 86, 148
Samaria, 13, 17
   Samaritan, 11, 72, 73, 123, 167, 183-84
sayings of Jesus, xvii, 73, 82, 100, 168, 182
scribes, 19, 21, 65, 70, 138, 142
Sepphoris, 5, 6, 8, 10, 17, 18, 105
silence, 139, 145, 162-63
sin, xviii, 44, 73
   sinners, 10, 47, 69, 83, 88, 93-96, 149
slave, 23, 63, 81, 92, 94, 97, 101, 115, 120, 136, 175, 179
   master and, 63, 81, 84, 92
   servant, 23, 31, 84, 120
social imagination, 3, 4, 58, 81, 202
Son of Man, xi, 36, 37, 62, 95, 157, 163
solitude, of Jesus, 11, 37-40, 68-69, 173, 191
space, 3, 15, 16, 26, 38, 39, 103, 108, 126, 145, 173
   dwelling, 16, 28, 30, 31, 104
synagogue, 13, 15-16, 34, 36, 40, 58, 70, 96

teaching, 11, 42, 51, 69, 84, 86, 88, 94, 98, 121, 158

Temple, of Jerusalem, 14-15, 18-22, 33, 36, 40, 70, 175
territory, 4-6, 8, 9, 11-12, 16-17, 24, 172. *See also* villages
text, xi, xiv-xv, 130, 178
   as cultural product, xiv
   theory of, 84, 178
   three levels of, xvii
thaumaturgy, 150, 151, 154, 217
   thaumaturge, 152.
   See also power, *dynamis*
time, 35-37
   of the itinerant, 35
   temporal dimension, xiii
   temporal location, 6
   temporal rhythm/cycle, 35-36
transfiguration, 152-54, 174
tunic, 136-37
   chiton, 136
   garments, 97, 135-37, 153
   See also clothing
Tyre, 8, 9, 12, 13, 27
   and Sidon, 8, 13, 14

Twelve (the), 51, 53-57, 69, 72
   twelve tribes of Israel, 99

uncertainty, of itinerants, 26, 33, 50, 171
   instability, 28, 30, 110
   precariousness, 26, 48, 85, 170

villages, 5-10, 13, 15, 16, 17, 24, 31, 171
   population and life of, 48, 105
   village-*oikoi* as centers of production, 107
visions, revelations, ecstasies, 38

women, 65-69, 76, 101, 104, 116, 118-19, 132
   as disciples of Jesus, 35, 52, 72, 111
workers, 14, 49, 81, 107, 193, 209
   work, 9, 26, 31, 33, 34, 36, 39, 48-50, 52, 94, 97, 103, 107, 108, 115, 124
   See also slave

www.ingramcontent.com/pod-product-compliance
Lightning Source LLC
Chambersburg PA
CBHW051938290426
44110CB00015B/2028